Fundamentals of United States Intellectual Property Law: Copyright, Patent, Trademark

Second edition

Sheldon W. Halpern,
Harold R. Tylor Chair of Law and Technology
Albany Law School

Craig Allen Nard
Tom J. E. and Bette Lou Walker Professor of Law and Director,
Centre for Law and Technology & the Arts
Case Western Reserve University Law School

Kenneth L. Port
Professor of Law and Director of Intellectual Property Law Studies
William Mitchell College of Law

INTERNATIONAL

Published by:
P.O. Box 316, 2400 AH Alphen aan den Rijn
The Netherlands
E-mail: sales@kluwerlaw.com
Website: http://www.kluwerlaw.com

Sold and Distributed in North, Central and South America by:
Aspen Publishers, Inc.,
7201 McKinney Circle, Frederick MD 21704, USA
Cambridge, MA 02139, USA

Sold and Distributed in all other countries by:
Turpin Distribution Services Ltd
Stratton Business Park,
Pegasus Drive, Biggleswade,
Bedfordshire SG18 8TQ, United Kingdom

This work was based on a monograph in the International
Encyclopedia of Laws, Intellectual Property

Cover design: Bearcomm.com, Penzance, United Kingdom

ISBN 90 411 2599 X

To Dorit and Miki
S.W.H.

To Lillian
C.A.N.

To Elissa, Emily, and Paula
K.L.P.

Preface

This book is designed to provide a detailed exposition of the United States laws concerning copyright, patent, and trademark. It offers a thorough analysis of this body of intellectual property law which, we believe, will prove useful to the student, the scholar, and the practitioner. Our aim was neither to supplant the existing compendious treatises in these areas nor to provide a simple introductory handbook. Rather, we have attempted to present and to develop, with appropriate authority, the fundamental concepts essential to an understanding of the law in each of the three fields covered.

Similarly, we have attempted to avoid an all-embracing approach to "intellectual property." While that phrase is used to cover a wide array of activities, it is fundamentally flawed; it both embraces too much and conveys too little information. Our focus, rather, is on the law in the United States of copyright, patent, and trademark, each of which may be considered part of this rather shapeless umbrella. We have chosen to exclude for these purposes the disparate areas of protection of ideas, trade secrets, and the right of publicity, which, although partaking of the flavor of "intellectual property" are the subject of more diffuse common law and state law development.

Copyright, patent, and trademark each are very distinct bodies of law. Their joinder under the rubric of "intellectual property" serves a useful purpose in distinguishing them as a body from other areas of law; it does not, however, support broad generalization about fundamental commonality.

For example, Congressional power to act with respect to copyright and patent is embedded in Article I of the Constitution, an explicit recognition by the founders of the need for the emerging republic to have a single, federal structure governing the nature and scope of copyright protection for the "writings" of "authors" and of patent protection for the "discoveries" of "inventors."[1] Trademark law is inherently different both in its scope and in its foundation, as Congress' constitutional authority to regulate trademarks derives from its more general power to act with respect to matters affecting interstate commerce. This is why "use" of a trademark in interstate commerce, rather than simply creation of the mark, is essential for federal protection. Indeed, unlike copyright and patent, trademark protection is ultimately a common law concept that exists independent of any statute.

---

[1] U.S. CONST., art. I, sec., 8, cl. 8.

The Supreme Court has reasoned that trademarks do not "depend upon novelty, invention, discovery, or any work of the brain. It requires no fancy or imagination, no genius, no laborious thought. Trademarks are simply founded on priority of appropriation."[2]

Copyright, on the other hand, requires, at bottom, an act of original authorship, crossing a threshold, however minimal, of creativity. Indeed, the Supreme Court has held that such originality and creativity is a constitutional prerequisite to protection.[3] Patent law, for its part, is distinct in being predicated on novelty of invention; originality and creativity themselves are not sufficient if the product of the creative process lacks novelty. In each case—copyright, patent, and trademark—we have attempted to build upon the forces underlying the legal construct to create a coherent and understandable description of the legal principles and the way in which they have been applied.

Much of the law here is counter-intuitive. Much is based upon the need to reconcile conflicting interests—political, economic, and social—and the inevitable compromises may not be consistent with any single, unifying theory or "natural" development. That is the source both of the joy and the pain in dealing with the difficult and absorbing legal issues that characterize these fields of study. We hope that we can, with this volume, ease that pain and share that joy.

This book grew out of a companion study which the authors undertook for Kluwer Law International in connection with Kluwer's International Encyclopaedia of Intellectual Property, and we would like to thank Kluwer for supporting this project.

S.W.H.
C.A.N.
K.L.P.

August, 2006

---

[2] The Trademark Cases, 100 U.S. 82, 94 (1879).

[3] Feist Publications, Inc. v. Rural Telephone Service, 499 U.S. 340, 111 S.Ct. 1282 (1991).

Summary of Contents

Table of Contents

PART III: TRADEMARK

Part I: Copyright

§ 1. CONGRESSIONAL POWER

1.1. Constitutional Grant of Power

The United States Congress alone has the power to regulate copyright. The power derives from Article I, section 8 of the United States Constitution:

> The Congress shall have power ... To promote the Progress of Science and useful Arts, by securing for limited Times to Authors and Inventors the exclusive Right to their respective Writings and Discoveries.

This language provides the basis for Congressional action—in the form of legislation—to grant, define, and limit copyright and patent.

The Constitutional language also sets the conceptual basis for copyright: to promote the public interest, the "author" of an appropriate "writing" will be given a *limited* monopoly. Implementing congressional action adumbrates the fundamental compromise harmonizing the desire to encourage intellectual creativity with the need to keep intellectual products flowing freely in society. Since the source of congressional power is the constitutional language, much of the development of the law of copyright with respect to the permissible scope of protection has been concerned with judicial determination of who are "authors" and what are "writings" as those terms are used in the Constitution.[1] With respect to the constitutional linkage of congressional power with a "purpose"–"to promote the progress of science and useful arts"–there has been some uncertainty over whether this language is an aspirational justification for the general grant of power or a condition, limiting specific exercise of the power. Finally, there remains an open question as to the extent to which Congress may use its overall power with respect to matters affecting interstate commerce to create copyright-like rights and remedies not otherwise within the scope of the constitutional grant of power.[2]

1.2. The Copyright Act

Congress has acted, from time to time, to implement its constitutional power through the enactment of comprehensive copyright legislation,

---

[1] *See infra,* § 3.2.1.

[2] *See, e.g., infra,* § 3.1.1

beginning with the first copyright statute in 1790, to the present statutory structure embodied in the Copyright Act of 1976.[3]

There is no federal non-statutory, "common-law" of copyright.[4] The Copyright Act, as amended from time to time, is the sole reference point for the granting and regulation of copyright. The various states and state courts play no significant role. While general principles of federal preemption would preclude enforceability of state copyright laws relating to published works,[5] at least with respect to areas in which Congress has acted,[6] prior to enactment of the 1976 Copyright Act, a so-called "common-law" or state law copyright was recognized, and enforced by the states, with respect to unpublished works.[7] The 1976 Act, the culmination of decades of effort, superseding the basic law which had been in effect since 1909, replaced the existing dual federal/state scheme with a unitary and virtually completely federal structure. Abolishing the "common-law" or state law copyright, the Act (and the power of Congress) completely preempts any state-created rights that are equivalent to any of the exclusive rights of a copyright owner provided by the Act "in works of authorship that are fixed in a tangible medium of expression and come within the subject matter of copyright."[8] The preemption provisions specifically do not apply to state action as to "subject matter that does not come within the subject matter of copyright as specified by sections 102 and 103, including works ... not fixed in any tangible medium of expression [or] activities violating legal or equitable rights that are not equivalent to any of the exclusive rights ... as specified by section 106."[9] Preemption goes directly to matters of jurisdiction and is of such seriousness that it may be raised by the court on its own motion; it even may be raised in a *habeas corpus* proceeding to attack collaterally a

---

[3] 17 U.S.C. §§ 101-810; 1001-1101.

[4] Wheaton v. Peters, 33 U.S. (8 Pet.) 591 (1834).

[5] Sears, Roebuck & Co. v. Stiffel Co., 376 U.S. 225, 84 S. Ct. 784 (1964); Compco Corp. v. Day-Brite Lighting, Inc., 376 U.S. 234, 84 S. Ct. 779 (1964).

[6] *See* Goldstein v. California, 412 U.S. 546, 93 S. Ct. 2303 (1973).

[7] *See* Estate of Hemingway v. Random House, 23 N.Y.2d 341, 296 N.Y.S.2d 771, 244 N.E.2d 250 (1968).

[8] 17 U.S.C. § 301 (a).

[9] 17 U.S.C. § 301 (b).

criminal conviction under a state law allegedly preempted by the federal copyright law.[10]

There has emerged an increasingly complicated body of federal case law dealing with the question of what rights are "equivalent" to the exclusive rights of a copyright owner under the Act and of what comes "within the subject matter of copyright" for the purposes of determining whether a state law claim has been preempted.

> Rights "equivalent to any of the exclusive rights within the general scope of copyright" are rights established by law—rights that restrict the options of persons who are strangers to the author. Copyright law forbids duplication, public performance, and so on, unless the person wishing to copy or perform the work gets permission; silence means a ban on copying. A copyright is a right against the world.[11]

It is clear that federal preemption is not predicated on a determination that the state law claim is one that could succeed as a federal copyright claim; it is sufficient for preemption that the matter involved in the state law claim, however it might be resolved, is generally within the subject matter of copyright, even if the material itself is uncopyrightable.[12] What is not nearly as clear is the determination of when a state law claim is "equivalent" to a copyright claim.

> Equivalency exists if the right defined by state law may be abridged by an act which in and of itself would infringe one of the exclusive rights...Conversely, if an extra element is required instead of or in addition to the acts of reproduction, performance, distribution or display in order to constitute a state-created cause of action, there is no preemption,

---

[10] Corcoran v. Sullivan, 112 F.3d 836 (7th Cir. 1997).

[11] ProCD, Inc. v. Zeidenberg, 86 F.3d 1447 (7th Cir. 1996).

[12] *See, e.g.*, National Basketball Ass'n v. Motorola, 105 F.3d 841 (2d Cir. 1997) ("Section 301 preemption bars state law misappropriation claims with respect to uncopyrightable as well as copyrightable elements"); ProCD, Inc. v. Zeidenberg, 86 F.3d 1447 (7th Cir. 1996) ("subject matter of copyright" must include "all works of a type covered by sections 102 and 103, even if federal law does not afford protection to them"); Wrench LLC v. Taco Bell Corp. 256 F.3d 446 (6th Cir. 2001) ("We join our sister circuits in holding that the scope of the Copyright Act's subject matter is broader than the scope of the Act's protections").

provided that the extra element changes the nature of the action so that it is qualitatively different from a copyright infringement claim.[13]

Although it is generally agreed that a claim will be preempted if it contains no essential elements in addition to those necessary for a copyright claim, there is not unanimity as to how one determines those elements.[14] The matter has been particularly troublesome in its application to contract claims, and especially so with respect to "shrink-wrap" contracts.[15]

The Copyright Act purports to be comprehensive; nevertheless, the United States common-law tradition of judicial interpretation, as well as the language of the Act, has made it subject to extensive judicial interpretation by the federal courts, from the various United States District Courts, to the Courts of Appeal, and the United States Supreme Court. Moreover, the 1976 Act, the first comprehensive revision in more than seventy years, was the product of more than two decades of congressional investigation and hearings, culminating in voluminous reports; that legislative history is significant in interpreting the Act.

1.3. Treaties and International Agreements

The United States is party to several international treaties and agreements, including the Berne Convention, the Universal Copyright Convention, the Geneva Convention for the Protection of Phonograms, and the WTO Agreement. Among other things, these agreements provide for reciprocal "national treatment" of foreign authors suing in the courts of member states for local infringement of their works.[16] The United States is bound by The Agreement on Trade-Related Aspects of Intellectual Property

---

[13] Wrench LLC v. Taco Bell Corp. 256 F.3d 446 (6th Cir. 2001).

[14] *Compare* ProCD, Inc. v. Zeidenberg, 86 F.3d 1447 (7th Cir. 1996) *and* National Car Rental System, Inc. v. Computer Associates, Int'l, 991 F.2d 426 (8th Cir. 1993), *cert. denied*, 510 U.S. 861, 114 S. Ct. 176 (1993) (both finding no preemption) *with* Vault Corp. v. Quaid Software, Ltd., 847 F.2d 255 (5th Cir. 1988) *and* Rano v. Sipa Press, Inc., 987 F.2d 580 (9th Cir. 1993) (both finding preemption). *See also* Baltimore Orioles v. Major League Baseball Players, 805 F.2d 663 (7th Cir. 1986).

[15] *See* Bowers v. Baystate Technoligies, Inc., F.3d 1317 (Fed. Cir. 2003).

[16] *See infra*, § 2.2.

Rights ("TRIPS"), which grew out of the General Agreement on Tariffs and Trade ("GATT"); as part of these obligations, the United States has signed and to a limited extent implemented,[17] the WIPO Copyright Treaty and the WIPO Performances and Phonograms Treaty.

§2. SUBJECT MATTER OF PROTECTION
2.1. Categories of Protected Works

Works of authorship within the subject matter of copyright include:
(1) literary works;

(2) musical works, including any accompanying words;

(3) dramatic works, including any accompanying music;

(4) pantomimes and choreographic works;

(5) pictorial, graphic, and sculptural works;

(6) motion picture and other audiovisual works;

(7) sound recordings; and

(8) architectural works.[18]

These categories are not meant to be exclusive. Rather, they function as administrative categories employed in registering copyrighted works. Thus, for example, as discussed below, computer software will come within the subject matter of copyright as a "literary work." The fundamental concept is that, except as specifically excluded, *all* original creative expression fixed in a tangible medium of expression is eligible for copyright protection.

2.2. National Origin

Unpublished works are subject to protection without regard to the nationality or domicile of the author.[19] Published works are subject to protection if—

(1) on the date of first publication, one or more of the authors is a national or domiciliary of the United States, or is a national, domiciliary, or sovereign authority of a treaty party, or is a stateless person, wherever that person may be domiciled; or

---

[17] *See infra*, § 11.

[18] 17 U.S.C. § 102 (a).

[19] 17 U.S.C. § 104 (a).

(2) the work is first published in the United States or in a foreign nation that, on the date of first publication, is a treaty party; or

(3) the work is a sound recording that was first fixed in a treaty party; or

(4) the work is a pictorial, graphic, or sculptural work that is incorporated in a building or other structure, or an architectural work that is embodied in a building and the building or structure is located in the United States or a treaty party; or

(5) the work is first published by the United Nations or any of its specialized agencies, or by the Organization of American States; or

(6) the work comes within the scope of a Presidential proclamation. ...[20]

A "treaty party" is a country or intergovernmental organization other than the United States that is a party to the Universal Copyright Convention, the Geneva Phonograms Convention, the Berne Convention, the WTO Agreement, the WIPO Copyright Treaty and Performances and Phonograms Treaty, or any other copyright treaty to which the United States is a party.[21]

When action is brought for infringement in the United States of a work of foreign authorship published in a nation that is a "treaty party," the choice of applicable law may differ as between issues of infringement and issues of ownership of the work.[22] "[T]hough the issues are related, the nature of a copyright interest is an issue distinct from the issue of whether the copyright has been infringed."[23] The principle of "national treatment" underlying the Berne Convention applies to assure that the substantive law of copyright protection of the country of infringement "will be applied

---

[20] 17 U.S.C. § 104 (b). "For purposes of paragraph (2), a work that is published in the United States or a treaty party within 30 days after publication in a foreign nation that is not a treaty party shall be considered to be first published in the United States or such treaty party, as the case may be." *Id.*

[21] 17 U.S.C. § 101 (definitions of "treaty party" and "international agreement"). Adherence of the United States to the Geneva Phonograms Convention or the WIPO Performances and Phonograms Treaty will not of itself be the basis for protection of any works other than sound recordings. 17 U.S.C. § 104 (d).

[22] Itar-Tass Russian News Agency v. Russian Kurier, Inc., 153 F.3d 82 (2d Cir. 1998).

[23] *Id.* at 91.

uniformly to foreign and domestic authors."[24] However, issues of initial ownership of the work and the rights attendant thereto are to be governed by the law of the country of origin.[25]

2.3. Excluded Works

2.3.1. Intangible Expression

The Copyright Act prescription that "[c]opyright protection subsists ... in original works of authorship *fixed* in any tangible medium of expression,"[26] also serves as a proscription: this language, together with the constitutional limitation of congressional power to "writings," excludes from protection any works *not* fixed in a tangible medium of expression. Thus, intangible expression—such as unfixed speeches, lectures, dance or other movements or performances—is outside the scope of protection unless and until reduced to some tangible form.[27] Since such intangible works are outside of the scope of protection of the federal scheme, they could form the subject matter of state law protection without conflicting with the preemption provisions of the 1976 Act.

2.3.2. Governmental Works

The Copyright Act also specifically excludes from protection "any work of the United States Government," although the government may enforce rights with respect to copyrighted works assigned to it.[28] Of course, questions of what is a "work of the United States Government"and what kind of assignment would properly vest rights in the government can become quite complex.[29]

---

[24] *Id.* at 89.

[25] *Id.* at 90-91.

[26] 17 U.S.C. § 102 (a) (emphasis added).

[27] *See infra*, § 3.1.1. Note the discussion there of the special treatment of "bootleg" unauthorized recordings of live performances and the definition of "fixed" in the Copyright Act ,which treats the live television broadcast of an athletic event as "fixed" if a simultaneous recording of that broadcast is made.

[28] 17 U.S.C. § 105.

[29] *See, e.g.*, Schnapper v. Foley, 667 F.2d 102 (D.C. Cir 1981), *cert denied*, 455 U.S. 948, 102 S. Ct. 1448 (1982).

The Act does not exclude copyright protection for works of state or local governments. However, while there is some controversy over the protectability of various state or local governmental works, state statutes, ordinances, and judicial opinions may not receive copyright protection.[30]

2.3.3. The Idea/Original Expression Continuum

2.3.3.1. Generally

It is fundamental that copyright protection extends only to the original "expression" of an idea and not to the "idea" itself. As set out in Section 102(b), which was intended to codify the Supreme Court opinion in *Baker v. Selden*:[31]

> In no case does copyright protection for an original work of authorship extend to any idea, procedure, process, system, method of operation, concept, principle, or discovery, regardless of the form in which it is described, explained, illustrated, or embodied in such work.[32]

To amplify this principle, and the statutory language, the Copyright Office Regulations[33] provide examples of excluded material—matter which may indeed be "expressive" but does not rise to the level of protectable works:

> § 202.1 Material not subject to copyright.
>
> The following are examples of works not subject to copyright and applications for registration of such works cannot be entertained:
>
> (a) Words and short phrases such as names, titles, and slogans; familiar symbols or designs; mere variations of typographic ornamentation, lettering or coloring; mere listing of ingredients or contents;
>
> (b) Ideas, plans, methods, systems, or devices, as distinguished from the particular manner in which they are expressed or described in a writing;

---

[30] John G. Danielson, Inc. v. Wincheswter-Conant, 322 F.3d 26 (1st Cir. 2003) ("it is well-established that judicial decisions and statutes are in the public domain"); *see* Callaghan v. Myers, 128 U.S. 617 (1888); Building Officials & Code Administrators International, Inc. v. Code Technology, Inc., 628 F.2d 730 1st Cir. 1980). *Cf.* Veeck v. S. Bldg. Cong. Int'l, Inc., 293 F.3d 791 (5th Cir. 2002) *and* Practice Management Information Corp. v. American Medical Association, 121 F.3d 516 (9th Cir. 1997).

[31] 101 U.S. 99 (1879).

[32] 17 U.S.C. §102 (b).

[33] 37 C.F.R. § 202.1.

(c) Blank forms, such as time cards, graph paper, account books, diaries, bank checks, scorecards, address books, report forms, order forms and the like, which are designed for recording information and do not in themselves convey information;

(d) Works consisting entirely of information that is common property containing no original authorship, such as, for example: Standard calendars, height and weight charts, tape measures and rulers, schedules of sporting events, and lists or tables taken from public documents or other common sources;

(e) Typeface as typeface.

The Regulations' exclusion of simple words and phrases recognizes that copyrightability is predicated on original expression.[34] "[C]opyright does not protect ideas; it protects only the author's particularized expression of the idea."[35] However, more broadly, the bedrock proposition that copyright protection extends only to the *expression* of ideas and not to the ideas themselves, requires a set of standards for separating protected "expression" from unprotected "idea." Except for the general language of §102(b), the Copyright Act provides no further guidance; that separation process has become quite complex, and defies broad generalization. The complexity arises from the proposition that copyright protection extends beyond the taking of *literal* expression; non-literal, structural elements of a copyrighted work may be protected if they are detailed and concrete enough.[36] Accordingly, under appropriate circumstances, the details of the plot of a literary work, the detailed structure of a play or motion picture, the harmonic and rhythmic structure of a musical work, and the arrangement of a set of algorithms in a computer program, may all come within the ambit of protection so that their taking could constitute infringement of the copyrighted works to which they relate.

With such an expansive view of "expression," it necessarily follows that with respect to the elements of any given work, there is a spectrum ranging

---

[34] CMM Cable Rep, Inc . v. Ocean Coast Properties, Inc., 97 F.3d 1504 (1st Cir. 1996); Narrell v. Freeman, 872 F.2d 907 (9th Cir. 1989).

[35] Mattel, Inc. v. Goldberger Doll Manufacturing Co., 365 F.3d 133 (2d. Cir. 2004).

[36] Nichols v. Universal Pictures Corp., 45 F.2d 119, *cert denied*, 282 U.S. 902, 51 S. Ct. 216 (1931); Sheldon v. Metro- Goldwyn Pictures Corp., 81 F.2d 49, *cert denied*, 98 U.S. 669, 56 S. Ct. 835 (1936).

from the clearly unprotected abstract idea underlying the work to the literal expression constituting the work as a whole. In a given case, where the defendant is alleged to have infringed the plaintiff's work, it is frequently necessary to determine where, on that spectrum, the material allegedly taken lies.[37] Thus, for example, courts have diverged in their attempts to separate protected expression from unprotected "ideas" or "processes" involved in computer software.[38] As one court observed, "[t]he first axiom of copyright is that copyright protection covers only the expression of ideas and not ideas themselves. ... The second axiom of copyright is that the first axiom is more of an amorphous characterization that it is a principled guidepost."[39] Nevertheless, while the process of differentiation becomes, in practice, essentially ad hoc, the courts have articulated helpful analytic concepts, such as the doctrine of merger and the unprotectability of "scenes à faire."

2.3.3.2. Merger

To avoid the impermissible protection of an idea, courts may withhold protection of matter that is clearly expressive, if that expression is one of only a very limited number of ways of expressing that idea. The expression is said to have merged into the idea, so that protection for the expression would in, effect, improperly grant a monopoly on the idea. The doctrine was first articulated in a 1967 First Circuit opinion[40] and has been restated with approval (albeit frequently in dicta) by most of the circuits which have dealt with the question.[41] As the Eighth Circuit describes it:

---

[37] See infra, § 9.2.

[38] See infra, § 2.4.1.

[39] Chuck Blore & Don Richman Inc. v. 20/20 Advertising Inc., 674 F.Supp. 671, 676 (D. Minn. 1987).

[40] Morissey v. Procter & Gamble Co., 379 F.2d 675 (1st Cir. 1967).

[41] See, e.g., John G. Danielson, Inc. v. Wincheswter-Conant, 322 F.3d 26 (1st Cir. 2003); Gates Rubber Co. v. Bando Chemical Industries, Ltd., 9 F.3d 823 (10th Cir. 1993); Allen v. Academic Games League of America, 89 F.3d 614 (9th Cir. 1996); Concrete Machinery Co. v. Classic Lawn Ornaments, Inc., 843 F.2d 600 (1st Cir.1988); Warren Publishing Inc. v. Microdos Data Corp., 115 F.3d 1509 (11th Cir. 1997); Toro Company v. R&R Products, 787 F.2d 1208 (8th Cir. 1986); Educational Testing Services v. Katzman, 793 F.2d 533 (3d Cir. 1986).

Under the copyright law doctrine of merger, a close cousin to the idea/expression dichotomy, copyright protection will be denied to even some *expressions* of ideas if the idea behind the expression is such that it can be expressed only in a very limited number of ways. The doctrine is designed to prevent an author from monopolizing an idea merely by copyrighting a few expressions of it.[42]

However, conflict has emerged beween the "copyrightability" and the "nfringement"analytic models of the merger doctrine. Thus, while some opinions in the Second Circuit expressly follow the classic statement of the merger doctrine denying copyrightability to expression essentially dictated by the idea,[43] other opinions reject the "non-copyrightability" approach to merger and hold instead that the issue is one of infringement, and that where the expression is one of only a limited number of ways of expressing the idea, then only a literal, verbatim taking of that expression will support a claim of infringement.[44]

Application of the merger doctrine, finding that a given expression is so closely related to the idea expressed as to give rise to merger, requires a determination of precisely what is the underlying "idea," a task that can often engender judicial disagreement in the same case.[45] Moreover, the Second Circuit has held that for these purposes distinctions should be made between "hard" ideas, "those ideas that undertake to advance the understanding of phenomena or the solution of problems," and "soft" ideas, those that "are infused with the author's taste or opinion"; and as to the latter, the court may well exercise its discretion to "withhold" application of the merger doctrine.[46]

---

[42] Toro Company v. R & R Products Co., 787 F.2d 1208, 1212 (8th Cir. 1986).

[43] *See, e.g.,* Mywebgrocer, LLC v. Hometown Info, Inc., 375 F.3d 190 (2d Cir. 2004); Computer Associates, International, Inc. v. Altai, Inc., 982 F.2d 693 (2d Cir. 1992) ("In order not to confer a monopoly of the idea upon the copyright owner, such expression should not be protected").

[44] Continental Casualty Co. v. Beardsley, 253 F.2d 702 (2d Cir.), *cert denied* 358 U.S. 816, 79 S. Ct. 25 (1958); Kregos v. Associated Press, 937 F.2d 700 (2d Cir. 1991); CCC Information Services, Inc. v. Maclean Hunter Market Reports, Inc., 44 F.3d 61 (2d Cir. 1994). *cert. denied*, 116 S. Ct. 72 (1995).

[45] *Cf.* Kregos v. Associated Press, 937 F.2d 700 (2d Cir. 1991).

[46] CCC Information Services, Inc. v. Maclean Hunter Market Reports, Inc., 44 F.3d 61 (2d Cir. 1994). *cert. denied*, 116 S. Ct. 72 (1995).

11

2.3.3.3. Scenes à Faire

Similar to the concept of merger is the proposition that copyright protection will not extend to "scenes à faire," thematic concepts which necessarily must follow from certain similar plot situations.[47] The scenes à faire exclusion is not limited to literary or dramatic works, but has been extended to the analysis of claims involving computer software[48] and musical works.[49]

Inasmuch as "ideas" as such are not within the subject matter of copyright, state laws purporting to protect ideas may be enforceable and will not be subject to preemption. The states vary considerably in their approach to the protection of ideas.[50]

2.4. Special Categories of Works:

While the Copyright Act does not create special categories of works, with separate schema for protection (except for semi-conductor chips), the combination of certain specific provisions of the Act and judicial development have resulted in different, if not special, treatment for computer software, compilations and databases, historical and factual material, utilitarian works, architectural works, sound recordings, and fictional characters.

2.4.1. Computer Software

---

[47] Reyher v. Children's Television Workshop, 533 F.2d 87 (2d Cir.), *cert denied*, 429 U.S. 980, 97 S. Ct. 492 (1976); Hartman v. Hallmark Cards, Inc., 833 F.2d 117 (8th Cir. 1987) ("Copyrights do not protect thematic concepts or scenes a faire").

[48] Mitel, Inc. v. Iqtel, Inc., 124 F.3d 1366 (10th Cir. 1997) (extending scenes à faire analysis "to exclude from protection against infringement those elements of a work that necessarily result from external factors inherent in the subject matter of the work"); Computer Associates, International, Inc. v. Altai, Inc., 982 F.2d 693 (2d Cir. 1992); Apple Computer, Inc. v. Microsoft Corp., 35 F.3d 1435 (9th Cir. 1994), *cert. denied*, 115 S. Ct. 1176 (1995).

[49] Smith v. Jackson, 84 F.3d 1213 (9th Cir. 1996).

[50] *See, e.g.* Murray v. National Broadcasting Co., Inc., 844 F.2d 988 (2d Cir. 1988).

2.4.1.1. Software as a "Literary Work"

In connection with passage of the 1976 Act, Congress created the National Commission on New Technological Uses of Copyrighted Works ("CONTU"), whose task was to determine what, if any, special legislation was needed to deal with computer software. Ultimately, CONTU's deliberations resulted in minimal recommendations: the inclusion in the Act of a definition of a computer program and special provisions relating to permissible copying; in short, it was determined that broad, separate provisions dealing exclusively with computer software were not necessary.

Consistent with the CONTU recommendation, the Copyright Act defines a computer program as "a set of statements or instructions to be used directly or indirectly in a computer in order to bring about a certain result."[51] While so defining software, the Act does not address software specifically in its exemplary listing of "works of authorship" within the subject matter of copyright. Rather, such a "set of statements or instructions," if sufficiently original, would qualify for protection as a "literary work." In short, with certain highly specific exceptions, computer programs are not treated by the Copyright Act, or other legislation, as a special category of intellectual property, subject to idiosyncratic rules. The conceptual problem that results is whether computer programs, as literary works, are to be analyzed, and their protection determined and limited by the same standards applicable to traditional literary works.

2.4.1.2. Protection of the Code Itself

With respect to the literal work constituting the program—the "code" in which the literary work is written—certain propositions have been clearly enunciated by the courts: (1) so long as it meets the minimal requirements of originality, the code is a "work of authorship" subject to copyright, irrespective of whether it is "source code" or "object code" or written in a directly perceptible high-level programming language, or in machine language comprehensible only to the computer;[52] (2) the form in which it is "fixed" is irrelevant so long as it is "fixed" in some form—*i.e.*, it may be fixed as writing on paper, in magnetic form on disc or tape, or even

---

[51] 17 U.S.C. § 101.

[52] Williams Electronics, Inc. v. Artic International, Inc., 685 F.2d 870 (3d Cir. 1982).

embedded in a ROM chip;[53] (3) the function of the program, including whether it is an application used by the human user of the system or an internal control program, such as an operating system, that is addressed to the machine rather than to a person, is irrelevant—protection exists independent of the nature of the program.[54]

2.4.1.3. Protection of Structure and "Look and Feel"

The significant problems and controversial issues relating to computer programs concern the protectability of the non-literal, structural elements of a program and the program's "look and feel." Although the overall structure of a program is not protectable, other non-literal elements may be sufficiently concrete to constitute protected "expression," just as copyright protection will extend to sufficiently detailed, concrete non-literal elements of any other "literary work" to the extent those elements are sufficiently original and creative. The problem for the courts has been the development of standards to determine when and how to protect the detailed structure. The opposing lines were drawn in conflicting opinions from the Third and Second Circuits: *Whelan Associates, Inc. v. Jaslow Dental Laboratory, Inc.*[55] and *Computer Associates, International, Inc. v. Altai, Inc.*,[56] respectively.

In *Whelan*, the Third Circuit, in finding protection for the set of algorithms constituting the structure of a program, started with the proposition, now universally accepted, that "[b]y analogy to other literary works ... copyrights of computer programs can be infringed even absent copying of the literal elements of the program." Finding the structure of the program analogous to a compilation of routines and algorithms, the court could protect "the sequence and order" of that compilation,[57] if it contained the requisite originality and creativity, and if it was not subject to application of the doctrine of merger. The court's approach was expansive, particularly in the way it distinguished between idea and original expression in the compilation.

---

[53] *Id.*

[54] Apple Computer, Inc. v. Franklin Computer Corp., 714 F.2d 1240 (3d Cir, 1983).

[55] 797 F.2d 1222 (3d Cir), *cert. denied* 479 U.S. 1031,107 S. Ct. 877 (1987).

[56] 982 F.2d 693 (2d Cir. 1992).

[57] See *infra*, §2.4.2.

On the other hand, the Second Circuit's 1992 *Computer Associates* opinion took a far more restrictive approach to protection of the non-literal elements of computer programs. Expressly criticizing the then five year old *Whelan* for "the opinion's somewhat outdated appreciation of computer science," the court proposed "abstraction, filtration, comparison" tests to determine copyrightability and infringement of non-literal elements. Specifically, the court proposed that in looking at claims for protecting structure, first one must place that structure on a continuum from the literal code to the ultimate function of the program, eliminating that which is found to be too abstract and thus in the realm of idea; then sift out non-protectible matter and compare what remains to the allegedly infringing program. In the process of "sifting" it is necessary to separate out (i) expression that merges into the relevant ideas; (ii) elements of a program necessarily incidental to its function; (iii) scenes à faire; (iv) matter in the public domain; and (v) matter necessary for "efficiency." Anything of the structure that is left may be protected if found to have been taken. The court acknowledged the restrictive nature of its approach and its rather grudging acceptance of computer programs as "literary works:"

> [Plaintiff] and some amici argue against the type of approach that we have set forth on the grounds that it will be a disincentive for future computer program research and development. .... The interest of the copyright law is not in simply conferring a monopoly on industrious persons, but in advancing the public welfare through rewarding artistic creativity, in a manner that permits the free use and development of non-protectable ideas and processes.

> ...

> In the meantime, Congress has made clear that computer programs are literary works entitled to copyright protection. Of course, we shall abide by these instructions, but in so doing we must not impair the overall integrity of copyright law. ... If the test we have outlined results in narrowing the scope of protection, as we expect it will, that result flows from applying, in accordance with Congressional intent, long-standing principles of copyright law to computer programs. Of course, our decision is also informed by our concern that these fundamental principles remain undistorted.[58]

---

[58] Computer Associates, International, Inc. v. Altai, Inc., 982 F.2d 693, 711-712 (2d Cir. 1992).

The Ninth Circuit has echoed the criticism of *Whelan* and approved *Computer Associates*, as have the Fifth, Tenth, Eleventh, and Federal Circuits.[59]

The question of protecting a program's "look and feel"—where the taking involves neither the actual code nor the structure of a program, but rather the re-creation of its appearance and manner of operation—remains unsettled. In the leading case, *Lotus Development Corp. v. Borland Int'l., Inc.*,[60] the First Circuit found the command menu structure of a spreadsheet program to be an unprotectable "process," analogous to the controls of a VCR. The opinion was affirmed by an equally divided (4-4) United States Supreme Court,[61] and thus has limited precedential value. The First Circuit analysis appears to be directly contrary to that of the Tenth Circuit,[62] but seems to be supported by the Eleventh Circuit.[63]

Computer software remains in a peculiar, hybrid position. While it is recognized that computer software does not fit exactly within the patent or copyright constructs, it nevertheless can find protection, to a greater or

---

[59] *See* Sega Enterprises, Ltd. v. Accolade, Inc., 977 F.2d 1510 (9th Cir. 1992); Apple Computer, Inc. v. Microsoft Corp., 35 F.3d 1435 (9th Cir. 1994), *cert. denied*, 115 S. Ct. 1176 (1995); Engineering Dynamics, Inc. v. Structural Software, Inc., 26 F.3d 1335 (5th Cir. 1994), *rehearing denied*, 46 F.3d 408 (5th Cir. 1995); Mitel, Inc. v. Iqtel, Inc., 124 F.3d 1366 (10th Cir. 1997); Gates Rubber Co. v. Bando Chemical Industries, 9 F.3d 823 (10th Cir. 1993); Bateman v. Mnemonics, Inc., 79 F.3d 1532 (11th Cir. 1996); Atari Games Corp. v. Nintendo of America, Inc., 975 F.2d 832 (Fed. Cir. 1992).

[60] 49 F.3d 807 (1st Cir. 1995).

[61] 116 S. Ct. 804 (1996).

[62] Autoskill, Inc. v. National Education Support Systems, Inc., 994 F.2d 1476 (10th Cir.), *cert. denied*, 114 S. Ct. 307 (1993).

[63] *See* Mitek Holdings v. Arce Engineering, 89 F.3d 1548 (11th Cir. 1996). The Ninth Circuit, in Apple Computer, Inc. v. Microsoft Corp., 35 F.3d 1435 (9th Cir. 1994), *cert. denied*, 115 S. Ct. 1176 (1995), dealt "for the first time, with a claim of copying a computer program's artistic look as an audiovisual work instead of program codes registered as a literary work." In a context limited by the parties' license agreement, the court upheld the use of "the limiting doctrines of originality, functionality, standardization, scenes a faire and merger to find no copying of protectable elements" with respect to Apple's graphical user interface.

lesser extent, as a species of "literary works" under the Copyright Act. The courts have had to apply traditional copyright concepts to this quite untraditional form of intellectual property. The judicial discomfort has been clearly expressed:

> To be frank, the exact contours of copyright protection for non-literal program structure are not completely clear. ... Indeed, it may well be that the Copyright Act serves as a relatively weak barrier against public access to the theoretical interstices behind a program's source and object codes. This results from the hybrid nature of a computer program, which, while it is literary expression, is also a highly functional, utilitarian component in the larger process of computing.
>
> Generally, we think that copyright registration—with its indiscriminating availability—is not ideally suited to deal with the highly dynamic technology of computer science. Thus far, many of the decisions in this area reflect the courts' attempt to fit the proverbial square peg in a round hole. [N]ow that more than 12 years have passed since CONTU issued its final report, the resolution of this specific issue could benefit from further legislative investigation—perhaps a CONTU II.[64]

As of the summer of 2006, there was no significant movement for the creation of a *sui generis* scheme for protection of computer programs. At the same time, the recent expansiveness in the scope of patent protection—particularly with respect to computer programs— has to some extent shifted the focus of concern away from copyright.[65]

2.4.2. Compilations and Databases

"Copyright law and compilations are uneasy bed fellows."[66] The Copyright Act provides that "the subject matter of copyright ... includes compilations ... ."[67] It defines a "compilation" as "a work formed by the collection and assembling of preexisting materials or of data that are selected, coordinated, or arranged in such a way that the resulting work as

---

[64] Computer Associates, International, Inc. v. Altai, Inc., 982 F.2d 693 (2d Cir. 1992).

[65] *See generally,* § 2.6.2, *infra.*

[66] Eckes v. Card Prices Update, 736 F.2d 859, 862 (2d Cir. 1984).

[67] 17 U.S.C. § 103.

a whole constitutes an original work of authorship."[68] In protecting an original compilation, the Act distinguishes between the compilation— the arrangement or selection of the material—and the material itself. As one court has observed: "The law of copyright defies the laws of logic ... since it affords to the summation of one hundred ... individual facts and their unadorned expression a significant measure of protection while affording none to the facts themselves. ...The whole of a compilation ... is greater than the sum of its parts."[69]

Irrespective of the material constituting the compilation, it is the originality of the compilation itself that determines the nature and extent of copyright protection. In *Feist Publications, Inc. v. Rural Telephone Service Co., Inc.,*[70] the United States Supreme Court resolved some conflict in the circuits over the role of effort, as opposed to originality, in establishing copyrightability for compilations. The Court firmly put to rest the notion that effort, "sweat of the brow," such as involved in creation of an alphabetical listing of names and telephone numbers in a telephone directory, can render copyrightable a compilation that is otherwise lacking in originality. The Court's language (O'Connor, J.) is unequivocal:

> It may seem unfair that much of the fruit of the compiler's labor may be used by others without compensation. [T]his is not "some unforeseen byproduct of a statutory scheme." ... It is, rather, "the essence of copyright," ... and a constitutional requirement. The primary objective of copyright is not to reward the labor of authors, but "to promote the Progress of Science and useful Arts." Art. I, § 8, cl. 8. ... To this end, copyright assures authors the right to their original expression, but encourages others to build freely upon the ideas and information conveyed by a work.[71]

---

[68] 17 U.S.C. § 101.

[69] Financial Information, Inc. v. Moody's Investors Services, Inc., 751 F.2d 501, 505 (2d Cir. 1984).

[70] 499 U.S. 340, 111 S. Ct. 1282 (1991).

[71] *Id.* at 349-350, 111 S. Ct. at 1289-1290 (quoting from Justice Brennan's dissenting opinion in Harper & Row Publishers, Inc. v. Nation Enterprises, 471 U.S. 539, 105 S. Ct. 2218 (1985).

For compilations, just as for any other work for which copyright protection is sought, "the *sine qua non* of copyright is originality."[72] Again, the language in *Feist* is instructive: "the 1976 revisions to the Copyright Act leave no doubt that originality, not 'sweat of the brow,' is the touchstone of copyright protection in directories and other fact-based works."[73] The originality threshold, however, is not very high. While a mechanical arrangement, or one dictated by the material itself, not involving any creative effort, will not be protected,[74] where originality can be found in the arrangement or selection of the material, the compilation will be copyrightable.[75] Even when the compilation is sufficiently original to be protected, that protection may be quite "thin"; protection extends only to that which is original in the compilation, leaving much of the work itself available to others.[76]

---

[72] *See infra* § 3.2.2.

[73] *Feist*, 499 U.S. at 359-360, 111 S. Ct. at 1295.

[74] *Feist*, 499 U.S. at 349-50, 111 S. Ct. at 1289-90. *See* Financial Information, Inc. v. Moody's Investors Services, Inc., 808 F.2d 204 (2d Cir. 1986), *cert. denied*, and 484 U.S. 820 (1987); *see also* Mid America Title Co. v. Kirk, 59 F.3d 719 (7th Cir.), *cert. denied*, 116 S. Ct. 520 (1995) (refusing to protect a selection that is "too rote and mechanical a task to constitute an original element of the work."); Warren Publishing Inc. v. Microdos Data Corp., 115 F.3d 1509 (11th Cir. 1997) (alphabetical listing of communities served by cable systems lacks sufficient originality in selection to warrant protection for the compilation).

[75] CCC Information Services, Inc. v. Maclean Hunter Market Reports, Inc., 44 F.3d 61 (2d Cir. 1994), *cert. denied*, 116 S. Ct. 72 (1995) (protecting a compilation of selected used car valuations):

> The compilation author typically chooses which facts to include, in what order to place them, and how to arrange the collected data so that they may be used effectively by readers. These choices as to selection and arrangement, so long as they are made independently by the compiler and entail a minimal degree of creativity, are sufficiently original that Congress may protect such compilations through the copyright laws.

See Lipton v. Nature Co., 71 F.3d 464 (2d Cir. 1995) (protecting a compilation of "terms of venery,"—sets of collective nouns, ranging from "a pride of lions" to "a bench of judges"—which plaintiff had selected and compiled from a variety of texts and manuscripts).

[76] *See, e.g,*, Kregos v. Associated Press, 937 F.2d 700 (2d Cir. 1991); same, 795 F. Supp. 1325 (S.D.N.Y. 1992), *aff'd*, 3 F.3d 656 (2d Cir. 1993), *cert. denied*, 114 S. Ct. 1056 (1994).

The problem of copyrightability of compilations is closely related to the question of protection of data and databases. Data as such, either in the form of individual datum or in the aggregate in a database, does not come within the subject matter of copyright. Facts, as ideas, have not been protectable individually or in the aggregate. As the Supreme Court made clear in *Feist*:[77] "That there can be no valid copyright in facts is universally understood. The most fundamental axiom of copyright law is that 'no author may copyright his ideas or the facts he narrates.'"[78] Justice O'Connor explains:

> This is because facts do not owe their origin to an act of authorship. The distinction is one between creation and discovery: the first person to find and report a particular fact has not created the fact; he or she has merely discovered its existence. ... The same is true of all facts—scientific, historical, biographical, and news of the day. They may not be copyrighted and are part of the public domain available to every person.[79]

Notwithstanding the effort that may be involved in individual instances of fact gathering and database creation, copyright protection, if any, can be found only in the way in which the data is selected and/or arranged. The result has been a sophisticated focus on the originality involved in data *selection* (rather than arrangement) in the more recent cases involving compiled databases.[80] Concomitantly, there has been increased interest in, and serious debate over, *sui generis* database protection, similar to that adopted by the European Union.[81]

2.4.3. Historical and Factual Material

A corollary of the proposition that facts as such are outside the scope of copyright, is the more limited copyright protection accorded historical, biographical, and other factual works. Neither historical facts nor

---

[77] 499 U.S. 340, 111 S. Ct. 1282 (1991).

[78] *Id.* at 344-345, 111 S. Ct. at 1287 (citing Harper & Row, Publishers, Inc. v. Nation Enterprises, 471 U.S. 539, 556 (1985)).

[79] *Id.* at 347-348, 111 S. Ct. at 1288-1289 (citing Miller v. Universal City Studios, 650 F.2d 1365, at 1369 (5th Cir. 1981)).

[80] *See, e.g., Lipton v. Nature Co.* and *CCC Information Services, supra*, note 70.

[81] As of mid 2006, such legislation, which had been introduced in Congress, had not been adopted.

interpretive theories are protectable, and the labor of research will not form the basis for copyright protection: "To avoid a chilling effect on authors who contemplate tackling an historical issue or event, broad latitude must be granted to subsequent authors who make use of historical subject matter, including theories or plots."[82]

The courts look closely at claims of infringement of factual or historical works to distill the protected expression from the unprotected idea. Again, Justice O'Connor in *Feist* is informative: "This court has long recognized that the fact/expression dichotomy limits severely the scope of protection in fact-based works."[83] Although copyright protection certainly is available for such types of literary work, the scope of that protection is more limited than it is for fictional or other purportedly more creative material. Thus, for example, while cookbooks may well be protectable as compilations of recipes, assuming a modicum of creativity in the arrangement, the individual recipes will normally not be protected.[84] In essence, to avoid protecting the facts comprising the work, the courts will protect such works against only wholesale, literal appropriation.[85] As the Ninth Circuit has observed:

> Because authors who wish to express ideas in factual works are usually confined to a "narrow range of expression ..., similarity of expression may have to amount to verbatim reproduction or very close paraphrasing before a factual work will be deemed infringed."[86]

---

[82] Hoehling v. Universal City Studios, Inc., 618 F.2d 972 (2d Cir. 1980).

[83] *Feist*, 449 U.S. at 350, 111 S. Ct. at 1290.

[84] Publications International Ltd. v. Meredith Corp., 88 F.3d 473 (7th Cir. 1996).

[85] *Hoehling*, 618 F.2d at 972 ("In works devoted to historical subjects, ... a second author may make significant use of prior work, so long as he does not bodily appropriate the expression of another"); Nash v. CBS, Inc., 899 F.2d 1537 (7th Cir. 1990); Narell v. Freeman, 872 F.2d 907 (9th Cir. 1989).

[86] Worth v. Selchow & Righter, 827 F.2d 569, 572 (9th Cir. 1987), *cert. denied*, 108 S. Ct. 1271 (1988) (citing Landsberg v. Scrabble Crossword Game Players, Inc., 736 F.2d 485, 488 (9th Cir.), *cert. denied*, 469 U.S. 1037 (1984)).

Of course, bodily appropriation of an entire factual work may well be infringing.[87]

Generally, the courts will not speculate as to whether a given work is "factual" or "historical" as opposed to "fictional." Rather, for purposes of defining the scope of protection, the author's own characterization of the work can be determinative. Thus, a work that purports to be "historical fiction" will have a greater claim to protection than one that purports to be an accurate history.[88]

2.4.4. *Utilitarian Works and Industrial Design*
2.4.4.1. "Useful Articles"

The Copyright Act does not deal directly with "industrial design"[89] nor is there a separate body of law, outside of the law relating to design patent, to deal specifically with such utilitarian works. Rather, the Act distinguishes between copyrightable (and broadly defined) "pictorial, graphic, and sculptural works" and uncopyrightable "useful articles," defined as articles "having an intrinsic utilitarian function that is not merely to portray the appearance of the article or to convey information."[90]

The definitional questions, of course, can be of crucial importance.[91] The fact that a work is "useful" in that it performs, or can be employed to perform, some function, will not necessarily result in it being defined as a "useful article." Thus, toy models or toy objects can be protected as "sculptural works" without reference to their utility as toys.[92] Similarly, masks designed to resemble the noses of a pig, an elephant, and a parrot

---

[87] *See* Applied Innovations, Inc. v. Regents of University of Minnesota, 876 F.2d 626 (8th Cir. 1989) (psychological inventory); Educational Testing Services v. Katzman, 793 F.2d 533 (3d Cir. 1986) (standardized test).

[88] *See* Nash v. CBS, Inc., 899 F.2d 1537 (7th Cir. 1990).

[89] Except for the limited purposes of Chapter 13 with respect to "vessel hulls." 17 U.S.C. 1301; *see infra*, sec. D, 3.

[90] 17 U.S.C. § 101.

[91] *See* Poe v. Missing Persons, 745 F.2d 1238 (9th Cir. 1984).

[92] *See* Gay Toys, Inc. v. Buddy L Corp., 703 F.2d 970 (6th Cir. 1983) ("To be sure, a toy airplane is to be played with and enjoyed, but a painting of an airplane, which is copyrightable, is to be looked at and enjoyed. Other than the portrayal of a real airplane, a toy airplane, like a painting, has no intrinsic utilitarian function").

have been held to be copyrightable "sculptural works," and not "useful articles."[93] So too, while mannequins in the form of a human torso designed to display clothing have been held to be "useful articles,"[94] forms in the shape of animals, used by taxidermists to hold animal skins, are considered sculptural works as "any utilitarian aspect of the mannequin exists 'merely to portray the appearance' of the animal."[95] On the other hand, clothing and theatrical and other costumes are considered "useful articles" not protectable as such but only upon satisfaction of the "separablility" test (discussed below).[96]

Although a model or photograph of an article may itself be copyrightable as a pictorial or sculptural work, such copyright does not extend to the manufacture of the useful article depicted.[97] Similarly, the copyright owner of a work that is lawfully reproduced in useful articles that "have been offered for sale or other distribution to the public" may not prevent "the making, distribution, or display of pictures or photographs of such articles in connection with advertisements or commentaries related to the distribution or display of such articles, or in connection with news reports."[98]

2.4.4.2. Separability of Form and Function

Although a useful article as such is not copyrightable, its design may, under certain circumstances, be protected as a pictorial, graphic, or sculptural work. The operative question is whether the formal, esthetic elements of the article's design are separable from the functional, utilitarian

---

[93] Masquerade Novelty, Inc. v. Unique Industries, Inc., 912 F.2d 663 (3d Cir. 1990) ("That nose masks are meant to be worn by humans to evoke laughter does not distinguish them from clearly copyrightable works of art like paintings. [T]he utilitarian nature of an animal nose mask ... inheres solely in its appearance").

[94] Carol Barnhart Inc. v. Economy Cover Corp., 773 F.2d 411 (2d Cir. 1985). *Cf.*

[95] Superior Form Builders, Inc. v. Dan Chase Taxidermy Supply Co., 74 F.3d 488 (4th Cir.), *cert. denied,* 117 S. Ct. 53 (1996); *see also* Hart v. Dan Chase Taxidermy Supply Co., 86 F.3d 320 (2d Cir. 1996).

[96] *See, e.g.,* Whimsicality, Inc. v. Rubie's Costume Co., 891 F.2d 452 (2d Cir. 1989).

[97] 17 U.S.C. § 113 (b).

[98] 17 U.S.C. § 113 (c).

elements. In the language of the Act, copyrightable pictorial, graphic, and sculptural works include:

> works of artistic craftsmanship insofar as their form but not their mechanical or utilitarian aspects are concerned; the design of a useful article ... shall be considered a pictorial, graphic, or sculptural work only if, and only to the extent that, such design incorporates pictorial, graphic, or sculptural features that can be identified separately from, and are capable of existing independently of, the utilitarian aspects of the article.[99]

The statutory language is an attempt[100] to codify the United States Supreme Court opinion in *Mazer v. Stein,*[101] in which the Court held that a statuette incorporated into the design of a lamp was copyrightable as a sculptural work, even if it might also be the subject of a design patent. In so doing, the court restated the "non-discrimination" doctrine to the effect that copyright is not limited to the fine arts and made clear that an otherwise copyrightable work (*e.g.* a sculpture) does not lose its copyrightability by virtue of being incorporated into a commercial, useful article.[102] The crucial issue concerned the separability of the aesthetic from the functional.

In *Mazer*, it was quite easy to separate the "sculpture" from the rest of the lamp; it was obviously physically separable. Physical separability, however, is not the only factor to be considered. The House Committee Report relating to the 1976 Act, in commenting on the language of "separability" in the definition of "pictorial, graphic, and sculptural works" and a "useful article," referred to elements that "physically *or conceptually*, can be identified as separable from the utilitarian aspects of that article."(Emphasis added) In a series of not entirely consistent opinions the courts have attempted to refine and apply the idea of conceptual separability for determining copyrightability of the design of a useful article. Thus, divided panels held that the aesthetic elements were not conceptually

---

[99] 17 U.S.C. § 101.

[100] In conjunction with 17 U.S.C. § 113.

[101] 347 U.S. 201,74 S. Ct. 460 (1954).

[102] 17 U.S.C. § 113 incorporates *Mazer* by providing:
(a) ... the exclusive rights to reproduce a copyrighted pictorial, graphic, or sculptural work in copies ... includes the right to reproduce the work in or on any kind of article, whether useful or otherwise.

separable from the utilitarian in mannequins in the form of human torsos used to display clothing[103] and in a bicycle rack,[104] while mannequins for mounting animal skins were found both to be not useful articles and to demonstrate conceptual separability of form and function.[105] While the courts recognize that "conceptual separability is ... alive and well, [t]he problem ... is determining exactly what it is and how it is to be applied."[106] The problem is perhaps best exemplified by the language of the Second Circuit in denying copyright protection for the design of a bicycle rack:

> Form and function are inextricably intertwined in the rack, its ultimate design being as much the result of utilitarian pressures as aesthetic choices. [The designer] has achieved ... the highest goal of modern industrial design, that is, the harmonious fusion of function and aesthetics. Thus there remains no artistic element ... that can be identified as separate and "capable of existing independently of, the utilitarian aspects of the article."[107]

2.4.4.3. *Sui Generis* Protection for "Mask Works": The Semiconductor Chip Protection Act[108]

---

[103] Carol Barnhart Inc. v. Economy Cover Corp., 773 F.2d 411 (2d Cir. 1985).

[104] Brandir International, Inc. v. Cascade Pacific Lumber Co., 834 F.2d 1142 (2d Cir. 1987).

[105] Pivot Point International, Inc. v. Charlene Products, 372 F.3d 913 (7th Cir. 2004); Superior Form Builders, Inc. v. Dan Chase Taxidermy Supply Co., 74 F.3d 488 (4th Cir.), *cert. denied*, 117 S. Ct. 53 (1996); Hart v. Dan Chase Taxidermy Supply Co., 86 F.3d 320 (2d Cir. 1996).

[106] Carol Barnhart Inc. v. Economy Cover Corp., 773 F.2d 411 (2d Cir. 1985). *See* Pivot Point International, Inc. v. Charlene Products, 372 F.3d 913 (7th Cir. 2004) in which the court reviews the various analytic models; *cf.* Galiano v. Harrah's Operating Company, Inc., 416 F.3d 411 (5th Cir. 2005) (proposing a sui generis approach to clothing and costume design).

[107] Brandir International, Inc. v. Cascade Pacific Lumber Co., 834 F.2d 1142 (2d Cir. 1987).

[108] For a more detailed discussion of this material *see* RICHARD H. STERN, SEMICONDUCTOR CHIP PROTECTION (Law & Business, Inc. 1986); PAUL GOLDSTEIN, COPYRIGHT § § 15.26 *et seq.* (Little Brown & Company 1989).

2.4.4.3.1. Generally

The nature of semiconductor chips is such that, in the normal course, they would not meet the stringent requirements for patent protection, nor, as inherently "useful articles," could they qualify for copyright protection. The circuit designs or technical drawings from which the chip is produced could possibly be protected as pictorial works, but neither the "mask" used to produce the embedded patterns in the chip, nor the patterns, nor the chip itself, would receive protection. While initial development of a particular semiconductor chip can be the product of significant expenditure of effort and resources, once manufactured, a chip may be analyzed and reproduced, through reproduction of the mask, at comparatively low cost. In response to industry concerns over copying, Congress enacted The Semiconductor Chip Protection Act of 1984,[109] as Chapter Nine of the Copyright Act, "Protection of Semiconductor Chip Products,"[110] to protect "mask works"[111] embodied in semiconductor chips.

Congress was quite clear in stating that this legislation, although technically incorporated into the Copyright Act, is not "a part of the Copyright Act's general provisions, but is "a sui generis form of intellectual property right, similar in many respects to existing copyright law but differing from copyright law in many ways."[112] Avoiding the somewhat murky issue of whether semiconductor chip protection is a proper exercise of Congress' power with respect to "writings" under Article I, section 8 of

---

[109] Pub. L. No. 98-620, 98 Stat.3335, 3347-3356 (1984).

[110] 17 U.S.C. § 901 et seq.

[111] A "mask work" is

a series of related images, however fixed or encoded—

(A) having or representing the predetermined, three-dimensional pattern of metallic, insulating, or semiconductor material present or removed from the layers of a semiconductor chip product; and

(B) in which series the relation of the images to one another is that each image has the pattern of the surface of one form of the semiconductor chip product.

17 U.S.C. § 901(a) (2). The House Report with respect to the Semiconductor Chip Protection Act describes the mask work as "the layout determination and the sum total of the individual masks, set upon each other, used to fabricate the entire chip." H.R. Rep. No. 781, 98th Cong., 2d Sess. (1984).

[112] H.R. Rep. No. 781, 98th Cong., 2d Sess. (1984). Implementing that idea, § 912 (b) specifically states that, with a minor exception, the other provisions of the Copyright Act are not applicable to Chapter Nine.

the Constitution,[113] as opposed to the general Congressional power with respect to interstate commerce, protection is limited to remedies for acts of infringement "by conduct in or affecting commerce."[114]

The legislation is designed to provide the exclusive source for protection of mask works, as its provisions expressly "preempt the laws of any State to the extent those laws provide any rights or remedies with respect to a mask work which are equivalent to those rights or remedies provided by [Chapter Nine]."[115] On the other hand, it expressly does not preempt any federal copyright or patent claims which might be applicable to a semiconductor chip,[116] such as, for example, copyright claims with respect to computer programs embedded in a chip, or patent claims if a chip design can pass the stringent tests of patentability.

Protection under the Chip Protection Act extends only to "a mask work fixed in a semiconductor chip product, by or under the authority of the owner of the mask work."[117] It is the "mask work" used as the template for etching the circuitry into the chip, not the chip itself, that is protected. Since protection is limited to mask works fixed in semiconductor chips, other technologies, accomplishing similar results but without the use of semiconductors or masks in the manufacturing process, would not come within the ambit of protection. On the other hand, the Act is not limited to any particular kind of semiconductor material.

Protection for a qualifying mask work commences on the earlier of the date on which the work is registered or the date on which the work is first commercially exploited anywhere in the world, and endures for a period of

---

[113] *Cf. supra* § 1.

[114] 17 U.S.C. § 910 (a).

[115] 17 U.S.C. § 912 (c).

[116] 17 U.S.C. § 912 (a).

[117] 17 U.S.C. § 902 (a) (1). A "semiconductor chip product" is the final or intermediate form of any product—
A) having two or more layers of metallic, insulating, or semiconductor material, deposited or otherwise placed on, or etched away or otherwise removed from, a piece of semiconductor material in accordance with a predetermined pattern; and
(B) intended to perform electronic circuitry functions.
17 U.S.C. § 901(a) (1).

ten years thereafter.[118] However, if protection commences by virtue of commercial exploitation, the protection will terminate (prospectively) if application for registration is not made within two years after such commencement date.[119]

Mirroring the Copyright Act,[120] the Chip Protection Act excludes from protection mask works "prepared by an officer or employee of the United States Government as part of that person's official duties," while recognizing the right of the United States Government to hold and enforce rights it receives as a transferee from one not an officer or employee.[121]

2.4.4.3.2. Substantive Conditions of Protection

As with copyright, protection is limited to "original expression,"[122] which requires both independent origin and some minimal degree of creativity, and it may be presumed that this standard will be applied to mask work protection in a manner similar to that in which it is generally applied.[123] Indeed, it is even more explicit than the overall copyright standard in denying protection to staple, commonplace, or familiar articles.[124]

Further, the Chip Protection Act follows the Copyright Act verbatim in limiting protection to "expression" rather than "idea."[125] Although there is a rich body of copyright law attempting to grapple with the problem of separating "idea" from "expression,"[126] given the nature of the work

---

[118] 17 U.S.C. § 904. For these purposes, terms of protection run to the end of the calendar year in which they would otherwise expire.

[119] 17 U.S.C. § 908 (a).

[120] See supra § 2.3.2.

[121] 17 U.S.C. § 903 (d).

[122] 17 U.S.C. § 902 (b) (10).

[123] See supra, § 2.3.3. and infra, § 3.2.2.

[124] 17 U.S.C. § 902 (b) (2).

[125] 17 U.S.C. § 902 (c): "In no case does protection ... for a mask work extend to any idea, procedure, process, system, method of operation, concept, principle, or discovery, regardless of the form in which it is described, explained, illustrated, or embodied in such work."

[126] See, generally, infra § 3.2.2.

involved, it is not likely that the same degree of complexity will attach to this analysis with respect to mask works.

Protection is further limited to mask works whose owners are nationals or domiciliaries of the United States at the time the work is registered or is first commercially exploited anywhere in the world, whichever occurs first (or whose owners are nationals or domiciliaries of foreign nations that are parties to a treaty, to which the United States is also party, protecting mask works, or whose owners are stateless persons); or that are first commercially exploited in the United States; or are the subject of a special Presidential proclamation.[127]

2.4.4.3.3. Formal Conditions of Protection

The Chip Protection Act again follows the Copyright Act in conditioning protection for a mask work on "fixation." However, unlike the Copyright Act, fixation must be in a particular medium, "a semiconductor chip product."[128] A mask work is "fixed" in a semiconductor chip product when its embodiment in the product is sufficiently permanent or stable to permit the mask work to be perceived or reproduced from the product for a period of more than transitory duration."[129]

The Chip Protection Act protects mask works fixed in a semiconductor chip product upon registration or upon the date, if earlier, on which the work is first "commercially exploited" anywhere in the world.[130] To "commercially exploit" a mask work "is to distribute to the public for commercial purposes a semiconductor chip product embodying the mask work."[131] The term also includes an offer to sell or transfer a semiconductor

---

[127] 17 U.S.C. § 902 (a) (1). The President may extend protection to mask works whose owners are nationals or domiciliaries of a foreign nation, who would not otherwise come within the provisions of this section, upon finding that that nation extends equivalent protection to masks works of owners who are nationals or domiciliaries of the United States. 17 U.S.C. § 902 (a) (2).

[128] 17 U.S.C. § 902 (a) (1).

[129] 17 U.S.C. § 901 (3).

[130] 17 U.S.C. §§ 902 (a), 904 (a).

[131] 17 U.S.C. § 901 (a) (5).

chip product "when the offer is in writing and occurs after the mask work is fixed in the semiconductor chip product."[132]

While protection is framed in the disjunctive (registration or commercial exploitation) in fact registration is essential to continuing protection, inasmuch as any protection for a mask work will terminate "if application for registration ... is not made ... within two years after the date on which the mask work is first commercially exploited anywhere in the world."[133] Since registration or exploitation is essential for the commencement of protection, the effect of this provision is to make registration mandatory for continuing protection.

Registration is accomplished by the filing of appropriate forms, as prescribed by the Register of Copyrights, accompanied by the necessary fees and deposit of specified identifying material.[134] The application is examined, much the same way as examination of copyright applications; if in order, a certificate of registration is issued, effective as of the date on which the application, together with appropriate fees and identify material, is received in the copyright office.[135] If registration is refused, the applicant may bring an action for judicial review in the United States District Court within sixty days after the date of refusal.[136]

Registration entitles the registrant to bring actions for infringement with respect to the protected mask work.[137] In much the same way as with copyrighted works,[138] the Chip Protection Act makes the certificate of registration prima facie evidence of the facts stated therein and of compliance with the registration requirements (although it does not mirror the Copyright Act's further presumption of validity).[139] If registration has been refused and the applicant has not directly appealed the refusal, the applicant may nevertheless institute a civil action for infringement if notice

---

[132] *Id.*

[133] *Id.*

[134] 17 U.S.C. § 908 (c) and (d).

[135] 17 U.S.C. § 908 (e).

[136] 17 U.S.C. § 908 (g).

[137] 17 U.S.C. § 910 (b) (1).

[138] *See infra* § 3.1.4.3.

[139] 17 U.S.C. § 908 (f).

thereof, together with a copy of the complaint, is served on the Register of Copyrights, who may then choose to become a party to the action.[140]

Notice may be placed upon protected mask works and semiconductor chip products embodying protected mask works so as "to give reasonable notice of such protection."[141] While notice is not a condition to protection, it does constitute prima facie evidence of notice of protection,[142] and therefore where it is present, it would essentially preclude the availability of the limitations on liability accorded innocent infringers. The Register of Copyrights, pursuant to statutory direction, has prescribed, by regulation, exemplary methods of fixation of notice.

2.4.4.3.4. Ownership and Transfer

The "owner" of a mask work is "the person who created the mask work, the legal representative of that person if that person is deceased or under a legal incapacity, or a party to whom all the rights ... of such person or representative are transferred."[143] Where a mask work has been made within the scope of a person's employment, "the owner is the employer for whom the person created the mask work or a party to whom all the rights ... of the employer are transferred."[144] Presumably, in determining whether a work has been made within the scope of a person's employment, the "work for hire" standards developed by the courts under the Copyright Act would be applicable.[145] Unlike the Copyright Act's definitions, the Chip Protection Act does not contemplate an alternative employer for hire status for specially commissioned work not within an employee's scope of employment. Presumably, a mask work might be developed jointly and the

---

[140] 17 U.S.C. § 910 (b) (2) ("the failure of the Register to become a party to the action shall not deprive the court of jurisdiction to determine [eligibility for registration]").

[141] 17 U.S.C. § 909. Notice is to be in the form of the words "mask work," the symbol "*M*," or the symbol "Ⓜ" ("M" in a circle) together with the name of the owner or owners of the work

[142] *Id.*

[143] 17 U.S.C. § 901 (a) (6).

[144] *Id.*

[145] *See infra* § 4.6.1.

Copyright Act's standards with respect to determining joint authorship should be helpful.[146]

As opposed to "ownership" of copyrighted works, which may involve multiple owners of exclusive rights relating to the infinitely divisible bundle of rights constituting copyright,[147] ownership of mask works is essentially unitary.

The Chip Protection Act expressly recognizes the right of the owner of "the exclusive rights" in a mask work to "transfer all of those rights, or license all or less than all of those rights."[148] Such transfer or license, however, even for a non-exclusive license, may be made only by a written instrument signed by the "owner" or the owner's authorized agent.[149] Transfer or license may also be effected by operation of law, by will, and by the applicable state laws of intestate succession.[150]

Transfers, and any other document "pertaining to a mask work" may be recorded in the Copyright office, if properly executed; record nation of a transfer all license "gives all persons constructive notice of the facts stated in the recorded document concerning the transfer or license."[151] Recording, and the concomitant constructive notice, will determine the resolution of conflicting transfers.[152]

2.4.4.3.5. Nature of the Rights

The Chip Protection Act grants a broad reproduction right with respect to the mask work, covering any means of reproduction, an exclusive distribution and importation right, and a right against contributory

---

[146] *See infra* § 4.4.

[147] *See infra*, § 4.2.

[148] 17 U.S.C. § 903 (b).

[149] *Id.*

[150] *Id.*

[151] 17 U.S.C. § 903 (c) (1).

[152] 17 U.S.C. § 903 (c) (2):
In any case in which conflicting transfers of the exclusive rights in a mask work are made, the transfer first executed shall be void as against a subsequent transfer which is made for a valuable consideration and without notice of the first transfer, unless the first transfer is recorded ... within three months after the date on which it is executed, but in no case later than the day before the date of such subsequent transfer.

infringement.[153] Rather than providing for a general "fair use" defense to infringement claims, the Chip Protection Act limits the exclusive reproduction right by providing an exception for "reverse engineering" and limits the distribution/importation right with a "first sale" exemption.

The Copyright Act generally does not deal with reverse engineering, so that the courts have applied fair use principles to reverse engineering of computer programs.[154] The Chip Protection Act, however, expressly exempts certain forms of reverse engineering from liability for infringement of the exclusive reproduction right.[155] The effect of this provision is to allow a competitor to use the results of a reverse engineering analysis to create a competing product that does not simply incorporate the protected mask work.[156]

As a limitation upon the exclusive rights to import or distribute a semiconductor chip product in which the mask work is embodied, the Chip Protection Act follows the Copyright Act[157] in creating a "first sale"

---

[153] The exclusive rights of the owner of a mask work are limited to the rights:
(1) to reproduce the mask work by optical, electronic, or any other means;
(2) to import or distribute a semiconductor chip product in which the mask work is embodied; and
(3) to induce or knowingly to cause another person to do any of the acts described in paragraphs (1) and (2).
17 U.S.C. § 905. For these purposes, "the distribution or importation of a product incorporating a semiconductor chip product as a part thereof is a distribution or importation of that semiconductor chip product." 17 U.S.C. § 901 (b).

[154] See infra § 7.4.

[155] Specifically,
it is not an infringement of the exclusive rights of the owner of a mask work for—
(1) a person to reproduce the mask work solely for the purpose of teaching, analyzing, or evaluating the concepts or techniques embodied in the mask work or circuitry, logic flow, or organization of components used in the mask work; or
(2) a person who performs the analysis or evaluation described in paragraph (1) to incorporate the results of such conduct in an original mask work which is made to be distributed.
17 U.S.C. § 906 (a).

[156] See Brooktree Corp. v. Advanced Micro Devices, Inc., 705 F.Supp. 491 (S.D. Cal. 1988).

[157] See infra § 6.3.2.

exemption.[158] The importation/distribution right (but not the reproduction right) is further limited by provisions completely immunizing from liability an innocent purchaser of an infringing semiconductor chip product who imports or distributes units of that infringing product before such innocent purchaser has notice of protection of the mask work embodied therein.[159] Moreover, such an innocent purchaser of an infringing product who, subsequent to the purchase, receives notice of protection and thereafter imports or distributes the product will be liable "only for a reasonable royalty on each unit of the infringing semiconductor chip product" so imported or distributed;[160] absent voluntary resolution, the amount of such a royalty is to be determined by the court in an action for infringement.[161] The innocent purchaser immunity and damages limitation provisions will apply to "any person who directly or indirectly purchases an infringing semiconductor chip product from an innocent purchaser."[162]

2.4.4.3.6. Infringement and Remedies

Except to the extent specifically exempted, "any person who violates any of the exclusive rights of the owner of a mask work ... by conduct in or affecting commerce, shall be liable as an infringer of such rights."[163] An action for infringement must be commenced within three years after the claim accrues.[164] Just as with respect to copyright infringement claims, registration is a condition to the institution of actions for infringement with

---

[158] 17 U.S.C. § 906 (b):

The owner of a particular semiconductor chip product made by the owner of the mask work, or by any person authorized by the owner of the mask work, may import, distribute, or otherwise dispose of or use, but not reproduce, that particular semiconductor chip product without the authority of the owner of the mask work.

[159] 17 U.S.C. § 907 (a) (1).

[160] 17 U.S.C. §§ 907 (a) (2) and (d).

[161] 17 U.S.C. § 907 (b).

[162] 17 U.S.C. § 907 (c). An "innocent purchaser" is defined as "a person who purchases a semiconductor chip product in good faith and without having notice of protection with respect to the semiconductor chip product," and, for these purposes, "having notice of protection" is defined as "having actual knowledge that, or reasonable grounds to believe that, a mask work is protected ... ." 17 U.S.C. § 901 (a) (8).

[163] 17 U.S.C. § 910 (a).

[164] 17 U.S.C. § 910 (d).

respect to the protected mask work.[165] Similarly, if registration has been refused the applicant may institute a civil action for infringement if notice thereof, together with a copy of the complaint, is served on the Register of Copyrights.[166] As opposed to actions for infringement of copyright, it is only the "owner" of a protected mask work, or "the exclusive licensee of all rights" to a protected mask work, who may institute a civil action for infringement with respect to the mask work.[167]

The Chip Protection Act specifically makes the states and state instrumentalities subject to its provisions and expressly abrogates any immunity which a state or state instrumentalities might claim under the Eleventh Amendment of the Constitution.[168] As discussed below in connection with copyright,[169] there are serious open questions as to the constitutionality of such abrogation of immunity. Unlike the Copyright Act,[170] the Chip Protection Act contains no provisions criminalizing infringement.

The Act authorizes injunctive relief (both temporary and permanent), the award of actual damages, as well as the non-duplicative profits of the infringer, the alternative of statutory damages (in an amount up to $250,000), as well as impoundment, seizure, and disposition of infringing physical items.[171] For the most part, the language is identical to that in the Copyright Act and presumably will be interpreted in much the same way. Given the similarity of statutory language, the United States Supreme Court holding of a constitutional right to jury determination in claims involving statutory damages for copyright infringement,[172] and its determination that prevailing plaintiffs and prevailing defendants are to be treated alike in the

---

[165] 17 U.S.C. § 910 (b) (1).

[166] 17 U.S.C. § 910 (b) (2) ("the failure of the Register to become a party to the action shall not deprive the court of jurisdiction to determine [eligibility for registration]").

[167] 17 U.S.C. § 910 (b) (1).

[168] 17 U.S.C. §§ 910 (a) and 911 (g).

[169] *See infra* § 9.1.6.

[170] *See infra* § 9.4.

[171] 17 U.S.C. § 911.

[172] *See infra* § 10.2.2.3.

exercise of the court's discretion in awarding attorney's fees,[173] would appear to be applicable to claims under the Chip Protection Act.

2.4.4.4. *Sui Generis* Protection for Vessel Hulls

In October 1998, Congress enacted similar *sui generis* protection for the design of vessel hulls. With the "Vessel Hull Design Protection Act," it added to the Copyright Act a new Chapter 13, "Protection of Original Designs,"[174] modeled substantially upon the Semiconductor Chip Protection Act. It provides, to the designer of an original design, sharply limited protection for a ten-year term, with respect to the making, importation, selling, or distributing, of vessel hulls embodying that design.[175] Provision is made for registration and a unique notice.[176] There are detailed provisions with respect to remedies, immunity for innocent infringement, ownership and transfer, and similar matters. Protection under these provisions terminates upon issuance of a design patent for a protected design.[177]

The legislation was clearly experimental and of an interim nature, as it originally contained a "sunset" provision, directing that Chapter 13 remain in effect only for two years following the date of enactment. In addition, there were to be two joint studies of the Vessel Hull Protection Act's effect, to be conducted by the Register of Copyrights and the Commissioner of Patents and Trademarks, culminating in reports to Congress, originally within two years. However, with the Intellectual Property and Communications Omnibus Reform Act of 1999, Congress repealed the "sunset" provision as well as the requirement for two reports. Instead, it required a single joint report by the Register and the Under Secretary of Commerce for Intellectual Property and Director of the United States Patent and Trademark Office. That report, when issued, found only "scant and anecdotal" evidence that the Act was effective in suppressing

---

[173] *See infra* § 10.3.

[174] 17 U.S.C. § 1301 *et seq.*

[175] 17 U.S.C. §§ 1301 and 1305 and 1308.

[176] 17 U.S.C. §§ 1306 and 1310. Notice is to be in the form of the words "Protected Design," or "Prot'd Des.," the symbol "*D*," or the symbol "Ⓓ" ("D" in a circle), together with the name of the owner or owners of the design.

[177] 17 U.S.C. § 1329.

infringement, but it concluded "that it is too soon to tell whether the VHDPA has had significant overall effect on the boat building industry."

2.4.5. Architectural Works

Architectural works would appear to be quintessentially "useful articles" and subject to the same analytic model and constraints as other utilitarian works. Prior to December 1, 1990, and for all architectural works constructed prior to the date, the "useful articles" paradigm was indeed applicable to architectural works; *i.e.* buildings and similar structures, as "useful articles," were not themselves copyrightable.[178] A distinction was drawn, however, between the structure and the plans or drawings upon which it was based; while the former was unprotectable as a useful article, the plans or drawings, as "pictorial or graphical works," could be protected. "One may construct a house which is identical to a house depicted in architectural plans, but one may not directly copy those plans and then use the infringing copy to construct the house."[179] Moreover, while protection was limited to the plans or drawings, the courts were quite expansive in determining damages when plans were copied. Thus, it was held that one who infringed the plans and built a building from those plans, could be held responsible not merely for the direct value of the plans, but also for losses to the plaintiff resulting from the infringer's *use* of the plans[180] or profits the infringer realized upon resale of the structure built from the plans.[181]

Prompted both by the United States accession to the Berne Convention in 1989, as well as to sharp criticism of the existing state of the law, Congress passed the Architectural Works Copyright Protection Act, which became effective on, and covers works created after, December 1, 1990. That legislation defines "architectural works" as:

> the design of a building as embodied in any tangible medium of expression, including a building, architectural plans, or drawings. The work includes the over all form as well as the arrangement and

---

[178] Imperial Homes Corp. v. Lamont, 458 F.2d 895 (5th Cir. 1972).

[179] *Id.; see also* Robert R. Jones Associates, Inc. v. Nino Homes, 858 F.2d 274 (6th Cir. 1988).

[180] *Robert R. Jones Associates, supra..*

[181] Arthur Rutenberg v. Dawney, 647 F.Supp. 1214 (D. Fla. 1986).

composition of spaces and elements in the design, but does not include individual standard features.[182]

More significantly, it adds "architectural works" to the enumeration of "works of authorship,"[183] thereby distinguishing such works from "pictorial, graphic, and sculptural works" and rendering them no longer subject to the "useful article" and separability standards.[184] The House Committee Report underlying the legislation contemplates a "two-step analysis":

> First, an architectural work should be examined to determine whether there are original design elements present, including overall shape and interior architecture. If such design elements are present, a second step is reached to examine whether the design elements are functionally required. If the design elements are not functionally required, the work is protectable without regard to physical or conceptual separability.[185]

The result is that, subject to the standards of originality applicable to all works, "the aesthetically pleasing overall shape of an architectural work" is protected.[186]

Protection for architectural works, however, is not quite as broad as that for other works. Thus, the architect retains no moral rights in the work and may not object to alteration or destruction of the structure.[187] Moreover, ownership of copyright in an architectural work embodied in a building "located in or ordinarily visible from a public place" does not prevent the making, distribution, or display of photographs or other pictorial representations of the work.[188]

---

[182] 17 U.S.C. § 101.

[183] 17 U.S.C. § 102 (8).

[184] As the House Committee Report observes:

By creating a new category of protectable subject matter ..., and, therefore, by deliberately not encompassing architectural works as pictorial, graphic, or sculptural works ..., the copyrightability of architectural works shall not be evaluated under the separability test applicable to pictorial, graphic, the sculptural works embodied in useful articles.

H.R. Rep. No. 101-735, 101st Cong. 2d Sess. 20 (1990).

[185] *Id.* at 21.

[186] *Id.*

[187] 17 U.S.C. § 120 (b).

[188] 17 U.S.C. § 120 (a).

2.4.6. Sound Recordings

The Copyright Act recognizes "sound recordings" as a special class of works of authorship, and distinct both from the works (musical or other sounds) of which the sound recordings are composed and from the physical form—"the phonorecords"—in which they are embodied. Sound recordings are defined as "works that result from the fixation of a series of musical, spoken, or other sounds [excluding the sounds accompanying audiovisual works] and regardless of the nature of the material objects ... in which they are embodied."[189]

The sound recording copyright is limited and highly specific: it is designed essentially to protect a specific performance of a work. Sound recordings, as such, were not protected by copyright prior to the effectiveness of the 1971 Sound Recording Amendment providing for a copyright in the performance of work independent of the copyright in the work being performed.[190] This legislation, directed at "record piracy"—the unauthorized commercial duplication of phonograph and other recordings—was incorporated into the 1976 Act with the recognition of "sound recordings" as a work of authorship.[191] It is consistent with the 1971 Geneva Convention for the Protection of Producers of Phonograms against Unauthorized Duplication of Their Phonograms, which entered into force in the United States in 1974.

The sound recording copyright is essentially limited to the prevention of unauthorized copying of recordings, that purpose. The owner of the sound recording copyright has the exclusive rights: to "duplicate the sound recording in the form of phonorecords or copies that directly or indirectly recapture the actual sounds fixed in the recording"; to create derivative works "in which the actual sounds fixed in the sound recordings are rearranged, re-mixed, or otherwise altered in sequence or quality"; publicly to distribute copies of the sound recording (for which purpose, internet

---

[189] 17 U.S.C. § 101.

[190] *See* the historical discussion by the New York Court of Appeals of the sound recording copyright and "common-law"copyright in Capitol Records, Inc. v. Naxos of America, Inc., 4 N.Y.3d 540, 830 N.E.2d 250, 797 N.Y.S.3d 352.

[191] 17 U.S.C. § 102 (7).

uploading is considered a "distribution"; and publicly to perform the sound recording "by means of a digital audio transmission."[192]

It has been suggested that "[t]he analysis that is appropriate for determining infringement of a musical composition copyright, is not the analysis that is to be applied to determine infringement of a sound recording" and that matters such as "substantial similarity"[193] and de minimis copying are not appropriate to a sound recording infringement inquiry.[194]   Except for the performance by "digital audio transmission," the sound recordings copyright does not give the owner any public performance rights with respect to the sound recordings.[195] The limited performance right was created by the Digital Performance Right in Sound Recordings Act of 1995, and expanded by the Digital Millenium Act of 1998, and is effectively limited to subscription or interactive digital audio transmissions.[196]

Although this legislation creates a sharply limited performance right in sound recordings—essentially directed to those applications that displace the market for the recordings, as opposed to those (such as over the air broadcast) that could enhance the market—there are continuing legislative efforts to broaden the performance right in sound recordings to make the United States law more closely comparable to that in the European Community and to make United States eligible to adhere to the Rome Convention for the Protection of Performers, Producers of Phonograms, and Broadcasting Organizations, to which United States is not presently a party.

2.4.7. Fictional Characters

Fictional characters may be quite valuable. Merchandising rights, television production and advertising, and an array of commercial development may be based upon exploitation of fictional characters. Such exploitation may give rise to rights under the law of trademark or unfair

---

[192] 17 U.S.C. § 114.

[193] *See infra* § 9.2.1.

[194] Bridgeport Music, Inc. v. Dimension Films, 410 F.3d 792 (6th Cir. 2005).

[195] 17 U.S.C. § 114 (a).

[196] 17 U.S.C. § 114 (d); see *infra*, § 6.6.

competition. The position of fictional characters in the law copyright, however, is not clear. Essentially it reflects a long-standing division between the Second and Ninth Circuits.

The Copyright Act does not expressly include "characters" within the umbrella of "works of authorship." Of course, the work in which a character appears will normally be within the subject matter of copyright. The problem arises when a "character" is used by one other than the copyright owner of that work in another work. One mode of analysis would be to ask whether such a taking of the character is an infringement of the work in which the character was first created.[197] The reality of the exploitation of characters, however, makes the question more difficult. It has, in short, become one of the protectability of the character as such apart from the setting in which it first appeared.

The issue is more academic than real when dealing with purely pictorial characters such as cartoons. Such works may easily be analyzed as "pictorial" works for determining copyrightability and infringement and their status as "characters" is not really significant.[198] However, with respect to literary characters and those taken from audiovisual works, the issue is not so easily resolved. The Second Circuit, building on *dicta* of Judge Learned Hand,[199] has essentially assumed the copyrightability and protectability of characters as such to the extent that they are developed.[200] The Ninth Circuit, however, began, in 1954, with the absolute position that characters as such are not copyrightable and will be protected only to the

---

[197] M. NIMMER & D. NIMMER, NIMMER ON COPYRIGHT 2.12 (1997) ("the issue of whether a character from a work of fiction is protectible apart from the story in which such character appears, is in a sense more properly framed as relating to the degree of substantial similarity required to constitute infringement rather than in terms of copyrightability *per se*"). *See* Leslie A. Kurtz, *The Independent Legal Lives of Fictional Characters*, 1986 WISC. L. REV. 429.

[198] *See, e.g.*, Walt Disney Productions v. Air Pirates, 581 F.2d 751 (9th Cir. 1978), *cert. denied*, 439 U.S. 1132, 99 S. Ct. 1054 (1979); Detective Comics v. Bruns Publications, 111 F.2d 432 (2d Cir. 1940).

[199] Nichols v. Universal Pictures Corporation, 45 F.2d 119 (2d Cir. 1930), *cert. denied*, 282 U.S. 902, 51 S. Ct. 216 (1931) ("the less developed the characters, the less they can be copyrighted").

[200] Silverman v. CBS Inc., 870 F.2d 40 (2d Cir.), *cert. denied* 492 U.S. 907, 109 S. Ct. 3219 (1989).

extent they "really constitute" the story of which they are a part.[201] Subsequent Ninth Circuit cases have appeared to ameliorate the absolute rejection of independent copyrightability,[202] but the situation remains unclear.[203]

§ 3. CONDITIONS OF PROTECTION

3.1. Formal Requirements

3.1.1. Fixation as the Point of Attachment of Copyright

The 1976 Act effectively eliminated the earlier formal requirements for attachment of copyright, focusing instead on fixation of the work. Prior to January 1, 1978 (the effective date of the Copyright Act of 1976), the essential formal element for the attachment of copyright and invocation of the federal copyright scheme was "publication" of the work with appropriate notice of copyright. Prior to publication, a work was protected by state law, the so-called "common-law copyright," and the act of publication terminated that protection. Upon such publication, a work would become protected by the federal scheme, if publication was accompanied with appropriate notice, or, if not so accompanied, all protection would be lost, and the work would fall into the public domain. This formal requirement of publication with proper notice produced a substantial judicial gloss on the definition of "publication"[204] and "notice."

---

[201] Warner Bros. Pictures v. Columbia Broadcasting System, 216 F.2d 945 (9th Cir. 1954), *cert. denied*, 348 U.S. 971, 75 S. Ct. 532 (1955).

[202] Olson v. N.B.C., 855 F.2d 1446 (9th Cir, 1988); Walt Disney Productions v. Air Pirates, 581 F.2d 751 (9th Cir. 1978), *cert. denied*, 439 U.S. 1132, 99 S. Ct. 1054 (1979).

[203] *See* Anderson v. Stallone, 11 U.S.P.Q. 2d 1161 (C.D. Cal. 1989). *See also* Gaiman v. McFarlane, 360 F.3d 644, 660 (7th Cir. 2004) (suggesting that the Ninth Circuit "has killed" its 1954 decision).

[204] *See* La Cienega Music Co. v. ZZ Top, 53 F.3d 950 (9th Cir.), *cert. denied*, 116 S. Ct. 331 (1995); *cf.*, Rosette v. Rainbow Record Mfg. Corp., 546 F.2d 461 (2d Cir. 1976). The *La Cienega* decision, which held that public distribution of a recording was "publication" under the 1909 Act, was overruled by legislation in 1997 (17 U.S.C. § 303 (b)), which provides that "the distribution before January 1, 1978, of a phonorecord shall not for any purpose constitute a publication of the musical work embodied therein").

One of the most significant changes effected by the 1976 revision was the elimination of common-law copyright, with its distinction between published and unpublished works, and the concomitant formalities attendant to the attachment of copyright. Instead, copyright attaches, and protection begins, once an "original work of authorship" has been "fixed in any tangible medium of expression"[205] by or under the authority of the author. The nature of that medium is immaterial, so long as it is such that the work "can be perceived, reproduced, or otherwise communicated, either directly or with the aid of a machine or device"[206] and "is sufficiently permanent or stable to permit it to be perceived, reproduced, or otherwise communicated for a period of more than transitory duration."[207] Thus, assuming it meets the test of originality, and the fixation is done by, or on behalf of the author, a work is "fixed" and copyright protection attaches, whether that fixation takes the form of a writing on paper, magnetic impulses on media such as audio or video tape, or a computer hard drive, or a floppy disk, or etching embedded in a silicone chip. With the constitutional grant of power to deal with copyright predicated upon the "writings" of "authors," the requirement of "fixation" in a tangible medium of expression would appear to be constitutionally mandated.[208]

Unrecorded speech or live musical performances, or other ephemera, would not be considered fixed and therefore not subject to copyright protection. To deal with the problem of "bootleg" unauthorized recordings of live performances (performances, even of newly created work, which would not be considered "fixed" and would therefore involve works not protected by copyright) Congress enacted the Uruguay Round Agreements Act, signed in December, 1994, implementing the General Agreement on Tariffs and Trade, which added a new Section 1101, "Unauthorized Fixation and Trafficking in Sound Recordings and Music Videos," specifically protecting against the unauthorized making and distribution of recordings

---

[205] "Copyright protection subsists ... in original works of authorship fixed in any tangible medium of expression." 17 U.S.C. § 102.

[206] *Id.*

[207] 17 U.S.C. § 101.

[208] *See* U.S. v. Moghadam, 175 F.3d 1269, 1273-1274 (1999), *cert denied*, 529 U.S. 1036 (2000).

of live performances.[209] Recognizing the difficulty this legislation poses as a proper exercise of Congress' constitutional power under Article I, Section 8, which deals with "writings," the Eleventh Circuit upheld the statute as a proper exercise of the general congressional power to deal with matters affecting interstate commerce.[210] Similar protective legislation, largely for the benefit of organized sports, is contained in the definition of "fixed" in the Copyright Act, which treats as "fixed" for the purpose of attachment of copyright, works "consisting of sounds, images, or both, that are being transmitted ... if a fixation of the work is being made simultaneously with its transmission."[211] Thus, the live television broadcast of an athletic event would be subject to copyright protection as "fixed" if a simultaneous recording of that broadcast were made.[212]

3.1.2. Publication

With the 1976 Act abolition of common-law copyright, the defining role of "publication" also came to an end. Publication of a work is no longer required for the attachment of copyright. Of course, for works published before January 1, 1978 the rich judicial development elaborating upon what

---

[209] 17 U.S.C. § 1101. Section 1101(a) provides:
Anyone who, without the consent of the performer or performers involved—(1) fixes the sounds or sounds and images of a live musical performance in a copy or phono-record, or reproduces copies or phonorecords of such a performance from an unauthorized fixation, (2) transmits or otherwise communicates to the public the sounds or sounds and images of a live musical performance, or (3) distributes or offers to distribute, sells or offers to sell, rents or offers to rent, or traffics in any copy or phonorecord fixed as described in paragraph (1), regardless of whether the fixations occurred in the United States, shall be subject to the remedies provided in sections 502 through 505, to the same extent as an infringer of copyright.
The legislation expressly does *not* preempt state law (17 U.S.C. § 1101(d).

[210] U.S. v. Moghadam, *supra*; *but see* U.S. v. Martignon, 346 F.Supp.2d 413 (S.D.N.Y. 2004), criticizing the holding in Moghadam and holding, alternatively, that Congress may not use its Commerce Clause power generally to provide copyright-like rights or that, in any event, the anti-bootlegging statute may not be so upheld because it appears to create "perpetual" rights, inconsistent with the "limited times" condition of Article I, Sections 8.

[211] 17 U.S.C. § 101.

[212] *See, e.g.*, Baltimore Orioles, Inc. v. Major League Baseball Players Association, 805 F.2d 663 (7th Cir. 1986), *cert denied*, 480 U.S. 941 (1987).

constitutes "publication" for the purpose of divesting copyright remains applicable. Moreover, publication may still have serious consequences under the Act. It can, for example, affect the duration of copyright and right of termination, as well as rights under the Berne Convention and Universal Copyright Convention. "Publication" is defined as:

> the distribution of copies or phonorecords of a work to the public by sale or other transfer of ownership, or by rental, lease, or lending. The offering to distribute copies or phonorecords to a group of persons for purposes of further distribution, public performance, or public display, constitutes publication. A public performance or display of a work does not of itself constitute publication.[213]

Generally, the owner of copyright in a published work must, within three months after publication, deposit with the Library of Congress two copies of the "best edition" of the work.[214]

3.1.3. Notice

While the Copyright Act contains numerous provisions concerning notice,[215] the shift from "publication" to "fixation" as the point of copyright attachment has minimized the formerly central importance of notice. The Act provides that notice of copyright "may" (rather than "shall") be placed on publicly distributed copies of a work.[216] Appropriate notice of copyright is still advisable and the better practice, but that formality no longer is determinative of the vesting of rights. Where there is proper notice, a claim of innocent infringement would generally not serve to mitigate damages.[217] The Act prescribes the form of notice: generally, the word "Copyright," or the abbreviation "Copr.," or the symbol "©"; the year of first publication; and designation of the copyright owner.[218]

Under the Act, defects in notice, or even omission of notice, no longer have the fatal impact they had under the prior law. Moreover, the Berne

---

[213] 17 U.S.C. § 101.

[214] 17 U.S.C. § 407.

[215] 17 U.S.C. §§ 401-412.

[216] 17 U.S.C. § 401(a).

[217] 17 U.S.C. § 401(d).

[218] 17 U.S.C. § 401(b).

Convention Implementation Act of 1988 (effective March 1, 1989) substantially reduces, if not entirely eliminates, the consequences of failure to affix notice to a copyrighted work. Nevertheless, notice, or its omission, can be significant, particularly for certain works of U.S. origin. Omission of notice can serve to insulate an innocent infringer, at least with respect to works publicly distributed prior to 1 March, 1989. Such omission, from works distributed prior to 1 March, 1989, if authorized by the copyright owner, can serve to forfeit copyright if the works were distributed in substantial copies and if no registration of copyright was made within five years of publication.[219]

Consistent with Berne Convention implementation, the Uruguay Round Agreements Act provides for restoration of copyright in certain *foreign* works which had become unprotected in the United States (while remaining protected in their country of origin) because of failure to comply with formalities such as notice.[220] These provisions are quite elaborate, as they seek to protect the rights of innocent parties ("reliance parties") who had relied on the earlier public domain status of such works.

3.1.4. Registration and Deposit

3.1.4.1. Registration

Under the Act, the Copyright Office, a division of the Library of Congress, administers the copyright registration and deposit system. Registration of copyright in a work, accompanied by deposit of copies of the work, provides a central place for the recording, and constructive notice of, the copyright interest in the work; it also ensures that copies of the work will be publicly accessible. Except with respect to renewal of copyright term for certain pre-1976 Act works,[221] registration is permissive and does not affect the existence or vesting of copyright.[222] Nonetheless, registration remains an important procedure, with serious consequences for the copyright owner.

---

[219] 17 U.S.C. § 405(a).

[220] 17 U.S.C. § 104A.

[221] *See infra*, § 8., for discussion of renewal for pre-1976 Act works.

[222] 17 U.S.C. § 408 (a).

3.1.4.2. Registration Procedure

Registration is accomplished by filing with the Copyright Office a completed official application form, together with payment of a rather modest fee and deposit of copies of the work;[223] registration will be effective as of the date of receipt by the Copyright Office, irrespective of the length of time for processing the application. The completed application is examined, in a process much less extensive and time-consuming than in the case of a patent application, and a certificate of registration is issued by the Register of Copyright, unless registration is denied because of infirmity in the process or because the work does not properly come within the subject matter of copyright. The vast majority of registration applications are granted; under a "rule of doubt," registration will issue as long as there is at least a reasonable doubt in favor of copyrightability. Action by the Register of Copyright denying registration is appealable to the federal courts.

3.1.4.3. Benefits

Registration, while not mandatory for the attachment of copyright to a work, is a prerequisite to the institution of actions for infringement[224] of a "United States work."[225] The limitation to a "United States work" is

---

[223] 17 U.S.C. §§ 408-409. Deposit of copies with the Library of Congress pursuant to 17 U.S.C. § 407 will satisfy the registration deposit requirement.

[224] Other than claims for violation of the attribution and integrity rights of works of visual art protected by § 106A. See *infra* § 6.7.2.

[225] 17 U.S.C. § 411. For purposes of § 411, a work is a "United States work" only if—

(1) in the case of a published work, the work is first published—-
(A) in the United States;
(B) simultaneously in the United States and another treaty party or parties, whose law grants a term of copyright protection that is the same as or longer than the term provided in the United States;
(C) simultaneously in the United States and a foreign nation that is not a treaty party; or
(D) in a foreign nation that is not a treaty party, and all of the authors of the work are nationals, domiciliaries, or habitual residents of, or in the case of an audiovisual work legal entities with headquarters in, the United States;
(2) in the case of an unpublished work, all the authors of the work are nationals, domiciliaries, or habitual residents of the United States, or, in the case of an unpublished audiovisual work, all the authors are legal entities with headquarters in the United

designed to keep the United States copyright laws consistent with the Berne Convention and other treaty prohibitions on conditioning protection for foreign authors upon compliance with domestic formalities. If proper application for registration has been made and refused, the applicant may nevertheless institute an action for infringement if notice of such action, together with a copy of the complaint, is served on the Register of Copyrights.[226]

Moreover, in an action for infringement, registration provides procedural and remedial advantages, unavailable for unregistered works, even works for which registration is not a prerequisite to suit. If the work was registered within five years after first publication, the certificate of registration is *prima facie* evidence of the validity of the copyright and of the facts stated in the certificate.[227] Further, registration can have a significant influence on damages in an infringement action. The successful plaintiff may recover statutory damages and attorneys fees, but only if registration preceded the acts of infringement; or, if the infringement preceded registration of an unpublished work, or, if the infringement began after first publication and before registration, if registration is made within three months after first publication.[228]

3.1.4.4. Recordation and Registration

Registration is also significant, and in fact essential, with respect to protecting rights of transferees or holders of security interests in a work. Thus, while the Act contains provisions for recording, in the Copyright Office, of documents relating to transfers of copyright ownership or the

---

States; or
(3) in the case of a pictorial, graphic, or sculptural work incorporated in a building or structure, the building or structure is located in the United States.
17 U.S.C. § 101. A "treaty party" is a country or intergovernmental organization other than the United States that is a party to the Universal Copyright Convention, the Geneva Phonograms Convention, the Berne Convention, the WTO Agreement, the WIPO Copyright Treaty, the WIPO Performances and Phonograms Treaty; and any other copyright treaty to which the United States is a party (definitions of "treaty party" and "international agreement"). *Id.*

[226] 17 U.S.C. § 411.

[227] 17 U.S.C. § 410(c).

[228] 17 U.S.C. § 412.

granting of any other interest in a copyrighted work, with recordation serving as constructive notice of the facts stated in the recorded document,[229] such recordation will be effective only if the work to which it relates has been registered.[230] Proper recordation in the Copyright Office of a security interest in a work is a necessary condition to the establishment of a priority for that interest, irrespective of any filings that may be made under state law.[231] Such recordation, and concomitant priority, however, is possible only if the underlying work has been registered. There is some uncertainty as to the determination of priorities of interests in unregistered works.

3.1.4.5. Deposit

As noted above, in the case of works published in the United States, with notice of copyright, two copies or phonorecords of the work must be deposited for use by the Library of Congress and failure to make such deposit can invoke a series of fines. Proper deposit for the Library of Congress will satisfy the deposit requirements for registration (which, in fact, require only one copy).

3.1.5. Domestic Manufacture

The 1976 Act carried forward, albeit with some modification, provisions of the earlier law requiring that English language books or periodicals, and foreign language books written by American authors, be manufactured in the United States. The 1976 Act provisions, while less inclusive and less draconian, nevertheless prohibited, until July 1, 1986, importation and or public distribution in the United States "of copies of a work consisting primarily of nondramatic literary material that is in the English language ... unless the portions consisting of such material have been manufactured in the United States or Canada."[232] There are a number of exceptions to this requirement, and noncompliance did not result in

---

[229] 17 U.S.C. § 205 (a)-(c).

[230] 17 U.S.C. § 205 (c)(2).

[231] 17 U.S.C. § 205 (d). *See* National Peregrine, Inc. v. Capitol Federal Savings and Loan Association of Denver, 116 B.R. 194 (D.C. Cal. 1990).

[232] 17 U.S.C. § 601 (a).

forfeiture of copyright.[233] What is most significant, however, is the fact that, by its terms, this prohibition on importation and distribution expired on July 1, 1986.

3.2. Substantive Requirements: "Writings" of "Authors" Consisting of "Original Expression"

3.2.1 "Authors" and their "Writings"

To be protected under the Copyright Act, a work must be a "writing" of an "author." The interpretation of these constitutionally required terms is crucial to the development of the law. Beginning with the 1884 United States Supreme Court opinion in *Burrow-Giles Lithographic Company v. Sarony*,[234] holding that a photographer may be an "author" whose photograph is a "writing," there has been a consistent expansive interpretation of these terms. With the Supreme Court's defining statement that "[a]n 'author' is one to whom anything owes its origin," it has readily been accepted that not only "authors" in the traditional sense, but also artists, sculptors, composers, photographers, and other expressive creators are "authors," whose works, if appropriately fixed, are "writings" in the sense constitutionally required for protection. As the House Committee Report in connection with the 1976 Act notes: "The history of copyright law has been one of gradual expansion in the types of work accorded protection .... "

This expansion has taken the form of both direct congressional action to include certain types of expression as works of authorship (*e.g.*, photographs, motion pictures, choreography, architectural works) and judicial recognition that new forms of creative expression are simply extensions of already recognized copyrightable subject matter. Recognizing that "authors are continually finding new ways of expressing themselves, but it is impossible to foresee the forms that these new expressive methods will take," the House Report makes clear that it was not intended "either to freeze the scope of copyrightable technology or to allow unlimited expansion into areas completely outside the present congressional intent."

---

[233] 17 U.S.C. § 601 (b)-(d).

[234] 111 U.S. 53, 4 S. Ct. 279 (1884).

Presumably, "author"infers the existence of a human creative force, rather than mechanical or other non-human generation of a work.[235] Referring to the question of "authorship "of computer-generated works, the Commission on New Technological Uses Report noted: "the eligibility of any work for protection by copyright depends not upon the device or devices used in its creation, but rather upon the presence of at least minimal human creative effort at the time the work is produced."[236]

Generally, the author of a work is not simply the person who mechanically fixes it, but the intellectual creator of the subject matter.[237] There are situations, of course, such as the work for hire context, in which the "author" for copyright purposes is a corporate entity, but the generative force is still human.

3.2.2. Original Expression
3.2.2.1. Generally

In *Feist Publications, Inc. v. Rural Telephone Service Co., Inc.*,[238] the United States Supreme Court made clear that "the *sine qua non* of copyright is originality," and that originality is a constitutional prerequisite to copyrightability.[239] Such "originality" embodies both the concept of independent origin and a minimal level of creativity, some modest amount of intellectual labor. Justice O'Connor there observed that "[o]riginal ... means only that the work was independently created by the author (as opposed to copied from other works), and that it possesses at least some minimal degree of creativity."[240] The constitutional requirement of

---

[235] *Cf.* Urantia Foundation v. Maaherra, 114 F.3d 955 (9th Cir. 1997), in which "[b]oth parties believe that the words in the [book at issue] were 'authored' by non-human spiritual beings "; the work was nevertheless held copyrightable because the "human" intervention by the producers of the book in selecting and arranging these non-human revelations "was not so mechanical as to preclude creativity."

[236] Report of the Commission on New Technological Uses, p. 45.

[237] *See* Andrien v. Southern Ocean County Chamber Of Commerce, 927 F.2d 132 (3d Cir. 1991).

[238] Feist Publications, Inc. v. Rural Telephone Service Co., Inc., 499 U.S. 340, 348, 111 S. Ct. 1282, 1289 (1991).

[239] *Id.* at 348, 111 S. Ct. at 1289.

[240] *Id.*

originality, therefore, carries within it a further requirement of "creativity."[241] However, as *Feist* further notes, "the requisite level of creativity is extremely low; even a slight amount will suffice."[242]

On the other hand, the fact that a work as a whole meets the originality/creativity standard and is therefore subject to protection, does not serve to extend copyright protection to everything contained in that work; rather, copyright protection will extend only to those portions of the work which are considered original expression.[243]

Underlying the determination whether a work purporting to be original expression is copyrightable, is the principle of non-discrimination; that is, esthetic or artistic judgments as to the inherent worth or cultural value are to be avoided. A work that is original, creative expression, otherwise eligible for copyright protection, will not be denied such protection because it may have been created for commercial purposes, or as an advertisement, or may be considered pedestrian or lacking in esthetic value.[244] "Any original literary work may be copyrighted. The necessary degree of 'originality' is low, and the work need not be aesthetically pleasing to be 'literary.'"[245]

---

[241] *See* Baltimore Orioles v. Major League Baseball Players, 805 F.2d 663 (7th Cir. 1986) ("The requirement of originality actually subsumes two separate conditions, *i.e.*, the work must possess an independent origin and a minimal amount of creativity. ... A work is original if it is the independent creation of its author. ... A work is creative if it embodies some modest amount of intellectual labor").

[242] *See* Atari Games v. Oman, 979 F.2d 242 (D.C. Cir. 1992) in which the court reversed denial of registration of a simple geometric "paddle" video game. Judge (now Justice) Ruth Bader Ginsburg emphasized how minimal the creativity standard is ("We are mindful ... of the teaching of *Feist* that '[t]he vast majority of works make the [copyright] grade quite easily.'").

[243] *See* Boisson v. Banian, Ltd., 273 F.3d 262, 266 (2d Cir. 2001) ("Plaintiffs must also demonstrate 'substantial similarity' between defendants' [works] and the *protectable* elements of their own [works]") (emphasis in original).

[244] Bleistein v. Donaldson Lithographing Co., 188 U.S. 239, 23 S. Ct. 298 (1903) ("it would be a dangerous undertaking for persons trained only to the law to constitute themselves final judge of the worth of pictorial illustrations, outside of the narrowest and most obvious limits"); Mazer v. Stein, 347 U.S. 201, 74 S. Ct. 460 (1954).

[245] American Dental Association v. Delta Dental Plans Association, 126 F.3d 977, 979 (7th Cir. 1997) (holding copyrightable a taxonomy of dental procedures).

The House Report in connection with the 1976 Act expresses the clear congressional intention to follow the existing case law providing for only minimal standards of originality and creativity, embodying the judicial pronouncement that "[t]he least pretentious picture"[246] can meet the originality standard:

> The phrase "original works of authorship," which is purposefully left undefined, is intended to incorporate without change the standard of originality established by the courts under the present [1909] copyright statute. This standard does not include requirements of novelty, ingenuity, or esthetic merit, and there is no intention to enlarge the standard of copyright protection to require them."

Thus, it is generally accepted that virtually all but the most mechanical photographs contain sufficient originality and creativity for copyright protection.[247] So too, there is sufficient originality/creativity in the decisions as to camera placement, choice of shots, and the like in creating the television broadcast of an athletic event to make that broadcast copyrightable.[248]

It is clear, of course, that copyright in an image—a pictorial representation meeting standards of originality—does not confer any rights with respect to the subject as such. As Justice Holmes said in *Bleistein*, "[o]thers are free to copy the original. They are not free to copy the copy.... the copy is the personal reaction of the individual upon nature."One may generally take a photograph of the same scene that is the subject of another's photograph, without infringing the rights of the first photographer. However, the deliberate re-creation of a scene depicted by another, as opposed to portraying the same general subject matter, may constitute an infringing "copy" of the "copy."[249]

---

[246] *Bleistein, supra.*

[247] *See* Burrow-Giles Lithographic Company v. Sarony, 111 U.S. 53, 4 S. Ct. 279 (1884); Ets-Hokin v. Skyy Spirits, Inc., 225 F.3d 1068 (9th Cir. 2000); Time, Inc. v. Bernard Geis Associates, 293 F.Supp. 130 (S.D.N.Y. 1968).

[248] Baltimore Orioles v. Major League Baseball Players, 805 F.2d 663 (7th Cir. 1986).

[249] *See* Leibovitz v. Paramount Pictures Corp., 137 F.3d 109 (2d Cir. 1998); Gross v. Seligman, 212 Fed 930 (2d Cir. 1914); Kisch v. Ammirati & Puris Inc., 657 F.Supp. 380 (S.D.N.Y 1987).

3.2.2.2. Originality in Derivative Works

The above words of Justice Holmes have proven troublesome, if not cryptic, in dealing with the issue of the originality standard for derivative works. That is, where one creates a derivative work, a work based upon a pre-existing work, what quantum of originality is necessary for that derivative work itself to be protected? The issue arises usually where the derivative work is based upon a work in the public domain or is one created with the consent of the copyright owner of the underlying work. "The requirement of originality is significant chiefly in connection with derivative works, where if interpreted too liberally it would paradoxically inhibit rather than promote the creation of such works by giving the first creator considerable power to interfere with the creation of subsequent derivative works from the same underlying work."[250]

Consequently, more is required in the case of derivative works than other works to meet the low originality threshold;[251] there must be substantial difference or more than a trivial variation between the underlying work and the derivative work.[252] Effort alone, however sophisticated or intensive, in reproducing an earlier work, appears no longer to be sufficient to create a copyrightable derivative work.[253] For a work based on pre-existing works to be protected, it must contribute "a distinguishable variation from the older works [which] variation must be substantial and not merely trivial."[254] Further, the original aspects of a derivative work must

---

[250] Gracen v. Bradford Exchange, 698 F.2d 300 (7th Cir. 1983).

[251] *See, e.g.*, Entertainment Research v. Genesis Creative Group, 122 F.3d 1211 (9th Cir. 1997) ("the copyright protection afforded to derivative works is more limited that it is for original works of authorship").

[252] Gracen v. Bradford Exchange, 698 F.2d 300 (7th Cir. 1983); L. Batlin & Son, Inc. v. Snyder, 536 F.2d 486 (2d Cir.), *cert. denied*, 429 U.S. 857, 97 S. Ct. 156 (1976); Durham Industries, Inc. v. Tomy Corp., 630 F.2d 905 (2d Cir. 1980); Hearn v. Meyer, 664 F.Supp. 832 (S.D.N.Y. 1987).

[253] *Id.* The cases, beginning with *Batlin, supra,* appear to have overruled earlier, less demanding cases such as Alfred Bell & Co. v. Catalda Fine Arts, 191 F.2d 99 (2d Cir. 1951). *See* The Bridgeman Art Library, Ltd. v. Corel Corporation, 36 F.Supp.2d 191 (S.D.N.Y. 1999).

[254] Norma Ribbon & Trimming, Inc. v. Little, 51 F.3d 45 (5th Cir. 1995); Entertainment Research Group, Inc. v. Genesis Creative Group, Inc., 122 F.3d 1211 (9th Cir. 1997).

reflect the degree to which it relies on preexisting material and must not in any way affect the scope of any copyright protection in that preexisting material.[255] Thus, the Copyright Office will allow registration as derivative works of "colorized" versions of black and white films if the colorization constitutes more than a trivial variation with respect to the underlying work. On the other hand, a wooden version of the traditional paper doll has been held to be an unprotectible idea rather than a copyrightable derivative work,[256] and the extraordinarily exact digital reproduction of public domain art has been held to be unprotectible as a derivative work, notwithstanding its technological advance, because of its slavish "copying."[257]

§ 4. OWNERSHIP

4.1. Ownership of Copyright v. Ownership of the Material Object

Ownership of copyright in a work must be distinguished from ownership of the physical object in which the work is embodied. One who writes a poem in a letter mailed to another continues to own the copyright in the poem, while the recipient of the letter owns the physical object, the piece of paper on which the poem was written. Thus, mailing the letter neither divests the author of the copyright interest in the poem nor invests the recipient with such interest.[258] This principle of separation is codified in the 1976 Act:

---

[255] Durham Industries, Inc. v. Tomy Corp., 630 F.2d 905, 909 (2d Cir. 1980), cited with approval in Entertainment Research v. Genesis Creative Group, 122 F.3d 1211 (9th Cir. 1997).

[256] Country Kids 'N' City Slicks, Inc. v. Sheen, 77 F.3d 1280 (10th Cir. 1996).

[257] The Bridgeman Art Library, Ltd. v. Corel Corporation, 36 F.Supp.2d 191 (S.D.N.Y. 1999).

[258] See, e.g. Salinger v. Random House, Inc., 811 F.2d 90 (2d Cir. 1987), cert. denied, 484 U.S. 890, 108 S. Ct. 213 (1987). This principle was illustrated in the unexpected context of a tax case; in Norwest Corp v. Commissioner, 108 T.C. No. 18, 1997 WL 211303 (U.S. Tax Ct., 1997), a sharply divided (9-8) panel of the Tax Court held that computer software acquired by a company for use in its business is tangible personal property eligible for the investment tax credit, rather than intangible property, so long as the company acquired the software without acquiring any copyright or other intangible property rights in it.

§ 202. Ownership of copyright as distinct from ownership of material object

Ownership of a copyright, or of any of the exclusive rights under a copyright, is distinct from ownership of any material object in which the work is embodied. Transfer of ownership of any material object, including the copy or phonorecord in which the work is first fixed, does not of itself convey any rights in the copyrighted work embodied in the object; nor, in the absence of an agreement, does transfer of ownership of a copyright or of any exclusive rights under a copyright convey property rights in any material object.[259]

4.2. Divisibility

The owner of copyright in a work possesses a right that is virtually infinitely divisible. That is, "copyright" should really be considered "copyrights," as the copyright interest really consists of an array, or bundle, of separate exclusive rights, each of which may be owned separately, transferred, and further subdivided. The divisibility of copyright interests is expressly recognized by the 1976 Act:

> Any of the exclusive rights comprising copyright, including any subdivision of any of the rights ..., may be transferred ... and owned separately. The owner of any particular exclusive right is entitled, to the extent of that right, to all of the protection and remedies accorded to the copyright owner ... .[260]

Thus, an assignee of the right to reproduce a work is the "owner" of the work to the extent of that right and may maintain an action for infringement of that right. For these purposes, an exclusive license (but not a non-exclusive license) is equivalent to an assignment.[261]

4.3. Authorship

Copyright "vests initially in the author or authors of the work."[262] Authorship is the central concept for the creation of a copyright interest. However, while vesting initial rights in the "author" of a work, the Act itself

---

[259] 17 U.S.C. § 202.

[260] 17 U.S.C. § 201 (d)(2).

[261] *See infra*, §§ 5.1 and 9.1.4.

[262] 17 U.S.C. § 201(a).

does not define the term. Rather, ownership issues begin with the proposition, as noted above, that "an 'author' is one to whom anything owes its origin."[263]

The author, as the one in whom copyright initially vests, is possessed of all the rights of a copyright owner and therefore may license or transfer all or any of these rights (except for moral rights under the Visual Artists Rights Act, Section 106A) and terminate such transfer or other grant.[264] Similarly, it is the nature of the author (*e.g.*, identified individual, joint author, employer of an employee for hire, anonymous creator) that will determine the duration of the copyright term, as well as rights of renewal in connection with pre-1976 Act works.[265]

4.4. Joint Works/Multiple Authorship

Joint authorship issues arise when a single work is purportedly created by more than one individual. The property interests in such a work are analogous to the interests in other jointly held property. The first inquiry is definitional, determining if a given work is a "joint" work, as distinct from a work in which each participant has his or her own, severable copyright interest. The consequences of the appropriate definition are quite serious. For example, the term of copyright for a joint work is generally measured by the life of the last surviving joint author.[266] Of greater significance is the fact that the "authors of a joint work are co-owners of copyright in the work."[267] As such, each joint author, with an undivided interest in the whole, can deal with the work, or grant non-exclusive license rights to it or exploit it, without the consent of the other joint authors, subject to a duty to account for profits realized upon any such dealing or exploitation.[268] In

---

[263] Burrow-Giles Lithographic Company v. Sarony, 111 U.S. 53, 4 S. Ct. 279 (1884).

[264] *See infra*, § 5.

[265] *See infra*, § 8.

[266] *Id.*

[267] 17 U.S.C. § 201.

[268] *See, e.g.*, Shapiro Bernstein & Co. v. Jerry Vogel Music Co., 221 F.2d 569 (2d Cir. 1955). As the congressional Committee Reports note, "co-owners of copyright would be treated generally as tenants in common, with each co-owner having an independent right to use or license the use of a work, subject to a duty of accounting to

short, and subject to a duty to account, each joint owner of a work may exercise all the rights of a copyright owner with respect to that work, except only the right to transfer all rights to the work (*i.e.* an assignment or other complete grant of rights to the work or exclusive license).

The 1976 Act defines a "joint work" as "a work prepared by two or more authors with the intention that their contributions be merged into inseparable or interdependent parts of a unitary whole."[269] The earlier copyright act did not expressly define joint works; the result was case-by-case determination that was not always consistent. The 1976 Act, departing from the earlier case law, creates a definition predicated upon the *contemporaneous intention* of the parties. The House Committee Report is clear in expressing the importance of intention:

> The touchstone here is the intention, at the time the writing is done, that the parts be absorbed or combined into an integrated unit, although the parts themselves may be either 'inseparable' (as in the case of a novel or painting) or 'interdependent' (as in the case of a motion picture, opera, or the words and music of a song).[270]

The cases under the Act have underlined the primacy of contemporaneous intention of the parties for determining whether a given work is a "joint work." For a work to be a "joint work," (i) it must be contemplated by each of the parties (when each makes a contribution) that the contribution will be part of a unitary work to which another will make or already has made a contribution; and (ii) each purported joint author must intend to contribute to a joint work at the time his or her alleged contribution is made.[271] As the Second Circuit has observed:

> Examination of whether the putative co-authors ever shared an intent to be co-authors serves the valuable purpose of appropriately confining the bounds of joint authorship arising by operation of copyright law, while leaving those not in a true joint authorship relationship with an author

---

the other co-owners for any profits." H.R. Rep. No. 1476, 94th Cong., 2d Sess. 121 (1976); S. Rep. No. 473, 94th Cong., 1st Sess. 104 (1975).

[269] 17 U.S.C. § 101.

[270] H.R. Rep. No. 1476, 94th Cong., 2d Sess. 120 (1976).

[271] Weissmann v. Freeman, 868 F.2d 1313 (2d Cir.), *cert. denied*, 493 U.S. 883,110 S. Ct. 219 (1989); *see* Childress v. Taylor, 945 F.2d 500 (2d Cir. 1991); Erickson v. Trinity Theatre, Inc., 13 F.3d 1061 (7th Cir. 1994).

free to bargain for an arrangement that will be recognized as a matter of both copyright and contract law. [Joint authorship] should be reserved for relationships in which all participants fully intend to be joint authors.[272]

Even the contribution of significant original material to a work will not itself make the contributor a joint author in the absence of evidence of co-authorship intention by the original author.[273]

It is not necessary that the participants actually work together or within the same time frame, or even that they know one another, so long as each participant created his or her contribution with the intention of integrating that contribution into a single unitary product. There is some uncertainty as to the nature of the contribution of each purported joint author. It has been held that for a participant to be considered a joint author, even with such contemporaneous intention to merge that participant's contribution into a "unitary whole," his or her contribution itself must contain sufficient originality to be independently copyrightable.[274] Thus, providing ideas, direction or editorial guidance, however valuable, will not suffice to make one a joint author. However, this "requirement" has been questioned, at least in the Seventh Circuit.[275]

Under certain limited circumstances, the status of joint ownership—an undivided interest in the work—may result from acts apart from the process by which the work was created and rights initially vested. A subsequent transferee of a work from the copyright owner, by contract, or by the laws of inheritance or state property laws, may have a joint interest in the work. In such circumstances, the joint *ownership* rights are independent of issues of joint *authorship*.

4.5. Collective Works

Contributions to collective works must be distinguished from joint works. A "collective work" "is a work, such as a periodical issue, anthology, or encyclopedia, in which a number of contributions, constituting separate and independent works in themselves, are assembled into a collective

---

[272] Childress v. Taylor, 945 F.2d 500 (2d Cir. 1991).

[273] Thomson v. Larson, 147 F.3d 195 (2d Cir. 1998).

[274] Childress v. Taylor, 945 F.2d 500 (2d Cir. 1991); Erickson v. Trinity Theatre, Inc., 13 F.3d 1061 (7th Cir. 1994).

[275] Gaiman v. McFarlane, 360 F.3d 644, 660 (7th Cir. 2004).

whole."[276] The creator of the individual contribution has, and retains, the sole copyright interest in that contribution, whereas the owner of copyright in the collective work itself, absent express transfer of rights, acquires only the right to reproduce and distribute that contribution as part of that particular collective work or any revision of that work.[277]

Section 201(c) of the 1976 Act significantly changed the law and balance of rights with respect to the individual contributions in a collective work in specifically keeping the copyright interest in the creator of that contribution. Thus, the Supreme Court has held that a freelance, independent author of a newspaper article, may object to the reproduction of that article for use in an online database of the newspaper's material; such digital reproduction is not a "revision" of the collective work and the copyright owner of the collective work has no right so to deal with that contribution.[278] On the other hand, it has been held that a digital version of a complete issue of a collective work is such a "revision" and the individual contributor may not object.[279]

4.6. Works Made for Hire

The 1976 Act continues the earlier law's recognition of a distinct status for works made for hire. It provides that, in the case of such works, "the employer or other person for whom the work was prepared is considered the author for purposes of [the Act], and, unless the parties have expressly agreed otherwise in a written instrument signed by them, owns all the rights comprised in the copyright."[280] The hiring party, while not the actual creator of the work, is the "author" entitled to all of the rights of an author (and the actual creator has none of those rights), except as those rights may be specifically limited.

Recognizing the different creative posture of an employer for hire "author," the Act provides for a fixed term (rather than one measured by the life of the author) for works for hire and excludes such works from the

---

[276] 17 U.S.C. § 101.

[277] 17 U.S.C. § 201 (c).

[278] New York Times Co, Inc. v. Tasini, 533 U.S.483, 121 S. Ct. 2381 (2001).

[279] Faulkner v. Mindscape, Inc., 409 F.3d 26 (2d Cir. 2005).

[280] 17 U.S.C. § 201 (b).

termination right and from the moral rights provisions of the Visual Artists Rights Act (§ 106A).[281]

With fundamental ownership rights dependent upon the employer/employee status, determination of whether a given work is a "work for hire" is a serious and important matter. The Act attempts to define "a work made hire" and in so doing creates two radically different ways in which that status can be created. The first, broad definition, defines "a work made for hire" as "a work prepared by an employee within the scope of his or her employment"; while the alternative, more limited definition, refers to certain specially commissioned works.[282]

4.6.1. Work Prepared by an Employee Within the Scope of Employment

A work prepared by an employee within the scope of his or her employment is considered a work for hire, and the employer is considered the "author" of the work, unless the parties have signed a writing expressly agreeing otherwise. Prior to the United States Supreme Court opinion in *Community for Creative Non-Violence v. Reid*[283] the Courts of Appeal had divided over the meaning of "employee" for purposes of determining if a work was a work made for hire, with some courts construing the term broadly enough to include independent contractors under certain circumstances, depending upon the degree of control exerted by the hiring party, and others construing it quite narrowly, limiting it to the traditional master-servant relationship, or even to a formal, salaried employee/employer relationship. Purporting to resolve the conflict, the Supreme Court held that the appropriate question is whether the creator of the work would be considered an "employee" under the master-servant definition of the "general common-law of agency."

While the Supreme Court thus purported to eschew the "control" tests of some of the lower courts, in fact, the issue of control becomes one of the significant factors in determining whether one is an "employee" under the common-law of agency. The Court relies upon Section 220 of the

---

[281] See *infra* §§ 6 and 8.

[282] 17 U.S.C. § 101.

[283] 490 U.S. 730, 109 S. Ct. 2166 (1989).

61

Restatement (Second) of Agency, which itself enumerates ten factors, including control over the details of the work. The result, therefore, is that while it would appear that a true "independent contractor" could not be considered an "employee for hire," the Court's less than explicit guidance for the lower courts has nevertheless created uncertainty. In an attempt at clarity, the Second Circuit has suggested that, of these ten factors, "[s]ome ... will often have little or no significance [while] there are some factors that will be significant in virtually every situation. These include: (1) the hiring party's right to control the manner and means of creation; (2) the skill required; (3) the provision of employee benefits; (4) the tax treatment of the hired party; and (5) whether the hiring party has the right to assign additional projects to the hired party."[284]

Determination of whether a work is a work made for hire is a legal conclusion based upon the underlying facts defining the relationship between the parties. Thus, it has been held that a work was created as part of an employment relationship and was therefore a work made for hire notwithstanding a co-authorship and co-ownership agreement between the parties.[285]

4.6.2. Specially Commissioned Works

The Act alternatively provides that certain works, even if clearly created by an independent contractor and not by an "employee for hire," will be considered works made for hire. This category of work is limited to nine types of specially ordered or commissioned works. Specifically, the work must be:

> specially ordered or commissioned for use as a contribution to a collective work, as a part of a motion picture or other audiovisual work, as a

---

[284] Aymes v. Bonelli, 980 F.2d 857 (2d Cir. 1992); *compare* Graham v. James, 144 F.3d 229 (2d Cir. 1998) (applying *Aymes* and relying on the high level of skill involved and lack of benefits to find no empoloyment for hire) *and* Carter v. Helmsley-Spear, Inc., 71 F.3d 77 (2d Cir. 1995), *cert. denied*, 116 S. C t.. 1824 (1996) (applying *Aymes* and relying heavily on the fifth factor to find an employment for hire).

[285] Saenger Organization, Inc. v. Nationwide Insurance Licensing Associates, Inc., 119 F.3d 55 (1st Cir. 1997).

translation, as a supplementary work, as a compilation, as an instructional text, as a test, as answer material for a test, or as an atlas,[286]

and the parties must "expressly agree in a written instrument signed by them that the work shall be considered a work made for hire."[287] The Act, in contradistinction to the earlier law,[288] thus sharply limits the kinds of commissioned works that may be considered works for hire; the statutory listing is quite specific and a commissioned work must fit squarely within the enumeration to meet the definition of a work for hire. Thus, for example, the reference to "audiovisual work" does *not* encompass a work that is solely "audio" or solely "visual." Moreover, in a change from the earlier law, the Act creates no presumption from the fact of the commissioning of a work that the commissioning party will be treated as the author of the work. Rather, the parties must jointly and expressly acknowledge that status in writing.

For works created prior to January 1, 1978 (the effective date of the 1976 Act), the earlier, case-based definition of a work for hire retains significance. For those works, the law created a presumption in favor of the hiring or commissioning party, and relevant factors were the right to supervise and control the work. With respect to commissioned works, it had been held "that an independent contractor is an 'employee' and a hiring party an 'employer' ... if the work is made at the hiring party's 'instance and

---

[286] 17 U.S.C. § 101. The "supplementary work" referred to in the definition is further defined as

a work prepared for publication as a secondary adjunct to a work by another author for the purpose of introducing, concluding, illustrating, explaining, revising, commenting upon, or assisting in the use of the other work, such as forewords, afterwords, pictorial illustrations, maps, charts, tables, editorial notes, musical arrangements, answer material for tests, bibliographies, appendixes, and indexes," and an "instructional text" "is a literary, pictorial, or graphic work prepared for publication and with the purpose of use in systematic instructional activities.

[287] 17 U.S.C. § 101.

[288] *See* Playboy Enterprises, Inc. v. Dumas, 53 F.3d 549 (2d Cir.), *cert. denied*, 116 S. Ct. 567 (1995); 20th Century Fox Film Corp. v. Entertainment Distributing, 429 F.3d 869 (9th Cir. 2005).

expense,' [*i.e.,*] when the 'motivating factor in producing the work was the employer who induced the creation.'"[289]

Of course, even if a work is neither a joint work nor a work made for hire, other parties, whether participants, commissioning parties or strangers, may succeed to rights by transfer or assignment of all or part of those rights. Such successors, however, are not "authors" for purposes of the Act.

§ 5. TRANSFER OF COPYRIGHT INTERESTS

5.1. Transfer Defined

As discussed above, copyright ownership is virtually infinitely divisible, so that all or part of all or any of the rights comprising a copyright owner's interest (except for the limited moral right created by section 106A) may be transferred or licensed to others. For purposes of the Act, a "transfer of copyright ownership" is broadly defined as:

> an assignment, mortgage, exclusive license, or any other conveyance, alienation, or hypothecation of a copyright or of any of the exclusive rights comprised in a copyright whether or not it is limited in time or place of effect, but not including a nonexclusive license.[290]

Thus, if the author/copyright owner of a book grants to a motion picture producer the exclusive right to make a motion picture of that book, there has been a "transfer" of a subset of the author's exclusive right to prepare derivative works. On the other hand, if the composer/copyright owner of a song grants to a singer the *nonexclusive* right to sing that song at a concert, there has been no "transfer" of any part of the composer's exclusive right publicly to perform the work;[291] whereas, a "transfer" will

---

[289] *Playboy Enterprises, supra.* As the Ninth Circuit put it: "It has been well established within this circuit that [1909 Act] works by independent contractors may qualify as works-for-hire so long as they were created at the instance and expense of the commissioning party." *20th Century Fox Film Corp, supra.* The court expressly rejects the argument that the Supreme Court's *CCNV* decision alters this result with respect to 1909 Act works ("No part of [that] decision rests on the meaning of the work-for-hire provision in the 1909 Act").

[290] 17 U.S.C. § 101.

[291] Johnson v. Jones, 149 F.3d 494, 500 (6th Cir. 1998) ("It is ... well settled that a non-exclusive license is not a transfer of ownership").

have occurred if the singer is given the *exclusive* right to sing that song at concerts, even if that grant is limited to one week or to a specific geographic area.

In short, there is no distinction between exclusive licenses and other kinds of transfers, assignments, or conveyances, while there is a sharp distinction between exclusive and nonexclusive licenses.

5.2. Requirement of a Writing

Since the ownership of copyright in a work is distinct from ownership of the material object embodying that work,[292] prior to the effectiveness of the 1976 Act there was dispute with respect to the extent to which unconditional transfer of such material object would carry, by implication, transfer of the copyright in the work. Resolution of the question of transfer involved determination of matters of intent and inconsistent presumptions. To buttress the separation between the intangible copyright interest and the interest in the tangible material object, and to put to rest dispute as to when transfer of ownership of an object might carry with it, by implication, transfer of the copyright interest in the work, the Act expressly requires a "writing" to effectuate a valid transfer of copyright ownership:

> A transfer of copyright ownership, other than by operation of law, is not valid unless an instrument of conveyance, or a note or memorandum of the transfer, is in writing and signed by the owner of the rights conveyed or such owner's duly authorized agent.[293]

The Act does not specify any particular form of writing to meet the statutory requirement and there is some controversy among the Courts of Appeal over whether the transfer of copyright can be inferred from broad language of a writing.[294] Nevertheless, it is clear that there must be some

---

[292] *See supra*, § 4.1.

[293] 17 U.S.C. § 204 (a).

[294] *Compare* Playboy Enterprises, Inc. v. Dumas, 53 F.3d 549 (2d Cir.), *cert. denied*, 116 S. Ct. 567 (1995) (checks in payment for pictorial works endorsed by the author/payee that contained the legend, "payee acknowledges payment in full for the assignment . . . of all right, title, and interest in and to" specified art works held not to be a sufficient writing) *and* Schiller & Schmidt, Inc. v. Nordisco Corp., 969 F.2d 410 (7th Cir. 1992) (holding sufficient a written transfer agreement that did not mention "copyright" expressly where the circumstances surrounding the agreement showed that

writing in connection with the transfer and the writing requirement goes to the very validity of the transfer.

> Section 204(a)'s requirement, while sometimes called the copyright statute of frauds, is in fact different from a statute of frauds. ...Rather than serving an evidentiary function and making otherwise valid agreements unenforceable, under §204(a) "a transfer of copyright is simply 'not valid' without a writing.[295]

The writing requirement applies to conveyances of copyright interests, but does not apply to a non-exclusive license, which, as the statutory definition quoted above makes clear, is not considered a transfer, and therefore may be granted orally.[296] Indeed, an invalid oral exclusive license may, by virtue of the conduct of the parties, be treated as an implied and enforceable non-exclusive license.[297]

5.3. Termination of Transfers and Grants

5.3.1. Nature of the Right

As is discussed below in connection with duration of copyright,[298] the 1976 Act creates a single term of copyright commencing with the fixation of an original work of authorship in a tangible medium of expression and lasting generally for the life of the author plus fifty (now seventy) years. This scheme replaced the earlier dual-term structure which provided for an initial twenty-eight year term, commencing with publication of the work with proper notice, and a renewal term of like duration commencing at the expiration of the initial term if proper registration for renewal were made. While it was the apparent intention of Congress in creating that structure to give the author a recapture right with respect to the renewal term—the ability to undo, licenses, transfers, and other grants made during the initial term—the renewal right was not inalienable,[299] and, therefore, an author

---

the parties intended to transfer copyright by the agreement).

[295] Lyrick Studios, Inc. v. Big Idea Productions, Inc., 420 F.3d 388 (5th Cir. 2005) (citation omitted).

[296] See, e.g., Johnson v. Jones, 149 F.3d 494, 500 (6th Cir. 1998).

[297] Jacob Maxwell, Inc. v. Veeck, 110 F.3d 749 (11th Cir. 1997).

[298] Infra, § 8.

[299] Fred Fisher Music Co. v. M. Witmark & Sons, 318 U.S. 643 (1943).

was frequently pressured to assign the renewal right in connection with any grants. With the 1976 Act, Congress more effectively implemented the idea of giving the author a right to recapture rights which had been the subject of grants, licenses and other transfers after a suitable period of time within which the transferee could exploit those rights.

The Act[300] grants to the author, or to specified statutory successors (the surviving spouse, children, or grandchildren of the author, or, if none survive, the author's estate), the right, during a five year period, to terminate any and all grants and recapture the rights granted, provided that the notice and other statutory procedures are meticulously followed. The termination right does not apply to grants made with respect to works made for hire.[301] The right is inalienable.[302] The scope of the termination right has been held to be broad enough to make an oral license with an indeterminate term terminable only after expiration of the statutory period, preempting state law making such a license terminable at will.[303]

The notice must state the effective date of termination, which must be within the permissible five-year termination period. The notice must be served at least two years, and not more than ten years, before that date; it must comply with regulations issued by the Register of Copyrights; and it must be recorded in the Copyright Office before the effective date of termination.[304] The notice provisions are quite stringent, and any failure to comply will forfeit the right to terminate.[305]

---

[300] 17 U.S.C. §§ 203 (a) (2), 304 (c) (2). The author's estate was added as ultimate owner of the right by the 1998 Copyright Term Extension Act.

[301] 17 U.S.C. §§ 203 (a), 304 (c).

[302] 17 U.S.C. §§ 203 (a) (5), 304 (c) (5): " Termination of the grant may be effected notwithstanding any agreement to the contrary, including an agreement to make a will or to make any future grant."

[303] Rano v. Sipa Press, Inc., 987 F.2d 580 (9th Cir. 1993). A contrary result—holding no preemption of state law for a license terminable at will—was reached by the Seventh and Eleventh Circuits: Walthal v. Rusk, 172 F.3d 481 (7th Cir. 1999); Korman v. HBC Florida, Inc., 182 F.3d 1291 (11th Cir. 1999).

[304] 17 U.S.C. §§ 203 (a) (4), 304 (c) (4).

[305] 17 U.S.C. §§ 203 (a) (4) (A)-(B), 304 (c) (4) (A)-(B). See Burroughs v. Metro-Goldwyn-Mayer, Inc., 683 F.2d 610 (2d Cir. 1982).

The termination right vests on the date that proper notice of termination is given. Accordingly, if an individual in whom the right vests dies prior to the actual reversion, the reverted rights will pass to that person's estate. So too, since the successors to the termination right of an author who dies prior to its exercise are fixed by statute, that succession cannot be changed by the author's will; "the purpose of the [termination right] is to protect the rights of widows and children in copyrights [and] is not necessarily a provision for the effectuation of the author's 'intent'."[306] For purposes of the termination right, the Act distinguishes between terminating grants made prior to January 1, 1978 and terminating grants made after that date.

5.3.2. Grants Made Prior to January 1, 1978

The 1976 Act essentially extends the renewal term for works in copyright at the effective date of the Act by thirty-nine (originally, nineteen) years. Assignments, grants, or licenses, exclusive or nonexclusive, made prior to the effective date of the 1976 Act and during the *renewal* term of the copyright in the work subject to the grant, may be terminated during the five-year period beginning at the end of 56 years from the date copyright was originally secured in the work (or beginning January 1, 1978, if later).[307] In operation, the termination right here recaptures the extension of the renewal term. The right may be exercised by the "author" who executed the grant or, if the author does not survive to the time for effecting termination, the author's surviving spouse and children or grandchildren, or estate[308] (for grants executed by an author's statutory successor,[309] termination may be effected by the surviving person or persons who executed the grant).[310] These termination provisions do not relate to grants (made prior to January 1, 1978) during the *initial* term of then subsisting copyrights since the grantor, at least theoretically, has a limited "recapture" right in connection with the renewal term.

---

[306] Larry Spier, Inc. v. Bourne Co., 953 F.2d 774 (2d Cir. 1992).

[307] 17 U.S.C. § 304 (c) (3).

[308] Issues of survivorship and determination of who are qualifying spouses and children are governed by applicable state law.

[309] As defined in 17 U.S.C. § 304 (a) (1) (C).

[310] 17 U.S.C. § 304 (c) (1), (2).

The 1998 amendments extending the duration of copyright by twenty years,[311] also provide for a limited restoration of the termination right with respect to that twenty-year extension as to works in their renewal term as of the effective date of the amendments and for which the termination right, previously unexercised, had expired; the restored right may be exercised by notice given during the five-year period commencing seventy-five years after the date copyright was originally secured.[312]

5.3.3. Grants Made from and after January 1, 1978

Grants, transfers, or other licenses made by the "author" and executed on or after January 1, 1978 may be terminated by the author (or the author's statutory survivors) at any time during the five-year period commencing at the expiration of thirty-five years from the date of execution of the grant, or, if the grant included a right of publication, the earlier of thirty-five years after publication or forty years after the date of execution of the grant.[313] For these purposes, it is immaterial when the copyright in the work began; the only consideration is the date of the grant.

5.3.4. The Effect of Termination: Derivative Works

With proper notice, termination will be effective on the date specified in the notice, and on that date the rights granted will revert to the author or to those holding the termination interest.[314] However, such termination cannot impair rights with respect to continued exploitation of derivative works "prepared under authority of the grant before its termination," and such works "may continue to be utilized under the terms of the grant," although such utilization "does not extend to the preparation after the termination of other derivative works based upon the copyrighted work covered by the terminated grant."[315] The question of exactly what is a derivative work "utilized under the terms of the grant" has been quite troublesome, particularly with respect to the rights of intermediate grantees.

---

[311] *See infra*, § 8.

[312] 17 U.S.C. § 304 (d).

[313] 17 U.S.C. § 203 (a).

[314] 17 U.S.C. §§ 203 (b), 304 (c) (6).

[315] 17 U.S.C. §§ 203 (b) (1), 304 (c) (6) (A).

It gave rise to a sharply divided United States Supreme Court decision in *Mills Music, Inc. v. Snyder.*[316]

> *Mills Music* appears to require that where multiple levels of licenses govern use of a derivative work, the "terms of the grant" encompass the original grant from author to publisher and each subsequent grant necessary to enable the particular use at issue. ... If one of those grants requires payment of royalties by licensees to an intermediary, such as a publisher, then continued utilization of derivative works "under the terms of the grant" requires continued payments to the intermediary. ... The effect of *Mills Music*, then, is to preserve during the post-termination period the panoply of contractual obligations that governed pre-termination uses of derivative works by derivative work owners or their licensees.[317]

§ 6. SCOPE OF EXCLUSIVE RIGHTS

Section 106 enumerates the exclusive rights of the owner of copyright. Except for the limited moral rights accorded certain authors of certain works of visual art under Section 106A (discussed below), the enumeration is complete and exhaustive and no other rights may be inferred. The owner of copyright has the exclusive rights to do and to authorize any of the following:

(1) to reproduce the copyrighted work in copies or phonorecords;

(2) to prepare derivative works based upon the copyrighted work;

(3) to distribute copies or phonorecords of the copyrighted work to the public by sale or other transfer of ownership, or by rental, lease, or lending;

(4) in the case of literary, musical, dramatic, and choreographic works, pantomimes, and motion pictures and other audiovisual works, to perform the copyrighted work publicly;

(5) in the case of literary, musical, dramatic, and choreographic works, pantomimes, and pictorial, graphic, or sculptural works, including the

---

[316] 469 U.S. 153, 105 S. Ct. 638 (1985).

[317] Woods v. Bourne Co., 60 F.3d 978 (2d Cir. 1995) (holding that "when a musical arrangement is contained within an audiovisual work produced under license from a publisher prior to termination, the publisher is entitled to receive royalties from post-termination performances of the audiovisual work under the terms of pre-termination licenses governing performance rights").

individual images of a motion picture or other audiovisual work, to display the copyrighted work publicly; and

(6) in the case of sound recordings, to perform the copyrighted work publicly by means of a digital audio transmission.[318]

The rights granted the owner of copyright are subject to the highly specific limitations and exemptions of Sections 108 through 121 of the Act and, as is discussed in Section 7, below, the broad fair use limitation of Section 107 of the Act.

6.1. The Right to Reproduce the Work

6.1.1. The Broadly Defined Right

The exclusive right to reproduce the copyrighted work is the most basic element in the bundle of rights constituting copyright. That right is infringed when one other than the copyright owner makes "copies" or "phonorecords" of the work. Those terms are broadly defined in the Act:

"Copies" are material objects, other than phonorecords, in which a work is fixed by any method now known or later developed, and from which the work can be perceived, reproduced, or otherwise communicated, either directly or with the aid of a machine or device. The term "copies" includes the material object, other than phonorecords, in which the work is first fixed.[319]

"Phonorecords" are material objects in which sounds, other than those accompanying a motion picture or other audiovisual work, are fixed by any method now known or later developed, and from which the sounds can be perceived, reproduced, or otherwise communicated, either directly or with the aid of a machine or device. The term "phonorecords" includes the material object in which the sounds are first fixed.[320]

The Act thus makes clear that questions as to the nature of the copying device, or the medium or the method used for copying, are all irrelevant to

---

[318] 17 U.S.C. § 106.

[319] 17 U.S.C. § 101.

[320] Id.

the determination of whether a "copy" has been made of a copyrighted work.[321]

In practice, certain types of reproduction, subsets of the reproduction right, receive specialized treatment and, in practice, are known by specific terms of art. For example, the "copying" involved in incorporating a sound recording into an audiovisual work, synchronizing the sound with the pictures, as is done with sound tracks for motion pictures, is, if done without consent, violative of the owner's exclusive "synchronization right" and industry practice has developed around procedures for license and exercise of that right. "Synchronization right" is an extra-statutory term of art for a special case of the exclusive reproduction right.[322]

Similarly, one speaks of the copyright owner's "mechanical right" in referring to the exclusive right to embody a copyrighted work in a phonorecord, and, as discussed below, a similar specialized practice, based upon compulsory license provisions of the Act, has developed for dealing with exercise of that right.

6.1.2. Specific Statutory Limitations and Compulsory Licenses

Conditioning the broad reproduction right, number of provisions of the Act exempt certain types of copying from infringement claims, while compulsory license provisions exempt certain activities upon compliance with the license terms. The compulsory license device, where it applies, is the product of a congressional determination that the principal value of a certain use is economic and that the copyright owner should be satisfied with a fixed compensation for that use. With a compulsory license the copyright owner, in exchange for a fee, relinquishes the right to determine

---

[321] *See, e.g.,* MAI Systems Corp. v. Peak Computer, Inc., 991 F.2d 511 (9th Cir. 1993), *cert. dismissed,* 510 U.S. 1033, 114 S. Ct. 671 (1994) (holding that copying an operating system into computer memory makes a "copy" of the program for purposes of the Act).

[322] *See* Agee v. Paramount Communications, Inc., 59 F.3d 317 (2d Cir. 1995) (holding that the exclusive right to reproduce a sound recording is infringed by Paramount's unauthorized copying ("synchronization") of the recording onto the audio track of a video tape that was broadcast only once and was not distributed to the public for sale or rental); *see also* ABKCO Music, Inc. v. Stellar Records, Inc., 96 F.3d 60 (2d Cir. 1996).

who may exercise certain of the owner's rights. In connection with certain of the compulsory licensing and related provisions, the Librarian of Congress, in consultation with the Register of Copyright, is directed to "appoint 3 full-time Copyright Royalty Judges...to make determinations and adjustments of reasonable terms and rates of royalty payments as provided in Sections 112(e), 114, 115, 116, 118, 119 and 1004."[323]

6.1.2.1. Library and Archival Copying:

Section 108 of the Act specifically exempts from infringement claims certain reproduction or distribution activities by libraries and archives. The exemption relates generally to noncommercial reproduction or distribution of not more than one copy or phonorecord of a work by libraries or archives that are open to the public or are available to persons, in addition to researchers affiliated with such libraries or archives, doing research in specialized fields.[324]

The exemption extends as well to (i) reproduction and distribution of not more than three copies or phonorecords of an unpublished work in the collections of the library or archives "solely for purposes of preservation and security or for deposit for research use in another library or archives" if any such copy or phonorecord that is reproduced in digital format is not otherwise distributed in that format and is not made available to the public in that format outside the premises of the library or archives; and (ii) reproduction of not more than three copies of a published work "solely for the purpose of replacement of a copy or phonorecords that is damaged, deteriorating, lost, or stolen, or if the existing format in which the work is stored has become obsolete," if the library or archives has, after reasonable effort, determined that an unused replacement cannot be obtained at a fair price and any such copy or phonorecord that is reproduced in digital format

---

[323] 17 U.S.C. § 801. Sections 801-805, enacted in late 2004, establish the Copyright Royalty Judges, amending and superceding the earlier "Copyright Arbitration Royalty Panels" created in Chapter 8.

[324] 17 U.S.C. § 108 (a).

is not made available to the public in that format outside the premises of the library or archives in lawful possession of such copy.[325]

Also exempt is reproduction and distribution "of no more than one article or other contribution to a copyrighted collection or periodical issue, or a copy or phonorecord of a small part of any other copyrighted work," at the request of a user or another library or archive; and reproduction and distribution of an entire work at the request of the user or another library if it has been determined, "on the basis of reasonable investigation, that a copy or phonorecord of the copyrighted work cannot be obtained at fair price." These exemptions are further conditioned on absence of notice that the copy "would be used for any purpose other than private study, scholarship, or research" and upon the library or archives prominently displaying appropriate notice of copyright and warning of infringement.[326]

The 1998 Copyright Term Extension Act, which effectively added twenty years to the duration of copyright,[327] provides a special exemption for library and archival copying. During the last twenty years of the copyright term of a published work, such institutions may reproduce, distribute, display, or perform a copy or phonorecord of the work for purposes of preservation, scholarship, or research, unless "the work is subject to commercial exploitation," or a copy or phonorecord can be obtained at a reasonable price, or the copyright owner has provided notice of the existence of either of these conditions.[328] This exemption originally excluded musical works, pictorial, graphical and sculptural works, and most audiovisual works,[329] but that exclusion was removed in 2005.

6.1.2.2. Ephemeral Recordings

A broadcasting station, or other "transmitting organization" that is licensed or otherwise has the right to transmit to the public a performance

---

[325] 17 U.S.C. §§ 108 (b) and (c); "a format shall be considered obsolete if the machine or device necessary to render perceptible a work stored in that format is no longer manufactured or is no longer reasonably available in the commercial marketplace." 17 U.S.C. § 108 (c).

[326] 17 U.S.C. §§ 108 (d) and (e).

[327] See infra, § 8.

[328] 17 U.S.C. § 108 (h).

[329] 17 U.S.C. § 108 (i).

or a display of a work, or a broadcast transmission of a performance of a sound recording in a digital format on a nonsubscription basis, may make a single copy or phonorecord of that transmission for its own use for archival preservation, or, if the copy or phonorecord is destroyed within six months from the date of first transmission, for purposes of security or for transmission within its own service area.[330] If, for the purposes of making such permitted copy, it is necessary to circumvent technological measures, and the copyright owner does not make available the necessary means for making such copy, then such circumvention will not be a violation of the prohibition on circumvention of copyright protection systems contained in Section 1201 of the Copyright Act.[331] Similarly, a transmitting organization with a statutory license or otherwise authorized under Section 411 to transmit a performance of a sound recording[332] may, upon compliance with the further statutory conditions, make no more than one phonorecord of that recording.[333]

If the transmitting entity is a governmental body or other nonprofit organization, it may make up to 30 copies or phonorecords of a transmission, provided that all but one archival copy are destroyed within seven years from the date of first transmission. Moreover, if the work is a performance or sound recording of a nondramatic musical work of a religious nature, a governmental body or other nonprofit organization may make and distribute, without charge, one copy or phonorecord of a transmitted nondramatic musical religious work for use by broadcasters licensed to transmit the work, provided that all copies, but one archival copy, are destroyed within one year of the date of first transmission. Further, a governmental body or other nonprofit organization entitled to transmit a performance of a work to certain handicapped recipients may make up to ten copies of such work for purposes of such transmission or for archival preservation or security, so long as no charge is made for such use.[334]

---

[330] 17 U.S.C. § 112 (a).

[331] 17 U.S.C. § 112 (a) (2). *See infra,* § 11.

[332] *See infra,* § 6.6.

[333] 17 U.S. C. § 112 (e).

[334] 17 U.S.C. § 112 (b)-(d).

6.1.2.3. Certain Copies of Computer Programs

In response to the CONTU report[335] Congress provided, in Section 117 of the 1976 Act, that the reproduction right is not infringed when the owner of a copy of a computer program makes "another copy or adaptation of that computer program" if that copy or adaptation is used only "as an essential step in the utilization of the computer program in conjunction with a machine," or is made only for archival purposes.[336]

Under Section 117, copying a program into a computer's random access memory in order to use it is not infringing, even if the "use" is not that for which the program was intended.[337] However, it has been held that that immunity will not extend to such copying by one who is not the "owner" of the copy of the program, but only a licensee.[338] To reverse that holding as applied to the specific facts before the court, Congress, in 1998, amended Section 117 to provide that copying of an authorized copy of a computer program that results solely from the activation of a machine by the owner *or lessee* of that machine is not an infringement if it is done only for purposes of maintenance or repair of that machine.[339] The safe harbor provisions of § 117(c) have been interpreted broadly:

[T]he general policy underlying the enactment of section 117(c) ... was "to ensure that independent service organizations do not inadvertently

---

[335] *See supra*, § 2.4.1.1.

[336] 17 U.S.C. § 117 (a).

[337] *See* Vault Corp. v. Quaid Software, Ltd., 847 F.2d 255 (5th Cir. 1988).

[338] MAI Systems Corp. v. Peak Computer, Inc., 991 F.2d 511 (9th Cir. 1993), *cert. dismissed*, 510 U.S. 1033, 114 S. Ct. 671 (1994) (loading by a computer servicing company of a licensed operating system into the licensee's computer RAM (an act incidental to turning on the computer) was "copying" not insulated by §117). See Krause v. Titleserve, Inc., 402 F.3d 119 (2d Cir.), *cert. denied*, 126 S.Ct. 622 (2005); noting that the exemption protects only "the owner of a copy of a computer program," the court emphasizes the distinction between owning the program and owning "a copy" of the program in attempting to determine when "possession" becomes "ownership" of a copy. For these purposes, formal transfer of title is not essential: "Instead, courts should inquire into whether the party exercises sufficient incidents of ownership over a copy of the program to be sensibly considered the owner of the copy for purposes of §117(a)." *See also* Wall Data, Inc. v. Los Angeles County Sheriff's Department, 447 F.3d 769 (9th Cir. 2006).

[339] 17 U.S.C. § 117 (c).

become liable for copyright infringement merely because they have turned on a machine in order to service its hardware components." H.R.Rep. No. 105-551, pt. 1, at 27. Congress thus sought to protect the class of companies that fix and maintain computer systems, as opposed to those that would make other commercial use of copyrighted material.[340]

6.1.2.4. Reproductions for the Blind or Other People with Disabilities

The exclusive reproduction right is not infringed by the reproduction (or distribution of copies or phonorecords) "of a previously published, nondramatic literary work if such copies or phonorecords are reproduced or distributed in specialized formats exclusively for use by blind or other persons with disabilities."[341] The exemption is specifically limited to "nondramatic literary works" reproduced in specialized formats, with appropriate notice, and does not apply to tests and testing material, or to computer programs.[342] Further, the exemption applies only to "a nonprofit organization or a governmental agency that has a primary mission to provide specialized services relating to training, education, or adaptive reading or information access needs of blind or other persons with disabilities."[343] Special exemption is provided for publishers of "print instructional materials for use in elementary or secondary schools" to create and distribute to the National Instructional Materials Access Center, under specified conditions, copies of certain electronic files that the publisher is entitled to distribute in print format.[344]

6.1.2.5. Home Audio Taping

The Act specifically immunizes from infringement actions "the noncommercial use by a consumer" of digital or analog recording devices or media "for making digital musical recordings or analog musical

---

[340] Storage Technology Corp. v. Custom Hardware Engineering & Consulting, Inc., 421 F.3d 1307 (Fed. Cir. 2005).

[341] 17 U.S.C. § 121.

[342] 17 U.S.C. § 121 (b).

[343] 17 U.S.C. § 121 (d).

[344] 17 U.S.C. § 121 (c).

recordings."[345] Digital audio taping technology ("DAT") provided the impetus for this exemption for noncommercial copying of musical works.

DAT technology, which preceded the introduction of inexpensive and easily usable devices for duplicating CDs, enabled the user to make extremely high fidelity copies of recorded works (particularly digitally encoded compact discs). The recording industry, which had tolerated home *analog* tape recording, mounted a strong campaign against the importation of DAT equipment. The Congressional response was the addition to Title 17 of Chapter 10—Digital Audio Recording Devices and Media,[346] which, while exempting such "noncommercial use by a consumer," prohibits the "importation, manufacture, and distribution" of digital audio recording devices unless such devices are so constructed as to prevent "serial copying," defined as "the duplication in a digital format of a copyrighted musical work or sound recording from a digital reproduction of a digital musical recording."[347] The Act seeks to prevent the making of digital copies of digital copies of a digitally recorded work; it is directed to wholesale copying of a work, rather than simple, even multiple copying from the original.[348]

A royalty obligation is imposed upon the manufacturer or importer of permitted digital audio equipment or media (*i.e.*, digital audio tape, discs, or other recording medium). The Copyright Office distributes 2/3 of the royalty fund to the record companies and performers and 1/3 to publishers and composers.[349]

Time, and technological development, have undermined the assumptions that underlay the congressional action. Focusing on digital tape technology, neither Congress nor the music industry, was prepared either for the ease with which CDs may be directly copied onto other CDs or for the distribution of music through the Internet and the use of MP3 compression to facilitate such distribution. As the Ninth Circuit observed, neither Congress nor the interested parties contemplated a "revolutionary

---

[345] 17 U.S.C. § 1008.

[346] 17 U.S.C. § 1001 *et seq.*

[347] 17 U.S.C. § 1001.

[348] 17 U.S.C. § 1002.

[349] 17 U.S.C. §§ 1003-1007.

new method of music distribution made possible by digital recording and the Internet; ...the brave new world of Internet music distribution."[350]

Consequently, applying the specific statutory language in § 1008, the Ninth Circuit held that a computer hard drive is not a "digital audio recording device," nor is an MP3 player, and that therefore, the manufacturer of an MP3 player that records from a hard drive is not subject to the inhibitions and royalty provisions of Chapter 10.[351] Applying the same reasoning, the Ninth Circuit also held that the noncommercial downloading of copyrighted music from the internet by means of a computer is not immunized by § 1008.[352]

6.1.2.6. Compulsory License for Mechanical Reproduction

The 1976 Act significantly expanded the use of compulsory licenses and it continued the principal compulsory license created under the older, 1909 Act, the "compulsory license for making and distributing phonorecords."[353] This is, in essence, a license to make "cover" recordings of previously recorded works. It permits, upon compliance with the compulsory license terms, the making and distribution of phonorecords of nondramatic musical works without the consent of the copyright owner of those works; the compulsory license can obviate the need for a specific "mechanical license" from the copyright owner of the work.

By its terms, the compulsory license applies to the making and distribution of mechanical copies, in the form of phonorecords, only of *nondramatic* musical works, phonorecords of which have theretofore been distributed to the public in the United States under the authority of the copyright owner, and only if the primary purpose in making such new phonorecords is to distribute them to the public for private use. The Digital Performance Right in Sound Recordings Act of 1995 extends the compulsory license to digital audio delivery of the nondramatic musical

---

[350] Recording Industry Association of America v. Diamond Systems, Inc., 180 F.3d 1072 (9th Cir. 1999).

[351] *Id.*

[352] A&M Records v. Napster, 239 F.3d 1004 (9th Cir. 2001) ("the Audio Home Recording Act does not cover the downloading of MP3 files to computer hard drives").

[353] 17 U.S.C. § 115.

works.[354] In short, once the copyright owner of a nondramatic musical work has authorized the making and distribution of phonorecords of that work in the United States, anyone else may similarly make phonorecords of that work for similar distribution to the public upon compliance with the compulsory license provisions. The provisions, limitations, and procedure for acquisition of the compulsory license and for determination and payment of royalties are set out in detail in Section 115 of the Act.[355]

Since the compulsory license is limited to *nondramatic* musical works, it cannot be used to make a recording of an opera, or the entirety of a musical play. So too, the compulsory license to make a new recording of an existing nondramatic musical work does not authorize, without the consent of the owner of copyright in the sound recording, the duplication of an existing sound recording in which that work may be embodied.[356] The license covers only the making and distribution of "phonorecords" and not any and all other kinds of reproductions of the works. Thus, a compact disc or other device that includes both the music of songs and a visual display of their lyrics (for example, for karaoke or sing-along purposes) is not a "phonorecord" for purposes of the compulsory license.[357]

The license does include "the privilege of making a musical arrangement of the work to the extent necessary to conform it to the style or manner of interpretation of the performance involved," so long as such arrangement does "not change the basic melody or fundamental character of the work"; and in any event, the arrangement itself cannot be protected as a derivative work without the express consent of the copyright owner.[358]

Although the creation of the compulsory mechanical license was a significant factor in implementing a policy favoring the proliferation of recorded music, that statutory mechanism itself is not the primary means by which phonorecords are commercially made and distributed; indeed, it is rarely used. Rather, the bulk of such recordings are made under license

---

[354] 17 U.S.C. § 114 (d).

[355] 17 U.S.C. §§ 115 (b) and (c).

[356] 17 U.S.C. § 115 (a) (1).

[357] ABKCO Music, Inc. v. Stellar Records, Inc., 96 F.3d 60 (2d Cir. 1996). The court also noted that even if a compulsory license were otherwise applicable, it would not cover the visual display of the lyrics.

[358] 17 U.S.C. § 115 (a) (2).

from the copyright owner through a voluntary system (administered by the Harry Fox Agency, a subsidiary of the National Music Publishers Association) pursuant to which nonexclusive licenses of the copyright owners' right to make reproductions of nondramatic musical works are granted to those seeking to make "cover" recordings, under essentially the same royalty terms as are provided by the statutory compulsory license, but without the more onerous accounting provisions of the statute. Of course, neither the statutory compulsory license nor these voluntary collective arrangements preclude direct negotiations between a copyright owner and one seeking to record the work.

6.1.2.7. Compulsory License for Public Broadcasting:

Section 118 of the Act creates a compulsory license granting "public broadcasting entities" a limited right to reproduce published nondramatic musical works and published pictorial, graphic, and sculptural works in connection with the broadcast of the performance and display of such works. Rather than set the license fee, the Act contemplates negotiations setting voluntary royalty rates between public broadcasters and organized copyright owners (with the rate to be determined in the absence of agreement by a copyright arbitration royalty panel convened by the Librarian of Congress).[359]

6.2. The Right to Prepare Derivative Works

The creation of a "derivative work" can raise two independent issues. As discussed above,[360] there is the question of the independent copyrightability of a non-infringing derivative work; this involves the issue of the quantum of creativity and originality distinguishing the derivative work from the original upon which it is based. On the other side of that coin is the question of whether one who creates a work based on a copyrighted work infringes the copyright owner's exclusive right under Section 106 (2) "to prepare derivative works based upon the copyrighted work."

The Act defines a "derivative work" as

---

[359] 17 U.S.C. § 118.

[360] *Supra*, § 3.2.2. 2.

a work based upon one or more pre-existing works, such as a translation, musical arrangement, dramatization, fictionalization, motion picture version, sound recording, art reproduction, abridgement, condensation, or any other form in which a work may be recast, transformed, or adapted. A work consisting of editorial revisions, annotations, elaborations, or other modifications which, as a whole, represent an original work of authorship, is a "derivative work."[361]

For purposes of determining whether a purported "derivative work" is itself copyrightable it must, as noted, pass the test of originality and must be fixed in a tangible medium of expression. On the other hand, one may be found to have infringed the exclusive right to prepare derivative works without having made a copy of the original work or without having fixed the infringing work.[362] As the Congressional Committee Reports make clear, "the preparation of a derivative work … may be an infringement even though nothing is ever fixed in tangible form."[363]

The exclusive right to prepare a derivative work is not an omnibus shield against any and all appropriation; it protects against the taking of the underlying work through one or another form of transformation, as in, for example, the transformation of a novel into a motion picture.[364]

To be an infringing derivative work, "the infringing work must incorporate a portion of the copyrighted work in some form; a detailed commentary on a work or programmatic musical composition inspired by

---

[361] 17 U.S.C. § 101.

[362] Lewis Galoob Toys, Inc. v. Nintendo of America, Inc., 964 F.2d 965 (9th Cir. 1992), *cert. denied*, 507 U.S. 985, 113 S. Ct. 1582 (1993).

[363] H.R. Rep No. 1476, 94th Cong., 2d Sess. 62 (1976); S. Rep. No 473, 94th Cong., 1st Sess. 58 (1975).

[364] The definition of "transformation" has produced some conflict in the Courts of Appeal over whether an infringing derivative work is created when one in lawful possession of a copy of a copyrighted work of visual art frames and remounts it and sells the finished product without reproducing or changing the works themselves. *Compare* Mirage Editions, Inc. v. Albuquerque A.R.T. Co., 856 F.2d 1341 (9th Cir. 1988), *cert. denied*, 489 U.S. 1018, 109 S. Ct. 1135 (1989) *and* Lee v. A.R.T. Co., 125 F.2d 580 (7th Cir. 1997).

a novel would not normally constitute infringements ... ."[365] Moreover, it has been held that to be considered an infringing derivative work the offending work must be "substantially similar" to the original, so that even if there is actual "incorporation" of the original, the new work would not be infringing if the final product is not "substantially similar" to the original.[366]

Just as it does in the case of the exclusive right to reproduce a copyrighted computer program, Section 117 of the Act creates a limited exemption for "adaptation" of a copyrighted computer program by the lawful owner of a copy of the program if such adaptation "is created as an essential step in the utilization of the computer program in conjunction with a machine and that it is used in no other manner" and such adaptation may not be transferred without the consent of the copyright owner of the underlying work.[367] In reliance on Section 117 and the CONTU report, it has been held that the owner of a copy of a computer program was entitled to make modifications to the program—*i.e.*, create a derivative work— without consent of the copyright owner so long as the changes "were necessary measures in [the] continuing use of the software" for no purpose other than the owner's "internal business needs."[368]

---

[365] *Id.*; Lewis Galoob Toys, Inc. v. Nintendo of America, Inc., 964 F.2d 965 (9th Cir. 1992), *cert. denied*, 507 U.S. 985, 113 S. Ct. 1582 (1993) (holding that the defendant's device, that allows the user to alter features of plaintiff's video games, was not itself a "derivative" work because of the absence of actual physical incorporation of the underlying work).

[366] Castle Rock Entertainment, Inc. v. Carol Publishing Group, Inc., 150 F.3d 132 (2d Cir. 1998):

> if the secondary work sufficiently transforms the expression of the original work such that the two works cease to be *substantially similar*, then the secondary work is not a derivative work and, for that matter, does not infringe the copyright of the original work.

Id. at 143; *see also*, Atkins v. Fischer, 351 F.3d 988 (D.C. Cir, 2003); Well-Made Toy Mfg. v. Goffa International Corp., 354 F.3d 112 (2d Cir. 2003); Litchfield v. Spielberg, 736 F.2d 1352 (9th Cir. 1984), *cert. denied*, 470 U.S. 1052, 105 S. Ct. 1753 (1985); Micro Star v. Formgen, 154 F.3d 1107 (9th Cir. 1998). *See infra*, § 9.2.1, for discussion of "substantial similarity."

[367] 17 U.S.C. § 117. See Wall Data, Inc. v. Los Angeles County Sheriff's Department, 447 F.3d 769 (9th Cir. 2006).

[368] Aymes v. Bonelli, 47 F.3d 23 (2d Cir. 1995).

6.3. The Right to Distribute

6.3.1. The Right of First Publication

The copyright owner has the exclusive right "to distribute copies or phonorecords of the copyrighted work to the public by sale or other transfer of ownership, or by rental, lease, or lending."[369] This public distribution right is, in essence, a recasting of the old common-law right of first publication, the right of the creator of a work to determine when that work will first be exposed to the public.[370] As with each of the enumerated exclusive rights, the public distribution right is distinct from the other rights, so that permission, for example, to copy, or to perform a work, would not include permission to make public distribution of those copies.

"Distribution" is not defined in the Act, although for most purposes the definition of "publication" as the "distribution of copies or phonorecords of a work to the public by sale or other transfer of ownership, or by rental, lease or lending,"[371] would be sufficient. However, concern over the nature of infringement of works through digital transmission has provoked legislative efforts more specifically to recognize such transmission as an actionable "distribution." In the mid-1990s, the Working Group on Intellectual Property Rights of the Information Infrastructure Task Force, directed by the Commissioner of Patents and Trademarks, recommended an amendment to Section 106(3) to include "transmission" as a "distribution" so that "transmission" of a work would be an infringing "distribution" even when the transmitter retains a copy of the work. It proposed conforming amendments to define "transmit" to include transmission of a reproduction of a work as well as of a performance or display of a work, to make a "transmission" from abroad an "importation" under Section 602,[372] and to define "publication" to include "transmission." Although Congress did not act on these proposals, the courts have, as it has been held that internet transmission of a sound recording (as opposed to a

---

[369] 17 U.S.C. §106 (3).

[370] *Cf.* Harper & Row Publishers, Inc. v. Nation Enterprises, 471 U.S. 539, 105 S. Ct. 2218 (1985) ("from the beginning, those entrusted with the task of revision recognized the 'overbalancing reasons to preserve the common-law protection of disseminated works until the author or his successor chooses to disclose them'").

[371] 17 U.S.C. § 101.

[372] See *infra,*§ 6.3.4.

television or radio "broadcast"),[373] is an infringing "distribution" of the sound recording and of the copyrighted music contained therein.[374]

6.3.2. The First Sale Doctrine

Section 109 of the Act provides: "The owner of a particular copy or phonorecord lawfully made ..., or any person authorized by such owner, is entitled ... to sell or otherwise dispose of the possession of that copy or phonorecord."[375] This provision codifies the prior case law which established the "first sale doctrine."[376] Through these provisions, the "first sale" or its equivalent by a copyright owner terminates the public distribution right. Of course, the first sale doctrine has no effect on rights other than the distribution right and, therefore, will not shield infringement of the right to reproduce the work or the right to perform the work.[377] In the case of foreign works which had fallen into the public domain in the United States but whose copyright has been restored,[378] the owner of copies or phonorecords of such works which had been manufactured prior to the date of restoration may sell or otherwise dispose of them without the authorization of the owner of the restored copyright, but such disposition "for purposes of direct or indirect commercial advantage" may be made only during the twelve-month period following notice of restoration or publication of notice of intention to file for restoration.[379]

The right to distribute a copy or phonorecord of a copyrighted work by one other than the copyright owner is limited to the lawful "owner" of that copy or phonorecord. Therefore, a lease or license by the copyright owner, rather than a transfer of "title" to that copy or phonorecord, will not serve to invoke the first sale doctrine or to divest a copyright owner of the

---

[373] The broadcast would be treated as a "performance," rather than a "distribution." Agee v. Paramount Communications, Inc., 59 F.3d 317 (2d Cir. 1995).

[374] A&M Records v. Napster, 239 F.3d 1004 (9th Cir. 2001).

[375] 17 U.S.C. § 109.

[376] See, e.g., Bobbs-Merrill Co. v. Straus, 210 U.S. 339 (1908); Independent News Company v. Williams, 293 F.2d 510 (3d Cir. 1961).

[377] See, e.g., Columbia Pictures Industries, Inc. v. Redd Horne, Inc., 749 F.2d 154 (3d Cir. 1984).

[378] 17 U.S.C. § 104A.

[379] 17 U.S.C. § 109 (a).

distribution right.[380] For these purposes, the substance, and not the form, of any transaction between the copyright owner and the recipient of a copy will be determinative.

Apart from the specific exceptions, discussed below, the first sale doctrine as embodied in Section 109 broadly permits any and all kinds of distribution or transfer by the lawful owner of a copy or a phonorecord of a work. There is no United States equivalent to the widely recognized public lending right of a copyright owner. The sale and rental of motion pictures on videotape, DVD, or other media, the dissemination of books by libraries, and similar activities involving the distribution of copyrighted works take place under the umbrella of the first sale doctrine.

6.3.3. The Record and Computer Program Rental Exceptions to the First Sale Doctrine

In response first to pressure from the recording industry and then from computer software developers, Congress sought to inhibit the unauthorized copying of recordings and computer programs by excluding commercial lending of recordings and computer programs from "first sale" protection. The Record Rental Amendment of 1984 and the Computer Software Rental Amendment Act of 1990 amended Section 109 to exclude from the shelter of the first sale doctrine the rental, lease, or lending, or their equivalent, "for the purposes of direct or indirect commercial advantage," of copies of computer programs or phonorecords without the consent of the owners of copyright in such programs and in the sound recordings and the musical works embodied in phonorecords.[381] This provision does not apply to the rental, lease, or lending of a phonorecord for nonprofit purposes by a nonprofit library or nonprofit educational institution[382] or to the lending of a computer program for nonprofit purposes by a nonprofit library;[383] nor does it apply to computer programs "used in conjunction with a limited purpose computer that is designed for playing video

---

[380] 17 U.S.C. § 109 (d) (the first sale doctrine "privileges ... do not ... extend to any person who has acquired possession of the copy or phonorecord from the copyright owner, by rental, lease, loan, or otherwise, without acquiring ownership of it").

[381] 17 U.S.C. § 109 (b) (1) (A).

[382] Id.

[383] 17 U.S.C. § 109 (b) (2) (A).

games."[384] The Record Rental and Computer Software Rental Amendments originally were considered "experimental" and had limited terms; however, these sunset provisions were repealed as part of the implementation of the NAFTA and GATT agreements.

6.3.4. Importation and the First Sale Doctrine

Section 602(a) of the Act expressly makes "importation into the United States, without the authority of the owner of copyright ..., of copies or phonorecords of a work that have been acquired outside the United States" an act of "infringement of the exclusive right to distribute copies or phonorecords under section 106."[385] Excluded from the ban on importation are copies or phonorecords imported for the use of the government of the United States or of any state or political subdivision, one copy or phonorecord imported for the private use of the importer and not for further distribution, or brought into the United States as part of the personal baggage of an individual, and not more than five copies or phonorecords imported by or for an organization operated for scholarly, educational, or religious purposes for its library or archival purposes or one copy of an audiovisual work solely for archival purposes.[386]

This section makes it an act of infringement of the distribution right to import into the United States copies of works acquired abroad even if those copies were lawfully made and acquired. The question that has caused considerable conflict and confusion is the extent to which, if any, the first sale doctrine of Section 109, limits application of the Section 602 (a) restraint on importation. The issue arises in several contexts, but the most troublesome appears to be in connection with "grey goods," or "parallel importation" of genuine goods purchased in foreign countries and imported into the United States for resale, generally at a price lower than that charged by authorized United States dealers. So long as there is no misrepresentation as to the goods and they are "genuine," such importation would not be an act of trademark infringement or unfair competition. However, if the packaging of the goods contains copyrighted material, then

---

[384] 17 U.S.C. § 109 (b) (1) (B) (ii).

[385] 17 U.S.C. § 602 (a).

[386] 17 U.S.C. § 602 (a) (1)-(3).

importation of the goods, as so packaged, could invoke the bar of Section 602 (a).[387]

The conflict played out in a series of cases. In *Sebastian International, Inc. v. Consumer Contacts (PTY) Limited*,[388] the Third Circuit appeared to hold that the first sale doctrine limited application of Section 602(a) if the goods had been made in the United States and then shipped abroad and subsequently imported back into the United States; *i.e*, the important question for the court was the place where the goods were originally made. The Ninth Circuit, in *Parfums Givenchy, Inc. v. Drug Emporium, Inc.*[389] held that the first sale doctrine did *not* apply to insulate importation of perfume boxes having a distinctive design if those boxes had been made and initially first sold abroad. The court noted that both the importer and one who purchases for resale from that importer are liable under Section 602(a) for infringing the distribution right. The court amplified its holding in *Denbicare U.S.A., Inc. v. Toys "R" Us, Inc.*,[390] pointing out that the effect of *Parfums Givenchy* was that "§109 applies to copies made abroad only if the copies have been sold in the United States by the copyright owner or with its authority."

However, shortly thereafter, another Ninth Circuit panel added to the confusion, in *L'Anza Research International, Inc. v. Quality King Distributors*,[391] as it rejected *Sebastian's* distinctions based upon the original sale of the goods, and held explicitly that Section 602(a) is not limited by the first sale doctrine (Section 109(a)). The United States Supreme Court granted *certiorari* to resolve this issue, which it did in March, 1998.

Reversing the Ninth Circuit, the Court held that the first sale doctrine, Section 109 (a), is applicable to imported copies of works and therefore conditions Section 602 (a).[392] Noting that Section 602 (a) "does not categorically prohibit the unauthorized importation of copyrighted

---

[387] *See, e.g.*, Sebastian International, Inc. v. Consumer Contacts (PTY) Limited, 847 F.2d 1093 (3d Cir. 1988).

[388] *Id.*

[389] 38 F.3d 477 (9th Cir. 1994), *cert. denied*, 115 S. Ct. 1315 (1995).

[390] 84 F.3d 1143 (9th Cir.), *cert denied*, 117 S. Ct. 190 (1996).

[391] 98 F.3d 1109 (9th Cir. 1996).

[392] Quality King Distributors v. L'Anza Research International, Inc., _ U.S._, 118 S. Ct. 1125 (1998).

materials" but rather "provides that such importation is an infringement of the exclusive right to distribute copies 'under section 106,'" and that Section 106 is limited by Section 109 (a), Justice Stevens reads the statutory language as clearly making the first sale doctrine applicable to importation of copies lawfully made "under the United States Copyright Act" and acquired abroad.[393] The Court found that the two sections can "retain significant independent meaning" and that Section 602 (a) is not swallowed up by Section 109 (a), in that the importation provisions would still be applicable with respect to copies that were not lawfully made under the United States Copyright Act. Justice Ginsburg, concurring, suggests that "lawfully made under the United States Copyright Act" "must mean 'lawfully made in the United States,'"[394] essentially the position taken in *Sebastian.*

6.4. The Public Performance Right

6.4.1. Generally

The copyright owner is vested with the exclusive right "in the case of literary, musical, dramatic, and choreographic works, pantomimes, and motion pictures and other audiovisual works, to perform the copyrighted work publicly."[395] The right does not apply to all copyrighted works, as pictorial, graphic, and sculptural works, and, with a limited exception (discussed below), sound recordings, do not have performance rights. The growth of radio, television, motion pictures, and instantaneous digital communications has made the copyright owner's public performance right extremely valuable, as well as controversial.

The performance right has been particularly important to the music industry, with the virtually continuous use of music in connection with radio and television broadcasting and other forms of public communication. The performance right with respect to *dramatic* musical works ("grand performance rights") is often dealt with quite differently from that with respect to *nondramatic* musical works ("small performance rights"). For example, certain exemptions apply only to performance of

---

[393] *Id.* at 1130.

[394] *Id.* at 1135.

[395] 17 U.S.C. § 106 (4).

nondramatic musical works, and licenses may be limited to the "small performance rights." Because of this distinction, a license that covers only the performance of a nondramatic musical work will not protect the performance of a dramatized version of that same work; a license for performance of individual songs from a musical play will not insulate performance of the original cast album of that play or any other performance in which the songs are rendered sequentially, as that would constitute a "dramatic" version of the work.[396] Unfortunately, there is no clear line separating dramatic from nondramatic musical works or performances. The nature of the performance itself may be determinative—the relevant question being whether the musical work is "dramatized."

For the performance right to be implicated, there must be a "performance" of the copyrighted work and that performance must be "public"; the way in which these terms are defined has enormous significance in setting the scope and value of the right. These definitions are discussed below.

6.4.2. "Performance"

The Act defines "performance" broadly:

To "perform" a work means to recite, render, play, dance, or act it, either directly or by means of any device or process or, in the case of a motion picture or other audiovisual work, to show its images in any sequence or to make the sounds accompanying it audible.[397]

"Performance" is not limited to the act of a human being physically conveying the work to another. Certainly, an individual singing a song is performing it; an orchestra playing a symphony performs it; actors in a play give a performance of that play. If the works involved are copyrighted and these performances are public, then the public performance right has been violated and an action for infringement will lie if the copyright owners have not consented to the performances. In this context, the "performance" has been done by "performers" as that term is generally understood.

---

[396] *See, e.g.*, Robert Stigwood Group, Limited v. Sperber, 457 F.2d 50 (2d Cir. 1972).

[397] 17 U.S.C. § 101.

However, a "performer" in that sense is not essential to invocation of the performance right. If a recording of an individual singing a song is played, a "performance" takes place and the person performing the copyrighted work (*i.e.*, the song) is the person who has caused the record to be played. While "performance" is broadly defined, simple use of a copyrighted work for its intended purpose may not necessarily constitute performance; thus, a copyrightable game is not "performed" when it is played, even when played by large groups of people at a public tournament.[398]

Consistent with the broad definition of performance is the recognition of multiple performances arising out of a single event. If a performance of a play in a theater is simultaneously televised, then while the actors perform the play, the television station also "performs" it, as does a restaurant owner who shows the television broadcast to patrons by means of a television set in the restaurant. In short, the single event of the performance of the play gives rise to multiple performances, each one of which may separately amount to an act of infringement; and permission which may have been granted by the copyright owner with respect to the underlying event will not insulate the performances for which permission was not granted. Using the above example, the copyright owner may have consented to the theatrical performance of the play and to the broadcast of that play, but such consent will not shield the restaurant owner from liability for the performance that arises from turning on the television set in the restaurant.[399]

The issue of retransmission of a broadcast as a "performance" has been a troublesome one. The multiple performance concept, discussed above, in which separate public performances occur when an event is broadcast and the transmission simultaneously received and further communicated, or retransmitted, was first recognized by the United States Supreme Court in *Buck v. Jewell-LaSalle Realty Company*,[400] which involved a hotel "piping" radio broadcasts into guest rooms. However, more than 35 years later, the Supreme Court cast serious doubt on this doctrine in two cases involving

---

[398] Allen v. Academic Games League of America, 89 F.3d 614 (9th Cir. 1996).

[399] *See generally*, David E. Shipley, *Copyright Law and Your Neighborhood Bar and Grill: Recent Developments in Performance Rights and the Section 110 (5) Exemption*, 29 ARIZONA L. REV. 475 (1987).

[400] 283 U.S. 191, 51 S. Ct. 410 (1931).

the retransmission of broadcast signals by cable television systems,[401] and essentially eviscerated the doctrine in a case involving a radio broadcast heard in a fast food restaurant.[402] The matter was put to rest, however, with the 1976 Act, which effectively reinstated *Buck v. Jewell-LaSalle* and reversed the later cases. The Act now makes clear that a separate and, if done without consent or if not within any of the specific exceptions, actionable "performance" occurs when there is a transmission or retransmission of a performance of a copyrighted work.

6.4.3. "Public"

To invoke the performance right, a performance must be "public." The Act attempts to be comprehensive in its definition:

To perform or display a work "publicly" means–

(1) to perform or display it at a place open to the public or any place where a substantial number of persons outside of a normal circle of a family and its social acquaintances is gathered; or

(2) to transmit or otherwise communicate a performance or display of the work to a place specified by clause (1) or to the public, by means of any device or process, whether the members of the public capable of receiving the performance or display receive it in the same place or in separate places and at the same time or at different times.[403]

Thus, one alternative prong of the definition looks at the place at which the work is performed. If it occurs in a place that is open to the public, even a very limited space which can accommodate only a few people at any one time, it is nevertheless "public" and the performance will be actionable even if there was virtually no audience for it. Accordingly, in *Columbia Pictures Industries, Inc. v. Redd Horne, Inc.,*[404] a videocassette rental store was deemed to have publicly performed videocassettes by providing customers with private "screening" rooms, accommodating no more than four people at a time, to which a rented videocassette was

---

[401] Fortnightly Corp. v. United Artists Television, Inc., 392 U.S. 390, 88 S. Ct. 2084 (1968); Teleprompter Corp. v. Columbia Broadcasting System, Inc., 415 U.S. 394, 94 S. Ct. 1129 (1974).

[402] Twentieth Century Music Corp. v. Aiken, 422 U.S. 151, 95 S. Ct. 2040 (1975).

[403] 17 U.S.C. § 106.

[404] 749 F.2d 154 (3d Cir. 1984).

transmitted; since the store was "a place open to the public," the performance of the videocassette was public irrespective of the size of the place or the composition of the audience.[405]

Alternatively, a performance that occurs in what is clearly a private place, one not open to the public, will nevertheless be considered "public" if the audience to whom the performance is directed consists of "a substantial number of persons outside of a normal circle of a family and its social acquaintances." There are no clear standards for determining what size group will be considered such a "substantial number," but that determination will depend not only upon the absolute size of the group but also the nature of the occasion and the relationship among the members of the group.[406]

Transmission of a performance to a place open to the public, as in *Redd Horne,* or generally to the public, as in the case of a radio or television broadcast, will constitute a public performance under the Act, whether the recipients receive it simultaneously or sequentially. Thus, a hotel that electrically transmits a copyrighted motion picture to individual rooms upon request of the guests would be publicly performing the work, as it would if it played tapes or discs of the motion picture on a monitor in the hotel lobby or other common room; on the other hand, if it rented the motion picture individually to guests for use in private guest rooms equipped with their own players, the performance would not be "public."[407]

6.4.4. Statutory Exemptions: Generally

Under the 1909 Act, the public performance right for nondramatic musical works was limited to performances made "for profit." With the growth of broadcast of recorded music and the concomitant increasing importance of the performance right for nondramatic musical works, a rich

---

[405] *Id.* at 158-159.

[406] *See* Columbia Pictures Industries, Inc. v. Aveco, Inc., 800 F.2d 59 (3d Cir. 1986) (videocassette rental store held liable as a contributory infringer for renting videocassettes to customers to be played on cassette players located in separate on-premises screening rooms, rather than by means of transmission from a central location).

[407] *See* Columbia Pictures Industries, Inc. v. Professional Real Estate Investors, Inc., 866 F.2d 278 (9th Cir. 1989).

body of case law developed over the issue of what constitutes a performance "for profit," with the courts making it clear that any benefit, direct or indirect, from the performance (such as a pianist playing background music in a restaurant or recorded music being played over the air) would be sufficient to constitute a performance "for profit." [408]

The 1976 Act eliminated the "for profit" limitation for nondramatic musical works. Section 106(4) makes the performance right applicable to all works (except for sound recordings and pictorial, graphic and sculptural works) without conditioning any rights upon the "profit" nature of the performance. Rather, the Act creates a broad performance right and then provides an array of highly specific exemptions, defining specific noncommercial or nonprofit situations in which performances are exempt, many of which, as discussed below, are refinements of the older, broader general not-for-profit exemption.

6.4.5. The Specific Statutory Exemptions:

The exemptions are set out in Sections 110, 111, 118 and 119 of the Act. The Section 110 exemptions cover a wide variety of situations; Section 111 exempts certain secondary transmissions; that section and Section 119 create compulsory license mechanisms for certain secondary transmissions; and Section 118 exempts public performances by certain noncommercial broadcasting entities under negotiated licenses.

Section 110 specifically exempts ten closely defined performances.[409] Performances that come strictly within the literal terms of these exemptions "are not infringements of copyright."[410] Sections 110 (1)-(4), (6), and (8)-(10) are concerned with various types of not for profit performances while Sections 110 (5) and (7) are narrowly defined commercial exemptions.

6.4.5.1. Sections 110(1) and 110(2): Classroom Exemption

An exemption is provided for "performance or display of a work by instructors or pupils in the course of face-to-face teaching activities of a non-profit educational institution, in a classroom or similar place devoted

---

[408] *See, e.g.* Herbert v. Shanley, 242 U.S. 591, 37 S. Ct. 232 (1917).

[409] 17 U.S.C. § 110.

[410] *Id.*

to instruction," provided that, if the work is a motion picture or other audiovisual work, the exemption will not apply if the performance is "by means of a copy that was not lawfully made" and if "the person responsible for the performance knew or had reason to believe" that it was not lawfully made.[411] This exemption covers performances of all copyrightable subject matter and will apply to face-to-face teaching situations in non-profit educational institutions. Accordingly, if an instructor, in the course of classroom instruction, plays on a player and video monitor in the classroom, a lawfully obtained copy of a copyrighted motion picture relating to the course of instruction, the instructor's performance of the motion picture will be exempt.

The focus of the exemption is the instructional, classroom nature of the performance, and any opening up of the situation so that the performance becomes directed to a wider audience, for other purposes, would place it outside the protection of the exemption. So, too, the exemption would be lost, even if the audience were limited to the students in that instructor's class, if, instead of playing the copy in a player located in the classroom, the instructor arranged for the motion picture to be transmitted to that classroom from an external location.

Section 110 (2) expands the instructional exemption from the face-to-face teaching context to instructional "transmissions." That exemption, as originally enacted, was limited to performances of *nondramatic literary or musical works* and would not include audiovisual works, motion pictures, or dramatic literary or musical works; so too, "transmission" of a performance of such works would be exempt only under limited circumstances related to classroom use. The growth of distance education, particularly through the internet, prompted re-examination of these instructional exemptions. Responding to a directive in the 1998 Digital Millennium Copyright Act, the Register of Copyrights sent to Congress a Report on Copyright and Digital Distance Education and, in 2002 Congress enacted the "Technology, Education and Copyright Harmonization Act" ("the TEACH Act") implementing some of the recommendations. Section 110(2) as so amended, broadens the "transmission" exemption to accommodate some of the exigencies of distance education, by expanding the kinds of works to which the exemption applies and broadening its scope

---

[411] 17 U.S.C. § 110 (1).

beyond the classroom; but it retains several serious limitations, it is not a broad "educational" transmission exemption, and the educational institutions seeking to use the exemption must meet an array of stringent requirements.[412]

6.4.5.2. Section 110(3): Religious Organizations

The section exempts performance, as part of religious services, "of a nondramatic literary or musical work or of a dramatico-musical work of a religious nature."[413]

6.4.5.3. Section 110(4): General Not for Profit Exemption for Nondramatic Works

This section attempts to preserve, to a much more limited extent, part of the 1909 Act "profit" limitation of the performance right. It exempts from liability performance of a nondramatic literary or musical work if that performance is not in a transmission to the public and is given "without any purpose of direct or indirect commercial advantage and without payment of any fee or other compensation for the performance to any of its performers, promoters, or organizers."[414] Further, the exemption requires either (a) that there be no direct or indirect admission charge or (b) that the proceeds from any direct or indirect admission charge (after deduction of expenses) be used "exclusively for educational, religious, or charitable purposes and not for private financial gain"; as to the latter, even if the proceeds are so dedicated, the exemption will not apply if the copyright owner of the work has served written notice of objection to the performance, with a statement of the reasons for the objection, upon the person responsible for that performance at least seven days before the performance date.[415] Interestingly, the Act does not explicitly require the sponsor of the event to notify the copyright owner of the intention to use the work.

---

[412] 17 U.S.C. § 110 (2).

[413] 17 U.S.C. § 110 (3).

[414] 17 U.S.C. § 110 (4).

[415] 17 U.S.C. § 110 (4) (B).

6.4.5.4. Section 110(6): Governmental Agricultural Organizations

Performance of a nondramatic musical work is exempt if it is done by a governmental body or a non-profit agricultural or horticultural organization in the course of an annual agricultural or horticultural fair or exhibition; the exemption extends to any vicarious liability which might otherwise be imposed upon the sponsoring organization for infringing activities of concessionaires or others at such agricultural fair or exhibition (but does not protect such individual infringers).[416]

6.4.5.5. Sections 110(8)and (9): Performance and Transmissions to Certain Handicapped Persons

Performance of a *nondramatic* literary work will be exempt if it occurs in the course of

> a transmission specifically designed for and primarily directed to blind or other handicapped persons who are unable to read normal printed material ..., or deaf or other handicapped persons who are unable to hear the aural signals accompanying the transmission of visual signals, if the performance is made without any purpose of direct or indirect commercial advantage and its transmission is made through the facilities of: (i) a governmental body; or (ii) a noncommercial educational broadcast station..; or (iii) a radio subcarrier...; or (iv) a cable system.[417]

The exemption applies only to nondramatic literary works and therefore will not cover the performance of a play or of any musical or audiovisual works.

A limited exemption is provided for a single performance, on only one occasion, of a *dramatic* literary work in a transmission "specifically designed for and primarily directed to blind or other handicapped persons who are unable to read normal printed material" if the performance is made without any purpose of direct or indirect commercial advantage and the transmission is made through the facilities of a radio subcarrier. Moreover, for the exemption to apply, the work must have been published at least ten years before the date of the performance.[418]

---

[416] 17 U.S.C. § 110 (6).

[417] 17 U.S.C. § 110 (8).

[418] 17 U.S.C. § 110 (9).

6.4.5.6. Section 110(10): Fraternal and Veterans Organizations, for Charitable Purposes

Performance of a nondramatic literary or musical work is exempt if it is done "in the course of a social function which is organized and promoted by a non-profit veterans' organization or a non-profit fraternal organization to which the general public is not invited ... if the proceeds from the performance, after deducting the reasonable costs of producing the performance, are used exclusively for charitable purposes and not for financial gain" (for these purposes, a college or university fraternity or sorority will be included only if the social function "is held solely to raise funds for a specific charitable purpose").[419] This exemption was added to the Act to give these organizations somewhat broader rights than they would have under the Section 110 (4) exemption.

6.4.5.7. Section110(5): Communication of Transmission of a Performance

6.4.5.7.1. The "Aiken" Exemption for "Home" Type Equipment

As discussed above,[420] the 1976 Act resolved controversy over the application of the performance right to multiple performances and secondary transmissions by overturning the series of Supreme Court opinions that had culminated in *Twentieth Century Music Corp. v. Aiken*;[421] the Act effectively reinstates *Buck v. Jewell-LaSalle Realty Company*,[422] making each of the elements of the multiple performances of a single event a separate "performance" for the purposes of the Act. However, at the same time, Congress attempted to codify the *result* in *Aiken* by exempting performances occurring in a context similar to that of that case. Specifically, Section 110 (5) (a) exempts a performance which consists of the public reception "on a single receiving apparatus of a kind commonly used in private homes" of a transmission embodying a performance of a work, unless a direct charge is made to see or hear the transmission or there is a

---

[419] 17 U.S.C. § 110 (10).

[420] *Supra*, § 6.4.2.

[421] 422 U.S. 151, 95 S. Ct. 2040 (1975).

[422] 283 U.S. 191, 51 S. Ct. 410 (1931).

98

further transmission of the work to the public.[423] In short, the section would exempt a performance consisting of having a simple radio or television receiver turned on in a restaurant. The exemption is limited specifically to communication of a *transmission* and, therefore, would not exempt playing of a compact disc or recording or a videotape or disc under the same circumstances and on a similarly simple device.

The crucial issue for determining applicability of the exemption is the characterization of the receiving apparatus as being "of a kind commonly used in private homes." The intention behind the exemption is to allow the use of ordinary radio and television sets in small commercial establishments. In considering the applicability of the exemption, one must consider both the size of the establishment and the nature of the receiving apparatus. The House Committee Report suggests that the factors to be considered are "the size, physical arrangement, and noise level of [the premises] and the extent to which the receiving apparatus is altered or augmented."[424] The Report suggests that the exemption will not be applicable where "the commercial establishment is of sufficient size to justify ... a subscription to a commercial background music service."[425] For these purposes, the relevant "size" is that of the individual establishment, so that an installation in each small store of an affiliated chain will be evaluated on an individual store basis and the court will not aggregate the stores; so long as each store uses equipment "of a kind commonly used in private homes" the use will be exempt.[426]

6.4.5.7.2. Nondramatic Musical Works in Licensed Broadcast Transmissions

Changing technology and increased sophistication of audio and video equipment has altered the boundaries of the definition of the statutory words. It is no longer so easy to differentiate "home" from "commercial" equipment. The result has been a lack of clear definitional rules or

---

[423] 17 U.S.C. § 110 (5) (a).

[424] H.R. Rep. No. 94-1476, 94th Cong., 2d Sess. 87 (1976).

[425] *Id.* at 75.

[426] *See* Broadcast Music, Inc. v. Claire's Boutiques, Inc., 949 F.2d 1482 (7th Cir. 1991), *cert. denied*, 112 S. Ct. 1942 (1992).

consistency in application.[427] In response both to the problem of technology and to concerns over the activities of ASCAP and the other performing rights societies, Congress enacted the "Fairness in Music Licensing Act of 1998," creating a further exemption with respect to performance or display of nondramatic musical works.[428]

These provisions exempt communication by a business establishment of a transmission (or of a retransmission) originated by a licensed radio or television broadcast station, or, if an audiovisual transmission, by a cable system or satellite carrier, embodying a performance or display of a nondramatic musical work intended to be received by the general public if: no direct charge is made to see or hear the transmission or retransmission, and the transmission or retransmission is not further transmitted beyond the establishment where it is received, and the transmission or retransmission is licensed by the copyright owner of the work. The exemption is further limited by the requirement that if the establishment has 2,000 or more (or, in the case of a food service establishment, 3,750 or more) gross square feet of space, the communication may not involve: (i) in the case of an audio performance, or of the audio portion of an audiovisual performance, more than six loudspeakers (with no more than four located in any one room or adjoining outdoor space) and (ii) in the case of the visual portion of an audiovisual performance, more than four audiovisual devices (with no more than one located in any one room) of audiovisual devices having a diagonal screen size greater than fifty-five inches.[429]

---

[427] *Cf.* Broadcast Music, Inc. v. Claire' s Boutiques, Inc., 949 F.2d 1482 (7th Cir. 1991), *cert. denied*, 112 S. Ct. 1942 (1992); Cass County Music Co. v. Muedini, 55 F.3d 263 (7th Cir. 1995), in which the Seventh Circuit examined and applied its *Claire's* opinion, to a different conclusion, holding that the addition to a standard receiver of a sophisticated control panel and 9 recessed speakers, connected with a powerful transformer, resulted in a system in defendant's restaurant that is not "commonly found in homes" and is therefore not exempt. *See* National Football League v. McBee & Bruno's, Inc., 792 F.2d 726 (8th Cir. 1986) (holding the use of antenna dishes to receive blacked-out television signals on a simple television set located in a bar was not exempt; while the receiving set meets the requirements, use of the large antenna to pick up the signal infringes).

[428] 17 U.S.C. § 110 (5) (b).

[429] *Id.*

The addition of Section 110 (5) (B) significantly expands the exemption for communication of a transmission of a nondramatic musical work. This expansion has put into bold relief the problem of harmonizing United States copyright law, and its array of exemptions and compulsory licenses, with the Berne Convention. In general, the Berne Convention leaves room for some limitation of copyright owner rights, as member countries reserve the right to impose "minor reservations" on the public performance right. However, in June 2000, a World Trade Organization dispute resolution panel, responding to the complaint by copyright owners in Ireland about the scope of Section 110 (5) (B), found that the section placed the United States in violation of the TRIPs (Trade Related Aspects of International Property) Agreement, specifically Article 13, a recodification of Article 9.2 of the Berne Convention, which limits exemptions to those "that do not conflict with a normal exploitation of the work." The panel held that the section, in its breadth and with its significant economic implications, does so conflict. By contrast, the panel upheld the Section 110 (5) (A) *Aiken* exemption for homestyle equipment as comparatively minimal and not inconsistent with the Berne Convention. No enforcement action has been taken against the United States, and the Congress has not acted to amend the section.

With respect to the exemptions under Section 110 (5), a proprietor of an establishment[430] who asserts the exemption as a defense to an infringement claim, without reasonable grounds to believe it was applicable, will be liable, in addition to any other damages, for twice the license fee that should have been paid, for up to the preceding three years.[431]

6.4.5.8. Section 110(7): Performance Ancillary to Retail Sales

The Act exempts performance of a nondramatic musical work "by a vending establishment open to the public at-large without any direct or indirect admission charge, where the sole purpose of the performance is to promote the retail sale of copies or phonorecords of the work, or of the audiovisual or other devices utilized in such performance, if the performance is not transmitted beyond the place where the establishment is located and is made "within the immediate area where the sale is

---

[430] As these terms are defined in 17 U.S.C. § 101.

[431] 17 U.S.C. 504 (d).

occurring."[432] As is clear from the language, the exemption is designed to protect performance of a work to enhance sales of phonorecords of the work or associated equipment.[433] Thus, playing a compact disc by means of a player and speakers located near the cash register of the music department of a department store would be exempt, whereas playing a videocassette of a motion picture through a cassette player and monitor located near the cash register of a video rental store would not be exempt since the motion picture is not a nondramatic musical work; so, too, the exemption would be lost by the department store in the case of the compact disc if the music were further transmitted from the music department to other parts of the store.

6.4.5.9. Section 111: Exemptions for Secondary Transmissions

Section 111 creates a limited exemption, under certain circumstances, for "secondary transmissions of a primary transmission embodying a performance or display of a work"[434]; the exemption deals essentially with the retransmission of over the air broadcast signals. It specifically exempts a secondary transmission, other than one made by a cable system, in the form of relaying transmissions by licensed broadcast stations "by the management of a hotel, apartment house, or similar establishment," "to the private lodgings of guests or residents of such establishment," if no direct charge is made to see or hear that secondary transmission.[435] The Act here seeks to exempt the *Buck v. Jewell-LaSalle* situation of a simple relay of a broadcast signal to private rooms (simply placing a radio or television receiver in a private hotel room is not a public performance or actionable in any event).

Section 111 further exempts secondary transmissions as part of the systematic instructional activities of a governmental body or nonprofit educational institution under the circumstance set out in Section 110(2)

---

[432] 17 U.S.C. § 110 (7).

[433] The inclusion of audiovisual or other devices utilized in the performance was added by the "Fairness in Music Licensing Act" of 1998.

[434] 17 U.S.C. § 111 (a).

[435] 17 U.S.C. § 111 (a) (1).

(discussed above);[436] secondary transmissions made by a "passive" carrier, one with no control over the content of the primary transmission or with the recipients of the secondary transmission, but merely a provider of hardware and communications channels for the use of others;[437] secondary transmissions "made by a satellite carrier for private home viewing pursuant to a statutory license under section 119 [of the Act];"[438] and secondary transmissions made by a governmental body or other nonprofit organization without charge to the recipients other than assessments necessary to defray the actual and reasonable costs of maintaining and operating the secondary transmission service.[439]

The foregoing exemptions under Section 111(a) will not be applicable if the secondary transmission is of a primary transmission that is "controlled and limited to reception by particular members of the public" unless that primary transmission is made by a licensed broadcast station and the secondary transmitter is required under the rules of the Federal Communications Commission to carry that signal and the signal is not altered.[440]

Finally, Section 111 deals with secondary transmissions by cable systems and creates a complex compulsory licensing scheme by which such cable systems pay royalties, based upon the size of the respective systems, and such royalties are allocated and distributed by the Library of Congress on recommendation from the Register of Copyrights. The statute contemplates an elaborate procedure for determining both the amount to be distributed and the proper parties to receive payment of the royalty fees.[441] To be protected by the compulsory license, a cable system may not change the content of the primary broadcast.

Peculiar problems have been created by satellite carrier companies, organizations that retransmit television programming signals by means of satellite to home satellite receiving dishes. If such carriers are "cable

---

[436] 17 U.S.C. § 111 (a) (2).

[437] 17 U.S.C. § 111 (a) (3).

[438] 17 U.S.C. § 111 (a) (4).

[439] 17 U.S.C. § 111 (a) (5).

[440] 17 U.S.C. § 111 (b).

[441] 17 U.S.C. § 111 (c)-(f).

systems," they would come within Section 111 if they otherwise met its provisions, whereas, absent some other exemption, their retransmissions would be infringing if they are not cable systems. To fill any void in the system, Congress enacted the Satellite Home Viewer Act of 1988, creating a compulsory license mechanism for "secondary transmissions of super stations and network stations for private home viewing."[442] It is not all clear how these carriers may be properly categorized. In response to an Eleventh Circuit holding that such a carrier is a "cable system,"[443] the Copyright Office issued regulations providing that such carriers were *not* "cable systems" for purposes of Section 111, and these regulations were upheld.[444]

6.4.5.10. Section 118: Noncommercial Broadcasting

The compulsory license for noncommercial broadcasters under Section 118 of the Act, discussed above,[445] includes the right to perform or display a work "in the course of a transmission made by a noncommercial educational broadcast station."[446]

6.4.6. Performing Rights Societies

While the Act clearly recognizes the performance right, enforcement of the right can be difficult, particularly with respect to the "small performance right," the performance right with respect to nondramatic musical works. Quite apart from the difficulty of any copyright owner tracking live performances of copyrighted works, the ubiquity of broadcast recorded music makes individual enforcement of performance rights a virtual impossibility. The difficulty was recognized almost as soon as

---

[442] 17 U.S.C. § 119.

[443] National Broadcasting Co., Inc. v. Satellite Broadcast Network, Inc., 940 F.2d 1467 (11th Cir. 1991).

[444] Satellite Broadcasting and Communications Ass'n of America v. Oman, 17 F.3d 344 (11th Cir. 1994), *cert. denied* 115 S. Ct. 88 (1994) ("Although the new regulations conflict with our interpretation of the term 'cable system' in SBN, they are neither arbitrary, capricious, nor in conflict with the clear meaning of the statute. They are therefore valid exercises of the Copyright Office's statutory authority to interpret the provisions of the compulsory licensing scheme, and are binding on this circuit").

[445] *Supra*, § 6.1.2.7.

[446] 17 U.S.C. § 118.

recorded music began and the solution was found in collective action with the formation in 1914 of the American Society of Composers Authors and Publishers ("ASCAP"), primarily through the efforts of the well-known composer Victor Herbert and the lawyer, Nathan Burkan.

ASCAP, the first and still largest of the performing rights societies,[447] is essentially a licensing, collection and distribution body. Its members—composers, authors, and publishers of copyrighted musical works—assign to the society the non-exclusive right to license the small performance rights (the nondramatic musical performance rights) to their works collectively. With the license from the individual members, the society then negotiates blanket licenses with broadcast stations, restaurants, bars, health clubs, and any other entities desiring to perform any of the works; in exchange for payment of the annual fee, the licensee then may exercise the nondramatic musical rights attaching to any and all of the society's works. The accumulated license fees, after expenses, are then distributed to the members more or less on the basis of the frequency of performance of their works, as determined by statistical samples.[448]

Dissatisfaction both by composers with the weighting distribution system employed by ASCAP, which allegedly favored older, more established composers, and by broadcasters, concerned about ASCAP's pricing practices, resulted in the formation, under the auspices of broadcasters, of a competing performing rights society, Broadcast Music Inc. ("BMI"). Several other, considerably smaller, special purpose performing rights societies also exist. What they all have in common is collective action and a practice of blanket licenses. This inevitably invited scrutiny and attack under the U.S. antitrust laws, with the result that ASCAP and BMI operate under consent decrees putting constraints on their activities. For example, ASCAP may acquire only non-exclusive licenses from its members, who remain free to negotiate licenses individually, and

---

[447] A "performing rights society" is "an association, corporation, or other entity that licenses the public performance of nondramatic musical works on behalf of copyright owners of such works, such as the American Society of Composers, Authors and Publishers (ASCAP), Broadcast Music, Inc (BMI), and SESAC, Inc." 17 U.S.C. § 101.

[448] *See* Korman and Koenigsberg, *Performing Rights in Music and Performing Rights Societies,* 33 JOURNAL OF THE COPYRIGHT SOCIETY 332 (1986).

105

ASCAP must make available to users a per program license as well as a blanket license.[449]

As part of the "Fairness in Music Licensing Act of 1998,"[450] Congress enacted Section 512 of the Copyright Act giving an individual proprietor owning fewer than seven establishments that publicly perform nondramatic musical works, the right to institute proceedings against any performing rights society that operates under a consent decree, to determine a reasonable license fee.[451]

The performing rights societies, and particularly ASCAP, vigorously enforce their rights and regularly institute litigation against entities who exercise the small performing rights without consent. Similarly with respect to motion pictures, the Motion Picture Association, while not a performing rights society, nevertheless quite actively monitors motion picture performances and arranges appropriate licenses. As discussed above,[452] there are other organizations which seek to facilitate licensing of various rights, although they are not licensing organizations as such but rather agents for copyright owners.

6.5. The Display Right

The exclusive rights of the owner of copyright include the right "to display the copyrighted work publicly."[453]

6.5.1. The Nature of The Right

To "display" a work

means to show a copy of it, either directly or by means of a film, slide, television image, or any other device or process or, in the case of a motion

---

[449] *See, e.g.,* Alan J. Hartnick, *The Newest Blanket License Triumphant: The Fourth Round of The ASCAP-BMI/CBS Litigation,* 2 COMM. & L. 49 (1980); Ralph Oman, *Source Licensing: The Latest Skirmish in an Old Battle,* 11 COLUM.-VLA J.L. & ARTS 251 (1987).

[450] *See supra,* § 6.4.5.7.2.

[451] 17 U.S.C. § 512.

[452] *Supra,* § 6.1.2.6.

[453] 17 U.S.C. § 106 (5) ("in the case of literary, musical, dramatic, and choreographic works, pantomimes, and pictorial, graphic, or sculptural works, including the individual images of a motion picture or other audiovisual work").

picture or other audiovisual work, to show individual images non-sequentially.[454]

As with a performance, one may "transmit" the display, *i.e.*, "communicate it by any device or process whereby images or sounds are received beyond the place from which they are sent."[455]

The display right has not been the subject of a great deal of elaboration or development, and functions to a great extent as a placeholder for technological change. Nevertheless, it does have significant practical impact upon the bundle of rights of a copyright owner. The display right was not explicitly recognized prior to the 1976 Act, but arose largely from concern over the possibility of harm to copyright owners from exhibition of works on mass communication devices or other forms of communication which might not necessarily amount to performance or distribution of a work but could nevertheless result in wide dissemination of that work to the public. Explicit recognition of the right reflects an intention to give the copyright owner control over direct showings of copyrighted work, as well as the projection of images and electronic transmission of images of such work.

In many respects, the display right parallels the public performance right. The right is concerned with *public* display of a work and that term is defined for purposes of the display right the same as it is defined for purposes of the performance right.

6.5.2. Limitations on the Display Right

To a large extent, the exemptions and limitations upon the display right parallel those attendant to the performance right. Specifically, the performance right exemptions in Sections 110(1) (face-to-face teaching), 110(2) (instructional broadcast), 110(3) (religious services), 110(5) (communication of a transmission), 111(c) (secondary transmissions by cable systems), and 118 (activities of public broadcasting stations)[456] all apply equally to the display right.

---

[454] 17 U.S.C. § 101.

[455] *Id.*

[456] *Supra*, § 6.4.5.

Moreover, an analog to the first sale doctrine[457] limits the display right. In addition to the right to make transfers or dispositions, the owner of a lawfully made copy of a work may

> display that copy publicly, either directly or by the projection of no more than one image at time, to viewers present at the place where the copy is located.[458]

Thus, a museum that has purchased artwork (without acquiring the copyright in that work) need not have the consent of the copyright owner to display that work at the museum. Just as with the first sale doctrine, the person seeking the benefit of the exemption must be the owner of a lawfully made copy of the work. Further, so long as the display takes place where the copy of the work is located, it may be displayed both directly or indirectly, such as by projection. The exemption is also limited to the display of not more than "one image at a time" and therefore it would not apply to a transmission made available to a number of people by the use of multiple images or multiple receiving devices, such as computer terminals.

6.6. The Limited Performance Right for Sound Recordings

As discussed above,[459] the 1976 Act, in creating the sound recording copyright, explicitly refuses generally to include performance rights as part of the exclusive rights of the owner of copyright in a sound recording;[460] consequently, the United States cannot adhere to the Rome Convention for the Protection of Performers, Producers of Phonograms, and Broadcasting Organizations.

However, with the passage, in 1995, of The Digital Performance Right in Sound Recordings Act, there was created a sharply limited performance right in sound recordings, directed essentially to those applications that displace the market for the recordings, as opposed to those (such as over the air broadcast) that could enhance the market. That 1995 Act effectively limited the right to subscription or interactive digital audio transmissions and a defined class of non-subscription transmissions.

---

[457] *Supra,* § 6.3.2.

[458] 17 U.S.C. § 109 (c).

[459] *Supra,* § 2.4.6.

[460] 17 U.S.C. § 114 (a).

The Digital Performance Right in Sound Recordings Act grants to the owner of copyright in a sound recording the exclusive right "to perform the copyrighted work publicly by means of a digital audio transmission."[461] "Digital transmission"is defined as "a transmission in whole or in part in a digital or other non-analog format"[462] and therefore the performance right would not apply to an analog transmission of a sound recording, such as was usually done by radio broadcast stations. Similarly, the right is limited to "transmission" and therefore would not apply to other forms of performance of sound recordings, such as playing prerecorded music in restaurants or other public places; nor can the right apply to the transmission of any audiovisual work.[463] Most significant is the complex set of limitations and exceptions which effectively tailor the performance right in sound recordings to digital "subscription transmissions" (and selected "eligible non-subscription transmissions"), transmissions to a controlled group of recipients who pay to receive them.[464]

The Digital Millennium Copyright Act of 1998 significantly expanded the scope and complexity of Section 114 (making it now one of the most complex and densely worded provisions of the 1976 Act), which now extends to Internet performances and contains a statutory and voluntary compulsory licensing scheme and measures related to that Act's anti-piracy provisions.[465] These amendments were part of an effort "to ensure that recording artists and record companies will be protected as new technologies affect the ways in which their creative works are used ... and to create fair and efficient licensing mechanisms that address the complex issues facing copyright owners and copyright users as a result of the rapid growth of digital audio services."[466]

Concerned over the economic impact of this limited performance right in sound recording on royalties payable to owners of the underlying musical

---

[461] 17 U.S.C. § 106 (6). *See, generally*, Sobel, *A New Music Law for the Age of Digital Technology*, 17 ENTER. L. REP. (No. 6) 3 (1995).

[462] 17 U.S.C. § 101.

[463] 17 U.S.C. § 114 (j)(3).

[464] 17 U.S.C. § 114 (d)-(j).

[465] *See infra*, § 11.

[466] Conference Report, Joint Explanatory Statement of the Committee of Conference,105th Cong., 2d Sess (1998).

works, Congress expressly provided: "It is the intent of Congress that royalties payable to copyright owners of musical works for the public performance of their works shall not be diminished in any respect as a result of the rights granted by section 106(6)."[467]

6.7. Moral Right[468]

6.7.1. Background

The so-called "moral right" is predicated on the idea that an artist invests his or her work with the artist's personality,[469] so that the creation of the work invokes personality rights which are independent of economic interests in the work. As so understood, the moral right in American society must conflict not only with rooted property principles but also with egalitarian norms. While we translate the French *droit moral* almost (but not quite) literally into the phrase "moral right," the translation of this civil law concept into its American incarnation cannot be nearly so literal.[470] The Civil Law's comfort and the common-law's unease with the bundle of personality interests protected by the moral right is manifest.[471]

---

[467] 17 U.S.C. § 114 (i).

[468] *See generally,* Roberta Rosenthal Kwall, *How Fine Art Fares Post VARA*, 1 MARQ. INTELL. PROP. L. REV. 1, 3-4. (1997); Sheldon W. Halpern, *Of Moral Right and Moral Righteousness*, 1 MARQ. INTELL. PROP. L. REV. 65 (1997); SHELDON W. HALPERN, THE LAW OF DEFAMATION, PRIVACY, PUBLICITY, AND MORAL RIGHT, Part Four— Moral Right (4th ed. 2000).

[469] Martin A. Roeder, The Doctrine of Moral Right: A Study in the Law of Artists, Authors and Creators, 53 HARV. L. REV. 540 (1940):

When an artist creates, be he an author, a painter, a sculptor, an architect or a musician, he does more than bring into the world a unique object having only exploitive possibilities; he projects into the world part of his personality and subjects it to the ravages of public use.

[470] The translation of the words leaves something to be desired. *See* Roberta Rosenthal Kwall, *Copyright and the Moral Right: Is an American Marriage Possible?* 38 VAND. L. REV. 1 (1985). Professor Kwall suggests that "moral right" is not an adequate rendering of the term *droit moral*, which connotes "a right that exists in an entity's ultimate being." *Id.* at n. 6.

[471] It was bountifully documented almost sixty years ago in Martin A. Roeder, *The Doctrine of Moral Right: A Study in the Law of Artists, Authors and Creators*, 53 HARV. L. REV. 540 (1940).

Although there are significant variations among the different Civil Law moral right schemes, there is no dichotomy, or mutual exclusivity in the Civil Law generally between "copyright" and "moral right." The moral right is an inherent part of the intellectual property scheme, a structure that accommodates, definitionally, both economic and noneconomic rights of the "creator." The law reflects a societal consensus with respect to artistic creation. At the very least, this consensus relates to a creator's rights of attribution and integrity, *i.e.*, the right to have one's name attached to one's work, with the corollary right not to have one's name attached to someone else's work, and the right to object to distortion of the work. These principal components of the moral right are set out in Article 6*bis* of the Berne Convention.[472]

In the United States, there is not a similar consensus and American law has not been hospitable to the moral right construct. As a general matter, the common-law in the United States rejected moral right as an independent basis for recognition of creator's rights of attribution or integrity and actionable independent of ownership of copyright in a work.[473] Over time, the courts, through interpretation of contracts, construction of the copyright laws, and extension of the laws of trademark, adopted cognates to enforce, by proxy, some of the essence of the moral right, without adopting the construct itself.[474]

By the late 1980s there was significant interest in comprehensive moral right legislation, driven by the perceived need for the United States to accede to the Berne Convention. Ultimately, the consortium of interests behind legislative action abandoned moral rights legislation upon being convinced that the judicial development of basic moral right cognates

---

[472] "Independently of the author's economic rights, and even after the transfer of the said rights, the author shall have the right to claim authorship of the work and to object to any distortion, mutilation or other modification of, or other derogatory action in relation to, the said work, which would be prejudicial to his honour or reputation." Berne Convention for the Protection of Literary and Artistic Property, as revised in Paris on July 24, 1971, art. 6bis.

[473] *See generally* SHELDON W. HALPERN, THE LAW OF DEFAMATION, PRIVACY, PUBLICITY, AND MORAL RIGHT, Part Four— Moral Right (4th ed. 2000).

[474] *See, e.g.*, Gilliam v. American Broadcasting Companies, 538 F.2d 14 (2d Cir. 1976); Lamothe v. Atlantic Recording Corporation, 847 F.2d 1403 (9th Cir. 1988); Granz v. Harris, 198 F.2d 585 (2d Cir. 1952).

permitted United States adherence to the Berne Convention without such legislation, and the Berne Convention Implementation Act of 1988 was adopted without reference to moral right or a counterpart to Article 6*bis* of the Berne Convention.[475]

Congress did take a step in the direction of preservation of works, in response to objections to the colorization of black and white films, with creation of the National Film Preservation Board,[476] which can add twenty-five films every year into a National Film Registry so that unaltered versions of those films will always be available. Then, in 1990, Congress adopted the Visual Artists Rights Act,[477] a tentative move toward incorporation of moral right principles into the federal copyright scheme.

6.7.2. The Visual Artists Rights Act

Embodied in Section 106A,[478] the Visual Artists Rights Act creates limited rights of attribution and integrity for certain works of visual art. These rights vest in the "author" rather than in the "copyright owner" and are designed to secure a personal right independent of the economic attributes of copyright ownership,[479] rights that would survive transfer of ownership of any copy of the work of visual art or transfer of the copyright in that work.[480] The "author" contemplated by these provisions is an individual (or individual co-authors); the definition of works of visual art to which the section is applicable specifically excludes "any work made for hire."[481] The Visual Artists Rights Act specifically preempts any state law claims equivalent to those created by Section 106A.[482]

---

[475] *See* Ralph S. Brown, *Adherence to the Berne Copyright Convention: The Moral Rights Issue*, 35 J. COPYRIGHT SOCIETY 196 (1988); *see also*, Roberta Rosenthal Kwall, *How Fine Art Fares Post VARA*, 1 MARQ. INTELL. PROP. L. REV. 1, 3-4. (1997).

[476] Pub.L. No. 100-446 (1988).

[477] Pub.L. No. 101-650 (1990).

[478] 17 U.S.C. § 106A.

[479] 17 U.S.C. § 106A (b) ("Only the author of a work of visual art has the rights conferred by subsection (a) in that work, whether or not the author is the copyright owner").

[480] 17 U.S.C. § 106A (e).

[481] 17 U.S.C. § 101.

[482] 17 U.S.C. § 301 (f).

6.7.2.1. The Attribution and Integrity Rights

The "author"of a work of visual art within that section is given the right "to claim authorship of that work," and "to prevent the use of his or her name as the author of any work of visual art which he or she did not create."[483]

The author is also given the right "to prevent the use of his or her name as the author of the work of visual art in the event of the distortion, mutilation, or other modification of the work which would be prejudicial to his or her honor or reputation." Further elaborating on this right of integrity, the author is given the right "to prevent any intentional distortion, mutilation, or other modification of that work which would be prejudicial to his or her honor or reputation"; and the author has the right "to prevent any destruction of a work of recognized stature."[484]

The integrity right here is rather convoluted, but it is clearly limited to acts which "would be prejudicial" to the author's "honor or reputation." This formula was taken directly from Article 6*bis* of the Berne Convention, but neither the Copyright Act nor any other constructs in American law provide a definition of "honor." Serious problems may arise in determining what is "prejudicial to ... honor and reputation" in order to fix liability. "Reputation" as used in the moral rights context has not been coextensive with its use in defamation; nor has American jurisprudence had much occasion to deal with the concept of "honor" as a juridical construct.

There has, as yet, been little judicial examination of the terms. There has been only one, District Court, attempt to define them, but the court did so without reference to the Civil Law experience; rather, it relied solely on

---

[483] 17 U.S.C. § 106A (a) (1).
[484] 17 U.S.C. § 106A (a) (2), (3).

a dictionary definition.[485] Nor is it clear what makes a work of visual art one of "recognized stature."[486]

6.7.2.2. Exclusions and Limitations

The Act defines a "work of visual art" quite narrowly, limiting it to *single* copies of "a painting, drawing, print, or sculpture" or "a still photographic image produced for exhibition purposes only" or to signed and numbered copies of such works in limited editions of not more than 200 copies; motion pictures, books, periodicals and a wide array of other types of work are specifically excluded, as are works made for hire.[487] Moreover, the attribution and integrity rights will not apply "to any reproduction, depiction, portrayal, or other use of a work in, upon or in any connection with" any of the above excluded works; nor will any such reproduction, depiction, portrayal, or other use of a work in connection with such excluded works be considered violative of the integrity right.

The integrity right is further limited. Modification of a work of visual art "which is a result of the passage of time or the inherent nature of the materials is not distortion, mutilation or other modification" for purposes of that right, nor is modification "which is the result of conservation, or of the public presentation, including lighting and placement, of the work... unless the modification is caused by gross negligence."[488]

For a work of visual art that has been incorporated in or made part of a building "in such a way that removing the work from the building will cause the destruction, distortion, mutilation, or other modification of the work" contemplated by the integrity right, the integrity right will not apply

---

[485] Carter v. Helmsley-Spear, Inc., 861 F. Supp. 303 (S.D.N.Y. 1994), *rev'd on other grounds*, 71 F.3d 77 (2d Cir. 1995), *cert. denied*, 116 S. Ct. 1824 (1996) (relying on' *Webster's Third New International Dictionary (unabridged)* (1971): "'Honor' is commonly understood to mean 'good name or public esteem.' ... 'Reputation' is commonly understood to mean 'the condition of being regarded as worthy or meritorious'").

[486] *Id.* (a plaintiff must make a two-tiered showing: (1) that the visual art in question has 'stature,' i.e. is viewed as meritorious, and (2) that this stature is 'recognized' by art experts, other members of the artistic community, or by some cross-section of society"). *Cf.* Martin v. City of Indianapolis, 192 F.3d 608 (7th Cir. 1999).

[487] 17 U.S.C. § 101.

[488] 17 U.S.C. § 106A (c).

to its removal, if a written instrument has been signed by the owner of the building and the author specifying that installation of the work may subject it to destruction or other modification upon removal (such consent need not be in writing if the work was installed prior to the effective date of the Visual Artists Rights Act).[489] If a work has been incorporated in or made part of a building and *can* be removed without destruction or other modification and the owner wishes to remove that work, the integrity right will apply to acts occurring during such removal unless the owner has "made a diligent, good-faith attempt without success to notify the author of the owner's intended action," or such notice has been given and the author has failed either to remove the work or to pay for its removal within ninety days after receipt of such notice (if the author does remove the work, then title to that copy of the work shall be vested in the author).[490] For purpose of such notice, the Register of Copyrights is required to maintain a system for recording the address and identity of the author of a work of visual art incorporated in a building.[491]

The rights will inhere in works created on or after June 1, 1991 (and to works created earlier if title has not been transferred prior to that date) and will generally endure only for the lifetime of the author.[492] The statute, while prohibiting transfer of the rights, does expressly recognize their waivability by a properly executed instrument. The matter of waiver is one of the salient differences between the statute and "moral right" as it exists in most other countries, and Congress directed the Copyright Office to undertake a study of the impact of this provision.[493] The studies have proven inconclusive.

The Visual Artists Rights Act is a first, tentative step by Congress to move expressly into the "moral rights" issue. As limited, of course, it does not apply to the motion picture "colorization" dispute nor does it appear, even within its own terms, to be coextensive with the Civil Law approach.

---

[489] 17 U.S.C. § 113 (d) (1).

[490] 17 U.S.C. § 113 (d) (2). *See* Martin v. City of Indianapolis, 192 F.3d 608 (7th Cir. 1999).

[491] 17 U.S.C. § 113 (d) (3).

[492] 17 U.S.C. § 106A (d).

[493] 17 U.S.C. § 106A (e). *See* Roberta Rosenthal Kwall, *How Fine Art Fares Post VARA*, 1 Marq. Intell. Prop. L. Rev. 1 (1997) for analysis of the results of the first study.

Whether these provisions, together with the earlier judicial gloss creating moral right analogues,[494] amount to full compliance with the Berne Convention remains to be determined.

The limited works of visual art to which the Visual Artists Rights Act applies; the wholesale exemption from coverage of works made for hire; the limited duration of the term of protection; the federal preemption of state action; and the waivability of the rights created, all of which set it apart from the generally accepted model of moral right, has produced much criticism[495] but there is not as yet any significant pending legislation to broaden the scope of the limited moral right provided by that Act.

6.7.3. State Moral Rights Statutes

Prior to enactment of the Visual Artists Rights Act, several states adopted legislation purporting to create variants of the "droit moral." None of the statutes approximate the broad sweep of the Civil Law concept. The New York[496] and California[497] statutes are exemplary. In each of these entertainment and artistic centers, this kind of legislation, balancing the interests of the creative artist and the entrepreneur and dealer, necessarily involves limiting compromise.[498]

---

[494] The impact of these analogues, particularly the extension of Lanham Act § 43(a), may have been attenuated by the Supreme Court's language in Dastar v. Twentieth Century Fox Film Corp., 539 U.S. 23 (2003). See, Jane C. Ginsburg, *The Right to Claim Authorship in U.S. Copyright and Trademarks Law*, 41 HOUS. L. REV. 263 (2004); Sheldon W. Halpern, *A High Likelihood of Confusion: Walmart, TrafFix, Moseley, and Dastar—The Supreme Court's New Trademark Jurisprudence*. 61 N.Y.U. ANNUAL SURVEY OF AMERICAN LAW 237 (2005)

[495] *See, e.g.*, Roberta Rosenthal Kwall, *How Fine Art Fares Post VARA*, 1 MARQ. INTELL. PROP. L. REV. 1 (1997).

[496] N.Y. ARTS & CULT. AFF. LAW §§ 14.01-08 (McKinney 1996).

[497] CAL. CIV. CODE § 987 (West 1980).

[498] For analysis of the legislation, see Petrovich, *Artists' Statutory Droit Moral in California: A Critical Appraisal*, 15 LOYOLA L.A. L. REV. 29 (1981); Taubman, *New York Artists' Authorship Rights Act of 1983: Waiver and Fair Use*, 3 CARDOZO ARTS & ENT. L. J. 113 (1984); Damich, *The New York Artists' Authorship Rights Act: A Comparative Critique*, 84 COLUMBIA L. REV. 1733 (1984).

The New York [499] and California statutes are limited to works of "fine art,"[500] which California further defines as "an original painting, sculpture, or drawing, or an original work of art in glass, of recognized quality."[501] The New York statute recognizes the attribution right with respect to "works of fine art or limited edition multiples of not more than three hundred copies knowingly displayed in a place accessible to the public, published or reproduced in this state," and limits the integrity right to the *public display or publication* of such works "in an altered, defaced, mutilated or modified form [if] damage to the artist's reputation is reasonably likely to result therefrom."[502] Approaching the problem from a different direction, the California statute is concerned principally with intentional physical defacement, mutilation, alteration, or destruction of works of fine art. Both statutes have numerous limitations and exceptions. As noted above, the Visual Artists Rights Act of 1990 contains explicit federal preemption provisions, and it is not clear how much of the existing state statutes remains operable.

6.7.4. Droit de Suite

While the *droit de suite*—the right of an artist to share in the proceeds of subsequent resales of the artist's work—is explicitly part of the Berne Convention (Article 14*ter*) and is recognized widely in the European Union, it is not recognized in the United States, except in California, which has adopted a limited *droit de suite* statute. California's Resale Royalties Act of 1976[503] provides that when a work of fine art is sold and the seller resides in California or the sale takes place in California, and the resale price is more than $1,000 and more than the original price paid by the seller, "the seller

---

[499] Statutes in Louisiana (LA REV. STAT.ANN. § 51:2151 et seq.), Maine (ME. REV. STAT. ANN. tit. 27, § 303), New Jersey (N.J. STAT. ANN. §2A: 24A-1 *et seq.*), and Rhode Island (R.I. GEN. LAWS. § 5-62-2 *et seq.*), are modeled on the New York statute.

[500] Of the state statutes, only that of Massachusetts is broader, covering "any original work of visual or graphic art of any media." MASS. GEN. LAWS ANN. Ch. 231 § 85S(b) (West Supp. 1987).

[501] CAL. CIV. CODE § 987 (b) (2) (1980).

[502] N.Y. ARTS & CULT. AFF. LAW §§ 14.03 (McKinney 1996); *see* Wojnarowicz v. American Family Association, 745 F. Supp. 130 (S.D.N.Y. 1990).

[503] CAL. CIV. CODE § 986 (1980).

or the seller's agent shall pay to the artist of such work of fine art or to such artist's agent [or, if the artist cannot be found, to the California Arts Council] 5 percent of the amount of such sale"; the right to such resale royalty is assignable by the artist, but is not waiveable and, upon the artist's death, will inure to the benefit of the estate for a period of 20 years.

The California Resale Royalties Act, like the state moral rights statutes, raises a question of federal preemption under the moral right preemption provisions of the Visual Artists Rights Act. While the matter is not clear, the legislative history of the Visual Artists Rights Act appears to support the position that resale royalty rights are not preempted.[504]

§ 7. Fair Use As a Limitation on Copyright Protection

7.1. The Fair Use Concept

Section 106 enumerates the fundamental rights of a copyright owner, the bundle of exclusive rights the unauthorized exercise of which gives rise to a claim of copyright infringement. Sections 108 to 122 provide highly detailed, narrowly tailored limitations upon the copyright owner's exclusive rights. To recapitulate, these specific exemptions are:

§108: Libraries and Archives

§109: "First Sale"

§110: Exempt Performances

§111: Secondary Transmissions: Hotels, Cable Systems

§112: Ephemeral Recordings

§113: Useful Articles

§114: Limitations on Sound Recordings

§115: Compulsory Mechanical License

§116: Jukeboxes

§117: Copying Computer Programs

§118: Public Broadcasting

§119: Secondary Transmission: Super Stations

§120: Pictures of Architectural Works

§121: Reproduction for the Blind

§122: Secondary Transmission: Satellite Carriers

---

[504] H.R.Rep. No. 101-514, 101st Cong., 2d Sess. 21 (1990).

Determination of infringement or non-infringement in cases involving these exemptions does not depend upon reasoning by analogy or application of common-law or equitable principles— it is simply a matter of construing the specific words of the statute. However, those statutory words do not necessarily do all that is necessary to maintain the balance between the rights of the copyright owner and the public interest underlying the Copyright Act. To perform that function, the courts have developed, and the 1976 Act has attempted to codify, the doctrine of "fair use."

"From the infancy of copyright protection, [the fair use doctrine] has been thought necessary to fulfill copyright's very purpose, '[t]o promote the Progress of Science and useful Arts.'"[505] "The ultimate test of fair use ... is whether the copyright law's goal of 'promot[ing] the Progress of Science and useful Arts,' ... would be better served by allowing the use than by preventing it."[506] It is a safety valve, by means of which a court can find that, notwithstanding the absence of any specific exemption, the defendant's use of the copyrighted material is such that, as a matter of policy, society gains most by a finding of non-infringement.

The doctrine of fair use has been called "the most troublesome in the whole law of copyright."[507] It is a judge-made concept, with origins in American law going back to 1841;[508] but it was not until 1984 that the United States Supreme Court first dealt with the doctrine, in a sharply divided opinion in *Sony Corp. of America v. Universal City Studios, Inc.*[509] This was followed by another divided opinion in *Harper & Row Publishers, Inc. v. Nation Enterprises,*[510] and by what appears to be a consensus in 1994 in *Campbell v. Acuff-Rose Music, Inc.*[511] These three cases are not necessarily

---

[505] Campbell v. Acuff-Rose Music, Inc., 510 U.S. 569, 575, 114 S. Ct. 1164 (1994) (quoting U.S. Const., art. I, § 8, cl. 8) ("in truth, in literature, in science and in art, there are, and can be, few, if any, things, which in an abstract sense, are strictly new and original throughout. Every book in literature, science and art, borrows, and must necessarily borrow, and use much which was well known and used before."

[506] Arica Inst., Inc. v. Palmer, 970 F.2d 1067, 1077 (2d Cir.1992).

[507] Dellar v. Samuel Goldwyn, Inc., 104 F.2d 661, 662 (2d Cir. 1939).

[508] Folsom v. Marsh, 9 F.Cas. 342 (C.C.D. Mass. 1841).

[509] 464 U.S. 417, 104 S. Ct. 774 (1984).

[510] 471 U.S. 539, 105 S. Ct. 2218 (1985).

[511] 510 U.S. 569, 114 S. Ct. 1164 (1994).

consistent with one another, apart from the general agreement that "fair use is 'a "rule of reason" fashioned by Judges to balance the author's right to compensation for his work, on the one hand, against the public's interest in the widest possible dissemination of ideas and information, on the other.'"[512]

> Although the law zealously protects the commercial interests of the artist from unscrupulous opportunistic interlopers, it recognizes that not all copying of artistic invention is necessarily undesirable piracy. Certain forms of copying of artistic creation are indispensable to education, journalism, history, criticism, humor and other informative endeavors; the statute therefore allows latitude in appropriate circumstances for copying of protected artistic expression and exempts such copying from a finding of infringement. The doctrine of *fair use* identifies this category of permissible copying.[513]

The purpose of the doctrine is quite clear—it "permits and requires courts to avoid rigid application of the copyright statute, when, on occasion, it would stifle the very creativity which that law is designed to foster"[514]—as is its peculiar status as a court-developed "rule of reason" residing, with varying degrees of discomfort, within a complex and comprehensive statute. What are not clear are the boundaries, standards and parameters of the doctrine necessary to a reasonable degree of predictability. The House Report on the 1976 Act succinctly describes the problem:

> Although the courts have considered and ruled upon the fair use doctrine over and over again, no real definition of the concept has ever emerged. Indeed, since the doctrine is an equitable rule of reason, no generally applicable definition is possible, and each case raising the question must be decided on its own facts.[515]

Judge Pierre Leval put it perhaps more forcefully:

---

[512] Triangle Publications, Inc. v. Knight-Ridder Newspapers, 626 F.2d 1171, 1174 (5th Cir. 1980)(quoting Sobel, *Copyright and the First Amendment: A Gathering Storm?*, 19 ASCAP COPYRIGHT L.SYMP. 43 (1971), quoting Latman, *Fair Use of Copyrighted Works* 5 (Sen. Comm.on Judiciary Study No. 141960).

[513] New Era Publications International v. Henry Holt and Co., 695 F.Supp. 1493 (S.D.N.Y. 1988) (Leval, J.).

[514] Campbell v. Acuff-Rose Music, Inc., 510 U.S. 569, 577 (1994).

[515] H.R. Rep. No. 94-1476.

What is most curious about this doctrine is that neither the decisions that have applied it ..., nor its eventual statutory formulation, undertook to define or explain its contours or objectives. ... Judges do not share a consensus on the meaning of fair use. ... Confusion has not been confined to judges. Writers, historians, publishers, and their legal advisers can only guess and pray as to how courts will resolve copyright disputes.[516]

7.2. Section 107— Codification of the Doctrine

7.2.1. Scope and Purpose

Section 107, in its entirety, reads as follows:

§ 107. Limitations on Exclusive Rights: Fair Use

Notwithstanding the provisions of sections 106 and 106A the fair use of a copyrighted work, including such use by reproduction in copies or phonorecords or by any other means specified by that section, for purposes such as criticism, comment, news reporting, teaching (including multiple copies for classroom use), scholarship, or research, is not an infringement of copyright. In determining whether the use made of a work in any particular case is a fair use the factors to be considered shall include—

(1) the purpose and character of the use, including whether such use is of a commercial nature or is for nonprofit educational purposes;

(2) the nature of the copyrighted work;

(3) the amount and substantiality of the portion used in relation to the copyrighted work as a whole; and

(4) the effect of the use upon the potential market for or value of the copyrighted work.

The fact that a work is unpublished shall not itself bar a finding of fair use if such finding is made upon consideration of all the above factors.[517]

The language makes clear that "fair use" conditions all of the exclusive rights granted by the Act ("notwithstanding the provisions of sections 106 and 106A, the fair use of a copyrighted work ... is not an infringement of copyright")[518] As the Supreme Court has observed: "Any individual may

---

[516] Leval, *Toward a Fair Use Standard,* 103 HARV. L. REV. 1105-07 (1990).

[517] 17 U.S.C. § 107.

[518] *Id.*

reproduce a copyrighted work for a 'fair use'; the copyright owner does not possess the exclusive right to such a use."[519]

Congress intended that, under Section 107, "courts continue the common law tradition of fair use adjudication."[520] "The statutory formulation of the defense of fair use in the Copyright Act reflects the intent of Congress to codify the common-law doctrine."[521] However, it is not always clear what that judicial doctrine is, in its details, and the statutory language itself leaves much room for interpretation. The House Report contemplates such an open-ended approach to fair use: "Beyond a very broad statutory explanation of what fair use is and some of the criteria applicable to it, the courts must be free to adapt the doctrine to particular situations on a case-by-case basis."[522] Fair use analysis, if not ad hoc, nevertheless ultimately "calls for case-by-case analysis."[523] However, both the human craving for order and the statutory language itself provide an impetus for the development of principles of general application.

7.2.2. Parsing the Statute

7.2.2.1. The Preamble: Productive and Transformative Uses

The opening sentence of Section 107 is quite rich: it says that "*the fair use* of a copyrighted work ... *for purposes* such as criticism, comment, news reporting, teaching ..., scholarship, or research, is not an infringement of

---

[519] Sony Corp. of America v. Universal City Studios, Inc., 464 U.S. 417, 433, 104 S. Ct. 774, 784 (1984); *see* Sundeman v. Seajay Society, Inc., 142 F.3d 194, 202 (4th Cir. 1998).

[520] Campbell v. Acuff-Rose Music, Inc., 510 U.S. 569, 577, 114 S. Ct. 1164, 1170 (1994). As the Congressional Reports note: "Section 107 is intended to re-state the present judicial doctrine of fair use, not change, narrow, or enlarge it any way." H.R.Rep. No. 94- 1476, p. 66 (1976); S.Rep. No. 94-473, p. 62 (1975), U.S. Code Cong. & Admin.News 1976, pp. 5659, 5679.

[521] Harper & Row Publishers, Inc. v. Nation Enterprises, 471 U.S. 539, 549, 105 S. Ct. 2218, 2224 (1985).

[522] H.R.Rep. No. 94- 1476, p. 66 (1976); S.Rep. No. 94-473, p. 62 (1975), U.S.Code Cong. & Admin.News 1976, pp. 5659, 5679.

[523] Campbell v. Acuff-Rose Music, Inc., 510 U.S. 569, 577, 114 S. Ct. 1164, 1170 (1994).

copyright."[524] This language seems to suggest that the application of fair use requires a two-part analysis: one must first determine whether there is a "fair use" and then determine if that use is for an appropriate purpose. The "factors" which then follow seem to be directed to the first question, whether there is a "fair use"; but the "purpose" analysis would appear to be central to the determination of whether such a "fair use" will be effective to insulate the activity. The United States Supreme Court has been neither entirely consistent nor clear in providing guidance as to the appropriate analytic model.

Sony Corp. of America v. Universal City Studios, Inc.,[525] the first of the Supreme Court's fair use cases, was a contributory infringement action brought on behalf of the major motion picture producers against the prominent maker of videocassette recorders. Resolution of the contributory infringement issue depended upon whether videotaping the over the air broadcast of copyrighted motion pictures for purposes of "time shifting" was infringing or a fair use. In a five to four opinion, the majority held the use to be a fair use, so that the defendant was not contributorily liable. Justice Stevens, speaking for the majority, while noting the character of fair use as an "equitable rule of reason,"[526] essentially ignored the opening language of Section 107 and appeared to concentrate, almost exclusively, on the enumerated factor analysis, emphasizing the personal, noncommercial nature of home videotaping. Justice Blackmun, for the dissenters, focused heavily on the preamble's exemplary uses, characterizing such uses ("criticism, comment, news reporting, teaching ..., scholarship, or research") as "productive" uses, "resulting in some added benefit to the public beyond that produced by the first author's work."[527] He suggested that while not every "productive use" was a fair use, to be a fair use, the use must be productive.

A year later the Supreme Court re-visited the fair use question in a radically different context. In *Harper & Row Publishers, Inc. v. Nation Enterprises*[528] a divided (6-3) Court rejected a fair use defense by the

---

[524] 17 U.S.C. § 107 (emphasis added).

[525] 464 U.S. 417, 104 S. Ct. 774 (1984).

[526] 464 U.S. at 448, 104 S. Ct. at 792.

[527] 464 U.S. at 478, 104 S. Ct. at 807.

[528] 471 U.S. 539, 105 S. Ct. 2218 (1985).

publisher of a magazine who had "scooped" the plaintiff by publishing excerpts from the not yet published memoirs of President Gerald Ford. Rejecting the idea that there is some overriding general "public interest" or First Amendment consideration that would shield as a fair use dissemination of copyrighted matter in which there was a strong public interest,[529] Justice O'Connor, for the majority emphasizes the general inapplicability of fair use to unpublished works.[530] Finding "that the unpublished nature of a work is '[a] key, though not necessarily determinative, factor' tending to negate a defense of fair use,"[531] she concludes that "the scope of fair use is narrower with respect to unpublished works."[532]

While the opinion says little about either "productive use" or the impact of the enumeration of purposes in the preamble, it does expressly note, in response to the claim that the defendant was entitled to special consideration because its activity was "news reporting," that the listing of "purposes" in Section 107 is merely exemplary, not exhaustive, and not designed "to single out any particular use as presumptively a 'fair' use."[533] Rather than issues of productive or unproductive use, the distinction between published and unpublished works significantly colors the application of the fair use factors. (That distinction produced a serious controversy exemplified in several highly charged Second Circuit opinions seeking to apply the *Harper & Row* limitation with respect to unpublished works.[534]) Ultimately, after extensive hearings, Congress amended Section 107 to read, as it now does, that "[t]he fact that a work is unpublished shall

---

[529] 471 U.S. at 558-59, 105 S. Ct. at 2229-30.

[530] 471 U.S. at 550-54 ("Under ordinary circumstances, the author's right to control the first public appearance of his undisseminated expression will outweigh a claim of fair use." *Id.* at 554).

[531] 471 U.S. at 554, 105 S. Ct. at 2233, quoting from the Senate Report.

[532] 471 U.S. at 564, 105 S. Ct. at 2232.

[533] 471 U.S. at 561, 105 S. Ct. at 2231.

[534] *See* Salinger v. Random House, Inc., 811 F.2d 90 (2d Cir.), *cert. denied* 484 U.S. 890, 108 S. Ct. 213 (1987); New Era Publications Int'l., ApS v. Henry Holt and Co., Inc., 873 F.2d 576 (2d Cir.), *re-hearing denied,* 884 F.2d 659 (1989), *cert. denied,* 493 U.S. 1094, 110 S. Ct. 1168 (1990); Wright v. Warner Books, Inc., 953 F.2d 731 (2d Cir. 1991).

not itself bar a finding of fair use if such finding is made upon consideration of all the [enumerated] factors."

In sum, the majority in *Sony* elided the centrality of "productive use" for fair use analysis and the *Harper & Row* majority refused to grant it any special consideration.[535] Nevertheless, lower courts continued to emphasize the importance to a fair use determination of the societal value derived from the defendant's use,[536] although not necessarily in terms of whether that use was "productive."[537] In 1994, the Supreme Court confronted the question directly in *Campbell v. Acuff-Rose Music, Inc.*[538] and firmly reinvigorated the productive use concept, under the rubric "transformative use," making it central to fair use analysis. The case itself, involving a rap music parody of a popular song, provided an opportunity for the court to address a series of issues (the question of application of fair use to parody is discussed below).

Justice Souter's opinion, by sharply limiting the previous two Supreme Court decisions to their facts, essentially writes on a clean slate and attempts to articulate and apply fundamental fair use principles. The opinion rests heavily on the opening language of Section 107. Justice Souter points out, however, that

> [t]he task is not to be simplified with bright-line rules, for the statute, like the doctrine it recognizes, calls for case-by-case analysis. [Moreover, the statute here] employs the terms "including" and "such as" in the preamble paragraph to indicate the illustrative and not limitative function of the examples given, ... which thus provide only general guidance about the sorts of copying that courts and the Congress most commonly had found to be fair uses.[539]

---

[535] "The fact that an article arguably is 'news' and therefore a productive use is simply one factor in a fair use analysis." Harper & Row Publishers, Inc. v. Nation Enterprises, 471 U.S. at 561, 105 S. Ct. at 2231.

[536] *See, e.g.* Los Angeles News Service v. Tullo, 973 F.2d 791 (9th Cir. 1992); Maxtone-Graham v. Burtchaell, 803 F.2d 1253, *cert. denied*, 481 U.S. 1059, 107 S. Ct. 2201 (1987); Pacific and Southern Company Inc. v. Duncan, 744 F.2d 1490, *cert. denied*, 471 U.S. 1004, 105 S. Ct. 1867 (1985).

[537] *See, e.g.,* Hustler Magazine, Inc. v. Moral Majority, Inc., 796 F.2d 1148 (9th Cir. 1986) (holding that defendant's use of the copyrighted material for "self-defense" supported a fair use determination).

[538] 510 U.S. 569,114 S. Ct. 1164 (1994).

[539] *Id.* at 577, 114 S. Ct. at 1170.

Nevertheless, the preamble relates to "the central purpose" of fair use investigation: to determine if the new work "adds something new, with a further purpose or different character, altering the first with new expression, meaning, or message; it asks, in other words, whether and to what extent the new work is 'transformative.'"[540] Echoing Justice Blackmun's observation in *Sony* with respect to "productive use," the opinion continues:

> Although such transformative use is not absolutely necessary for a finding of fair use,... the goal of copyright, to promote science and the arts, is generally furthered by the creation of transformative works. Such works thus lie at the heart of the fair use doctrine's guarantee of breathing space within the confines of copyright, ... and the more transformative the new work, the less will be the significance of other factors, like commercialism, that may weigh against a finding of fair use.[541]

Following *Campbell*, the Courts of Appeal have been more inclined to begin the fair use inquiry with the preamble and its categories of "illustrative" fair uses.[542] Nevertheless, as the Seventh Circuit has noted, notwithstanding *Campbell*'s rationalization of the analytic model, "the fair use defense defies codification."[543]

7.2.2.2. The Enumerated Factors

Campbell makes clear that the four enumerated factors are interrelated and are not to be "treated in isolation, one from another. All are to be explored, and the results weighed together, in light of the purposes of copyright."[544] As the Seventh Circuit observed:

---

[540] *Id.* at 580, 114 S. Ct. at 1171 (quoting from Leval, *Toward a Fair Use Standard,* 103 HARV. L. REV. 1105, 1111 (1990). *See* Ringgold v. Black Entertainment Television, Inc., 126 F.3d 70 (2d Cir. 1997) (rejecting a fair use defense in connection with the fleeting, background use in a television program of plaintiff's artwork: "the defendants have used [plaintiff's] work for precisely the central purpose for which it was created—to be decorative").

[541] 510 U.S. 580, 114 S. Ct. at 1171.

[542] *See, e.g.,* Infinity Broadcast Corp. v. Kirkwood, 150 F.3d 104 (2d Cir. 1998).

[543] Chicago Board of Education v. Substance, Inc., 354 F.3d 624, 629 (7th Cir. 2003).

[544] *Campbell,* 510 U.S.. at 578, 114 S. Ct. at 117; *see* Castle Rock Entertainment, Inc. v. Carol Publishing Group, Inc., 150 F.3d 132 (2d Cir. 1998).

"The important point is simply that...the four factors are a checklist of things to be considered rather than a formula for decision; and likewise the list of statutory purposes."[545]

7.2.2.2.1. The First Factor—Commercial or Noncommercial Purpose

The first analytic factor requires a consideration of "the purpose and character of the use, including whether such use is of a commercial nature or is for nonprofit educational purposes." In *Sony*, the majority used this factor to build a presumption: a use "for a commercial or profit-making purpose ... would presumptively be unfair" while a noncommercial use would raise a presumption of fairness.[546] The following year, in *Harper v. Row*,[547] Justice O'Connor suggested further that the "crux of the profit/nonprofit distinction is not whether the sole motive of the use is monetary gain but whether the user stands to profit from exploitation of the copyrighted material without paying the customary price."[548]

The *Sony* "presumptions," buttressed by *Harper & Row*, caused considerable problems for the Courts of Appeal in analyzing fair use cases in which the defendant received some commercial benefit, and these courts attempted to ameliorate the impact of the presumptions by finding some social benefit attendant to the commercial use.[549]

---

[545] Ty, Inc. v. Publications International, Ltd., 292 F.3d 512, 522 (7th Cir. 2002).

[546] Sony Corp. of America v. Universal City Studios, Inc., 464 U.S. 417, 449, 104 S. Ct. 774, 792 (1984). Justice Stevens was quite forceful in asserting that "every commercial use of copyrighted material is presumptively an unfair exploitation of the monopoly privilege that belongs to the owner of the copyright." *Id.* at 451, 104 S. Ct. at 793.

[547] Harper & Row Publishers, Inc. v. Nation Enterprises, 471 U.S. 539, 562, 105 S. Ct. 2218, 2231 (1985) ("The fact that a publication was commercial as opposed to non-profit ... tends to weigh against a finding of fair use").

[548] *Id.*

[549] *See, e.g.*, Maxtone-Graham v. Burtchaell, 803 F.2d 1253 (2d Cir.), *cert. denied*, 481 U.S. 1059, 107 S. Ct. 2201 (1987); Hustler Magazine, Inc. v. Moral Majority, Inc., 796 F.2d 1148 (9th Cir. 1986).

In *Campbell*, with its emphasis on transformative use, the Court appears to abandon these presumptions[550] and the special role of commerciality, as it reversed the lower court for "giving virtually dispositive weight to the commercial nature [of the defendant's use]":

> The language of the statute makes clear that the commercial or nonprofit educational purpose of a work is only one element of the first factor enquiry into its purpose and character. ... Accordingly, the mere fact that a use is educational and not for profit does not insulate it from a finding of infringement, any more than the commercial character of a use bars a finding of fairness. If, indeed, commerciality carried presumptive force against a finding of fairness, the presumption would swallow nearly all of the illustrative uses listed in the preamble paragraph of § 107, including news reporting, comment, criticism, teaching, scholarship, and research, since these activities "are generally conducted for profit in this country."[551]

Rather, for purposes of the first factor, the relevant issue is the overall one of "the purpose and character of the use," and the significant element in that analysis is the extent to which the use is "transformative"; "the more transformative the new work, the less will be the significance of other

---

[550] "In focusing the first factor inquiry upon the 'transformative' nature of the use, the Court abandoned the statement in *Sony*... that 'every commercial use of copyrighted material is presumptively... unfair'...." Leibovitz v. Paramount Pictures Corp., 137 F.3d 109, 113 (2d Cir. 1998).

[551] Campbell v. Acuff-Rose Music, Inc., 510 U.S. 569, 584, 114 S. Ct. 1164, 1174 (1994) (quoting from Justice Brennan's dissent in Harper & Row Publishers, Inc. v. Nation Enterprises, 471 U.S. 539, 574, 105 S. Ct. 2218, 2246 (1985)); *see* Castle Rock Entertainment, Inc. v. Carol Publishing Group, Inc., 150 F.3d 132, 142 (2d Cir. 1998) ("We ... do not give much weight to the fact that the secondary use was for commercial gain"). *See also* Sony Computer Entertainment America, Inc. v. Bleem, LLC, 214 F.3d 1022 (9th Cir. 2000):

> In this analysis, the commercial use of copyrighted material is not presumptively unfair; rather, commercial use is but one of four factors that we must weigh. The Supreme Court expressly rejected the irrebutability of the presumption against fair use in commercial contexts in *Campbell* when the court flatly reversed the Sixth Circuit for making just such a presumption...The Court emphasized that, although the fourth factor may be the most important, all factors must be considered, and the commercial nature of the copies is just one element in the broader calculus.

factors, like commercialism, that may weigh against a finding of fair use."[552] In short, the fair use calculus involves balancing and no single factor will create a presumptively fair or unfair use.

7.2.2.2.2. The Second Factor—Nature of the Copyrighted Work

The inquiry here requires categorizing the plaintiff's work; it "calls for recognition that some works are closer to the core of intended copyright protection than others, so that fair use is more difficult to establish when the former works are copied."[553] Thus, the second factor will militate against a finding of fair use where the copyrighted work is creative art or literary fiction, or other forms of creative expression, as opposed to factual, historical data or news reporting.[554] While this content based categorization for purposes of the second factor was elided by the Supreme Court in *Harper & Row,* which made a distinction between copyrighted works which had been published and those which had been unpublished, the Court in *Campbell* brought the analysis back to the fundamental distinction between those works which are "closer to the core" of copyright protection than those which are more removed.

7.2.2.2.3. The Third Factor—The Amount Taken

Here one must consider "the amount and substantiality of the portion used in relation to the copyrighted work as a whole." Asking how much the defendant took from the plaintiff, the question is both quantitative and qualitative; a quantitatively small amount may nevertheless be sufficient to encapsulate the copyrighted work and qualitatively be quite substantial.[555]

---

[552] *Campbell,* 510 U.S. at 579, 114 S. Ct. at 1171.

[553] *Id.* at 586, 114 S, Ct, at 1175.

[554] *Id.; see* Stewart v. Abend, 495 U.S. 207, 237, 110 S. Ct. 1750 (1990) ("in general, fair use is more likely to be found in factual works than in fictional works"); Castle Rock Entertainment, Inc. v. Carol Publishing Group, Inc., 150 F.3d 132, 143 (2d Cir. 1998) ("the scope of fair use is somewhat narrower with respect to fictional works ... than to factual works"); Twin Peaks Prods., Inc. v. Publications Int'l, Ltd., 996 F.2d 1366, 1376 (2d Cir.1993) (the second factor "favor[s] ... creative and fictional work").

[555] *Campbell,* 510 U.S. at 587, 114 S. Ct. at 1175 ("this factor calls for thought not only about the quantity of the materials used, but about their quality and importance, too"); *see also, Harper & Row, supra.*

Central to resolution of the third factor is the manner in which and purposes for which the copyrighted material is used by the defendant. By its terms, analysis under this factor focuses on the relationship between the material taken and the copyrighted work as a whole; whether the material taken constitutes a significant or insignificant portion of the *defendant's* work would seem to be irrelevant. However, since the analysis is qualitative, the fact that the defendant's work makes extensive use of material that is a quantitatively small part of the copyrighted work is evidence of the qualitative substantiality of the material taken.[556] Moreover, the extent to which the defendant has used to the material in a "transformative" manner can have a significant bearing upon whether the taking is to be considered excessive; a transformative use can support a qualitatively greater taking than can a non-transformative use.[557] As discussed below, this issue has been particularly important in parody fair use analysis.

7.2.2.2.4. The Fourth Factor—Economic Impact

This factor is directed to "the effect of the use upon the potential market for or value of the copyrighted work." While the four factors are not specifically weighted, the economic impact of the taking upon the plaintiff's work has generally been considered the most important of the factors.[558] The inquiry concerns the impact upon both the existing market for the plaintiff's work and potential markets for that work itself as well as for derivative works.[559] In short, the concern is with the present and future exploitative possibilities of the copyright in the work. In general, this factor "is concerned with secondary uses that, by offering a substitute for the original, usurp a market that properly belongs to the copyright-holder."[560]

---

[556] *Harper & Row, supra*; Iowa State University Research Foundation, Inc. v. American Broadcasting Companies, Inc., 621 F.2d 57 (2d Cir. 1980).

[557] *Campbell*, 510 U.S. at 587-88, 114 S. Ct. at 1176 ("a work composed primarily of an original, particularly its heart, with little added or changed, is more likely to be a merely superseding use, fulfilling demand for the original").

[558] "This last factor is undoubtedly the single most important element of fair use." Harper & Row Publishers, Inc. v. Nation Enterprises, 471 U.S. 539, 566, 105 S. Ct. 2218, 2234 (1985).

[559] "This inquiry must take account not only of harm to the original but also of harm to the market for derivative works." *Id.* at 568, 105 S. Ct. at 2234.

[560] Infinity Broadcasting Corp. v. Kirkwood, 150 F.3d 104 (2d Cir. 1998).

Within that context, the analysis presents certain logical problems. For example, in any given case in which the defendant has taken some copyrighted material, that defendant, and the use to which that material was put, theoretically constitute a potential market with respect to which the copyright owner might license the work. In effect, since every use is potentially a market, this factor, if analyzed literally, would simply swallow fair use.[561] In practice, however, the courts avoid this logical extreme, and focus on realistic potential markets for exploitation of the copyright.[562] The principal concern is whether the defendant's use can substitute for the copyrighted work or derivative works based thereon. Since the focus is on displacement of the copyrighted work, a use in criticism, a use disparaging the copyrighted work, that harms the market by suppressing demand rather than usurping the work, would not constitute a cognizable market harm. As the Supreme Court noted in *Campbell*:

> the role of the courts is to distinguish between "[b]iting criticism [that merely] suppresses demand [and] copyright infringement[, which] usurps it." ... This distinction between potentially remediable displacement and unremediable disparagement is reflected in the rule that there is no protectible derivative market for criticism. The market for potential derivative uses includes only those that creators of original works would in general develop or license others to develop.[563]

---

[561] " We have recognized the danger of circularity in considering whether the loss of potential licensing revenue should weight the fourth factor in favor of a plaintiff." Ringgold v. Black Entertainment Television, Inc., 126 F.3d 70, 81 (2d Cir. 1997).

[562] "We have endeavored to avoid the vice of circularity by considering 'only traditional, reasonable, or likely to be developed markets' when considering the challenged use upon a potential market." *Id.* at 81(2d Cir. 1997). See Leibovitz v. Paramount Pictures Corp., 137 F.3d 109, 117 (2d Cir. 1998) ("[Plaintiff's] only argument for actual market harm is that the defendant has deprived her of a licensing fee by using the work. ... But she is not entitled to a licensing fee for a work that otherwise qualifies for the fair use defense").

[563] *Campbell*, 510 U.S. at 593, 114 S. Ct. at 1179 (quoting from Fisher v. Dees, 794 F.2d 432, 438 (9th Cir. 1986)).

Similarly, the fact that the infringing use might well serve to revive or create a market for the copyrighted work, and thereby benefit the copyright owner, is immaterial if the effect of the infringement is market usurpation.[564]

In *Sony*, as noted above, the Supreme Court majority not only created and relied heavily upon presumptions of fairness or unfairness as a function of the commercial or noncommercial nature of the defendant's use, but also extended these presumptions into the fourth factor analysis. The majority appeared to hold that a commercial use creates a presumption of potential market harm, which the defendant is required to rebut, and a noncommercial use creates a presumption of lack of such harm, requiring a plaintiff to demonstrate the harm.[565] Limiting *Sony* to its facts, the Court in *Campbell* rejected these presumptions: "No 'presumption' or inference of market harm that might find support in *Sony* is applicable to a case involving something beyond mere duplication for commercial purposes. ... No such evidentiary presumption is available to address either the first factor, the character and purpose of the use, or the fourth, market harm, in determining whether a transformative use ... is a fair one."[566]

7.3. Parody as Fair Use

Parody has been defined as a "'literary or artistic work that imitates the characteristic style of an author or a work for comic effect or ridicule,' or as a 'composition in prose or verse in which the characteristic turns of thought and phrase in an author or class of authors are imitated in such a way as to make them appear ridiculous.'"[567] By its very nature, to be at all effective a parody must take qualitatively substantial and significant parts of the underlying work; if such work is protected by copyright, then, absent a fair use defense, the parody must necessarily be infringing. Since a parody, again, by its nature, serves to some extent as critical commentary, it would

---

[564] *See, e.g.*, Iowa State University Research Foundation, Inc. v. American Broadcasting Companies, Inc., 621 F.2d 57 (2d Cir. 1980).

[565] *Sony*, 464 U.S. at 451, 104 S. Ct. at 793 ("If the intended use is for commercial gain, [the] likelihood [of harm] may be presumed. But if it is for a noncommercial purpose, the likelihood must be demonstrated").

[566] *Campbell*, 510 U.S. at 591, 594, 114 S. Ct. at 1177, 1179.

[567] *Id.* at 580, 114 S. Ct. at 1172 (quoting from AMERICAN HERITAGE DICTIONARY 1317 (3d ed. 1992) and 11 OXFORD ENGLISH DICTIONARY 247 (2d ed. 1989).

appear to be peculiarly susceptible to fair use analysis. The judicial treatment of parody and fair use, however, has been complex and inconsistent, exemplified by the different approaches of the Second and Ninth Circuits.

The Ninth Circuit initially, in 1956, rejected the proposition that the parodic nature of a use created any special significance for fair use analysis, a position that an equally divided United States Supreme Court then left unresolved.[568] The Ninth Circuit modified its position in 1978, recognizing the particular applicability of fair use to parody, but focused analysis upon the third factor, the amount taken, holding that the parodist may take only so much as is necessary to "recall or conjure up" the original.[569] Although the court there seemed to rely upon dicta from an earlier Second Circuit case,[570] the Second Circuit took a significantly different position when it dealt directly with the matter in 1980. Rather, that court established a special place for parody in the fair use calculus, holding that "a parody is entitled *at least* to 'conjure up' the original. Even more extensive use would still be fair use, provided the parody builds upon the original, using the original as a known element of modern culture and contributing something new for humorous effect or commentary."[571] The Second Circuit has been unequivocal in finding that "parody and satire are valued forms of criticism, encouraged because this sort of criticism itself fosters the creativity protected by the copyright laws."[572] By 1986, the Ninth Circuit apparently moved to the Second Circuit position, finding parody to be a "potential"

---

[568] Benny v. Loew's Inc., 239 F.2d 532 (9th Cir. 1956), *aff'd by an equally divided court*, 356 U.S. 43, 78 S. Ct. 667 (1958).

[569] Walt Disney Productions v. Air Pirates, 581 F.2d 751 (9th Cir. 1978), *cert. denied*, 439 U.S. 1132 (1979).

[570] Berlin v. E.C. Publications, Inc., 329 F.2d 541 (2d Cir.), *cert. denied*, 379 U.S. 822 (1964).

[571] Elsmere Music, Inc. v. National Broadcasting Co., 623 F.2d 253 (2d Cir. 1980) (emphasis added).

[572] Rogers v. Koons, 960 F.2d 301, 310 (2d Cir. 1992).

fair use, with the parodist allowed to take enough "to accomplish reasonably its parodic purpose."[573]

Ultimately, in *Campbell*, the Supreme Court spoke definitively about the place of parody in fair use analysis.

> [P]arody has an obvious claim to transformative value. .... Like less ostensibly humorous forms of criticism, it can provide social benefit, by shedding light on an earlier work, and, in the process, creating a new one. We thus line up with the courts that have held that parody, like other comment or criticism, may claim fair use under § 107.[574]

Moreover, the Court made clear that in applying the fair use factors to parody, the extent to which the parody is "transformative" will play a significant role in determining the impact of each of the factors. Thus, with respect to the third factor, the Court affirms that "the parody must be able to 'conjure up' at least enough of [the] original to make the object of its critical wit recognizable. ... Copying does not become excessive in relation to parodic purpose merely because the portion taken was the original's heart. ... In parody ... context is everything, and the question of fairness asks what else the parodist did besides go to the heart of the original."[575]

For purposes of the third factor, the amount of permissible taking is a function of the nature of the use: a transformative use can support a qualitatively greater taking than can a non-transformative use.[576] Similarly, for the fourth factor, a "transformative" commentary whose adverse market impact arises out of the fact of criticism or disparagement may well be a fair use, as opposed to a blatant taking which simply usurps the market.[577] In

---

[573] Fisher v. Dees, 794 F.2d 432 (9th Cir. 1986). However, the Ninth Circuit most recently appears to have backtracked, and to have ignored the Supreme Court (see below), in reiterating the older "conjure up" limitation. Dr. Seuss Enterprises, L.P v. Penguin Books, 109 F.3d 1394 (9th Cir. 1997) ("This Court has adopted the 'conjure up' test where the parodist is permitted a fair use of a copyrighted work if it takes no more than is necessary to 'recall' or ' conjure up' the object of his parody").

[574] *Campbell*, 510 U.S. at 579, 114 S. Ct. at 1172.

[575] *Id.* at 588-89, 114 S. Ct. at 1176

[576] *Id.* at 587-88, 114 S. Ct. at 1176.

[577] *Id.* at 593, 114 S. Ct. at 1178.

assessing market impact, "the law looks beyond the criticism to the other elements of the work."[578]

With parody holding a preferred position in the fair use calculus, determining whether a given work is a "parody" is a significant task. "Parody emerges from [the] 'joinder of reference and ridicule'."[579] The determination of whether a work is a "parody" is one for the court, and is not a "factual" determination to be resolved by the weight of the evidence or other evidentiary factors: "The issue of whether a work is a parody is a question of law, not a matter of public majority opinion."[580]

Justice Souter's opinion in *Campbell* also is unequivocal in distinguishing "satire"— which uses the underlying work humorously to comment on societal matters without in some way ridiculing that work itself—from "parody." It is only the latter that may have special fair use protection:

> For the purposes of copyright law, the nub of the definitions, and the heart of any parodist's claim to quote from existing material, is the use of some elements of a prior author's composition to create a new one that, at least in part, comments on that author's works. ... If, on the contrary, the commentary has no critical bearing on the substance or style of the original composition, which the alleged infringer merely uses to get attention or to avoid the drudgery in working up something fresh, the claim to fairness in borrowing from another's work diminishes accordingly (if it does not vanish), and other factors, like the extent of its commerciality, loom larger. Parody needs to mimic an original to make its point, and so has some claim to use the creation of its victim's (or collective victims') imagination, whereas satire can stand on its own two feet and so requires justification for the very act of borrowing.[581]

While it is necessary, therefore, that a parody, to some extent, comment and criticize the underlying work, such criticism need not be devastating and

---

[578] *Id.* at 592, 114 S. Ct. at 1178.

[579] Mattel, Inc. v. Walking Mountain Productions, 353 F.3d 792, 802 (9th Cir. 2003) (quoting from *Campbell*, 510 U.S. at 583, 114 S. Ct. at 1164).

[580] *Id.* at 801.

[581] *Id.* at 580-81, 114 S. Ct. at 1172.

"[a] parodist need not demonstrate that the copyright owner would prohibit the use in order to qualify the copy as fair use."[582]

7.4. Fair Use of Utilitarian Works

Complex computer software cases have included issues resulting from the "dissection" and "disassembly" of a program for the purpose of reverse engineering to create a competing program. It has been held that while "disassembly is wholesale copying [that] falls squarely within the category of acts that are prohibited by the statute," such copying may be a fair use:

> We are not unaware of the fact that to those used to considering copyright issues in more traditional contexts, our result may seem incongruous at first blush. ...
>
> . . .
>
> We conclude that where disassembly is the only way to gain access to the ideas and functional elements embodied in a copyrighted computer program and where there is a legitimate reason for seeking such access, disassembly is a fair use of the copyrighted work, as a matter of law.[583]

7.5. Fair Use and Photocopying for Research and Academic Purposes

7.5.1. Library, Archival, and Research Copying

Although the Copyright Act contains specific exemptions with respect to certain enumerated kinds of copying by archives and libraries, the scope of a broader, fair use exemption for library and archival photocopying is not

---

[582] Leibovitz v. Paramount Pictures Corp., 137 F.3d 109, 115 n. 3 (2d Cir. 1998).

[583] Sega Enterprises Ltd v. Accolade, Inc., 977 F.2d 1510 (9th Cir. 1992). *Sega* was expressly adopted in Bateman v. Mnemonics, Inc., 79 F.3d 1532 (11th Cir. 1996) ("We find the Sega opinion persuasive in view of the principal purpose of copyright—the advancement of science and the arts"); *see also* Atari Games Corp. v. Nintendo of America Inc., 975 F.2d 832 (Fed. Cir. 1992) ("reverse engineering object code to discern the unprotectable ideas in a computer program is a fair use"). *See* Sony Computer Entertainment Amertica, Inc. v. Connectix Corp., 203 F.3d 595 (9th Cir.), *cert. denied* 121 S. Ct. 172 (2000).

clear.[584] Photocopying for research in a commercial context was the subject of *American Geophysical Union v. Texaco, Inc.*,[585] where the question was "whether it is lawful under the U.S. Copyright Act ... for a profit-seeking company to make unauthorized copies of copyrighted articles published in scientific and technical journals for use by the company's scientists employed in scientific research." The district court held that such copying was not a fair use. The divided Second Circuit affirmance focused on the non-transformative and "archival" nature of the copying: "to assemble a set of papers for future reference, thereby serving the same purpose for which additional subscriptions are normally sold, or ... for which photocopying licenses may be obtained." Such licenses are available from the Copyright Clearance Center, a central clearing-house established in the late 1970s to license photocopying, thereby facilitating inexpensive copying for research and obviating a difficult fair use question.

7.5.2. Academic, Classroom Copying

While the exemplary uses in Section 107 include making "multiple copies for classroom use," there is no general exemption for copying either for academic research or for classroom distribution. In response to various concerns, an agreement was reached among representatives of publishers, authors, and educational institutions concerning *Guidelines for Classroom Copying in Not-for-Profit Educational Institutions*; these "guidelines" were incorporated into the House Committee Report underlying the 1976 Act. Without having the direct force of law, they nevertheless establish a minimum safe harbor for copying for academic research and for limited, brief, and spontaneous copying for classroom distribution. There remains, however, the issue of the extent to which general fair use analysis applies to academic copying in excess of the guidelines. In that connection, it has been held that wholesale copying of copyrighted works for reproduction in

---

[584] *See, e.g.*, Williams & Wilkins Co. v. United States, 487 F.2d 1345 (1973), a four to three Court of Claims decision, that was *affirmed by an equally divided* Supreme Court, 420 U.S. 376, 95 S. Ct. 1344 (1975).

[585] 802 F. Supp. 1 (S.D.N.Y. 1992), *aff'd*, 60 F.3d 513 (2d Cir. 1994), *cert. dismissed*, 116 S. Ct. 592 (1995).

"coursepacks" or "anthologies" is both outside the guidelines and not a fair use.[586]

7.6. First Amendment Considerations

Periodically, it has been argued that First Amendment concerns provide an additional, unstated fair use factor, an extra-statutory gloss on fair use.[587] Justice O'Connor's opinion in *Harper & Row* appears firmly to reject that argument[588] and the Courts of Appeal have generally refused to recognize a first amendment defense separate from the fair use factors.[589]

> The Copyright Clause and the First Amendment, while intuitively in conflict, were drafted to work together to prevent censorship; copyright laws were enacted in part to prevent private censorship and the First Amendment was enacted to prevent public censorship...In copyright law, the balance between the First Amendment and copyright is preserved, in part, by the idea/expression dichotomy and the doctrine of fair use.[590]

Nevertheless, within the fair use analysis, "we must remain cognizant of the First Amendment protections interwoven into copyright law."[591]

---

[586] Princeton University Press v. Michigan Document Services, 99 F.3d 1381 (1996), *cert denied*, 117 S. Ct. 1336 (1997); Basic Books, Inc. v. Kinko's Graphics Corp., 758 F.Supp. 1522 (S.D.N.Y. 1991).

[587] *See, e.g.*, Triangle Publications v. Knight-Ridder Newspapers, 626 F.2d 1171 (5th Cir. 1980, Tate, J., concurring); *see also*, Maxtone-Graham v. Burtchaell, 803 F.2d 1253, *cert. denied*, 481 U.S. 1059, 107 S. Ct. 2201 (1987).

[588] Harper & Row Publishers, Inc. v. Nation Enterprises, 471 U.S. 539, 105 S. Ct. 2218 (1985).

> In view of the First Amendment protections already embodied in the Copyright Act's distinction between copyrightable expression and uncopyrightable facts and ideas, and the latitude for scholarship and comment traditionally afforded by fair use, we see no warrant for expanding the doctrine of fair use to create what amounts to a public figure exception to copyright.

Id. at 560, 105 S. Ct. at 2230.

[589] *See* Los Angeles News Service v. Tullo, 973 F.2d 791 (9th Cir. 1992); Twin Peaks Productions, Inc. v. Publications International, Ltd., 996 F.2d 1366 (2d Cir. 1993).

[590] Suntrust Bank v. Houghton Mifflin Company, 268 F.3d 1257, 1263 (11th Cir. 2001).

[591] *Id.* at 1265.

§ 8. DURATION OF COPYRIGHT PROTECTION

8.1. General Overview

By its express terms, Article I, Section 8 of the Constitution requires that the copyright monopoly may be granted only "for limited times." Accordingly, in exercising its constitutional power, Congress may not grant a perpetual copyright, but must define and set limits to the term of copyright. The determination of the copyright term, of course, has far-reaching consequences for the economic value of copyright.

8.1.1. The Pre-1976 Renewal Right and the Renewal Term

In the first Copyright Act, of 1790, Congress established a dual copyright term: an initial term (fourteen years) and a right in the copyright owner to renew the copyright for a second, renewal term of equal duration. Over the succeeding years the term of copyright under this dual term scheme was extended; the 1909 Act set initial and renewal terms of twenty-eight years each.

Under the 1909 Act, copyright attached to a work upon its publication with appropriate notice and endured for an initial fixed term of twenty-eight years from the date of publication. If no further action was taken with respect to copyright in the work thereafter, the copyright ended and the work fell into the public domain upon the expiration of that term. However, copyright in the work would continue for an additional, renewal term of twenty-eight years if appropriate action was taken prior to the expiration of the initial term by the persons entitled to renew the copyright.

8.1.1.1. Vesting Of The Renewal Right

The renewal right generally vested in the author of the work, the entity originally entitled to the initial copyright. Thus, an individual author who assigned and completely transferred his or her copyright interest in a work during the initial term would nevertheless own the renewal right and the transferee would have no interest with respect to the renewal term. In the case of an individual author, if that author did not survive the expiration of the initial term, then the right vested in specifically named and prioritized statutory successors, essentially the family, or the estate of the author.[592] There was some uncertainty as to how long the author had to survive for the renewal right, and the renewal term, to vest in the author or the author's assignee; *i.e.*, survival might be required up to the date of registration of the renewal application or through the initial term and to the beginning of the renewal term for the author or his or her assignee to own the copyright for the renewal term as against the statutory successors.[593] With the 1992 automatic renewal amendment, discussed below,[594] and its specific disposition of this question, the issue has become academic.

In the case of works made for hire, the employer was the entity entitled to renew. (As to works which had been in the first term at the effective date of the 1976 Act, determination of whether a work is" a work made for hire" for these purposes will be governed by the earlier, 1909 Act, standards rather than the definition of work for hire under the 1976 Act.[595])

To be renewed, a work had to have been registered and the application for renewal registration had to be filed with the copyright office by the person entitled thereto during the final year of the initial term. Upon expiration of the initial term, if proper renewal application had been filed, the renewal term would commence and vest in the person entitled thereto.[596]

8.1.1.2. The Renewal Term As a New, Independent Term

The renewal term was not simply an extension of the initial term. It was a completely new term, vesting only in the person entitled to renewal. Thus, assignments, transfers, licenses and other rights granted by the author during the initial term would endure only for that term and would not encumber the renewal term. Similarly, as the Supreme Court made clear in *Stewart v. Abend*,[597] such rights could not continue to be exercised during

---

[592] *See* Marascalco v. Fantasy, Inc., 953 F.2d 469 (9th Cir. 1991), *cert. denied*, 504 U.S. 931, 112 S. Ct. 1997 (1992).

[593] *Id.*

[594] *See infra* § 8.1.1.4.

[595] *See supra* § 4.6.

[596] *See* 17 U.S.C. § 304 (a) (3).

[597] 495 U.S. 207, 110 S. Ct. 1750 (1990).

the renewal term on the strength only of rights granted during the initial term; new arrangements would have to have been made with the owner of the renewal term.

8.1.1.3. Assignment of the Renewal Right

Since a grant, even of the entire copyright interest, endured only for the initial term of copyright, grantees often sought to secure for themselves rights in the renewal term. While it appeared to be the intent of Congress in creating a bifurcated duration structure to protect authors by limiting their transfers to the initial term, the United States Supreme Court held that an assignment of the renewal right by an author during the initial term was binding, if otherwise a valid contract, and gave the assignee a right to renew superior to that of the author.[598]

However, since the author's right to renew was contingent upon survival of the author to effect that renewal, the assignee's right was similarly contingent; if the author did not survive to the appropriate time for vesting of the renewal term, then the assignee could not exercise the renewal right and would have no rights in the renewal term—the assignment was only of a "mere expectancy."[599] Accordingly, it became common practice for grantees of rights to get assignments with respect to the renewal term not only from the author, but from as many statutory successors as could be located.

8.1.1.4. Automatic Renewal

In 1992, Congress amended the Copyright Act to alleviate some of the technical concerns over renewal for works copyrighted under the 1909 Act.

---

[598] Fred Fisher Music Company v. M. Witmark & Sons, 318 U.S. 643, 63 S. Ct. 773 (1943).

[599] Stewart v. Abend, 495 U.S. 207, 110 S. Ct. 1750 (1990) (holding that the producer of a motion picture made during the initial term of the short story upon which it was based, the author of which had granted the producer motion picture rights in the story and had assigned to the producer rights in the renewal term, infringed the copyright in the short story by exhibiting the motion picture during the renewal term since the author had died prior to the time for registration for renewal and renewal had in fact vested in the statutory successor, for whom appropriate filing of renewal had been made).

Section 304(a)[600] was amended to provide for *automatic* renewal, without registration, for works that were in their initial term at the effective date of the 1976 Act and were still in their initial term in 1992 (*i.e.*, works whose copyright term commenced between January 1, 1963 and December 31, 1977).[601]

However, in an effort to encourage renewal by registration, the amendments provided differing consequences from renewal by registration and automatic renewal. Thus, in setting vesting rights, the statute distinguishes between automatic renewal and renewal by application and registration. If proper renewal registration is made, then the renewal term will vest (once term begins) in the person entitled to renewal *at the time the application is made*; if renewal is automatic, without registration, the term will vest in the person entitled to renewal *as of the last day of the original term*.[602] Moreover, by virtue of these amendments, the creator of a derivative work authorized during the original term may continue to exploit that work during the renewal term if (and only if) the renewal is automatic, and not the result of registration, essentially limiting the rule of *Stewart v. Abend* to cases of renewal by registration.[603]

8.1.2. The 1976 Act Single Term

One of the most significant changes made by the 1976 Act was the abandonment of this dual term system, based upon absolutely fixed terms of years, and substitution of a single copyright term to endure, in general, for the life of the author plus a fixed term—originally fifty years. The 1998 Copyright Term Extension Act extended by twenty years the term for all works, including existing works then in copyright. (For those works in which no real person is identified as the author and for works made for hire, the term was fixed originally at one hundred years from creation (extended, in 1998, to one hundred and twenty years) or, if the work is unpublished, 75 years (extended to 95 years) from publication, whichever expires earlier.) The Supreme Court upheld the 1998 term extension, even with respect to

---

[600] 17 U.S.C. § 304 (a).

[601] 17 U.S.C. § 304 (a) (2).

[602] *Id.*

[603] 17 U.S.C. § 304(a)(4)(A).

existing copyrights, as within the constitutional "limited times" restriction and as a proper exercise of Congress' constitutional power:[604]

> Guided by text, history, and precedent, we cannot agree with petitioners' submission that extending the duration of existing copyrights is categorically beyond Congress' authority under the Copyright Clause.
>
> ...
>
> [W]e find that the CTEA is a rational enactment; we are not at liberty to second-guess congressional determinations and policy judgments of this order, however debatable or arguably unwise they may be. Accordingly, we cannot conclude that the CTEA–which continues the unbroken congressional practice of treating future and existing copyrights in parity for term extension purposes–is an impermissible exercise of Congress' power under the Copyright   Clause.[605]

The twenty-year extension adopted in October, 1998 is applicable to all works whose copyright had not by then expired, but does not serve to restore copyright in works which had theretofore fallen into the public domain.

The 1976 Act change to a fixed term was designed both to bring American law more closely into line with that of Berne Convention states and, in the view of Congress, more adequately to protect authors. As the House Committee Report notes:

> The present 56 year term is not long enough to insure an author and his dependents the fair economic benefits from the works. Life expectancy has increased substantially, and more and more authors are seeing their works fall into the public domain during their lifetimes, forcing later works to compete with their own early works in which copyright has expired.
>
> ...
>
> One of the worst features of the present copyright law is the provision for renewal of copyright. A substantial burden and expense, this unclear and highly technical requirement results in incalculable amounts of unproductive work. In a number of cases it is the cause of inadvertent and unjust loss of copyright. Under a life-plus-50 system the renewal device would be inapplicable and unnecessary.

---

[604] Eldred v. Ashcroft, 537 U.S. 186, 123 S. Ct. 769 (2003).

[605] *Id.* at 187, 208, 123 S. Ct. 770, 782

...

A very large majority of the world's countries have adopted a copyright term of the life of the author and 50 years after that author's death ... .[606]

As is clear from a detailed analysis of the duration provisions,[607] the assumption underlying these provisions was that the practical effect of their application would be to produce, on average, a copyright term of seventy-five years. With movement of the European Union toward a term of life of the author plus seventy years, and the passage of conforming legislation in the United States, adjustment of that assumption would appear to be necessary.

8.2. Works Created on or After the Effective Date of the 1976 Act (January 1, 1978)

In general, for works created on or after January 1, 1978, copyright attaches from the time the work is fixed in a tangible medium of expression and endures for the life of the author plus seventy years.[608] In the case of works of joint authorship, the term is measured by the life of the last surviving joint author (plus seventy years).[609]

To aid in the determination whether a copyright in a given work has expired, the Copyright Office is required to maintain current records of information as to the death of authors of copyrighted works, and, for such purposes, any person having an interest in a copyright may record in the Copyright Office a statement of the date of death of the author of that work, or statement that the author is alive as of a particular date.[610] Further, in the absence of such records with respect to the author of a particular work, after the expiration of the earlier of ninety-five years from the year of first publication of that work, or one hundred and twenty years from the year of its creation, it may be presumed that the author has been dead for at least

---

[606] H.R. Rep No. 94-1476 at 133.

[607] 17 U.S.C. §§ 302-305.

[608] 17 U.S.C. § 302 (a).

[609] 17 U.S.C. § 302 (b).

[610] 17 U.S.C. § 302 (d).

seventy years and reliance upon that presumption is a complete defense to any action for infringement.[611]

For anonymous works, pseudonymous works, and works made for hire, the term is fixed at ninety-five years from the year of first publication or, if the work is unpublished, one hundred and twenty years from the year of creation, whichever expires first.[612] With respect to anonymous or pseudonymous works, a person with an interest in the copyright in such works may record with the Copyright Office a statement identifying one or more authors of the work. If, prior to the expiration of the fixed term, such statement has been filed or the identity of one or more of the authors is otherwise revealed in records of registration for the work, then the term will be measured by the life of the last surviving author whose identity has been revealed (plus seventy years).[613]

8.3. Works Created but Not Published or Copyrighted Before January 1, 1978.

In abolishing the perpetual "common-law" copyright for unpublished works, Congress provided protection under the 1976 Act for works created but not published or copyrighted[614] or in the public domain as of the effective date of the Act. Copyright in such works subsists from January 1, 1978 and endures for the later of (a) the term that would apply had the work been created on or after January 1, 1978, (b) the period ending December 31, 2002, and (c) the period ending 31 December 2047, if the work is published on or before December 31, 2002.[615]

Thus, for example, copyright might attach to an unpublished manuscript created in 1920, even if the author had died by 1925, and such copyright would endure through 2002 and if published by that date, until 2047. Essentially, in exchange for removal of the perpetual protection

---

[611] 17 U.S.C. § 302 (e).

[612] 17 U.S.C. § 302 (c).

[613] *Id.*

[614] Under the 1909 Act, it was possible to secure federal copyright protection for certain unpublished works (for example, to secure protection for a play performed in the theater, which did not constitute "publication," prior to the time that the play itself might appear in book form).

[615] 17 U.S.C. § 303.

accorded unpublished works pursuant to the "common-law" copyright, the Act, for all practical purposes treats the author of an unpublished work who had died prior to the effective date of the Act as if such author had died on that date.

8.4. Works with Subsisting Copyright Protection As of January 1, 1978

The intention of the Act with respect to copyright subsisting as of the effective date was to extend their term from fifty-six years to seventy-five (now ninety-five) years. Thus, for copyrights in their first term as of that date, the first term continued to the completion of its twenty-eight years, followed by the renewal term (effected either by registration or automatically), for a further period of sixty-seven years.[616] For works which were in the renewal term or had been registered for renewal before January 1, 1978, that renewal term continued and was extended, originally by nineteen years, and currently, if the work was still in its renewal term as of the end of October, 1998, by thirty-nine years, to produce a total term of ninety-five years from the date copyright was originally secured.[617] As discussed above, in connection with termination of transfers,[618] it is this thirty-nine year extension that may be recaptured by the author, free of any intervening grants or transfers.

8.5. Restoration of Copyright in Certain Foreign Works

Legislation in 1993 implementing the North American Free Trade Agreement added a new provision, Section 104A, restoring copyright in certain Mexican and Canadian works which had entered the public domain in the United States. The GATT implementation amendments of 1994, effective January 1, 1996, substituted much broader language restoring copyright protection generally to foreign works under copyright protection in their "source" country but which had fallen into the public domain in the United States as a result of noncompliance with then existing statutory formalities, or for lack of subject matter protection. Restoration provides

---

[616] 17 U.S.C. § 304 (a) (1).

[617] 17 U.S.C. § 304 (b).

[618] *Supra*, § 5.

protection in the United States for the remainder of the term the work would have had had it not entered the public domain. There are detailed provisions as to "eligible" countries, protection for "reliance" parties, continued exploitation of pre-existing derivative works, and notice and procedural requirements.[619] The D.C. Circuit, relying on *Eldred*, upheld the constitutionality of the restoration provisions of Section 104A.[620]

§ 9. INFRINGEMENT

Anyone who violates any of the exclusive rights of the copyright owner as provided by sections 106 through 118 or of the author as provided in section 106A(a), or who imports copies or phonorecords into the United States in violation of section 602, is an infringer of the copyright or right of the author, as the case may be.[621]

9.1. Procedural Issues in Infringement Actions

9.1.1. Registration

Registration, while not mandatory for the attachment of copyright to a work, is a prerequisite to the institution of actions for infringement,[622] except for actions involving copyright in works first published in a Berne Convention country other than the United States.[623] If proper application for registration has been made and refused, the applicant may nevertheless institute an action for infringement if notice of such action, together with a copy of the complaint, is served on the Register of Copyrights.[624] Moreover, if the work was registered within five years after first publication, the certificate of registration is *prima facie* evidence of the validity of the

---

[619] 17 U.S.C. § 104A. *See* Dam Things from Denmark v. Russ Berrie & Co., Inc., 290 F.3d 548 (3d Cir. 2002).

[620] Luck's Music Library v. Gonzalez, 407 F.3d 1262 (D.C. Cir. 2005).

[621] 17 U.S.C. § 501 (a).

[622] Other than claims for violation of the attribution and integrity rights of works of visual art protected by 17 U.S.C. § 106A.

[623] 17 U.S.C. § 411.

[624] *Id.*

copyright and of the facts stated in the certificate,[625] creating a rebuttable presumption of validity.[626]

9.1.2. Subject Matter Jurisdiction

9.1.2.1. Exclusive Federal Jurisdiction

Jurisdiction of civil actions "arising under" the Copyright Act is vested exclusively in the federal district courts; it is "exclusive of the courts of the states."[627] A copyright infringement action, therefore, must be brought in federal court. Since subject matter jurisdiction is involved, the parties may not, directly or indirectly, circumvent this requirement to confer jurisdiction upon a state court; the court may, on its own motion, dismiss a claim as outside its jurisdiction.

The jurisdictional language, however, is not limited to actions for copyright infringement. Rather, the conferring of jurisdiction on the federal courts, and the ousting of state court jurisdiction, requires that the action be one "arising under any Act of Congress relating to" copyright. While an action for copyright infringement based upon a claimed unauthorized reproduction of a copyrighted work clearly must be brought in a federal district court and may not be brought in a state court, other kinds of actions might also "arise under" the Copyright Act. So, too, not every claim that may involve a copyrighted work will be considered to "arise under" the Act so as to confer jurisdiction upon the federal court. The leading interpretive formulation for setting boundaries for subject matter jurisdiction is that of Judge Friendly in *T.B. Harms Co. v. Eliscu:*[628]

> [The] jurisdictional statute does not speak in terms of infringement, and the undoubted truth that a claim for infringement 'arises under' the Copyright Act does not establish that nothing else can. ...

> ...

---

[625] 17 U.S.C. § 410(c).

[626] *See* Entertainment Research Group, Inc. v. Genesis Creative Group, Inc., 122 F.3d 1211, 1217 (9th Cir. 1997).

[627] 25 U.S.C. § 1338 (a): " The district court shall have original jurisdiction of any civil action arising under any Act of Congress relating to patents, plant variety protection, copyrights and trademarks. Such jurisdiction shall be exclusive of the courts of the states in patent, plant variety protection and copyright cases."

[628] 339 F.2d 823 (1964).

Mindful of the hazards of formulation in this treacherous area, we think that an action "arises under" the Copyright Act if and only if the complaint is for a remedy expressly granted by the Act, *e.g.*, a suit for infringement or for the statutory royalties for record reproduction, ... or asserts a claim requiring construction of the Act ... or, at the very least and perhaps more doubtfully, presents a case where a distinctive policy of the Act requires that federal principles control the disposition of the claim.[629]

Thus, a claim, even if not for infringement, that would require interpretation or construction of the Copyright Act would be within the exclusive jurisdiction of the federal court. While it is not clear how and when jurisdiction would be conferred because of the requirements of "a distinctive policy" of the Copyright Act, it is clear that "the general interest that copyrights, like all other forms of property, should be enjoyed by the true owner is not enough to meet this last test."[630] The issue has been most clearly presented in litigation involving disputes over contracts and licenses relating to copyrighted works. Although it had been suggested, contrary to *T.B. Harms Co.*, that the determinative factor is the centrality of Copyright Act interpretation to the principal dispute, "whether the plaintiff's infringement claim is only 'incidental' to the plaintiff's claim seeking a determination of ownership or contractual rights under the copyright,"[631]

---

[629] *Id.* at 828.

[630] *Id.*

[631] Schoenberg v. Shapolsky Publishers, Inc., 971 F.2d 926, 932-933 (2d Cir. 1992): [To determine] whether a suit "arises under" the Copyright Act when it alleges infringement stemming from a breach of contract [a] district court must first determine whether the plaintiff's infringement claim is only "incidental" to the plaintiff's claim seeking a determination of ownership or contractual rights under the copyright....If...the claim is not merely incidental, then a...court must next determine whether the complaint alleges a breach of a condition to, or a covenant of, the contract licensing or assigning the copyright. [I]f a breach of a condition is alleged, then the district court has subject matter jurisdiction....But if the complaint merely alleges a breach of a contractual covenant...then the court must undertake a third step and analyze whether the breach is so material as to create a right of rescission in the grantor. If the breach would create a right of rescission, then the asserted claim arises under the Copyright Act.

the Second Circuit has reasserted the continued viability of the *T.B. Harms Co* test.[632]

9.1.2.2. Pendent Jurisdiction

If a district court properly has jurisdiction over a copyright claim, it may, in certain cases, also adjudicate related, non-copyright pendent claims. Statutorily, such jurisdiction is authorized specifically for "any civil action asserting a claim of unfair competition when joined with a substantial and related claim under the copyright, patent, plant variety protection or trademark laws."[633] Thus, a district court having jurisdiction over a copyright claim may decide pendent nonfederal claims if the federal claim is both "substantial and "related" to the nonfederal claims. The relationship need not be based on absolutely identical facts, although there must be a strong factual tie between the two types of claims. While the statute speaks only of pendent "unfair competition" claims, it has been construed more broadly to include other types of claims, where appropriate.[634]

9.1.2.3. Suits in the United States for Acts of Infringement Abroad

Generally, a district court does not have jurisdiction to hear an infringement action based upon acts of infringement occurring in a foreign jurisdiction.[635] "It is settled that the Copyright Act does not apply extraterritorially."[636] It has been held that authorization within the United States of these foreign acts of infringement is not a sufficient domestic act

---

[632] Bassett v. Mashantucket Pequot Tribe, 204 F.3d 343 (2d Cir. 2000) ("When a complaint alleges a claim or seeks a remedy provided by the Copyright Act, federal jurisdiction is properly invoked").

[633] 28 U.S.C. § 1338 (b).

[634] *See, e.g.*, Lone Ranger Television, Inc. v. Program Radio Corp., 740 F.2d 718 (9th Cir. 1984).

[635] *See, e.g.*, Filmvideo Releasing Corp. v. Hastings, 668 F.2d 91 (2d Cir. 1981); Robert Stigwood Group Ltd. v. O'Reilly, 530 F.2d 1096 (2d Cir. 1976).

[636] Los Angeles News Service v. Reuters Television International, Ltd., 149 F.3d 987, 990 (9th Cir. 1998).

to support jurisdiction.[637] However, where there has been a completed act of infringement in the United States, the plaintiff "is entitled to recover damages flowing from exploitation abroad of the domestic acts of infringement."[638]

9.1.3. Personal Jurisdiction and Venue

There are no special personal jurisdictional rules for copyright infringement actions. Rather, jurisdiction over the person of the defendant is governed by the general *in personam* jurisdiction provisions of the Federal Rules of Civil Procedure. Similarly, with respect to venue, copyright actions, as other actions, may be instituted "in the district in which the defendant or his agent resides or may be found."[639]

9.1.4. Standing

Under the 1909 Act, standing to sue for infringement vested only in the owner of the entire copyright interest; a transferee of less than the whole was considered merely a licensee for these purposes. With the infinite divisibility of copyright under the 1976 Act,[640] any number of entities might *own* rights in a copyrighted work and the Act recognizes their rights to sue for infringement. Subject to the registration requirements,[641] an action may be brought by "the legal or beneficial owner of an exclusive rights under copyright ... for any infringement of the particular right committed while he or she is the owner of it."[642] The effect of this provision is to confer proper standing to sue for infringement on anyone owning *any* exclusive right in a copyright. For example, the owner of the exclusive right to make

---

[637] Subafilms, Ltd. v. MGM-Pathe Communications Co., 24 F.3d 1088 (9th Cir.), *cert. denied*, 115 S. Ct. 512 (1994) ("when the assertedly infringing conduct consists solely of the authorization within the territorial boundaries of the United States of acts that occur entirely abroad ... such allegations do not state a claim for relief under the copyright laws of the United States"); *cf.* Peter Starr Production Co. v. Twin Continental Films, Inc., 783 F.2d 1440 (9th Cir. 1986).

[638] *Los Angeles News Service*, 149 F.3d 987, 992.

[639] 28 U.S.C. § 1400 (a).

[640] 17 U.S.C. § 201 (d); *see supra*, § 4.2.

[641] 17 U.S.C. § 411; *see supra*, § 3.1.4.

[642] 17 U.S.C. § 501 (b).

a motion picture version of a book may sue for infringement of that motion picture. So too, an exclusive licensee would have standing to object to infringement of the licensed right. The beneficial owner of an exclusive right, such as a composer who had assigned copyright in exchange for percentage royalties, would similarly have standing to sue.[643] On the other hand, a non-exclusive licensee, whether the "legal" or beneficial" holder of the license, would not be considered an "owner" for these purposes. So, too, it has been held that the assignee of a cause of action for infringement does not have a sufficient interest by virtue alone of the assignment, to have standing to sue.[644]

To ameliorate the problem of multiplicity of litigation resulting from the divisibility of copyright "ownership," notice of a pending action must be served "upon any person whose interest is likely to be affected by a decision in the case," and the court may require notice to be served upon any person who is shown "to have or claim an interest in the copyright."[645]

9.1.5. Statute of Limitations

A civil action under the Copyright Act must be "commenced within three years after the claim accrued."[646] The statute may be tolled by the defendant's concealment of the infringement or for the period during which the plaintiff could not reasonably have learned of the infringement.[647] Criminal proceedings under the Act must, except as expressly provided otherwise in the Act, be "commenced within five years after the cause of action arose."[648]

---

[643] *See, e.g.,* Cortner v. Israel, 732 F.2d 267 (2d Cir. 1984).

[644] Silvers v. Sony Pictures Entertainment, Inc., 402 F.3d 881 (9th Cir. 2005) ("The bare assignment of an accrued cause of action is impermissible under 17 U.S.C. § 501 (b). Because that is all [plaintiff's assignor] conveyed to Silvers, Silvers was not entitled to institute and may not maintain this action against Sony for alleged infringement of the copyright").

[645] 17 U.S.C. § 501 (b).

[646] 17 U.S.C. § 507 (b).

[647] Taylor v. Meirick, 712 F.2d 1112 (7th Cir. 1983); *cf.* Roley v. New World Pictures, Ltd., 19 F.3d 479 (9th Cir. 1994).

[648] 17 U.S.C. § 507 (a).

9.1.6. Actions against State Instrumentalities

9.1.6.1. Sovereign Immunity under the Eleventh Amendment

The United States government has waived its sovereign immunity from suits for patents and copyright infringement.[649] However, the Eleventh Amendment to the Constitution appears to shield state instrumentalities from suit. It provides: "The Judicial power of the United States shall not be construed to extend to any suit in law or equity, commenced or prosecuted against one of the United States by Citizens of another State, or by Citizens or Subjects of any Foreign State." This provision has been construed to preclude any suit for copyright infringement against a state, or any of its instrumentalities. There had been confusion as to the effect of a clearly expressed congressional intention to abrogate that immunity and impose liability.[650]

9.1.6.2. Abrogation of Immunity

In 1989, in *Pennsylvania v. Union Gas Company,*[651] the United States Supreme Court appeared to hold that Congress could, by express resolution, abrogate a state's Eleventh Amendment immunity. Exercising that power, Congress in 1990 Congress enacted the Copyright Remedy Clarification Act, expressly stating that state instrumentalities "shall not be immune, under the Eleventh Amendment of the Constitution of the United States or under any other doctrine of sovereign immunity," from suit for copyright infringement.[652] However, in 1996, in *Seminole Tribe v. Florida,*[653] a case not involving copyright or patent issues, a sharply divided Supreme Court overruled *Pennsylvania v. Union Gas* and held that Congress could not use its powers under Article 1 to abrogate Eleventh Amendment immunity. Presumably, the ruling would apply to attempts to abrogate immunity from copyright infringement suits since Congress, in its

---

[649] 28 U.S.C. § 1498; note, however, that a plaintiff in an action against the United States may receive only damages, and not injunctive relief.

[650] *See, e.g.,* BV Engineering v. University of California, 858 F.2d 1394 (9th Cir. 1988), *cert. denied*, 489 U.S. 1090, 109 S. Ct. 1557 (1989).

[651] 491 U.S. 1, 109 S. Ct. 2273 (1989).

[652] 17 U.S.C. § 511.

[653] 517 U.S. 44, 116 S. Ct. 1114 (1996).

resolution, appears to have acted under its Article 1 powers. The *Seminole Tribe* opinion, however, seemed to leave room for congressional action under the Fourteenth Amendment.[654] In June, 1999, the Supreme Court, reversing the Federal Circuit, held that an identical abrogation resolution as to patent claims was unconstitutional, even under the Fourteenth Amendment.[655] In 2000 the Fifth Circuit reached the same conclusion with respect to the copyright abrogation resolution.[656]

9.1.7. Misuse of Copyright

Borrowing a concept from patent law, some courts have held that the copyright owner may forfeit the right to sue for otherwise actionable infringement if the copyright has been "misused." The public policy behind the limited monopoly of copyright "forbids the use of the copyright to secure an exclusive right or limited monopoly not granted by the Copyright Office."[657]

Put simply, our Constitution emphasizes the purpose and value of copyrights and patents. Harm caused by their misuse undermines their usefulness. Anticompetitive licensing agreements may conflict with the purpose behind a copyright's protection by depriving the public of the would-be competitor's creativity. The fair use doctrine and the refusal to copyright facts and ideas also address applications of copyright protection that would otherwise conflict with a copyright's constitutional goal...But it is possible that a copyright holder could leverage its copyright to restrain the creative expression of another without engaging in anti-competitive behavior or implicating the fair use and idea/expression doctrines.[658]

---

[654] *Cf.* College Savings Bank v. Florida Prepaid Post Secondary Education Expense Board, 148 F.3d 1343 (Fed. Cir. 1998); Chavez v. Arte Publico Press, 157 F.3d 282 (5th Cir. 1998); College Savings Bank v. Florida Prepaid Post Secondary Education Expense Board, 131 F.3d 353 (3d Cir. 1997).

[655] Florida Prepaid Post Secondary Education Expense Board v. College Savings Bank, 527 U.S. 627, 119 S. Ct. 2199 (1999).

[656] Chavez v. Arte Publico Press, 204 F.3d 601 (5th Cir. 2000).

[657] Lasercomb America, Inc. v. Reynolds, 911 F.2d 970, 979 (4th Cir. 1990).

[658] Video Pipeline, Inc. v. Buena Vista Home Entertainment, Inc., 342 F.3d 191, 204-205 (3d Cir. 2003), *cert. denied*, 540 U.S. 1178, 124 S. Ct. 1410 (2004).

While the patent model has generally been concerned with use of the monopoly in ways that violate the antitrust laws, the misuse of copyright defense has been applied to prevent the use of the copyright monopoly for anticompetitive or restrictive purposes going beyond the subject of the copyright itself, whether or not antitrust activities are implicated: "The question is not whether the copyright is being used in a manner violative of antitrust law ..., but whether the copyright is being used in a manner violative of the public policy embodied in the grant of copyright."[659]

9.2. Substantive Issues in Infringement Actions

When it is claimed that the defendant has copied the plaintiff's work, or created a derivative work, the plaintiff must prove "(1) ownership of a valid copyright, and (2) copying the constituent elements of the work that are original."[660] (While issues of "copying" may arise in actions involving the distribution right, the performance right, or the display right, in the usual course in such actions there is no real dispute as to whether the defendant has actually employed the plaintiff's work.) Ownership issues are generally straightforward. However, frequently, there is little or no direct evidence of copying available. Rather, the copying necessary to establish infringement must be demonstrated circumstantially by presenting proof of the defendant's access to the copyrighted work and of the "substantial similarity" between that work and the defendant's allegedly infringing

---

[659] Lasercomb America at 978. See Video Pipeline, *supra*, 342 F.3d at 2006 ("Thus, while we extend the patent misuse doctrine to copyright, and recognize that it might operate beyond its traditional anti-competition context, we hold it inapplicable here. On this record Disney's licensing agreements do not interfere significantly with copyright policy" (while holding to contrary might, in fact do so); *see also* Practice Management Information Corp. v. American Medical Association, 121 F.3d 516, 521 (9th Cir. 1997), *modified*, 133 F.3d 1140 (9th Cir. 1998) ("a defendant in a copyright infringement suit need not prove an antitrust violation to prevail on a copyright misuse defense"); DSC Communications Corp. v. DGI Technologies, 81 F.3d 597 (5th Cir. 1996). *See* generally Assessment Technologies of Wisconsin, Llc. v. Wiredata, Inc., 350 F.3d 640 (7th Cir. 2003).

[660] Feist Publications, Inc. v. Rural Telephone Service Company, 499 U.S. 340, 361, 111 S. Ct. 1282 (1991); Stenograph L.L.C. v. Bossard Associates, Inc., 144 F.3d 96, 99 (D.C. Cir. 1998).

copy.[661] "Substantial similarity" is an "elusive concept, not subject to precise definition."[662]

9.2.1. Substantial Similarity
9.2.1.1. Generally

Inasmuch as infringement consists of the copying of protected expression, in determining whether there is substantial similarity between two works so as to create an inference of copying, the analysis must be limited to a determination of substantial similarity of protectible *expression*. "When we determine that a work contains both protectible and unprotectible elements, we must take care to inquire only whether 'the protectible elements, standing alone, are substantially similar.'"[663] However, as noted above,[664] protectable "expression" can embrace structural elements and other matter beyond the literal text of a work; "two works need not be identical in order to be deemed 'substantially similar' for purposes of copyright infringement. ... Both literal and nonliteral similarity may warrant a finding of copyright infringement."[665]

---

[661] "To prove copyright infringement, the plaintiff must show (1) ownership of the copyright; (2) access to the copyrighted work; and (3) substantial similarity between the copyrighted work and the defendant's work." Litchfield v. Spielberg, 736 F.2d 1352,1355 (9th Cir. 1984), *cert. denied*, 470 U.S. 1052, 105 S. Ct. 1753 (1985) (noting, as well, that "a work is not a derivative work unless it has been substantially copied from the prior work.").

[662] Concrete Machinery Co., Inc. v. Classic Lawn Ornaments, Inc., 843 F.2d 600, 606 (1st Cir. 1988).

[663] Williams v. Crichton, 84 F.3d 58, 81 (2d Cir. 1996) (quoting from Knitwaves v. Lollytogs, Ltd., 71 F.3d 996, 1002 (2d Cir. 1995)). "In order to prove copying of legally protectible material, a plaintiff must typically show substantial similarity between legally protectible elements of the original work and the allegedly infringing work." Jacobsen v. Deseret Book Co., 287 F.3d 936 (10th Cir. 2002).

[664] *Supra*, § 2.3.

[665] Bateman v. Mnemonics, Inc., 79 F.3d 1532, n. 25 (11th Cir. 1996); *see also* Twin Peaks Productions, Inc. v. Publications International Limited, 996 F.2d 1366, 1372 (2d Cir. 1993) ("substantial similarity can take the form of 'fragmented literal similarity' or 'comprehensive nonliteral similarity'") (quoting from 3 Nimmer § 13.03 [A], at 13-28 to 13-29 (1992).

It has become necessary, therefore, for the courts to develop analytic tools to aid in the determination of whether the similarities between two works can be found at the level of "expression" rather than "idea." These tools provide only the starting point for analysis. The fundamental analytic concepts were set out by Judge Learned Hand, who nevertheless observed that "the test for infringement of a copyright is of necessity vague. ... Decisions must therefore inevitably be *ad hoc*."[666]

9.2.1.2. Modes of Analysis

Judge Hand suggested that in attempting to determine if there is "substantial similarity" between two works, in the absence of literal copying, the allegedly taken non-literal elements must be positioned on a spectrum ranging from "idea" to "expression," the position varying with the degree of "abstraction" or "concreteness" of the material.[667]

> To draw the distinction between ideas and their expressions, courts use the abstraction test first described by Judge Learned Hand with respect to a theatrical play.
>
> ...
>
> This test will only place a work's elements on a spectrum from more expression-like to more idea-like. It does not pick the point on the spectrum at which elements cease to be unprotected ideas and become protectible expressions. Nevertheless, it serves as a useful, if not dispositive, analytical tool in drawing these distinctions.[668]

The "abstraction analysis" has been used in a variety of circumstances, involving a wide array of copyrightable material, and, as noted above, has been the center of the dispute over the proper approach to take in dealing

---

[666] Peter Pan Fabrics, Inc. v. Martin Weiner Corp., 274 F.2d 487, 489 (2d Cir. 1960).

[667] *See* Nichols v. Universal Pictures Corp., 45 F.2d 119, *cert denied*, 282 U.S. 902, 51 S. Ct. 216 (1931); Sheldon v. Metro-Goldwyn Pictures Corp., 81 F.2d 49, *cert denied*, 98 U.S. 669, 56 S. Ct. 835 (1936).

[668] Murray Hill Publications, Inc. v. Twentieth-Century Fox, 361 F.3d 312, 319 (6th Cir. 2004).

with issues of nonliteral copying of computer programs.[669] Although Hand's analysis "has often been referred to as Hand's 'abstractions test,' in fact, as Judge Hand and others have noted, it is no test at all, but merely a way of perceiving the problem."[670]

Parallel with, and sometimes in opposition to the "abstraction" model is the "total concept and feel" construct, in which the inquiry is predicated not so much on dissection of the works at issue and close comparison of their details, as it is on examining the similarities and differences in the total concept and feel of the works.[671] That "test" is not always appropriate:

> The total concept and feel test ... is simply not helpful in analyzing works that, because of their different genres and media, must necessarily have a different concept and feel. Indeed, many 'derivative' works of different genres, in which copyright owners have exclusive rights, ... may have a different total concept and feel from the original work.[672]

9.2.1.3. Extrinsic/Intrinsic Tests, "Probative Similarity," and the Roles of Experts, Judge, and Jury

In its 1946 opinion in *Arnstein v. Porter*,[673] the Second Circuit adopted a two-step analytic scheme for determining substantial similarity. In the first step, the two works are analyzed and compared in detail, a process of

---

[669] *Supra*, § 2.4.1.3. As the Ninth Circuit observed in Apple Computer, Inc. v. Microsoft Corp., 35 F. 3d 1435, 1445 (9th Cir. 1994), *cert. denied*, 115 S. Ct. 1176 (1995), "graphical user interface audiovisual works are subject to the same process of analytical dissection as are other works."

[670] CCC Information Services, Inc. v. Maclean Hunter Market Reports, Inc., 44 F.3d 61, 69 (2d Cir. 1994), *cert. denied*, 116 S. Ct. 72 (1995).

[671] *See, e.g.*, Litchfield v. Spielberg, 736 F.2d 1352, 1356, 1357 (9th Cir. 1984), *cert. denied*, 470 U.S. 1052, 105 S. Ct. 1753 (1985) (finding listing and comparison of similarities and differences "inherently subjective and unreliable" the court concludes that "[t]o constitute infringement of expression, the total concept and feel of the works must be substantially similar"); Hartman v. Hallmark Cards, Inc., 833 F.2d 117, 120-21 (8th Cir. 1987) ("Infringement of expression occurs only when the total concept and feel of the works in question are substantially similar"); *see also* Williams v. Crichton, 84 F.3d 581 (2d Cir. 1996) ("consideration of the total concept and feel of a work").

[672] Castle Rock Entertainment, Inc. v. Carol Publishing Group, Inc., 150 F.3d 132, 140 (2d Cir. 1998).

[673] 154 F.2d 464 (2d Cir. 1946).

dissection, to determine if there are similarities of expression; this stage involves objective analysis of the works, an "extrinsic" test, for which purpose expert testimony is appropriate. It has been suggested that the initial issue is the existence of "probative" similarity, the search for similarities that are probative of copying.[674] If such analysis produces a reasonable basis for finding similarity of expression, then the inquiry moves to the second step, in which the trier of fact determines the *substantiality* of the similarity; this is a subjective process, an "intrinsic" test, in which the use of experts gives way to the subjective judgment of the "ordinary" lay observer. Building on the Second Circuit's analysis, the First Circuit articulated the "probative similarity" model as the first step in a two step "substantial similarity" analysis:

> Proof of wrongful copying is a two-step process. First, the plaintiff must show that copying actually occurred. This showing entails proof that, as a factual matter, the defendant copied the plaintiff's copyrighted material. [T]he plaintiff may satisfy his "first step" obligation indirectly by adducing evidence that the alleged infringer enjoyed access to the copyrighted work and that a sufficient degree of similarity exists between the copyrighted work and the allegedly infringing work to give rise to an inference of actual copying ... We have referred to that degree of similarity as "probative similarity." ... This requirement ... is somewhat akin to but different than [sic], the requirement of substantial similarity that emerges at the second stage in the progression. ...
>
> The substantial similarity requirement focuses holistically on the works in question and entails proof that the copying was so extensive that it rendered the works so similar that the later work represented a wrongful appropriation of expression.[675]

The bifurcated extrinsic/intrinsic model of analysis has generally been followed, albeit with a confusing detour in the Ninth Circuit. That court, while purporting to follow *Arnstein*, at first described the extrinsic test as an analysis of similarity of *ideas* and the intrinsic test as an analysis of similarity of *expression*.[676] After a series of opinions in which it expanded the scope of

---

[674] *Castle Rock Entertainment*, 150 F.3d 132 at 137; Repp v. Webber, 132 F.3d 882, 889 (2d Cir. 1998).

[675] Johnson v. Gordon, 409 F.3d 12 (1st Cir. 2005).

[676] Sid & Marty Krofft Television Productions, Inc. v. McDonald's Corp., 562 F.2d 1157 (9th Cir. 1977).

the constituent parts of protected expression,[677] the Ninth Circuit ultimately conformed its approach more closely to that of the Second Circuit as it articulated an "extrinsic" test comprised of an *objective analysis of expression* and an "intrinsic" test in the form of a *subjective analysis of expression.*[678] The Ninth Circuit, even more strongly than the Second, makes clear that the subjective judgment of the trier of fact, without the use of expert testimony, is the ultimate determinant of infringement. Accordingly, once the objective extrinsic test is satisfied, summary judgment is precluded and the case must proceed to the subjective intrinsic stage.[679]

---

[677] *See, e.g.*, Olson v. National Broadcasting Co., Inc., 855 F.2d 1446 (9th Cir. 1988); Narell v. Freemen, 872 F.2d 907 (9th Cir. 1989).

[678] Shaw v. Lindheim, 919 F.2d 1353 (9th Cir. 1990). The *Shaw* formulation was reaffirmed by the Ninth Circuit in Brownbag Software v. Symantec Corp., 960 F.2d 1465 (9th Cir. 1992), *cert. denied,* 113 S. Ct. 198 (1992) and in Smith v. Jackson, 84 F.3d 1213 (9th Cir. 1996); *see* Apple Computer, Inc. v. Microsoft Corp., 35 F.3d 1435, 1442 (9th Cir. 1994), *cert. denied,* 115 S. Ct. 1176, (1995) ("the extrinsic test now objectively considers whether there are substantial similarities in both ideas and expression, whereas the intrinsic test continues to measure expression subjectively"); Kouf v. Walt Disney Pictures & Television, 16 F.3d 1042 (9th Cir. 1994); *see also* Dr. Seuss Enterprises, L.P v. Penguin Books, 109 F.3d 1394 (9th Cir. 1997).

[679] *Shaw v. Lindheim,* 919 F.2d at 1359-60:

Satisfaction of the extrinsic test creates a triable issue of fact. ... Once a court has established that a triable question of objective similarity of expression exists, ... its inquiry should proceed no further. What remains is a subjective assessment of the concept and feel of two works of literature—a task no more suitable for a judge than for a jury.

See Metcalf v. Bochco, 294 F.3d 1069 (9th Cir. 2002). In Amini Innovation Corp. v. Anthony California, Inc., 439 F.3d 1365 (Fed. Cir. 2006), the Federal Circuit, applying Ninth Circuit law, reversed a district court's grant of summary judgment as misapplication of the extrinsic test:

In this case, the trial court erred in expanding its application of the "extrinsic" part of the infringement test to encompass an examination of "the total concept and feel of the works." Thus, the trial court mistakenly expanded the extrinsic elements of the infringement test to encompass the intrinsic elements as well. The trial court's error is significant because on summary judgment the Ninth Circuit places the extrinsic part of the infringement test within the court's purview, but disfavors application of the subjective-intrinsic part

There remains some dispute within the Ninth Circuit over whether the *Shaw* rule precluding summary judgment if a work passes the extrinsic test is limited to literary works. The conflict is discussed, but not resolved, in *Apple Computer, supra.*

While the Ninth Circuit's reaffirmation of *Arnstein* should eliminate any conflict among the circuits, the Fourth and Eighth Circuits appears still to follow the now superseded older Ninth Circuit rule,[680] while another purports to "apply a more stringent standard regarding when to allow expert testimony on the first part of the test."[681]

In applying the subjective, intrinsic test, the courts reiterate the primacy of the "ordinary" observer.[682] However, it has been suggested that it is more appropriate to consider the "intended audience" rather than the "ordinary observer": "The undisputed principles of copyright law ... require orientation of the ordinary observer test to the works' intended audience, permitting an ordinary lay observer characterization of the test only where the lay public fairly represents the works' intended audience."[683] Where the intended audience is specialized, expert testimony relating to that specialization is appropriate.[684]

---

[680] *See* Towler v. Sayles, 76 F.3d 579, 584 (4th Cir. 1996):

First, a plaintiff must show—typically with the aid of expert testimony—that the works in question are extrinsically similar because they contain substantially similar ideas that are subject to copyright protection. Second, a plaintiff must satisfy the subjective, or intrinsic, portion of the test by showing substantial similarity in how those ideas are expressed.

See also Taylor Corp. v. Four Seasons Greetings, LLC, 403 F.3d 958 (8th Cir. 2005); Schoolhouse, Inc. v. Anderson, 275 F.3d 726 (8th Cir. 2002):

we must first analyze the similarity of ideas extrinsically, focusing on any objective similarities in the details of the works. ... If the ideas behind the works are substantially similar, we must then evaluate similarity of expression intrinsically, according to the response of the ordinary, reasonable person.

[681] Murray Hill Publications, Inc. v. Twentieth-Century Fox, 361 F.3d 312, 318 (6th Cir. 2004).

[682] *See, e.g.*, Baxter v. MCA, Inc, 812 F.2d 421 (9th Cir.), *cert. denied*, 44 U.S. 954,108 S. Ct. 346 (1987); Concrete Machinery Co., Inc. v. Classic Lawn Ornaments, 843 F.2d 600 (1st Cir. 1988) ("whether there is substantial similarity between copyrightable expressions is determined by the 'ordinary observer' test").

[683] Dawson v. Hinshaw Music Inc., 905 F.2d 731, 733 (4th Cir.), *cert. denied*, 498 U.S. 981, 111 S. Ct. 511 (1990).

[684] *Id*; *see also* Whelan Associates, Inc. v. Jaslow Dental Laboratory, Inc., 797 F.2d 1222 (3d Cir. 1986), *cert. denied*, 479 U.S. 1031, 107 S. Ct. 877 (1987).

9.2.2. Access

In the absence of direct evidence of copying, a determination of infringement requires not only that there be substantial similarity of expression between the copyrighted work and the allegedly infringing work, but also evidence that the alleged infringer had access to the copyrighted work. Such access, as other elements of a claim, can be demonstrated circumstantially by a showing of a reasonable possibility of access, either because of the wide dissemination of the work or because of the availability of the work to the defendant via third parties.[685] On the other hand, clear evidence of independent creation by the alleged infringer, irrespective of circumstantial evidence of access, would defeat the infringement claim.[686]

A reciprocal relationship, an "inverse ratio rule," appears to exist between substantial similarity and access. Thus, it has been suggested that conceded or overwhelming proof of access may reduce the requisite quantum of proof of similarity,[687] although the subjective nature of the proof of similarity inhibits quantification. On a more practical level, convincing evidence of substantial similarity can serve to reduce the requisite quantum of proof of access. Where the similarity is "striking" access may be inferred; where the nature of the works and the similarities between them are such as reasonably to preclude coincidence or independent creation "striking similarity" can support a determination of infringement even in the absence of any proof of access:[688]

[A] similarity that is so close as to be highly unlikely to have been an accident of independent creation *is* evidence of access. ... Access (and

---

[685] Selle v. Gibb, 741 F.2d 896, 901 (7th Cir. 1984).

[686] *See, e.g.*, Benson v. Coca-Cola Co., 795 F.2d 973 (11th Cir. 1986).

[687] Sid & Marty Krofft Television Productions, Inc. v. McDonald's Corp., 562 F.2d 1157, 1172 (9th Cir. 1977).

[688] Ty, Inc. v. GMA Accessories, Inc., 132 F.3d 1167 (7th Cir. 1997); Repp v. Webber, 132 F.3d 882 (2d Cir. 1997); Gaste v. Kaiserman, 863 F.2d 1061 (2d Cir. 1988). Murray Hill Publications, Inc. v. Twentieth Century Fox, 361 F.3d 312 (6th Cir.), *cert. denied*, 543 U.S. 959 (2004), makes it clear that although "a bare possibility of access" is insufficient and "access may not be inferred through mere speculation or conjecture," striking similarity carries the burden of proof that the infringing work is sufficient[sic] similar as to intrude into the copyrighted work's protection and that the defendant must have had access to the copyrighted work, even if the plaintiff can provide no extrinsic proof of that fact.

copying) may be inferred if two works are so similar to each other and not to anything in the public domain that it is likely that the creator of the second work copied the first, but the inference can be rebutted by disproving access or otherwise showing independent creation ... .[689]

9.3. "Innocent" Infringement

The Act imposes liability for infringement on "anyone who violates any of the exclusive rights of the copyright owner."[690] It makes no distinction, for purposes of liability (as opposed to damages) among the willful copier who takes from another with knowledge of the infringing nature of the taking, the copier who believes either that the work is not protected or that the copying is defensible, and the copier who was unaware that he or she was in fact copying the work of another. In short, intention to infringe is not a necessary predicate for liability. Rather, the "innocent" infringer, one whose copying may be the product of a subconscious retention of the copyrighted work, will nevertheless be liable for infringement: "when a defendant's work is copied from the plaintiff's, but the defendant in good faith has forgotten that the plaintiff's work was the source of his own, such 'innocent copying' can nevertheless constitute an infringement. [C]opyright infringement can be subconscious."[691]

While "innocent" infringement, arising from either subconscious copying or copying predicated on a good faith belief that the material was not protected, will not shield the infringer from liability, it may serve to mitigate damages or otherwise have an impact on the remedies available to the copyright owner.[692]

---

[689] *Ty, Inc.,* 132 F.3d at 1170, 1171. The Seventh Circuit there attempted to harmonize *Gaste v. Kaiserman* with its earlier opinion in *Selle v. Gibb* which had held that even striking similarity cannot dispense totally with the need for some evidence of reasonable possibility of access.

[690] 17 U.S.C. § 501 (a).

[691] ABKCO Music, Inc. v. Harrisongs Music, Ltd., 722 F.2d 988, 998-99 (2d Cir. 1983; *see also* Sheldon v. Metro-Goldwyn Pictures Corp., 81 F.2d 49, 54 (2d Cir.), *cert. denied,* 298 U.S. 669, 56 S. Ct. 835 (1936) ("unconscious plagiarism is actionable quite as much as deliberate").

[692] *See infra,* § 10.

9.4. Criminal Infringement

It is a criminal offense to infringe a copyright "willfully either (1) for purposes of commercial advantage or private financial gain, or (2) by the reproduction or distribution, including by electronic means, during any 180-day period, of 1 or more copies or phonorecords of 1 or more copyrighted works, which have a total retail value of more than $1,000."[693] Depending upon the nature of the offense, the criminal infringer is subject to fines and/or imprisonment for terms ranging from one year to ten years.[694] Moreover, "all infringing copies or phonorecords and all implements, devices, or equipment used in the manufacture of such infringing copies of phonorecords" are subject to forfeiture and destruction.[695] As with other criminal offenses, the prosecution has the burden of proving the elements of the crime, including willfulness; for these purposes, "evidence of reproduction or distribution of a copyrighted work, by itself, shall not be sufficient to establish willful infringement."[696]

It is also a criminal offense, subject to a fine of up to $2,500, for one, acting with "fraudulent intent," knowingly to place a false notice of copyright on an article or knowingly to distribute publicly an article with such notice, or to remove or alter a notice of copyright, or knowingly to make a false representation of a material fact in an application for copyright registration.[697] In 2005, Congress made it acts of criminal infringement to record a motion picture in a theatre and to distribute a work not then otherwise distributed but "being prepared for commercial distribution."

9.5. Vicarious Liability and Contributory Infringement

In a variety of circumstances, a person not directly involved in infringing activity may be held liable as an infringer for the infringing conduct of another. Such liability may arise vicariously through the relationship between the infringer and the person sought to be held liable or, in the special case of contributory infringement, it may arise through a

---

[693] 17 U.S.C. § 506 (a).

[694] 18 U.S.C. § 2319.

[695] 17 U.S.C. § 506 (b).

[696] 17 U.S.C. § 506 (a).

[697] 17 U.S.C. § 506 (c)-(e).

person's activities that facilitate another's infringing conduct.[698] The issue has become particularly difficult with the development and growth of digital communication and dissemination of material through the Internet. The courts have been struggling with application of principles of vicarious liability and contributory infringement to Internet service providers as a result of infringing activities by individuals using these facilities. There has not yet been a coherent body of opinion from the Courts of Appeal and various attempts have been made in Congress to introduce immunizing or limiting legislation.

9.5.1. Vicarious Liability

In accordance with general principles of *respondeat superior*, an employer will be held liable for the infringing acts of an employee acting within the scope of employment.[699] However, for copyright infringement purposes, vicarious liability has a much broader scope than the narrow tort concept of *respondeat superior*. Rather, liability for the infringing acts of another will be imposed upon one who has power to supervise or control the infringer and a financial interest in the fruits of the infringer's activities; such liability will be imposed, where these conditions exist, irrespective of the knowledge, or lack of knowledge, of the infringing activity:

> When the right and ability to supervise coalesce with an obvious and direct financial interest in the exploitation of copyrighted materials—even in the absence of actual knowledge that the copyright monopoly is being impaired ... — the purposes of copyright law may be best effectuated by the imposition of liability upon the beneficiary of that exploitation.[700]

---

[698] *See, e.g.*, Ellison v. Robertson, 357 F.3d 1072, 1076 (9th Cir. 2004) ("We recognize three doctrines of copyright liability: direct copyright infringement, contributory copyright infringement, and vicarious copyright infringement").

[699] *See* Shapiro, Bernstein & Co. v. H.L. Green Co., 316 F.2d 304, 307 (2d Cir. 1963) ("It is quite clear ... that the normal agency rule of *respondeat superior* applies to copyright infringement by a servant within the scope of his employment").

[700] *Id.* Ellison v. Robertson, 357 F.3d 1072, 1076 (9th Cir. 2004) ("A defendant is vicariously liable for copyright infringement if he enjoys a direct financial benefit from *another's* infringing activity and 'has the right and ability to supervise' the infringing activity") (quoting from A & M Records v. Napster, Inc., 239 F.3d 1004 at 1022 (9th Cir. 2001).

Accordingly, owners of premises rented to others for use as bars and music halls, at which infringing performances of copyrighted music take place, will not be liable for those acts of infringement where the owners receive a fixed rental and exercise no supervision, but such liability will be imposed where the performances can have an impact upon the proprietor's income. Similarly, the operators of those premises will be held liable for infringing performances "whether the bandleader is considered, as a technical matter, an employee or independent contractor, and whether or not the proprietor has knowledge of the compositions to be played or any control over their selection."[701] Applying these principles, the operators of a "swap meet" flea market were held vicariously liable for the infringement by vendors selling counterfeit sound recordings; "control" was found from the operators' active promotion of the swap meet and ability to control and patrol the premises and to terminate the occupancy of any vendors, and "financial benefit" came from admission fees, concession stand sales, and parking fees, "all of which flow directly from customers who want to buy the counterfeit recordings at bargain basement prices."[702]

9.5.2. Contributory Infringement

"One who, with knowledge of the infringing activity, induces, causes, or materially contributes to the infringing conduct of another, may be held liable as a 'contributory' infringer."[703] Liability under these circumstances is imposed upon one who provides the wherewithal for another to infringe. Not everyone whose conduct may facilitate another's infringing activities will incur liability. The crucial issue will be the nature of that conduct, the person's awareness of its consequences for infringement, and the extent to which that conduct is otherwise permissible. Clearly, the fact alone that copying equipment is used by some people to make infringing copies would not be sufficient to impose liability upon the manufacturer of that equipment for those acts of infringement.

---

[701] *Shapiro, Bernstein & Co, supra,* (reviewing the cases).

[702] Fonovisa, Inc. v. Cherry Auction, Inc., 76 F.3d 259, 263 (9th Cir. 1996). *See also* RCA/Ariola v. Thomas & Grayston, 845 F.2d 773 (8th Cir. 1988).

[703] Gershwin Publishing v. Columbia Artists Management, 443 F.2d 1159, 1162 (2d Cir. 1971); Ellison v. Robertson, 357 F.3d 1072, 1076 (9th Cir. 2004).

The United States Supreme Court attempted to provide standards and guidance in *Sony Corp. of America v. Universal City Studios, Inc.*[704] Borrowing from the "staple article of commerce" doctrine of patent law, the court held that contributory infringement liability could not be imposed solely on the basis that the defendant sold equipment with constructive knowledge that customers may use that equipment to make unauthorized copies of copyrighted material; there must be a closer relationship between the direct infringer and the alleged "contributory" infringer, and some ability to control the activity. Contributory infringement cannot be found if the article at issue is "capable of substantial noninfringing uses":

> The staple article of commerce doctrine must strike a balance between a copyright holder's legitimate demand for effective—not merely symbolic—protection of the statutory monopoly, and the rights of others freely to engage in substantially unrelated areas of commerce. Accordingly, the sale of copying equipment, like the sale of other articles of commerce, does not constitute contributory infringement if the product is widely used for legitimate, unobjectionable purposes. Indeed, it need merely be capable of substantial noninfringing uses.[705]

On the other hand, "providing the site and facilities for known infringing activity is sufficient to establish contributory liability,"[706] as is the purported sale of the right to copyrighted material with knowledge by the seller of the seller's lack of rights to that material.[707] In each case, the defendant materially contributes to the infringing conduct of another.

The growth of the internet, together with technology facilitating the digital distribution of copyrighted music, motion pictures, and other material, has put a severe strain on the accepted definitions of vicarious and contributory infringement. Thus, in *A & M Records v. Napster, Inc.*,[708] the Ninth Circuit held that, at least for purposes of the pending preliminary injunction, a sufficient showing had been made to hold the operator of the Napster website that was used for the uploading and downloading by users of copyrighted music both vicariously and contributory liable for the

---

[704] 464 U.S. 417, 104 S. Ct. 774 (1984).

[705] *Id.* at 442, 104 S. Ct. at 788-89.

[706] Fonovisa, Inc. v. Cherry Auction, Inc., 76 F.3d 259, 264 (9th Cir. 1996).

[707] Casella v. Morris, 820 F.2d 362 (11th Cir. 1987).

[708] 239 F.3d 1004 (9th Cir. 2001).

infringing activities of the users. The situation became more complicated with the proliferation of "peer-to-peer networking software," allowing for the distribution among users without the use of a centralized entity that actually stores the material. In actions against the providers of the software, the circuits split over the issue of whether liability can be avoided by a showing of "capability" of noninfringing use alone or if the defendant must demonstrate the probability or quantitative significance of such use.[709] In its 2005 decision in *Metro-Goldwyn-Mayer Studios, Inc. v. Grokster, Ltd.*,[710] the Supreme Court declined the invitation broadly to reexamine the issue; instead, it held that contributory liability may properly be imposed on "one who distributes a device" (e.g., peer-to-peer software) with the object of promoting its use to infringe copyright, as shown by clear expression or other affirmative steps taken to foster infringement.

9.5.3. Online Infringement Liability Limitation
9.5.3.1. Generally

As part of the Digital Millennium Copyright Act of 1998, Congress enacted the Online Copyright Infringement Liability Limitation Act, embodied in Section 512 of the Copyright Act.[711] This section, essentially, limits the liability of online service providers who do not have notice of the existence of infringing material or activities on their systems for vicarious or contributory infringement resulting from the unauthorized transmission, system caching, or storage of copyrighted material, or linking to infringing locations, and who act expeditiously to remove infringing materials, or access thereto, upon receipt of proper notice of claimed infringement.[712] The limitations on liability, the "safe harbors,"[713] discussed below, apply only to a service provider who "accommodates and does not interfere with

---

[709] *Compare* In re Aimster Copyright Litigation, 334 F.3d 643 (7th Cir. 2003), *cert. denied* 540 U.S. 1107, 124 S. Ct. 1069 (2004) *and* Metro-Goldwyn-Mayer Studios, Inc. v. Grokster Ltd., 380 F.3d 1154 (9th Cir. 2004), *rev'd*, 125 S. Ct. 2764 (2005).

[710] 125 S. Ct. 2764 (2005).

[711] 17 U.S.C. § 512 (i).

[712] The nature and elements of effective "notification" are set out in detail in 17 U.S.C. § 512 (c) (3).

[713] *See* Ellison v. Robertson, 357 F.3d 1072 (9th Cir. 2004) and Costar Group, Inc. v. Loopnet, Inc., 373 F.3d 544 (4th Cir. 2004) (reviewing the "safe harbor" provisions).

standard technical measures," and who has adopted and reasonably implemented, and informs subscribers and account holders of, "a policy that provides for the termination in appropriate circumstances of subscribers and account holders of the service provider's system or network who are repeat infringers."[714]

To effectuate the purposes of these provisions, copyright owners must provide appropriate notice of infringing activity[715] and are granted the sharply circumscribed right to request the issue of subpoenas to service providers to identify alleged infringement.[716] In that connection, liability is imposed upon one who knowingly materially misrepresents that online material or activity is infringing or was mistakenly removed or disabled.[717]

9.5.3.2. Transmission

Specifically, the service provider[718] will not be liable for monetary relief for infringement of copyright resulting from that provider's "transmitting, routing, or providing connections for, material through a system more network controlled or operated by or for the service provider or by reason of the intermediate and transient storage of that material in the course of such transmitting, routing, or providing connections," if the service provider was involved neither in the initiation of the transmission, nor in the selection of the material or of the recipients of the material, and if no intermediate or transient storage copy is maintained on the system longer

---

[714] 17 U.S.C. § 512 (c).

[715] But mere technical defects in the notice will not be fatal. The "safe harbor" will not be available when the copyright owner has "substantially complied" with the notice provisions. ALS Scan, Inc. v. Remarq Communities, Inc., 239 F.3d 619 (4th Cir. 2001) ("Because we conclude that the service provider was provided with a notice of infringing activity that *substantially* complied with the Act, it may not rely on a claim of defective notice to maintain the immunity defense provided by the safe harbor").

[716] 17 U.S.C. § 512 (h).

[717] 17 U.S.C. § 512 (f).

[718] Defined, for this purpose, as "an entity offering the transmission, routing, or providing of connections for digital online communications, between or among points specified by a user, of material of the user's choosing, without modification to the content of the material as sent or received." 17 U.S.C. § 512 (k) (1) (A). For other purposes it is defined more broadly as "a provider of online services or network access, or the operator of facilities therefor." 17 U.S.C. § 512 (k) (1) (B).

than is necessary or is ordinarily accessible to anyone other than anticipated recipients, and if the material is transmitted without modification.[719] Injunctive relief with respect to a qualifying service provider is limited to an order preventing access by terminating the accounts of the subscriber or account holder engaged in infringing activity.[720]

9.5.3.3. System Caching

Similarly, the service provider will not be liable for monetary relief for infringement of copyright resulting from system caching, the intermediate and temporary storage of material on a system, if the material is made available online by a person other than the service provider, and it is transmitted from such person to another at the direction of that other person, and the storage is done through an automatic process that makes the material available to users of the system who request access to it from the person providing the material.[721] The limitation is further conditioned by requirements that the material be transmitted without modification, that the service provider act expeditiously to remove material upon notification of claimed infringement if it was made available online without authorization of the copyright owner and further detailed requirements with respect to access to the material.[722] Injunctive relief with respect to a qualifying service provider under these and the limitation on liability provisions discussed below, is limited to an order restraining the service provider from providing access to infringing material or activity, or providing access to a subscriber or account holder by terminating such person's accounts, or such other relief as is least burdensome to the service provider and necessary to prevent or restrain infringement of copyright.[723]

9.5.3.4. Storage

Nor will a service provider be liable for monetary relief for infringement resulting from the storage of material on the system or network, if the storage was done at the direction of a user of the system, if

---

[719] 17 U.S.C. § 512 (a).

[720] 17 U.S.C. § 512 (j) (1) (B).

[721] 17 U.S.C. § 512 (b) (1).

[722] 17 U.S.C. § 512 (b) (2).

[723] 17 U.S.C. § 512 (j) (1) (A).

the operator has, in accordance with the statutory provisions, designated an agent to receive notification of claimed infringement, and neither has knowledge of infringement nor awareness of facts or circumstances from which infringing activity is apparent, or acts expeditiously to remove or disable access to the material upon obtaining such knowledge or awareness or notice of claimed infringement, and if the operator, with the right and ability to control the infringing activity, does not receive a financial benefit directly attributable thereto.[724]

9.5.3.5. Links

A service provider will not be liable for monetary relief for infringement resulting from the linking of users to another online location containing infringing material or infringing activity if the service provider neither has knowledge of infringement nor awareness of facts or circumstances from which infringing activity is apparent, or acts expeditiously to remove or disable access to the material upon obtaining such knowledge or awareness or notice of claimed infringement, and if the operator, with the right and ability to control the infringing activity, does not receive a financial benefit directly attributable thereto.[725]

9.5.3.6. Further Limitations on Liability of Nonprofit Educational Institutions

If the service provider is a nonprofit educational institution, faculty members and graduate students who are employees of the institution and who perform teaching or research functions will be considered persons "other than the institution" and their knowledge or awareness of infringing activity will not be attributed to the institution, if such persons' infringing activities do not relate to instructional materials required are recommended within the preceding three-year period for courses taught by such persons, and if the institution has not received more than two valid notifications of claimed infringement by such persons within that three-year period, and if the institution provides to all users "materials that accurately describe, and

---

[724] 17 U.S.C. § 512 (c).
[725] 17 U.S.C. § 512 (d).

promote compliance with, the laws of the United States relating to copyright."[726]

9.5.3.7. Limitation on Liability for Removal of Material

In general, a service provider will not incur liability for any claim based upon the good faith disabling of access to, or removal of, material or activity claimed to be infringing or based on facts or circumstances from which infringing activity is apparent.[727] There are detailed provisions with respect to notification to one who has provided material that is removed, and to a duty to replace remove material upon proper "counter notification."[728]

§ 10. REMEDIES

10.1. Injunctive Relief

The Copyright Act expressly empowers the district court to "grant temporary and final injunctions on such terms as it may deem reasonable to prevent or restrain infringement of a copyright."[729] As an equitable remedy, injunctive relief is subject to the discretion of the court and the general principles governing such relief: the need for a showing of irreparable harm, the comparative threatened injury to the plaintiff and of the harm an injunction might inflict on the defendant and (in the case of preliminary relief) the reasonable likelihood of plaintiff's success.[730]

However, while injunctive relief is not automatic, it is quite common and follows from a generally accepted presumption that copyright infringement produces irreparable harm.[731] While it has been held that, once infringement has been found, the district court does not retain broad

---

[726] 17 U.S.C. § 512 (e).

[727] 17 U.S.C. § 512 (g) (1).

[728] 17 U.S.C. §§ 512 (g) (2) and (3).

[729] 17 U.S.C. § 502 (a).

[730] See, e.g., Atari, Inc. v. North American Philips Consumer Electronics Corp., 672 F.2d 607 (7th Cir. 1982).

[731] Apple Computer, Inc. v. Franklin Computer Corp., 714 F.2d 1240 (3d Cir. 1983), cert. denied, 464 U.S. 1033, 104 S. Ct. 690 (1984).

discretion to deny injunctive relief on general public interest grounds,[732] the court does retain discretion to balance harm,[733] and the Supreme Court has since noted the propriety of public interest considerations to temper the grant of injunctive relief, at least in close cases or where serious questions of fair use are involved:

> [W]hile in the "vast majority of cases, [an injunctive] remedy is justified because most infringements are simple piracy," such cases are "worlds apart from many of those raising reasonable contentions of fair use" where "there may be a strong public interest in the publication of the secondary work [and] the copyright owner's interest may be adequately protected by an award of damages for whatever infringement is found.[734]

10.2. Damages

Section 504 of the Act sets out alternative bases for the award of monetary damages: "an infringer of copyright is liable for either—(1) the copyright owner's actual damages and any additional profits of the infringer ...; or (2) statutory damages ... ."[735]

10.2.1. Actual Damages and Profits

"The copyright owner is entitled to recover the actual damages suffered by him or her as a result of the infringement, and any profits of the infringer that are attributable to the infringement and are not taken into account in computing the actual damages."[736] That is, the successful plaintiff in an infringement action may recover proven actual damages attributable to the infringement, which may also include profits lost by the plaintiff as a result

---

[732] New Era Publications International, ApS v. Henry Holt & Co., 873 F.2d 576 (2d Cir. 1989).

[733] Abend v. MCA, Inc., 863 F.2d 1465, 1479 (9th Cir. 1988) (finding "special circumstances that would cause "great injustice" to defendants and "public injury" were injunction to issue), aff'd sub nom. Stewart v. Abend, 495 U.S. 207, 110 S. Ct. 1750 (1990) (the Supreme Court did not reach this issue).

[734] Campbell v. Acuff-Rose, 510 U.S. 569, 578 fn. 10, 114 S. Ct. 1164, 1171 fn. 10 (citing, with approval, Abend v. MCA, Inc. and quoting from Pierre Leval, Toward a Fair Use Standard, 103 HARV. L.REV. 1105 (1990)).

[735] 17 U.S.C. § 504 (a).

[736] 17 U.S.C. § 504 (b).

thereof, and any nonduplicative profits of the infringer. As the House Report notes, this provision "recognizes the different purposes served by awards of damages and profits."[737]

10.2.1.1. Provable Damages

The plaintiff must prove damage attributable to the act of infringement, the injury caused by the infringer to the value of the copyrighted work.[738] While the fact of harm and the amount of damages may not be purely speculative, once the plaintiff does in fact demonstrate harm, the precise amount of damages need not be established with certainty and the burden will shift to the infringer to demonstrate the extent to which the harm was the result of circumstances other than the acts of infringement. To the extent provable, potential profits on demonstrated lost sales are recoverable as part of the plaintiff's damages, as is proven loss of licensing royalties. In short, if loss and causation—injury to the copyrighted work attributable to the acts of infringement—are established, the loss is compensable.

In the case of a proprietor of an establishment[739] who asserts, as a defense to a claim of violation of the performance right, the exemptions provided by Section 110 (5),[740] without reasonable grounds to believe it was applicable, will be liable, in addition to any other damages, for twice the license fee that should have been paid, for up to the preceding three years.[741]

10.2.1.2. Infringer's Profits

As noted above, to the extent that they are not duplicated in the plaintiff's lost profits,[742] the plaintiff may, in addition to provable damages, recover the defendant's profits arising out of the acts of infringement.

---

[737] H.R. Rep. No. 94-1476 at 160.

[738] Frank Music Corp. v. Metro-Goldwyn-Mayer, Inc., 772 F.2d 505 (9th Cir. 1985); see Mary Ellen Enterprises v. Camex, Inc., 68 F.3d 1065 (8th Cir. 1995).

[739] As these terms are defined in 17 U.S.C. § 101.

[740] See supra, § 6.4.5.7.

[741] 17 U.S.C. § 504 (d).

[742] See, e.g., Taylor v. Meirick, 712 F.2d 1112 (7th Cir. 1983).

Damages are awarded to compensate the copyright owner for losses from the infringement, and profits are awarded to prevent the infringer from unfairly benefitting from a wrongful act. Where the defendant's profits are nothing more than a measure of the damages suffered by the copyright owner, it would be inappropriate to award damages and profits cumulatively, since in effect they amount to the same thing. However, in cases where the copyright owner has suffered damages not reflected in the infringer's profits, or where there have been profits attributable to the copyrighted work but not used as a measure of damage [§504(b)] authorizes the award of both.[743]

Consistent with the purpose of the Act, a plaintiff might recover the infringer's profits significantly in excess of the plaintiff's actual losses; the deterrent effect of such a result is of greater significance than the unearned benefit derived by the plaintiff.[744] The more serious problem in dealing with the infringer's profits is the difficulty of determining with exactitude both the amount of "profits" realized by the infringer from a given act, and how much of those profits are specifically allocable to the act of infringement. Difficult and complex questions are frequently presented with respect to the nature and the amount of appropriate deductions and the allocation of profits to infringing and non-infringing activity.[745] The Act is clear in placing the burden with respect to both of these issues on the alleged infringer:

> In establishing the infringer's profits, the copyright owner is required to present proof only of the infringer's gross revenue, and the infringer is required to prove his or her deductible expenses and the elements of profits attributable to factors other than the copyrighted work.[746]

Although the burden is placed on the infringer to present proof of appropriate deductions from gross revenues in arriving at net profits and of "the elements of profit attributable to factors other than the copyrighted work," meeting that burden does not necessarily require exact proof: "where it is clear ... that not all the profits are attributable to the infringing

---

[743] H.R. Rep. No. 94-1476 at 161.

[744] *See, e.g.*, Taylor v. Meirick, 712 F.2d 1112 (7th Cir. 1983).

[745] *Id.; see also* Frank Music Corp. v. Metro-Goldwyn-Mayer, Inc., 772 F.2d 505 (9th Cir. 1985).

[746] 17 U.S.C. § 504 (b).

material, the copyright owner is not entitled to recover all of those profits merely because the infringer fails to establish with certainty the portion attributable to the non-infringing elements."[747] The court will make such apportionment as it deems proper.

10.2.2. Statutory Damages

It is frequently quite difficult to prove actual damages, even when infringement is clearly established. The Copyright Act provides for alternative monetary relief, statutory damages in lieu of proven actual damages. "[T]he copyright owner may elect, at any time before final judgment is rendered, to recover, instead of actual damages and profits, an award of statutory damages ... ."[748]

10.2.2.1. Registration as a Condition

The alternative of electing to recover statutory damages is not available as a remedy for infringement of copyright which commenced after the first publication of a work and prior to the effective date of its registration, "unless such registration is made within three months after the first publication of the work";[749] nor are statutory damages available for infringement of copyright in an unpublished work commenced before the effective date of its registration.[750] The requirement of timely registration for recovery of statutory damages is equally applicable to actions for infringement of works originating from Berne Convention countries (notwithstanding the fact that registration is not a condition to the institution of infringement actions for such works).

---

[747] Cream Records, Inc. v. Joseph Schlitz Brewing Co., 754 F.2d 826, 828 (9th Cir. 1985); *Frank Music Corp., supra; see* Sheldon v. Metro-Goldwyn Pictures Corp., 106 F.2d 45, 51 (2d Cir. 1939), *aff'd*, 309 U.S. 390, 60 S. Ct. 681 (1940) ("we are resolved to avoid the one certainly unjust course of giving the plaintiffs everything, because the defendants cannot with certainty compute their own share").

[748] 17 U.S.C. § 504 (c) (1).

[749] 17 U.S.C. § 412 (2).

[750] 17 U.S.C. § 412 (1).

10.2.2.2. Amount of Damages: Range of Discretion

Generally, statutory damages with respect to infringement for any one work (for which purposes, all the parts of a compilation or derivative work constitute one work) are recoverable in a range from $750 to $30,000, "as the court considers just."[751] Where multiple acts of infringement are involved, the award can be quite substantial. Thus, infringement of a television series, with each episode being considered a separate work, resulted in an award of nine million dollars in statutory damages.[752]

Since statutory damages are awarded "for all infringements involved in the action, with respect to any one work," there has been confusion as to the application of the language in cases of multiple acts of infringement, the issue being whether statutory damages are to be applied to each infringed work or to each infringement of a given work. The First Circuit has held that, in accord with its view of the prevailing reading in the circuits, "under §504(c) the total number of 'awards' of statutory damages that a plaintiff may recover in any given action against a single defendant depends on the number of *works* that are infringed and the number of individually liable infringers and is unaffected by the number of *infringements* of those works."[753]

Moreover, if the plaintiff proves that the defendant committed the acts of infringement "willfully," the court in its discretion may award statutory damages up to $150,000."[754] However, a finding that an infringer acted "willfully" requires more than a showing of conscious copying. It requires knowledge that the act constitutes an infringement or action in reckless disregard of the copyright owner's rights:

> Willfulness, under [the] statutory scheme, has a rather specialized meaning. ... "In other contexts [willfulness] might simply mean an intent to copy, without necessarily an intent to infringe. It seems clear that as here used, 'willfully' means with knowledge that the defendant's conduct constitutes copyright infringement. Otherwise, there would be no point

---

[751] 17 U.S.C. § 504 (c) (1).

[752] MCA Television Ltd. v. Feltner, 89 F.3d 766 (11th Cir. 1996); Columbia Pictures Television v. Krypton Broadcasting of Birmingham, Inc., 106 F.3d 284 (9th Cir.1997).

[753] Venegas-Hernandez v. Sonolux Records, 370 F.3d 183 (1st Cir. 2004).

[754] 17 U.S.C. § 504 (c) (2).

in providing specially for the reduction of minimum awards in the case of innocent infringement, because any infringement that was nonwillful would necessarily be innocent. This seems to mean, then, that one who has been notified that his conduct constitutes copyright infringement, but who reasonably and in good faith believes the contrary, is not 'willful' for these purposes." ...

[T]he issue is whether the copyright law supported the plaintiffs' position so clearly that the defendants must be deemed as a matter of law to have exhibited a reckless disregard of the plaintiffs' property rights.[755]

The willful infringement provisions of Section 504(c) were strengthened in connection with infringing activities conducted via the internet, as a new subsection 504(c)(3) was added at the end of 2004, providing in part:

> In a case of infringement, it shall be a rebuttable presumption that the infringement was committed willfully for purposes of determining relief if the violator, or a person acting in concert with the violator, knowingly provided or knowingly caused to be provided materially false contact information to a domain name registrar, domain name registry, or other domain name registration authority in registering, maintaining, or renewing a domain name used in connection with the infringement.[756]

On the other hand, if the infringer proves "that such infringer was not aware and had reason to believe that his or her acts constituted an infringement of copyright, the court in its discretion may reduce the award of statutory damages to a sum of not less than $200."[757] In certain limited circumstances, involving a reasonable belief that the act of infringement was a fair use in the case of infringing copying by employees or agents of nonprofit educational institutions, libraries, or archives, or infringing

---

[755] Princeton University Press v. Michigan Document Services, 99 F.3d 1381, 1392 (1996), *cert. denied*, 117 S. Ct. 1336 (1997), quoting from MELVILLE B. NIMMER & DAVID NIMMER, 3 NIMMER ON COPYRIGHT §14.04[B] [3] (1996); *see also* Peer International Corp. v. Pausa Records, Inc., 909 F.2d 1332, 1335 (9th Cir. 1990), *cert. denied*, 498 U.S. 1109 (1991) ("'willful' [means] with knowledge that the defendant's conduct constitutes copyright infringement").

[756] 17 U.S.C. § 504 (c) (3).

[757] 17 U.S.C. § 504 (c) (2).

performance or transmission by a public broadcasting entity, statutory damages are to be totally remitted.[758]

10.2.2.3. Right to Jury Determination

As is evident, since statutory damages are to be determined within a range "as the court considers just" the court retains a great deal of discretion in fixing the amount. Inasmuch as statutory damages are "damages" and serve as an alternative form of compensation, even though the statute refers to the *court's* discretion, a conflict developed among the Courts of Appeal as to the right of either party in an infringement action to a jury trial with respect to the amount of statutory damages. This conflict was resolved by the United States Supreme Court as it held in 1998 that, although the Copyright Act itself creates no right to a jury trial with respect to statutory damages, "the Seventh Amendment provides a right to a jury trial on all issues pertinent to an award of statutory damages under Section 504(c) of the Copyright Act, including the amount itself."[759] However, it has been held that if the plaintiff seeks only the minimum statutory damages, then there is no Seventh Amendment right to a jury trial. [760]

10.3. Costs and Counsel Fees

The court, in its discretion, may allow the recovery of costs by or against any party (other than the United States or an officer thereof) and may also award a reasonable attorney's fee to the prevailing party as part of such party's costs.[761] However, as with statutory damages, attorney's fees are not available to a prevailing plaintiff who has failed to make timely registration of the copyrighted work at issue (*i.e.*, where infringement occurs prior to registration, unless infringement occurs after first

---

[758] *Id.*

[759] Feltner v. Columbia Pictures Television, Inc., 118 S. Ct. 1279, 1288 (1998).

[760] BMG Music v. Gonzalez, 430 F.3d 888 (7th Cir. 2005):
When there is a material dispute of fact to be resolved or discretion to be exercised in selecting a financial award, then either side is entitled to a jury; if there is no material dispute and a rule of law eliminates discretion in selecting the remedy, then summary judgment is permissible.

[761] 17 U.S.C. § 505.

publication and registration is made within three months after first publication).[762]

While the Act authorizes discretionary award of attorney's fees to the prevailing party, there was disagreement among the Courts of Appeal as to whether prevailing plaintiffs and prevailing defendants were to be subject to the same standards.[763] In 1994, the United States Supreme Court resolved the matter by adopting an "even-handed" model in which prevailing plaintiffs and prevailing defendants are to be treated alike:[764]

> Because copyright law ultimately serves the purpose of enriching the general public through access to creative works, it is peculiarly important that the boundaries of copyright law be demarcated as clearly as possible. To that end, defendants who seek to advance a variety of meritorious copyright defenses should be encouraged to litigate them to the same extent that plaintiffs are encouraged to litigate meritorious claims of infringement. [A] successful defense of a copyright infringement action may further the policies of the Copyright Act every bit as much as a successful prosecution of an infringement claim by the holder of a copyright.
>
> . . .
>
> [W]e reject both the 'dual standard' adopted by several of the Courts of Appeals, and petitioner's claim that § 505 enacted the British Rule for automatic recovery of attorney's fees by the prevailing party. Prevailing plaintiffs and prevailing defendants are to be treated alike, but attorney's fees are to be awarded to prevailing parties only as a matter of the court's discretion.[765]

The Court's emphasis upon the discretionary nature of the award of attorney's fees (and costs), while requiring that the same standards be applicable to both plaintiffs and defendants, leaves unresolved the question of just what these standards are. The trial court determines both what are "reasonable" attorneys' fees and of the circumstances under which they ought to be awarded. These can be difficult determinations, reviewable for

---

[762] 17 U.S.C. § 412.

[763] *See, e.g.,* Lieb v. Topstone Industries, Inc., 788 F.2d 151 (3d Cir. 1986) (reviewing the distinctions).

[764] Fogerty v. Fantasy, Inc., 510 U.S. 517, 114 S. Ct. 1023 (1994).

[765] *Id.* at 527-28, 534, 114 S. Ct. at 1029-30, 1032.

abuse of the court's discretion.[766] The Court does appear to endorse the use of factors including "'frivolousness, motivation, objective unreasonableness (both in the factual and in the legal components of the case) and the need in particular circumstances to advance considerations of compensation and deterrence' [,] so long as such factors are faithful to the purposes of the Copyright Act and are applied to prevailing plaintiffs and defendants in an evenhanded manner."[767]

10.4. Impoundment and Disposition

While an action is pending, the court may, at any time, order the impoundment of infringing articles and devices used to produce them: "all copies or phonorecords claimed to have been made or used in violation of the copyright owner's exclusive rights, and ... all plates, and molds, matrices, masters, tapes, film negatives, or other articles by means of which such copies or phonorecords may be reproduced."[768] It is not clear what procedures must be followed in connection with impoundment orders and what showing one seeking impoundment must make; *i.e.,* the propriety of *ex parte* or summary impoundment orders.

At the conclusion of the action, as part of its final judgment, the court may similarly "order the destruction or other reasonable disposition" of all infringing articles and the devices used to produce them (as above defined).[769] This provision contemplates the alternative of destruction or a sale to the public, delivery to the plaintiff, or other appropriate disposition.

---

[766] *See, e.g.,* Entertainment Research Group, Inc. v. Genesis Creative Group, Inc., 122 F.3d 1211, 1217 (9th Cir. 1997).

[767] 510 U.S. at 535, n. 19, 114 S. Ct. at 1033 (quoting from *Lieb v. Topstone Industries, Inc., supra.,* 788 F.2d at 156).

[768] 17 U.S.C. § 503 (a).

[769] 17 U.S.C. § 503 (b).

§11. Copyright Protection Systems and Copyright Management Information

11.1. Generally

The Digital Millennium Copyright Act was enacted on October 28, 1998, to implement certain provisions of the World Intellectual Property Organization Copyright Treaty and Performances and Phonograms Treaty, which had been adopted by WIPO in Geneva in December, 1996. The centerpiece of this legislation is the addition to the Copyright Act of Chapter 12—"Copyright Protection and Management Systems."[770] These are anti-piracy provisions directed (i) to the circumvention of technological protection measures taken by copyright holders to limit access to copyrighted material, and (ii) to the facilitation of such circumvention and of circumvention of technological measures that inhibit infringing activities; there are also provisions designed to protect the integrity of "copyright management information." The legislation directs the Register of Copyrights and the Assistant Secretary for Communications and Information to evaluate, and to report thereon to Congress within twenty-four months, the effect of the legislation and the development of electronic commerce and associated technology on sections 109 ("first sale") and 117 (computer programs) of the Copyright Act and the relation between existing and emergent technology and the operation of those sections. The resultant report did not recommend significant change.

11.2. Circumvention of Copyright Protection Systems

11.2.1. Actionable Conduct

Chapter 12 enumerates as actionable specific conduct, both direct and contributory, relating to the circumvention of technology designed to limit access to or to protect all or portions of copyrighted works. These provisions are not intended either to enlarge or diminish rights or defenses with respect to copyright infringement or vicarious or contributory liability for copyright infringement as such, or to set standards for the design of consumer electronics, telecommunications, or computer products.[771]

---

[770] 17 U.S.C. §§ 1201-1205.

[771] 17 U.S.C. § 1201 (c).

11.2.1.1. Circumvention of Access Control

"No person shall circumvent a technological measure that effectively controls access to a [copyright protected] work."[772] The prohibition relates, essentially, to the circumvention of encryption or scrambling schemes that limit access to a work; it does not deal directly with circumvention of technological copy protection or other schemes that inhibit infringing activities. More specifically, to "circumvent a technological measure" means "to descramble a scrambled work, to decrypt an encrypted work, or otherwise to avoid, bypass, remove, deactivate, or impair a technological measure, without the authority of the copyright owner."[773] For these purposes, "a technological measure 'effectively controls access to a work' if the measure, in the ordinary course of its operation, requires the application of information, or a process or a treatment, with the authority of the copyright owner, to gain access to the work."[774]

Application of this prohibition was deferred until October 28, 2000 (the expiration of two years from the enactment date of the legislation).[775] During the two-year deferral period, and during each succeeding three-year period, the Librarian of Congress was required to institute a rulemaking proceeding to determine the existence of persons who are, or are likely to be, adversely affected by the prohibition in their ability to make non-infringing uses of a particular class of works.[776] If the rulemaking proceeding concludes that there are classes of copyrighted works with respect to which noninfringing uses are, or are likely to be, adversely affected, then, with respect to each succeeding three-year period, the prohibition will not apply to users of those classes of works.[777]

---

[772] 17 U.S.C. § 1201 (a) (1) (A).

[773] 17 U.S.C. § 1201 (a) (3) (A).

[774] 17 U.S.C. § 1201 (a) (3) (B).

[775] 17 U.S.C. § 1201 (a) (1) (A).

[776] 17 U.S.C. § 1201 (a) (1) (B) and (C).

[777] 17 U.S.C. § 1201 (a) (1) (D).

11.2.1.2. Facilitating Circumvention of Technological Protection Measures

There is a separate specific prohibition with respect to providing the means for circumvention of technological protection measures. It is a violation to "import, offer to the public, provide, or otherwise traffic in any technology, product, service, device, component, or part thereof, that": (A) is primarily designed or produced for the purpose of (i) "circumventing a technological measure that effectively controls access" to a copyrighted work or (ii) "circumventing protection afforded by a technological measure that effectively protects a right of a copyright owner ... in a work or a portion thereof"; or (B) has only limited commercially significant purpose or use other than to (i) "circumvent a technological measure that effectively controls access" to a copyrighted work or (ii) "circumvent protection afforded by a technological measure that effectively protects a right of a copyright owner ... in a work or a portion thereof"; or (C) is knowingly marketed for use in "circumventing a technological measure that effectively controls access" to a copyrighted work, or "circumventing protection afforded by a technological measure that effectively protects a right of a copyright owner ... in a work or a portion thereof."[778]

This language appears to create an express and specifically defined contributory infringement analog with respect to technology and devices used to circumvent technology either limiting access to copyrighted works or protecting copyrighted works from infringing activities. The provisions relating to facilitating circumvention essentially create a form of contributory liability independent of the standards for determining contributory copyright infringement generally with respect to copyrighted works.[779]

"[T]o 'circumvent protection afforded by a technological measure' means avoiding, bypassing, removing, deactivating or otherwise impairing a technological measure;" and "a technological measure 'effectively protects a right of a copyright owner...' if the measure, in the ordinary course of its operation, prevents, restricts, or otherwise limits the exercise of a right of a copyright owner ... ."[780] The statute is designed specifically to deal with

---

[778] 17 U.S.C. § 1201 (a) (2), (b) (1).

[779] *See supra*, § 9.5.2.

[780] 17 U.S.C. § 1201 (b) (2).

circumvention of limitations on access to *copyrighted* works, and not generally to impose liability for all acts of decryption or circumvention of technological measures.[781]

> [T]he DMCA applies ... when the product manufacturer prevents all access to the copyrightable material and the alleged infringer responds by marketing a device that circumvents the technological measure designed to guard access to the copyrightable material.
>
> ...
>
> Nowhere in its deliberations over the DMCA did Congress express an interest in creating liability for the circumvention of technological measures designed to prevent consumers from using consumer goods while leaving the copyrightable content of a work unprotected.[782]

These provisions of the DMCA have been upheld against constitutional, First Amendment, challenge.[783]

11.2.1.3. Limitation on Analog Videocassette Recorders

While the use of "black box" devices to defeat copy protection embedded in prerecorded videotaped motion pictures would appear clearly to be violative of Section 1201 (b) (2), discussed above, Chapter 12 further attempts to inhibit copying of copyrighted audiovisual works essentially by penalizing (i) new analog videocassette recorders that are not equipped with specified copy control technology;[784] and (ii) analog videocassette recorders whose design has been modified to eliminate pre-existing conformity to

---

[781] Lexmark International, Inc. v. Static Control Components, 387 F.3d 522 (6th Cir. 2004).

[782] *Id.* at 548, 549. *See* The Chamberlain Group, Inc. v. Skylink Technologies, Inc., 381 F.3d 1178, at 1183 (Fed. Cir. 2004), *cert. denied,* _ S. Ct. _, 2005 WL 218463 (2005) ("Chamberlain=s proposed construction of the DMCA ignores the significant differences between defendants whose accused products enable copying and those, like Skylink, whose accused products enable only legitimate uses of copyrighted software").

[783] Universal City Studios, Inc. v. Corley, 273 F.3d 429, 441 (2d Cir. 2001).

[784] 17 U.S.C. § 1201 (k) (1) (A). Such recorders must conform to the "automatic gain control copy control technology." The prohibition covers analog videocassette recorders in VHS, 8mm, Beta, and NTSC formats but will not apply to Beta until United States sales in any one calendar year are at least one thousand units or to an 8mm format analog videocassette recorder that is not an analog camcorder until United States sales in any one calendar year equal 20,000 units.

copy control technology .[785] The provisions as to new recorders become effective at the end of April, 2000 (eighteen months after the enactment of Chapter 12), and violations are to be treated as violations of Section 1201 (b) (1); the provisions with respect to modification of pre-existing conformity are effective immediately and violations will be deemed an "act of circumvention."[786] The various technical terms are defined in detail.[787]

The requirement of conformity to copy control technology does not apply to "professional" analog videocassette recorders or to the trafficking in legally manufactured, unmodified, previously owned cassette recorders, and is not required with respect to video signals received through a camera lens.[788] Moreover, the use of copy control technology on consumer videocassette recorders is limited[789] to the prevention of "the making of a viewable copy of a pay-per-view, near video on demand, or video on demand transmission or prerecorded tape or disk containing one or more motion pictures or other audiovisual works," without impairing the ability of consumers to make analog copies of other types of programming; "the basic and expanded basic tiers of programming services ... may not be encoded with these technologies at all."[790]

11.2.2. Exceptions and Limitations

As detailed below, Section 1201 contains a number of highly specific exemptions to the circumvention liability provisions. There is no general "fair use" exemption for circumvention activities, and, other than in

---

[785] 17 U.S.C. § 1201 (k) (1) (B). Specifically, this provision refers to pre-existing conformity to the "automatic gain control copy control technology" or to the "four-line color stripe copy control technology." The prohibition covers analog videocassette recorders in VHS or 8mm formats but the prohibition concerning modification of pre-existing four-line color stripe copy control technology does not apply to 8mm analog videocassette recorders that are not also 8mm analog videocassette camcorders.

[786] 17 U.S.C. § 1201 (k) (5).

[787] 17 U.S.C. § 1201 (k) (4).

[788] 17 U.S.C. § 1201 (k) (3).

[789] 17 U.S.C. § 1201 (k) (2).

[790] Conference Report, Joint Explanatory Statement of the Committee of Conference, 105th Cong., 2d Sess. (1998).

connection with the specific exemptions, the purpose for otherwise actionable circumvention is not relevant to determination of liability:

> [T]he DMCA targets the circumvention of digital walls guarding copyrighted material (and trafficking in circumvention tools), but does not concern itself with the use of those materials after circumvention has occurred. Subsection 1201(c)(1) ensures that the DMCA is not read to prohibit the "fair use" of information just because that information was obtained in a manner made illegal by the DMCA.
>
> ...
>
> It would be strange for Congress to open small, carefully limited windows for circumvention to permit fair use in subsection 1201(d) if it then meant to exempt in subsection 1201(c)(1) any circumvention necessary for fair use.
>
> ...
>
> Fair use has never been held to be a guarantee of access to copyrighted material in order to copy it by the fair user's preferred technique or in the format of the original.[791]

11.2.2.1. Non-Profit Libraries, Archives, and Educational Institutions

Nonprofit libraries, archives, and educational institutions are exempt from liability with respect solely to circumvention of access limitation technology engaged in for the purpose of determining whether to acquire a copy of a commercially exploited copyrighted work for noninfringing purposes, if an unprotected copy of the identical work is not reasonably available.[792] Repeated non-exempt circumvention of access limitations by an institution can result in forfeiture of the exemption.[793]

11.2.2.2. Law Enforcement, Intelligence, and Other Government Activities

A broad exemption with respect to all otherwise prohibited circumvention activity is provided for law enforcement, intelligence, and

---

[791] Universal City Studios, Inc. v. Corley, 273 F.3d 429, 443, 444, n. 13, 459 (2d Cir. 2001).

[792] 17 U.S.C. § 1201 (d).

[793] 17 U.S.C. § 1201 (d) (3) (B).

other governmental activities, including "activities carried out in order to identify and address the vulnerabilities of a government computer, computer system, or computer network."[794]

11.2.2.3. Reverse Engineering of Computer Programs to Achieve Interoperability

Circumvention of access limitation technology by one with the lawful right to use an access-protected copy of a computer program is exempt from liability if it is not otherwise infringing and if done "for the sole purpose of analyzing those elements of the program that are necessary to achieve interoperability of an independently created computer program with other programs ..."[795] For purposes of enabling such analysis, or achieving interoperability, the development and use of technological means to circumvent technological access limitation or protection is exempt from liability.[796]

11.2.2.4. Encryption Research on Published Works

It is not a violation of the prohibition on circumvention of technological access limitation applied to a copy, phonorecord, performance, or display of a published work if that circumvention is done by one in lawful possession of the encrypted work "in the course of an act of good faith encryption research."[797] For the exemption to apply, the act of circumvention must be necessary to conduct such encryption research, a good faith effort had to have been made to obtain authorization for it, and the act may not otherwise constitute an act of infringement.[798] "Encryption research" is defined as:

> activities necessary to identify and analyze flaws and vulnerabilities of encryption technology applied to copyrighted works, if these activities are

---

[794] 17 U.S.C. § 1201 (e).

[795] 17 U.S.C. § 1201 (f) (1). "Interoperability" means "the ability of computer programs to exchange inforjation, and of such programs mutually to use the information which has been exchanged." 17 U.S.C. § 1201 (f) (4).

[796] 17 U.S.C. § 1201 (f) (2).

[797] 17 U.S.C. § 1201 (g) (2).

[798] *Id.*

conducted to advance the state of knowledge in the field of encryption technology or to assist in the development of encryption products.[799]

Exemption is also provided with respect to the development and use of technological means to circumvent technological measures in order to perform such acts of encryption research.[800]

Factors to be considered in determining whether a person qualifies for the "encryption research" exemption include the extent and manner of dissemination of the information derived from the research—dissemination that is "reasonably calculated to advance the state of knowledge or development of encryption technology," as opposed to that which may facilitate infringement or violations of law; whether the person involved "is engaged in a legitimate course of study, is employed, or is appropriately trained or experienced, in the field of encryption technology;" and whether the person provides notice of the findings of the research, and appropriate documentation, to the copyright owner of the work involved.[801]

11.2.2.5. Protection of Personally Identifying Information

It is not a violation of the prohibition on circumvention of technological measures that control access to work, (i) if those measures, or the protected work, contain "the capability of collecting or disseminating personally identifying information reflecting the online activities of a natural person who seeks to gain access to the work protected," and collect and disseminate such information "without providing conspicuous notice of such collection of dissemination to such person, and without providing such person with the capability to prevent or respect such collection of dissemination;" and (ii) the only effect of the act of circumvention is identifying and disabling the capability of so collecting or disseminating personally identifying information, and is carried out solely for the purpose of preventing such collection or dissemination, and is not otherwise in violation of any law.[802]

---

[799] 17 U.S.C. § 1201 (g) (1) (A). "Encryption technology" means "the scrambling and descrambling of information using matehmatical formulas or algorithms." 17 U.S.C. § 1201 (g) (1) (B).

[800] 17 U.S.C. § 1201 (g) (4).

[801] 17 U.S.C. § 1201 (g) (3).

[802] 17 U.S.C. § 1201 (i) (1).

11.2.2.6. Security Testing

It is not a violation of the prohibition on circumvention of technological measures that control access to work, "to engage in an act of security testing," that does not otherwise constitute infringement or a violation of law,[803] or to develop or use technological means solely to perform such acts of security testing.[804] For these purposes, "security testing" means "accessing the computer, computer system, or computer network, solely for the purpose of good faith testing, investigating or correcting a security fall vulnerability, with the authorization of the owner or operator of such computer, computer system, or computer network."[805]

11.3. Copyright Management Information

"Copyright management information" refers to information identifying a copyrighted work, such as the name of the author, the title of the work, such information as is set forth in notice of copyright, terms and conditions for use of the work, identifying numbers or symbols linking referring to such information, the names of performers, writers, directors and others credited with a work (except with respect to public performances of works by radio and television broadcast stations), and such other information as the Register of Copyrights prescribes by regulation.[806]

11.3.1. Impairment of Copyright Management Information

Section 1202 subjects to liability (i) one who provides false copyright management information or distributes or imports or distribution false copyright management information, knowingly and with the intent to

---

[803] 17 U.S.C. § 1201 (j) (2).

[804] 17 U.S.C. § 1201 (j) (4).

[805] 17 U.S.C. § 1201 (j) (1). Factors to be considered in determining application of the exemption, include whether the information derived from the security testing "was used solely to promote the security of the owner or operator" of the computer or computer system involved are shared with the developer of such system, and whether the information was used are maintained in a manner that does not facilitate infringement or other violation of law. 17 U.S.C. § 1201 (j) (3).

[806] 17 U.S.C. § 1202 (c).

induce, enable, facilitate or conceal infringement;[807] and (ii) one who, without authority, and with knowledge or reasonable grounds to know that such action will induce, enable, facilitate or conceal infringement, intentionally removes or alters any copyright management information, distributes or imports for distribution copyright management information with knowledge that such information has been removed or altered, or distributes, imports for distribution or publicly performs works with knowledge that copyright management information has been removed or altered.[808]

11.3.2. Exemptions and Limitations

11.3.2.1. Law Enforcement and Other Government Activities

These provisions do not apply so as to prohibit "lawfully authorized investigative, protective, information security, or intelligence activity" of governmental bodies.[809]

11.3.2.2. Transmissions

No liability will attach to analog transmissions of broadcast stations, or cable systems, or those who provide programming to broadcast stations or cable systems that impair copyright management information if avoidance of the prohibited activity "is not technically feasible or would create an undue financial hardship" and if it was not intended by such activity to "induce, enable, facilitate, or conceal infringement."[810] Separate exemption is provided for digital transmissions, dependent upon the development of a voluntary industry standard for the placement of copyright management information (interim, tightly circumscribed exemptions are provided).[811]

---

[807] 17 U.S.C. § 1202 (a).

[808] 17 U.S.C. § 1202 (b).

[809] 17 U.S.C. § 1202 (d).

[810] 17 U.S.C. § 1202 (e) (1).

[811] 17 U.S.C. § 1202 (e) (2).

11.4. Enforcement and Remedies

11.4.1. Civil Remedies

"Any person injured by a violation of section 1201 or 1202 may bring a civil action in an appropriate United States district court for such violation."[812]

11.4.1.1. Injunctive and Related Relief

The court may, in its discretion, grant temporary and permanent injunctive relief to prevent or restrain a violation, "but in no event shall [the court] impose a prior restraint on free speech or the press protected under the first amendment to the Constitution."[813]

During the pendency of an action, the court may order the impounding "of any device or product that is in the custody or control of the alleged violator and that the court has reasonable cause to believe was involved in a violation."[814] As part of its final judgment or decree, where a violation is found, the court may order "the remedial modification or the destruction of any device or product involved in the violation that is in the custody or control of the violator or has been impounded."[815]

11.4.1.2. Damages: Actual and Statutory

The successful plaintiff is entitled to actual damages suffered as a result of the violation, and "any profits of the violator that are attributable to the violation and are not taken into account in computing the actual damages."[816]

In lieu of actual damages, the successful plaintiff may elect, at any time before final judgment is entered, to recover statutory damages ranging from $200 to $2,500 for each violation of section 1201 (relating to circumvention of technological measures) and ranging from $2,500 to $25,000 for each violation of section 1202 (copyright management information), the specific

---

[812] 17 U.S.C. § 1203 (a).

[813] 17 U.S.C. § 1202 (b) (1).

[814] 17 U.S.C. § 1203 (b) (2).

[815] 17 U.S.C. § 1203 (b) (6).

[816] 17 U.S.C. § 1203 (c) (2).

amount to be determined "as the court considers just."[817] Given the similarity of statutory language, the United States Supreme Court holding of a constitutional right to jury determination in claims involving statutory damages for copyright infringement[818] presumably is applicable to these statutory damages claims.

11.4.1.3. Increasing or Reducing Damages

Where the injured party proves that the defendant violated the sections 1201 or 1202 within three years after entry of a final judgment for another violation of those sections, "the court may increase the award of damages up to triple the amount that would otherwise be awarded, as the court considers just."[819]

Conversely, the court *may*, in its discretion, reduce or remit the total award of damages in any case in which the violator proves that it was not aware and had no reason to believe that its acts constituted a violation.[820] In the special case of violation by a nonprofit library, archives, or educational institution, the court *shall* remit damages if the library, archives, or educational institution proves that it was not aware and had no reason to believe that its acts constituted a violation.[821]

11.4.1.4. Costs and Counsel Fees

The court, in its discretion, may allow the recovery of costs by or against any party other than the United States or an officer thereof, and may award to the prevailing party reasonable attorneys' fees.[822] The United States Supreme Court determination that prevailing plaintiffs and prevailing defendants are to be treated alike in the exercise of the court's discretion in awarding attorney's fees[823] would appear to be applicable here.

---

[817] 17 U.S.C. § 1203 (c) (3).

[818] *See supra*, § 10.2.2.3.

[819] 17 U.S.C. § 1203 (c) (4).

[820] 17 U.S.C. § 1203 (c) (5) (A).

[821] 17 U.S.C. § 1203 (c) (5) (B).

[822] 17 U.S.C. §§ 1203 (b) (4) and (5).

[823] *See supra*, § 10.3.

11.4.2. Criminal Penalties

Willful violation, "for purposes of commercial advantage or private financial gain" (except by a nonprofit library, archives, or educational institution) may result in fines and/or imprisonment; criminal proceedings must be commenced within five years after the cause of action arose.[824]

---

[824] 17 U.S.C. § 1204. The fine may be up to $500,000 and/or imprisonment up to five years, or both, for the first offense; the fine may be up to $1,000,000 and/or imprisonment up to ten years, for any subsequent offense.

Part II: Patent

§1. SOURCES OF UNITED STATES PATENT LAW[1]

1.1. Constitutional Foundation

The foundation for American patent law, as for copyright law, is embodied in Article I, Section 8, Clause 8 of the United States Constitution. This constitutional provision empowers Congress:

> To promote the Progress of Science and useful Arts, by securing for limited Times to Authors and Inventors the exclusive Right to their respective Writings and Discoveries.[2]

The United States Supreme Court understands this clause to be "both a grant of power and a limitation." According to the Court:

> This qualified authority, unlike the power often exercised in the sixteenth and seventeenth centuries by the English Crown, is limited to the promotion of advances in the "useful Arts." It was written against this backdrop of the practices—eventually curtailed by the Statute of Monopolies—of the Crown in granting monopolies to court favorites in goods or businesses which had long before been enjoyed by the public. ... The Congress in the exercise of the patent power may not overreach the restraints imposed by the stated constitutional purpose.[3]

James Madison, one of America's more prominent founders, wrote in The Federalist #43 that "the utility of [Article I, Section 8, Clause 8] will scarcely be questioned. The copyright of authors has been solemnly adjudged, in Great Britain, to be a right of common law. The right to useful inventions seems with equal reason to belong to the inventors. The public good fully coincides in both cases with the claims of individuals."[4] Thus, the drafters of the American Constitution understood that patent law seeks to strike a balance between the promotion of technological creativity and the dissemination of its fruits.

---

[1] Much of the material of this Section is adapted from DONALD S. CHISUM, CRAIG ALLEN NARD, ET. AL., PRINCIPLES OF PATENT LAW (Foundation Press 1998).

[2] U.S. CONST. art. 1, § 8, cl. 8

[3] Graham v. John Deere Co., 383 U.S. 1, 5-6 (1966).

[4] THE FEDERALIST, No. 43 (James Madison).

1.2. Statutory Foundation

The present statutory scheme for American patent law is embodied in Title 35 of the United States Code. To fully appreciate what led up to Title 35, a brief history of the numerous statutory enactments may be helpful.

The Patent Act of 1790, America's first patent statute, was signed into law on April 10, 1790, by President George Washington.[5] The 1790 Act authorized the issuance of patents for "any useful art, manufacture, engine, machine, or device, or any improvement therein not before known or used."[6] The Act did not create a patent office, but instead designated a patent board that would *examine* patent applications, comprising a specification and drawings, to determine if "the invention or discovery [was] sufficiently useful and important" so as to merit a patent. The board, self-dubbed the "Commissioners for the Promotion of the Useful Arts," consisted of the Secretary of State (Thomas Jefferson), Secretary of War (Henry Knox), and the Attorney General (Edmund Randolph). The first patent under the 1790 Act was issued to Samuel Hopkins for a method of "making Pot ash and Pearl ash by a new apparatus and Process."

The examination system under the 1790 Act proved to be too burdensome on the three-member patent board, and in 1793 a new patent act was on the books. Although the 1793 Act contained several fundamental patent law concepts that are extant today, the Act did away with the patent board and the examination proceedings and implemented a registration system, clerical in nature, like that which existed in England.[7] Needless to say, the lack of an examination requirement attracted several fraudulent or

---

[5] Act of Apr. 10, 1790, ch. 7, 1 Stat. 109.

[6] A total of 55 patents were issued under the 1790 Act. It is interesting to note that the Patent Act of 1790 was passed, on April 5, 1790, by the Congress of twelve states. Rhode Island did not join the Union as the thirteenth state until May 29, 1790, 49 days after President Washington signed the bill. *See* KENNETH W. DOBYNS, THE PATENT OFFICE PONY - A HISTORY OF THE EARLY PATENT OFFICE 22 (1994).

[7] *Id.* at 35 ("The Act of 1793 went from the extreme of rigid examination to the opposite extreme of no examination at all. The Patent Board was abolished. The State Department was to register patents, and the courts were to determine whether the patents were valid").

duplicative patents.[8] Nevertheless, the registration system lasted for forty-three years, until, on July 4, 1836, Congress enacted what is generally acknowledged to be the foundation of the modern patent system in the United States.[9] The 1836 Patent Act reintroduced the requirement under the 1790 Act that patent applications be examined for novelty and utility.[10] In 1850, the Supreme Court, in *Hotchkiss v. Greenwood*,[11] established what is presently referred to as the nonobviousness requirement of patentability. Applicants, as under the 1790 and 1793 Acts, were required to submit a specification, drawings, and models with their application. In addition to the examination requirement, the 1836 Act, *by law*, made the Patent Office a distinct and separate bureau in the Department of State and created the position of Commissioner of Patents.[12] The Act also created the present patent numbering system[13] and allowed for a patent applicant to appeal an examiner's refusal to issue a patent. The appeal was heard by a three-member board appointed by the Secretary of State.

The next major statutory revisions came in 1870 and 1952. The 1870 Act essentially retained the 1836 Act's provisions. However, because the courts found it increasingly difficult to discover what the invention was and the distinction between new and old was sometimes blurred, the 1870 Act,

---

[8] *See* Edward C. Walterscheid, *To Promote the Progress of Useful Arts: American Patent Law and Administration, 1787-1836 (Part I)*, 79 J. PAT. & TRAD. OFF. SOC'Y 61, 73-74 (1997); BRUCE BUGBEE, GENESIS OF AMERICAN PATENT AND COPYRIGHT LAW 150-53 (1967).

[9] *See* BUGBEE, *supra*, note 8, at 152 (1967)("With the act of 1836, the United States patent system came of age."); Walterscheid, *supra*, note 8, at 61.

[10] As noted, the 1793 Act did away with the examination requirement of the 1790 Act which in turn led to fraudulent and duplicative patents. A Senate Report accompanying the 1836 Act cited these fraudulent and duplicative patents as some of the "evils" that existed under 1793 Act. *See* Senate Report Accompanying Senate Bill No. 239, 24th Cong., 1st Sess. (April 1836); *see also*, DONALD S. CHISUM, I CHISUM ON PATENTS OV-5-6 (1997).

[11] 52 U.S. (11 How.) 248 (1850).

[12] Henrey Leavitt Ellsworth (1791-1858), one of the twin sons of Justice Oliver Ellsworth, was appointed as the first Commissioner of Patents in 1836.

[13] Patent Number 1 was issued to Senator John Ruggles of Maine, who was primarily responsible for the passage of the 1836 Act. Prior to 1836, patents were identified by the date they were issued.

one could argue, placed more emphasis on the importance of the patent *claim* and required the patent applicant to define more distinctly what her invention was.[14]

A brief discussion of the Supreme Court's attitude towards patents prior to the 1952 Act will shed light on the Act itself as well as the driving forces behind the Act. From 1890 to 1930, patents were viewed favorably by the Court; but from about 1930 to 1950, the Court approached patents with a great deal of suspicion, emphasizing the monopolistic and social costs aspects of patents.

The 1952 Act was largely a response to the previous twenty years of the Supreme Court's anti-patent attitude. A significant portion of the 1952 Act, codified in Title 35 of the United States Code, governs American patent law to the present day. Further amendments to the patent laws occurred in 1984, and most recently, important changes were ushered in by the General Agreement on Tariffs and Trade (GATT) and the North American Free Trade Agreement (NAFTA). For example, the term for patents filed on or after June 8, 1995, is twenty years from date of filing. Prior to GATT, the term of a patent was seventeen years from date of issuance. Furthermore, evidence of inventive activity (*i.e.*, conception and reduction to practice) outside of the United States may be used to establish date of invention, whereas before, only inventive activity within the U.S. could be used.

---

[14] *See* RISDALE ELLIS, PATENT CLAIMS 3 (1949) (Claims under the 1836 Act "severed merely to call attention to what the inventor considered the salient features of his invention. The drawing and description were the main thing, the claims were a mere adjunct thereto. ... The idea that the claim is just as important if not more important than the description and drawings did not develop until the Act of 1870 or thereabouts"); *see also*, DELLER, PATENT CLAIMS (2d ed. 1971):

> Along with the development of the importance of the claim, there was another far-reaching change in the attitude of both the Patent Office and the courts as to the way in which claims should be drawn and interpreted. To appreciate this change, it is necessary to go back to the fundamental principles underlying the definition of what is new and the various modes of distinguishing what is new from what is old. Generally speaking, compliance with the requirements of the early statutes for a distinction between new and the old was not perfect. The problem of discovering in the early patents what invention was involved was a burden which was carried by the courts and the public. The desirability of shifting this burden to the Patent Office and to the patentee himself soon became apparent.

The most recent amendment to the patent law came in 1999 with the American Inventors Protection Act (AIPA). Prior to the AIPA, patents were kept secret by the PTO. The AIPA as codified in the United States Code and the Federal Regulations, however, authorizes publication of applications filed on or after 29 November 2000. Pursuant to 35 U.S.C. 122 (b) (1) (2000), subject to some exceptions, "each application for a patent shall be published...promptly after the expiration of a period of eighteen months from the earliest filing date." The exceptions to publication are set forth in 35 U.S.C. 122 (b) (2) (2001).

A particularly significant development in American patent law was the creation of the United States Court of Appeals for the Federal Circuit. The Federal Circuit was created by Congress in 1982[15] and is America's thirteenth federal appellate court. The court was created primarily in response to a spree of forum shopping in patent litigation, a lack of uniformity in our patent laws, and a high invalidity rate among litigated patents.[16]

The Federal Circuit sits in Washington, D.C., and in any place where the other regional circuit courts may sit pursuant to 28 U.S.C. Section 48(a), and comprises twelve active judges. Unlike the regional circuit courts, the Federal Circuit has unlimited geographic jurisdiction nationwide with broad subject matter jurisdiction. As such, the court enjoys exclusive jurisdiction over cases arising "under any Act of Congress relating to

---

[15] Federal Courts Improvement Act of 1982, P.l. 97-164, 96 Stat. 25 (April 2, 1982). This Act merged the Court of Claims, which had seven judges, and the Court of Customs and Patent Appeals, which had five judges. The Federal Circuit came into existence on October 1, 1982. *See* THE UNITED STATES COURT OF APPEALS FOR THE FEDERAL CIRCUIT: A HISTORY (1991).

[16] *See* H.R. REP. NO. 312, 97th Cong., 1st Sess. 20-22 (1981)("[S]ome circuit courts are regarded as 'pro-patent' and others 'anti-patent,' and much time and money is expended in 'shopping' for a favorable venue." Furthermore, "the validity of a patent is too dependent upon geography (*i.e.*, the accident of judicial venue) to make effective business planning possible . ... A single court of appeals for patent cases will promote certainty where it is lacking to a significant degree and will reduce, if not eliminate, the forum-shopping that now occurs"); *see also* S. REP. NO. 275, 97 Cong., 1st Sess. 5 (1981)("The creation of the Court of Appeals for the Federal Circuit will produce desirable uniformity in this area of [patent] law. Such uniformity will reduce the forum-shopping that is common to patent litigation").

patents," as well as over cases in several other areas of the law.[17] Furthermore, the court's jurisdiction includes appeals of non-patent claims that accompany patent claims. For example, an appeal regarding antitrust claims will go to the Federal Circuit if the case in the district court also involved claims arising under the patent laws. In this type of situation, although the court applies its own law when reviewing the patent claims, it applies the substantive law of that district court's regional circuit court when reviewing the antitrust claims.[18] Also, the Federal Circuit decides procedural issues that are unrelated to the patent issues in dispute by applying the law of the relevant regional circuit court.[19]

§2. CONDITIONS OF PATENTABILITY

Before the particulars of American patent law are discussed, it should be noted, as an initial matter, that inventors may opt for trade secret protection in lieu of patent protection. Trade secret law offers an extremely important means of protecting a firm's commercial information. Indeed, many industries rely heavily on trade secrecy *vis-à-vis* patent law, particularly for process-related inventions.[20] There are important distinctions between patent law and trade secret law. First, information eligible for trade secret protection may or may not be eligible for patent protection. Trade secrets include not only technologic information, but also customer lists, business plans, and marketing strategies. Also, there is no novelty requirement for trade secret protection; only that the commercial

---

[17] See 28 U.S.C. §§ 1338 and 1295. See also H.R. REP. NO. 312, supra, note 16, at 19 ("The proposed new court is not a 'specialized court.' Its jurisdiction is not limited to one type of case, or even to two or three types of cases. Rather, it has a varied docket spanning a broad range of legal issues and types of cases."); S. REP. NO. 275, supra, note 16, at 6 ("[The Federal Circuit's] rich docket assures that the work of the ... court will be a broad variety of legal problems. Moreover, the subject matter of the new court will be sufficiently mixed to prevent any special interest from dominating it").

[18] See Atari, Inc. v. JS & A Group, Inc., 747 F.2d 1422, 1438-40 (Fed. Cir. 1984).

[19] See Panduit Corp. v. All States Plastic Mgh. Co., 744 F.2d 1564 (Fed. Cir. 1984); see also, Joan E. Schaffner, Federal Circuit "Choice of Law": Erie Through the Looking Glass, 81 IOWA L. REV. 1173 (1996).

[20] See WESLEY M. COHEN, RICHARD R. NELSON, AND JOHN P. WALSH, PROTECTING THEIR INTELLECTUAL ASSETS: APPROPRIABILITY CONDITIONS AND WHY U.S. MANUFACTURING FIRMS PATENT (OR NOT) (NBER Working Paper Series 7552, 2000).

information provide an economic advantage. Second, trade secret protection can last in perpetuity as long as the information remains secret and maintains its value whereas a patent expires twenty years from its filing date. Third, with the exception of the Economic Espionage Act, trade secret protection is a creature of state law and is recognized in one form or another by every jurisdiction. Patent law is a strictly federal regime.

A patent applicant is entitled to a patent only if his invention is new,[21] adequately disclosed,[22] useful,[23] nonobvious,[24] and fits within statutorily defined subject matter.[25] These patentability requirements secure a *quid pro quo* for society. The disclosure requirements ensure that the patentee discloses to the public how to make and use the patented invention so that others, namely persons of ordinary skill in the art, can improve upon or design around the patentee's claimed invention. Because it would be nonsensical to grant a patent on an invention that already exists, the novelty requirement ensures that the inventor has contributed something new to society, something not previously known or used.[26] The utility requirement is fairly straightforward and requires that in exchange for patent protection, the patent applicant disclose an invention that is useful and operative. The nonobvious requirement builds upon the novelty requirement and raises the patentability hurdle by denying patent protection to inventions that are "obvious" to a person of ordinary skill in the art. Thus, even if an invention is novel, it may nevertheless be unpatentable. Lastly, the invention must fall

---

[21] 35 U.S.C. § 102 (1994).

[22] 35 U.S.C. § 112 (1994).

[23] 35 U.S.C. § 101 (1994).

[24] 35 U.S.C. § 103 (1994).

[25] 35 U.S.C. § 101 (1994).

[26] *See* Kewanee Oil Co. v. Bicron Corp., 416 U.S. 470, 481 (1974). Although it is accepted that prior art is knowledge that is available to the public, "it has been unusual that opinions have explained the real reason for the denial of patent rights, which is the basic principle (to which there are minor exceptions) that no patent should be granted which withdraws from the public domain technology already available to the public. It is available, in legal theory at least, when it is described in the world's accessible literature, including patents, or has been publicly known or in the public use or on sale 'in this country.'" Lamb-Weston, Inc. v. McCain Foods, Ltd., 78 F.3d 540, 549 (Fed. Cir. 1996) (Newman, J., dissenting) (*quoting* Kimberly-Clark Corp. v. Johnson & Johnson and Personal Prods. Co., 745 F.2d 1437 (Fed. Cir.1984)).

within statutorily classified subject matter (*e.g.*, process or composition of matter) and, for example, cannot be a naturally occurring substance or a fundamental mathematical formula (*e.g.*, $E = MC^2$). Taken collectively, these requirements assure that a patent applicant has made a genuine contribution to society in exchange for patent protection.[27]

2.1. Disclosure Requirements

It would be difficult to overstate the importance of the patent law's disclosure requirements, which are contained in the first two paragraphs of 35 U.S.C. § 112. The patent's disclosure provides the foundation for the claims and hence for the scope of patent protection.[28] Specifically, Section 112 provides in part:

[¶ 1] The specification shall contain a *written description* of the invention, and of the manner and process of making and using it, in such full, clear, concise, and exact terms as to *enable* any person skilled in the art to which it pertains, or with which it is most nearly connected, to make and use the same, and shall set forth the *best mode* contemplated by the inventor of carrying out his invention.

[¶ 2] The specification shall conclude with one or more claims *particularly pointing out and distinctly claiming* the subject matter which the applicant regards as his invention.[29]

---

[27] *See Kewanee Oil,* at 480-81. Patent law promotes the Constitutional provision for the progress of the useful arts "by offering a right of exclusion for a limited period as an incentive to inventors to risk the often enormous costs in terms of time, research, and development." *Id.* at 480. Further, patent law not only introduces new product and process technology into the economy, but also provides "employment and better lives ... ." *Id.*

[28] *Compare* O'Reilly v. Morse, 56 (15 How.) 62 (1854)(finding Morse's eighth claim too broad because specification was not enabling and not shown to have been invented, which claimed "every improvement where the motive power is the electric or galvanic current, and the result is the marking or printing intelligible characters, signs, or letters at a distance"), *and* United States v. American Bell Tel. Co., 128 U.S. 315 (1888) (upholding as enabling, Bell's claim to the "method of, an apparatus for, transmitting vocal or other sounds telegraphically, ... by causing electrical undulation" because the invention was limited to a method and apparatus).

[29] 35 U.S.C. § 112 (1994)(emphasis added).

These four requirements, (1) enablement, (2) best mode, (3) written description, and (4) clear claiming, must be satisfied for a patent to issue. The disclosure must support the scope of the patent claim. Section 112 requires the patentee to give the public "fair notice of what the patentee and the Patent and Trademark Office have agreed constitute the metes and bounds of the claimed invention"[30] and to disseminate to the public information concerning the patented subject matter. This dual notice/dissemination function allows third parties to avoid conduct that would infringe the patent while providing the interested public with information that enlarges the storehouse of knowledge, and may also help others to improve upon or design around the claimed invention—thus leading to further technological progress. As the Supreme Court stated in *Markman v. Westview Instruments, Inc.*:

> [t]he limits of a patent must be known for the protection of the patentee, the encouragement of the inventive genius of others and the assurance that the subject of the patent will be dedicated ultimately to the public. Otherwise, a zone of uncertainty which enterprise and experimentation may enter only at the risk of infringement claims would discourage invention only a little less than unequivocal foreclosure of the field, and [t]he public [would] be deprived of rights supposed to belong to it, without being clearly told what it is that limits these rights.[31]

2.1.1. Enablement

The enablement requirement of Section 112 demands the inventor provide sufficient information in the specification to enable a person skilled in the relevant art to make and use the claimed invention without "undue experimentation." The enablement requirement is often considered to be at the heart of the *quid pro quo* between the government and the inventor. In exchange for the powerful right to exclude, the inventor must inform the public how to make and use the invention so others, namely competitors of the inventor, can improve upon the claimed invention.[32]

---

[30] London v. Carson Pirie Scott & Co., 946 F.2d 1534, 1538 (Fed. Cir. 1991).

[31] 116 S.Ct. 1384, 1395 (1996).

[32] This policy was first expressed by Chief Justice Marshall in Grant v. Raymond, 31 U.S. (6 Pet.) 218 (1832) (stating the enablement requirement "is necessary in order to give the public, after the privilege shall expire, the advantage for which the privilege

Although the Section 112 does expressly resolve the question of at what time the disclosure must be enabling, the Federal Circuit and its predecessor court have held that the sufficiency of the patent's disclosure "must be judged as of its filing date."[33] Information that is developed or becomes available after that date cannot be considered in determining disclosure sufficiency. Similarly, post-filing date developments that enable previously unknown variations cannot be relied upon to establish nonenablement.[34]

The test for compliance with the enablement requirement is whether "undue experimentation" is required to make and use the claimed invention. In determining what constitutes undue experimentation, the Federal Circuit has applied a standard of reasonableness. The test is not merely quantitative because a significant amount of routine experimentation is permitted. The court will consider several factors in determining whether undue experimentation is needed, including: (1) the quantity of experimentation necessary, (2) the amount of direction or guidance presented, (3) presence or absence of working examples, (4) the nature of the invention, (5) the state of the prior art, (6) the relative skill of those in the art, (7) the predictability or unpredictability of the art, and (8) the breadth of the claims.[35]

In addition to serving as an information dissemination device, the enablement requirement also requires the specification's enablement be commensurate with the scope of the claims. A patentee cannot claim more than he discloses.[36] An example of the claim limiting function of the enablement requirement can be found in the famous case of *O'Reilly v. Morse*.[37] Samuel Morse, known principally for his work in telegraphy, owned a patent that had eight claims. The patent described

"a new and useful apparatus for, and a system of, transmitting intelligence between distant points by means of electro-

---

is allowed, and is the foundation of the power to issue the patent").

[33] *See* In re Glass, 492 F.2d 1228 (C.C.P.A. 1974).

[34] *See* United States Steel Corp. v. Phillips Petroleum Co., 865 F.2d 1247, 1251 (Fed. Cir. 1989); In re Hogan, 559 F.2d 595 (C.C.P.A. 1977).

[35] *See* In re Wands, 858 F.2d 731, 737 (Fed. Cir. 1988).

[36] *See* National Recovery Technologies, Inc. v. Magnetic Separation Systems, Inc., 166 F.3d 1190, 1195 (Fed. Cir. 1999).

[37] 56 U.S. 62 (1853).

magnetism, which puts in motion machinery for producing sounds or signs, and recording said signs upon paper or other suitable material, which invention I denominate the American ElectroBMagnetic Telegraph."

The patent also set forth the instruments to carry out the transmission and the famous "Code." Claims 1-7 were covered the machinery for "transmitting intelligence" by employing principles of electro-magnetism. But claim 8 was more expansive:

> I do not propose to limit myself to the specific machinery, or parts of machinery, described in the foregoing specifications and claims; *the essence of my invention being the use of the motive power of the electric or galvanic current, which I call electro-magnetism, however, developed,* for making or printing intelligible characters, letters, or signs, at any distances, being a new application of that power, of which I claim to be the first inventor or discovered.

The Supreme Court held claim eight invalid because the breadth of this claim was not commensurate with the specification, which did not disclose all uses and improvements of the motive power of the electric or galvanic current. In other words, Morse "claims an exclusive right to use a manner and process which he has not described and indeed had not invented, and therefore could not describe when he obtained his patent." The Court was particularly concerned with stifling the ability or willingness of others to improve on Morse's invention. According to the Court:

> If this claim can be maintained, it matters not by what process or machinery the result is accomplished. For aught that we now know some future inventor, in the onward march of science, may discover a mode of writing or printing at a distance by means of the electric or galvanic current, without using any part of the process or combination set forth in the plaintiff's specification...But yet if it is covered by this patent the inventor could not use it, nor the public have the benefit of it without the permission of this patentee. [W]hile he shuts the door against inventions of other persons, the patentee would be able to avail himself of new discoveries in the properties and powers of electromagnetism which scientific men might bring to light.[38]

---

[38] *Id. See also* The Incandescent Lamp Patent, 159 U.S. 465 (1895) (finding claims not commensurate with specification).

2.1.2. Best Mode

Compliance with Section 112 requires that "[t]he specification ... set forth the best mode contemplated by the inventor of carrying out his invention."[39] The best mode requirement prohibits an inventor from applying for a patent while concealing from the public a preferred embodiment of the invention, which the inventor has in fact conceived.[40]

The best mode analysis involves two inquiries, one subjective and the other objective: the first inquiry is whether the inventor subjectively contemplated and disclosed the best mode of practicing the claimed invention at the time of filing; and the second inquiry is whether, objectively, the specification adequately discloses the best mode such that a person of ordinary skill in the art could practice it.[41]

Because "Congress ... specifically limited the best mode requirement to that contemplated by the inventor," the best mode requirement is based upon the inventor's knowledge at the time that the patent application is filed.[42] Consequently, the Federal Circuit has held that there is no best mode violation even though the specification did not disclose a superior process that was known by the patentee's employees, but unknown to the actual inventor of the patented process.[43] Because only the inventor's knowledge

---

[39] 35 U.S.C. § 112, 1st ¶ (1994). The best mode requirement is distinct from the enablement requirement. See Glaxo Inc. v. Novopharm Ltd., 52 F.3d 1043, 1050 (Fed. Cir. 1995):

> "Enablement looks to placing the subject matter of the claims generally in the possession of the public." ... Best mode looks to whether specific instrumentalities and techniques have been developed by the inventor and known to him at the time of filing as the best way of carrying out the invention. ... The enablement requirement, thus, looks to the objective knowledge of one of ordinary skill in the art, while the best mode inquiry is a subjective, factual one, looking to the state of the mind of the inventor.

[40] See Chemcast Corp. v. Arco Indus. Corp., 913 F.2d 923, 926 (Fed. Cir. 1990); Spectra-Physics, Inc. v. Coherent, Inc., 827 F.2d 1524, 1532 (Fed. Cir. 1987); Dana Corp. v. IPC Limited Partnership, 860 F.2d 415, 419 (Fed. Cir. 1988).

[41] See Great Northern Corp. v. Henry Molded Prods., Inc., 94 F.3d 1569, 1571 (Fed. Cir. 1996); United States Gypsum Co. v. National Gypsum Co., 74 F.3d 1209, 1212 (Fed. Cir. 1996); Transco Prods., Inc. v. Performance Contracting, Inc., 38 F.3d 551, 560 (Fed. Cir. 1994).

[42] Glaxo, Inc., 52 F.3d at 1052.

[43] Id.

is relevant for a best mode violation, it is improper to impute a third party's knowledge of a preferred embodiment onto the inventor.[44] In addition, there is no duty to update the best mode disclosure *after* the application is filed, unless the applicant introduces new matter, in which case he would have to file a continuation-in-part application.[45]

Even when an inventor discloses the best mode, a Section 112 violation will occur if the disclosure is so objectively inadequate that it effectively conceals the best mode from the public.[46] That is, the "quality of an applicant's best mode disclosure is so poor" that those skilled in the art could not practice it.[47]

Notwithstanding the best mode disclosure requirement, an inventor is not required to disclose "commercial considerations" or "production details," such as particular materials, sources of materials, manufacturing methods, or specific techniques if the information is readily known in the art. For example, in *Wahl Instruments, Inc. v. Acvious, Inc.,*[48] Acvious defended an infringement suit on the ground that Wahl's patent failed to disclose "manufacturing techniques . . . materials and sources of supply for materials used in [the invention]."[49] The district court ruled that the claims were invalid for failure to disclose the best mode; however, the Federal Circuit reversed, holding that "there is no mechanical rule that a best mode violation occurs because the inventor failed to disclose particular manufacturing techniques beyond that information sufficient for enablement."[50] In addition to inquiring into the inventor's beliefs, the scope

---

[44] *Id.*

[45] *See* Transco Prod., Inc. v. Performance Contracting, Inc., 38 F.3d 551, 557-59 (Fed. Cir. 1994).

[46] *See* U.S. Gypsum Co., 74 F.3d at 1215; *Transco Prods.*, 38 F.3d at 560.

[47] *U.S. Gypsum,* 74 F.3d at 1215.

[48] 950 F.2d 1575 (Fed. Cir. 1991).

[49] *Id.* at 1580

[50] *Id.*:

[A] requirement for routine details to be disclosed because they were selected as the "best" for manufacturing or fabrication would lay a trap for patentees whenever a device has been made prior to filing for the patent. The inventor would merely have to be interrogated with increasing specificity as to steps or material selected as "best" to make the device. A fortiori, he could hardly say the choice is not what he thought was "best"

of an invention, and the skill in the art, one must consider whether any missing information would be readily known by those skilled in the art.[51] If it is known, then there is no best mode violation.

2.1.3. Written Description

The first paragraph of § 112 requires that the specification contain a "written description of the invention ... ."[52] Unlike the enablement requirement, which demands that an inventor disclose how to make and use an invention,[53] the purpose of the written description requirement is to convey with reasonable clarity to those skilled in the art that an inventor was in possession of the claimed subject matter when the patent application was filed.[54] As long as the disclosure reasonably conveys to persons skilled in the art that the inventor had possession of the subject matter in question, the written description requirement will be judged satisfied.[55] Under proper circumstances, drawings alone may provide an adequate written description.[56]

However, simply describing a large body of information is not sufficient to satisfy the written description requirement as to a particular subset of information contained therein.[57] To use a metaphor set out in *In re Ruschig*: "It is an old custom in the woods to mark trails by placing blaze marks on the trees. It is no help in finding a trail ... to be confronted simply by a large number of unmarked trees ... . We are looking for blaze marks which single out particular trees."[58] Following this reasoning, the Federal Circuit, in *Fujikawa v. Wattansin*, held that describing a large genus of

---

in some way. Thus, at the point he would testify respecting a step or material or source or detail which is not in the patent, a failure to disclose the best mode would, ipso facto, be established.

[51] *Id.*

[52] 35 U.S.C. § 112, 1ˢᵗ ¶ (1994).

[53] *See* discussion *supra,* § 2.1.1.

[54] *See* Vas-Cath, Inc. v. Mahurkar, 935 F.2d 1555, 1560 (Fed. Cir. 1991).

[55] *See* Fujikawa v. Wattansin, 93 F.3d 1559, 1570 (Fed. Cir. 1996).

[56] *See Vas-Cath,* 935 F.2d at 1563.

[57] *See Fujikawa,* 93 F.3d at 1570.

[58] 379 F.2d 990, 994-95 (C.C.P.A. 1967).

compounds is not sufficient to satisfy the written description requirement as to a particular species of sub-genus; a blanket disclosure does not reveal that the inventor knew the value of an exact subset of information.[59] Another example is where the patent applicant discloses a numerical range of 30 to 70 percent of a compound X, but claims, as the invention, a specific numerical value within that range (*e.g.*, 37.5%). A court is likely to hold that the written description requirement is not satisfied as to that claim.[60]

2.1.4. Definiteness Requirement

The second paragraph of Section 112 requires the patentee to "particularly point[ ] out and distinctly claim[ ]" the invention. The purpose of the definiteness requirement is to put the public, namely competitors, and the PTO on notice of what exactly is being claimed by the patentee. An assertion of indefiniteness requires an analysis of whether persons skilled in the art would understand the metes and bounds of the claim when read in light of the specification. A claim is indefinite if its legal scope is not clear enough that a person of ordinary skill in the art could determine whether a particular [product or method] infringes or not. The degree of precision necessary is a function of the nature of the subject matter; and, indeed, terms of degree such as "substantially" are frequently used in claim drafting. A claim is not indefinite because there is some ambiguity or the language poses a difficult issue of interpretation. As the Federal Circuit recently stated:

> We have held that a claim is not indefinite merely because it poses a difficult issue of claim construction; if the claim is subject to construction, i.e., it is not insolubly ambiguous, it is not invalid for indefiniteness. That is, if the meaning of the claim is discernible, "even though the task may be formidable and the conclusion may be one over which reasonable persons will disagree, we have held the claim sufficiently clear to avoid invalidity

---

[59] See *Fujikawa*, 93 F.3d at 1570. ("[S]imply describing a large genus of compounds is not sufficient to satisfy the written description requirement as to particular species or sub-genuses.").

[60] *See id.* ("Specific claims to single compounds require reasonably specific supporting disclosure and while ... naming [each species] is not essential, something more than the disclosure of a class of 1000, or 100, or even 48 compounds is required." (Quoting *In re Ruschig*, 379 F.2d at 994)).

on indefiniteness grounds." Exxon Research & Eng'g Co. v. United States, 265 F.3d 1371, 1375 (Fed. Cir. 2001)[61]

Even when claim language is subject to two plausible interpretations, one narrower than the other, but both supported by the specification, the Federal Circuit will adopt the narrower interpretation rather than invalidating the claim.[62]

2.2. Novelty

A basic requirement of American patent law is that an invention, to be patentable, must be novel. It makes no sense to grant someone a patent on an invention that already exists and is available to the public. The novelty requirement, as it is appropriately known, is embodied in subsections (a), (e), and (g) of 35 U.S.C. § 102. If an invention isn't new, it is said to be *anticipated* by the prior art. For example, if an inventor claims an apparatus comprising elements A, B, and C and a certain relationship among these three elements, and the prior art discloses explicitly or inherently the same apparatus comprising the same elements in the same relationship, the invention is said to be *anticipated* by the prior art.

A patent claim is considered "anticipated" by prior art only if each claim limitation is disclosed, "either expressly or inherently,"[63] in a *single* prior art reference that existed before the patent applicant's *date of invention.*[64]

2.2.1. *Date of Invention*

For a prior art reference to anticipate an invention, it must have existed prior to the patent applicant's date of invention (thus, the name *prior* art). Therefore, it is important to understand how one establishes date of

---

[61] Bancorp Services, L.L.C. v. Hartford Life Ins. Co., 359 F.3d 1367, 1371 (Fed. Cir. 2004).

[62] Athletic Alternatives, Inc. v. Prince Mfg., Inc., 73 F.3d 1573 (Fed. Cir. 1996).

[63] Rowe v. Dror, 112 F.3d 473, 477 (Fed. Cir. 1997).

[64] When an application is made for a patent claiming the same subject matter as another application or an issued patent, an interference is declared by the Patent & Trademark Office. An interference is a procedural mechanism to determine who is the first inventor (*i.e.*, who has priority of invention). *See* 35 U.S.C. § 135.

invention. In the United States, the date of invention is the date when the inventor reduces his invention to practice.[65] There are two types of reduction to practice (RTP): (1) Actual RTP; and (2) Constructive RTP. The latter occurs when a patent application is filed, regardless of whether anything is actually built as long as the applicant satisfies the disclosure requirements of § 112. Actual RTP occurs when the invention is shown to be suitable for its intended purpose.[66]

Alternatively, a "person 'who conceives, and, in a mental sense, first invents ... may date his patentable invention back to the time of its conception, if he connects the conception with its reduction to practice by reasonable diligence on his part, so that they are substantially one continuous act.'"[67] In short, "priority of invention 'goes to the first party to reduce an invention to practice unless the other party can show that it was the first to conceive the invention and that it exercised reasonable diligence in later reducing that invention to practice.'"[68] Conception occurs when the inventor has in his mind "'a definite and permanent idea of the complete and operative invention, as it is thereafter applied in practice.'"[69] Corroboration is required when the inventor seeks to establish conception

---

[65] See Mahurkar v. C.R. Bard, Inc., 79 F.3d 1572, 1577-78 (Fed. Cir. 1996).

[66] See id. ("Depending on the character of the invention and the problem it solves, this showing may require test results. Less complicated inventions and problems do not demand stringent testing. In fact, some invention are so simple and their purpose and efficacy so obvious that their complete construction is sufficient to demonstrate workability"); see also Estee Lauder Inc. v. L'Oreal S.A., 129 F.3d 588, 593 (Fed. Cir. 1997).

[67] Mahurkar, 79 F.3d at 1577. Diligence only comes into play when a party is the first to conceive, but the second to reduce to practice. The patent law favors prompt public disclosure, and therefore wants to know what this party was doing given the fact that another was the second to conceive, but the first to reduce practice. Thus, the party who was the first to conceive must show "reasonably continuous activity" from just prior to the other party's date of conception to the reduction to practice date of the party who was the first to conceive.

[68] Id.

[69] Id. ("The idea must be 'so clearly defined in the inventor's mind that only ordinary skill would be necessary to reduce the invention to practice, without extensive research or experimentation'").

through oral testimony rather than physical exhibits.[70] Without evidence of conception or actual reduction to practice, the filing date (*i.e.*, constructive RTP) acts as the date of invention.[71]

2.2.2. *Identity of Invention in Single Prior Art Reference*

To serve as anticipatory prior art, there must be identity of invention.[72] Identity of invention requires that "each element of the claim at issue is found, either expressly or under principles of inherency, in a single prior art reference, or that the claimed invention was previously known or embodied in a single prior art device or practice."[73] Under the doctrine of inherency, "[i]f an inventor seeks to claim an advantage or modification that flows necessarily from a prior art reference, the reference inherently anticipates the inventor's claim."[74]

The use of multiple references is not acceptable under § 102.[75] In other words, for a prior art reference to anticipate an invention, "all the claimed elements must be found in exactly the same situation and united in the same way to perform the identical function" in a single piece of prior art.[76]

---

[70] *Id.* (The courts assess corroboration of oral testimony with a rule of reason analysis, which evaluates "'all pertinent evidence must be made so that a sound determination of the credibility of the inventor's story may be reached.'" *Id.* (quoting Price v. Symsek, 988 F.2d 1187, 1195 (Fed. Cir. 1993)).

[71] *See* Hybritech Inc. v. Monoclonal Antibodies, Inc., 802 F.2d 1367, 1374 (Fed. Cir. 1986).

[72] *See* Minnesota Mining & Mfg. Co. v. Johnson and Johnson, 976 F.2d 1559, 1565 (Fed. Cir. 1992).

[73] *Id.*; *see also*, Scripps Clinic & Research Foundation v. Genetech, Inc., 927 F.2d 1565, 1576 (Fed. Cir. 1991) ("There must be no difference between the claimed invention and the reference as viewed by a person of ordinary skill in the field of the invention").

[74] Glaxo, Inc. v. Novopharm Ltd., 830 F.Supp. 871, 874 (E.D.N.C. 1993), *aff'd*, 52 F.3d 1043 (Fed. Cir. 1995); *see also*, In re Paulsen, 30 F.3d 1475, 1479-80 (Fed. Cir. 1994).

[75] Multiple references, however, may be used in a § 103 nonobviousness determination. *See* § 2.5, *infra*.

[76] Studiengesellschaft Kohle, m.b.H. v. Dart Indus., Inc., 762 F.2d 724, 726 (Fed. Cir. 1984).

2.2.2.1. Section 102(a) Prior Art

Section 102(a) of the Patent Act states that a person is entitled to a patent unless "the invention was known or used by others in [the United States], or patented or described in a printed publication in [the United States] or a foreign country, before the invention thereof by the applicant ... ."[77] Subsection (a) entails three significant limitations: A patent will not issue if someone other than the applicant (1) knew of or used the invention in the United States before the applicant's date of invention, (2) patented the invention in the United States or a foreign country before the applicant's date of invention, or (3) described the invention in a printed publication before the applicant's date of invention.

While at first glance these limitations seem fairly straightforward, a closer inspection reveals several underlying questions: how precise does a reference need to coincide with the claimed invention to qualify as anticipatory prior art? Under what conditions is an invention known or used? What considerations determine the foreign equivalent to a patent? What constitutes a printed publication? To answer these question one must turn to common law principles.

2.2.2.1.1. "Known or Used by Others"

As stated above, a patent applicant is entitled to a patent under Section 102(a) unless his invention was "known or used by others" (*i.e.*, by someone other than the inventor).[78] Courts have interpreted the "known or used" clause as *publically* known or used; that is, knowledge or use will not anticipate a claimed invention unless such knowledge or use is publically accessible.[79] One reason for this interpretation may be the public policy favoring the person who is the first to disclose the invention to the public,

---

[77] 35 U.S.C. § 102(a) (1994).

[78] *See* Pennock v. Dialogue, 27 U.S. (2 Pet.) 1, 18 (1829):

What then is the true meaning of the words "known or used before the application?" They cannot mean that the thing invented was not known or used before the application by the inventor himself, for that would prohibit him from the only means to obtain a patent. ... These words, then, to have any rational interpretation, must mean, not known or used by others before the application.

In other words, to put it somewhat awkwardly, an inventor cannot invent before he invents.

[79] *See* Galyer v. Wilder, 51 U.S. (10 How.) 477 (1850).

even though someone else may have made the discovery earlier. Public disclosure is a firmly embedded policy underlying our patent system.[80] Under this view, a previously invented, but unknown invention should not act as an anticipatory reference against one who was the first to disclose the invention to the public.

However, there is no requirement that a prior inventor make an effort to publicize an invention. Even if an invention is hidden from view, if it is used in the usual course of business without efforts to conceal it, the use qualifies as public.[81]

2.2.2.1.2. "Printed Publication"

A patent will not issue if the patent applicant's invention was, prior to the date of invention, described in a "printed publication." The term printed publication,[82] in the light of data storage and retrieval technologies,

---

[80] *Id.* at 497:

But if the [prior] discovery is not patented, nor described in any printed publication, it might be known or used in remote places for ages, and the people of this country be unable to profit by it. The means of obtaining knowledge would not be within their reach; and as their interest is concerned, it would be the same thing as if the improvement had never been discovered. It is the inventor here that brings [the invention] to [the public], and places it in their possession.

[81] *See* Rosaire v. Baroid Sales Division, 218 F.2d 72, 74 (5th Cir. 1955)(Section 102(a) does not "require some affirmative act to bring the work to the attention to the public at large."); W.L. Gore & Assoc., Inc. v. Garlock, Inc., 721 F.2d 1540, 1562 (Fed. Cir. 1983), *appeal after remand*, 842 F.2d 1275 (Fed. Cir. 1988)("The nonsecret use of a claimed process in the usual course of producing articles for commercial purposes is a public use"); Egbert v. Lippmann, 104 U.S. 333 (1881)("public use" found where the invention was corset steels which were hidden from public view by the clothing worn over the corset); *National Research Development Corp. v. Varian Associates, Inc.*, 28 USPQ2d 1436, 1447 (D.N.J. 1993)("A prior use is public even if there is no effort to show the invention to the public at large, ... even if the invention is completely hidden from view. ... There is simply no requirement that the prior user make an effort to make the invention publicly accessible, so long as he or she uses it in the ordinary course of business without efforts to conceal it").

[82] In 1836, when the term "printed" first appeared in § 102(a), actual printing was the only known means for disseminating or making information available. Today, however, there are obviously other means available. As the Court of Customs and Patent Appeals stated in *In re Wyer*, 655 F.2d 221, 226 (CCPA 1981), "[t]he traditional dichotomy between 'printing' and 'publication' is no longer valid. Given the state of

has been interpreted to mean any reference that is "sufficiently accessible to the public interested in the art;"[83] indeed, there is no requirement that a person of ordinary skill in the art actually obtain the reference.[84] To be a printed publication, a source must be catalogued or indexed in a library, or other place reasonably accessible, such that the material would be accessible with a *reasonably diligent search*.[85]

Likewise, a publication cannot become prior art before the public has access to it. Thus, the reference becomes prior art on the date it becomes accessible to the relevant public (*e.g.*, indexed, catalogued, or published).[86]

2.2.2.1.3. Geographical Limitations

Section 102(a) reads that an invention will be anticipated if it was "known or used *in this country*." However, foreign patents and foreign printed publications may act as prior art. Why is knowledge and use limited to the United States? This geographic distinction did not make its way into American patent law until 1836, but the Senate Report accompanying the 1836 Act offers little, if any, explanation. Common sense tells us that unpublished knowledge and use are less difficult for a U.S. inventor to discover in the U.S. as opposed to Europe or Japan. How does one search

---

technology in document duplication, data storage, and data-retrieval systems, the 'probability of dissemination' of an item very often has little to do with whether or not it is printed in the same sense of the word when it was introduced into the patent statute in 1836."

[83] Constant v. Advanced Micro-Devices, Inc., 848 F.2d 1560, 1568 (Fed. Cir. 1988). *See also*, In re Hall, 781 F.2d 897, 899 (Fed. Cir. 1986) ("'public accessibility' has been called touchstone in determining whether a reference constitutes a 'printed publication'").

[84] *See Constant*, 848 F.2d at 1568 ("[D]issemination and public accessibility are the keys to the legal determination whether a prior art reference was published ... . If accessibility is proved, there is no requirement to show that particular members of the pubic actually received the information.").

[85] *See In re* Cronyn, 890 F.2d 1158, 1161 (Fed. Cir. 1989). *See also* In re Klopfenstein, 380 F.3d 1345 (Fed. Cir. 2004) (finding printed publication for slide show when confidentiality agreements were not secured).

[86] *See In re* Bayer, 568 F.2d 1357, 1361 (CCPA. 1978)("The date on which the public actually gained access to the invention by means of the publication is the focus of the inquiry").

for unpublished knowledge in foreign lands without incurring a great deal of expense (*i.e.*, search costs). It is difficult enough to obtain such knowledge in the United States, let alone a foreign country. At least with many foreign publications and most foreign patents, there exist databases that one can search relatively cheaply today.

The Supreme Court has addressed the geographic distinction issue:

If the foreign invention had been printed or patented, it was already given to the world and open to the people of this country, as well as of others, upon reasonable inquiry. They would therefore derive no advantage from the invention here. It would confer no benefit upon the community, and the inventor therefore is not considered to be entitled to the reward. But if the foreign discovery is not patented, nor described in any printed publication, it might be known and used in remote places for ages, and the people of this country be unable to profit by it. The means of obtaining knowledge would not be within their reach; and, as far as their interest is concerned, it would be the same thing as if the improvement had never been discovered.[87]

2.2.2.2. Section 102(e) Prior Art

Under Section 102(e), prior art may assume two forms. First, the American Inventors Protection Act of 1999 amended the patent code to require, with certain exceptions, patent applications filed on or after 29 November 2000, to be published "promptly after the expiration of a period of eighteen months from the earliest filed date." 35 U.S.C. Section 122(b). (Under 37 C.F.R. 1.219, an applicant can have his application published "earlier" than eighteen months from the earliest filing date.) As such, Section 102(e)(1) was added to permit published applications to serve as prior art. This subsection reads:

A person shall be entitled to a patent unless:

(e)(1) an application for patent, published under Section 122(b), by another filed in the United States before the invention by the applicant for patent, except that an international application filed under the treaty defined in section 351(a) [Patent Cooperation Treaty] shall have the effect under this subsection of a national application published under Section 122(b) only if the international application designating the United States

---

[87] *Gayler*, 51 U.S. at 497.

was published under Article 21(2)(a) of such treaty in the English language.

Under Section 102(e)(1), once a United States patent application is *published* in the United States, its prior art effect is triggered, and its effective date reverts to its date of filing.

Of perhaps greater significance, however, is that an international patent application filed pursuant to the Patent Cooperation Treat (PCT) that designates the United States and is ultimately published in English will have prior art effect under Section 102(e)(1) as of its international filing date, which is the date the PCT application is filed. The international filing date is no more than twelve months from the priority date (i.e., the date of first filing in a PCT member country); and, under Article 21(2)(a) of the PCT, a PCT application is published eighteen months after its priority date. Of note is that a PCT application, which satisfies the English language and designation requirements, can serve as a prior art reference as of its international filing date, even though an application is never subsequently filed in the United States. *See* 35 U.S.C. Section 374.

The second form of Section 102(e) prior art falls under Section 102(e)(2). Under this section, international (or PCT) applications have no prior art effect; but United States patent applications are certainly eligible. A United States patent application that is not subject to publication (because, for example, the applicant certifies that he is not filing in a foreign country) is "kept in confidence by the PTO" under 35 U.S.C. Section 122(a). As a result, pending patent applications are not "known" (i.e., "publicly accessible" in the Section 102(a) sense); yet, such applications can serve as prior art references as of their filing date under Section 102(e)(2) if the application eventually issues as a patent. Why? According to Justice Holmes in *Alexander Milburn Co. v. Davis-Bournonville Co.*,[88] "delays in the Patent Office ought not to cut down the effect of what has been done." That is, but for the administrative delays present within the PTO in examining and ultimately issuing the patent, the basic fact is that someone other than the inventor previously disclosed the inventor's claimed invention.

Accordingly, information which is not known and is unknowable may act as anticipatory prior art so long as the patent does issue. The fact that the patent must issue before it can be used as prior art indicates that Section

---

[88] 270 U.S. 390, 400-01 (1926).

102(e) does have a publicity requirement, but it simply comes later in the game, acting as a condition precedent.

Two further points should be made with respect to § 102(e)(2) prior art. First, Section 102(e) prior art is limited to United States patent applications; second, patent applications under § 102(e)(2) are prior art only for what they disclose, not what they claim. If a previously filed patent application claims the same subject matter as a later filed application, Section 102(g)(1) would be applicable because now the issue is who *invented* first or who has priority of invention.[89]

2.2.2.3. Section 102(g)(2) Prior Art

Section 102(g) serves dual purposes. First, Section 102(g)(2) is the basis for what is known as a priority dispute or "interference." When an application is made for a patent claiming the same subject matter as another application or an issued patent, an interference may be declared by the Patent & Trademark Office. An interference is a procedural mechanism to determine who is the first inventor (i.e., who has priority of invention). Second, Section 102(g)(2) provides statutory grounds for "secret" prior art that may have a patent-defeating effect.[90] This section allows for patent-defeating inventive activity that is not subject to an interference, but the inventive activity must be "in this country" (i.e., the United States). For example, imagine that Smith, instead of filing a patent application, practices his invention, that he made *in the United States*, as a trade secret. A third party can use Smith's trade secret as a prior art reference against Mary's claimed invention, if Smith invented Mary's claimed invention before she did.

Although it may look like Section 102(g) incorporates Section 102(a) prior art, one basic distinction is that § 102(a) does not require continued use like § 102(g); that is, under § 102(g), the prior invention must not be abandoned, suppressed, or concealed. A court considers several factors in determining whether an invention was abandoned, suppressed, or concealed, including "not filing a patent application, not publicly

---

[89] *See infra*, 2.2.4.

[90] Thomson, S.A. v. Quixote Corp., 166 F.3d 1172 (Fed. Cir. 1999).

disseminating documents describing the invention, and not publicly using the invention."[91]

2.2.3. Derivation: Section 102(f)

Section 102(f) of Title 35 is known as the "derivation" provision. It provides that a person is entitled to a patent unless "he did not himself invent the subject matter sought to be patented." In other words, the named inventor *derived* the claimed subject matter from a third party and is, therefore, not the original inventor.

To show derivation, the party asserting invalidity must prove: (1) prior conception of the invention by another, and (2) communication of that conception to the patentee such that the communication enabled one of ordinary skill in the art to make the patented invention.[92] It is important to note that Section 102(f) applies to derivation that occurs in the United States or in a foreign country.

2.2.4. Priority

Priority of invention in the United States is based on a *first to invent* system. The United States is unique in this regard among industrialized nations in that other countries have adopted a *first to file* system of priority.[93] Thus, in the United States, a party who is second to file may nevertheless be awarded the patent if he can prove that he was the first to invent. The procedure by which priority (who invented first) is determined is called an *interference*.

As a general rule, priority is awarded to the inventor who first reduced the invention to practice. However, there are two exceptions to this rule: (1) an inventor who was the first to conceive the invention but the last to reduce it to practice will be awarded priority if he can show that he exercised *reasonable diligence* in reducing to practice from a time just prior to when

---

[91] *Oak Industries*, 726 F. Supp. at 1533. Although it should be noted that there is no requirement that an inventor file a patent application. *See* Checkpoint Systems, Inc. v. U.S. Int'l Trade Comm'n, 988 F.2d 1165 (Fed. Cir. 1993).

[92] *See* Gambro Lundia AB v. Baxter Healthcare Corp., 110 F.3d 1573, 1576 (Fed. Cir. 1997).

[93] There has been much discussion in recent years among commentators and members of the bar as to whether the United States should adopt a first to file system.

the first person who reduced to practice conceived the invention; and (2) the second inventor will be awarded priority if the first inventor *abandoned, suppressed, or concealed* the invention (after reducing it to practice). As the Federal Circuit has stated, the person "who first conceives, and, in a mental sense, first invents ... may date his patentable invention back to the time of its conception, if he connects the conception with its reduction to practice by reasonable diligence on his part, so that they are substantially one continuous act."[94]

2.2.4.1. Conception

In the 1897 case of *Mergenthaler v. Scudder*,[95] the Court of Appeals for District of Columbia laid down a definition for conception that has been adopted by the Federal Circuit:

> The conception of the invention consists in the complete performance of the mental part of the inventive act. All that remains to be accomplished in order to perfect the act or instrument belongs to the department of construction, not invention. It is, therefore, the formation in the mind of the inventor of a definite and permanent idea of the complete and operative invention as it is thereafter to be applied in practice that constitutes an available conception within the meaning of the patent law.[96]

Similarly, the Federal Circuit has stated:

> To have conceived of an invention, an inventor must have formed in his or her mind "a definite and permanent idea of the complete and operative invention, as it is hereafter to be applied in practice." The idea must be "so clearly defined in the inventor's mind that only ordinary skill would be necessary to reduce the invention to practice, without extensive research or experimentation."[97]

Subsequently, in *Amgen, Inc. v. Chugai Pharmaceutical Co., Ltd.*,[98] the Federal Circuit added that:

---

[94] *Mahurkar, supra,* note 72, at 1577.

[95] 1897 C.D. 724 (1897).

[96] *Id.* at 731.

[97] *Mahurkar, supra,* note 72, at 1577(citing Burroughs Wellcome Co. v. Barr Laboratories, Inc., 40 F.3d 1223, 1228 (Fed. Cir. 1994)).

[98] 927 F.2d 1200 (Fed. Cir. 1991).

[i]n some instances, an inventor is unable to establish a conception until he has reduced his invention to practice through a successful experiment. This situation results in simultaneous conception and reduction to practice. ...."[99]

Because conception "is a mental act, courts require corroborating evidence of a contemporaneous disclosure that would enable one skilled in the art to make the invention."[100] "[C]ourts apply a rule of reason analysis. Under a rule of reason analysis, '[a]n evaluation of all pertinent evidence must be made so that a sound determination of the credibility of the inventor's story may be reached.'"[101]

2.2.4.2. Reduction to Practice

There are two types of reduction to practice (RTP): constructive and actual. *Constructive* RTP results when the patent application is filed. Constructive RTP may occur even if the applicant never built or tested his invention as long as the applicant satisfies sECTION 112.[102] The policy behind constructive RTP is to encourage early disclosure of the invention.

---

[99] *Id.* at 1206. In referring to the problem of "conception" in the context of a patent concerning DNA sequences for encoding a chemical compound, the court observed:
A gene is a chemical compound, albeit a complex one, and it is well established in our law that conception of a chemical compound requires that the inventor be able to define it so as to distinguish it from other materials, and to describe how to obtain it. Conception does not occur unless one has a mental picture of the structure of the chemical, or is able to define it by its method of preparation, its physical or chemical properties, or whatever characteristics sufficiently distinguish it. It is not sufficient to define it solely by its principal biological property, e.g., encoding for [EPO], because an alleged conception having no more specificity than that is simply a wish to know the identity of any material with that biological property. We hold that when an inventor is unable to envision the detailed constitution of a gene so as to distinguish it from other materials, as well as a method for obtaining it, conception has not been achieved until reduction to practice has occurred, i.e., until after the gene has been isolated.
Id.

[100] Burroughs Wellcome Co. v. Barr Laboratories, Inc., 40 F.3d 1223, 1228 (Fed. Cir. 1994).

[101] *Mahurkar, supra,* note 72, at 1577.

[102] *See* Fiers v. Revel, 984 F.2d 1164, 1169 (Fed. Cir. 1993) ("While one does not need to have carried out one's invention before filing a patent application, one does need to be able to describe that invention with particularity.")

Requiring actual testing may delay disclosure. *Actual* RTP occurs when the invention is shown to be suitable for its intended purpose, that is, when the invention is physically made and tested (*e.g.*, a prototype).[103]

To prove actual RTP, an inventor must construct the invention (*e.g.*, prototype) and test it to determine if it works for its intended purpose. There must be some recognition of successful testing for an invention to be actually reduced to practice[104] It is clear that actual working conditions are not required. Indeed, laboratory tests may be sufficient if they simulate actual working conditions. The Federal Circuit referred to a "common sense approach" with respect to sufficiency of testing:

> This common sense approach prescribes more scrupulous testing under circumstances approaching actual use conditions when the problem includes many uncertainties. On the other hand, when the problem to be solved does not present myriad variables, common sense similarly permits little or no testing to show the soundness of the principles of operation of the invention.[105]

There is a difference between proving that the invention works for its intended purpose and proving that the invention works in the commercial sense. Neither perfection nor commercial viability is required to show actual RTP.[106]

---

[103] *See* DSL Sciences, Ltd. v. Union Switch & Signal, Inc., 928 F.2d 1122, 1124 (Fed. Cir. 1991):
> [P]roof of actual reduction to practice requires a showing that "the embodiment relied upon as evidence of priority actually worked for its intended purpose" .... On the other hand, tests performed outside the intended environment can be sufficient to show reduction to practice if the testing conditions are sufficiently similar to those of the intended environment.

[104] *See* Estee Lauder Inc. v. L'Oreal S.A., 129 F.3d 588 (Fed. Cir. 1997).

[105] Scott v. Finney, 34 F.3d 1058, 1063 (Fed. Cir. 1994). *See also Mahurkar, supra,* note 72, at 1578 (Fed. Cir. 1996):
> To show actual reduction to practice, an inventor must demonstrate that the invention is suitable for its intended purpose. ... Depending on the character of the invention and the problem it solves, this showing may require test results. ... Less complicated inventions and problems do not demand stringent testing. ... In fact, some inventions are so simple and their purpose and efficacy so obvious that their complete construction is sufficient to demonstrate workability.

[106] *See DSL Sciences,* 928 F.2d at 1126.

As with conception, an inventor must be able to corroborate independently his actual reduction to practice. This can be done through the submission of affidavits analyzing and describing the experiments, the dates of the experiments, etc. As with conception, the Federal Circuit applies a "rule of reason" standard when evaluating the sufficiency of the corroborating evidence.[107]

2.2.4.3. Abandonment, Suppression, and Concealment

Consistent with the patent policy favoring prompt disclosure, an inventor who was the first to reduce to practice may lose his right of priority if he abandons, suppresses, or conceals his invention. Consider the following scenario:

> Inventor 1 reduces to practice invention X, but neither files a patent application, nor markets invention X. A year later, inventor 2, ignorant of inventor 1 and his invention X, invents X and files a patent application. Upon learning of inventor 2, inventor 1 is "spurred" into activity and claims that he is the first to invent X.

The law favors inventor 2 in this instance because it is he who brought invention X to the public, whereas inventor 1 abandoned, suppressed, and concealed invention X and only came to the fore once he found out about inventor 2. However, if inventor 2 never came into the picture, or if inventor 1 resumed inventive activity prior to inventor 2's inventive activity, inventor 1 may still apply for and obtain a patent, even though there was a delay.[108] Indeed, there is no duty to file a patent application.[109]

Diligence comes into play only when a party is the first to conceive but the second to reduce to practice. The patent law favors prompt disclosure and, therefore, wants to know what this party was doing, given the fact that another was the second to conceive, but the first to reduce to practice. The party who was the first to conceive but the second to reduce to practice must show continuous and reasonable diligence from a date just prior to the

---

[107] *See* Holmwood v. Balasubramanyan Sugavanam, 948 F.2d 1236, 1238 (Fed. Cir. 1991).

[108] *See* Paulik v. Rizkalla, 760 F.2d 1270 (Fed. Cir. 1985). *See also* Fujikawa v. Wattanasin, 93 F.3d 1559 (Fed. Cir. 1996).

[109] *See* Checkpoint Sys., Inc. v. United States ITC, 54 F.3d 756, 762 (Fed. Cir. 1995).

other party's conception to its reduction to practice. As the Board of Patent Appeals & Interferences explained:

> A party that seeks to establish reasonable diligence must account for the entire period during which diligence is required; that period commences from a time just prior to the senior party's [party who was the first to RTP] date to the junior party's [party who was the second to RTP] reduction to practice, either actual or constructive. ... Public policy favors early disclosure, ... and thus the law is reluctant to displace an inventor who was the first to disclose to the public his invention. ... During this period there must be "reasonably continuous activity". ... Evidence which is of a general nature to the effect that work was continuous and which has little specificity as to dates and facts does not constitute the kind of evidence required to establish diligence in the critical period.[110]

While a showing of constant effort is not required to prove diligence, the inventor must account for the entire critical period. The question is whether the applicant was pursuing his goal "in a reasonable fashion."[111] Thus, periods of inactivity may not be fatal to a showing of diligence if the inventor has an adequate excuse such as (1) poverty or illness of the inventor,[112] (2) obligations of the inventor's regular employment,[113] or (3) excessive workload of the inventor's patent attorney, provided the attorney "takes up work in a reasonable order—for example, handling applications in the chronological order in which they are submitted."[114]

2.2.4.4. Inventorship

U.S. patent law requires that a patent issue to the correct inventive entity, and there is a rebuttable presumption that the inventors named on an issued patent are correct. With multiple inventors, the "theory of

---

[110] Hunter v. Beissbarth, 230 USPQ 365, 368 (Bd. Pat. App. & Int'f 1986).

[111] Hybritech, Inc. v. Abbott Laboratories, 4 USPQ2d 1001, 1006 (C.D. Calif. 1987), aff'd, 849 F.2d 1446 (Fed. Cir. 1988).

[112] See Christie v. Seybold, 55 F. 69, 77 (6th Cir. 1893) ("the sickness of the inventor, his poverty, and his engagement in other inventions of similar kind are all circumstances which may affect the question of reasonable diligence").

[113] See Gould v. Schawlow, 363 F.2d 908, 919 (CCPA 1966) ("reasonable diligence does not require that one abandon his means of livelihood to further his reduction to practice").

[114] DONALD S. CHISUM, 3 CHISUM ON PATENTS § 10.07[4][e].

inventorship entity" postulates that "the joint work of two or more persons is treated as being by an 'inventorship entity' separate and distinct from the work of each person solely or in other joint entities."[115]

This requirement does not mean that joint inventors must make equal contributions or that each inventor must contribute to the subject matter in each and every claim. Section 116 of Title 35, as amended in 1984, reads:

> When an invention is made by two or more persons jointly, they shall apply for a patent jointly and each make the required oath, ... Inventors may apply for a patent jointly even though (1) they did not physically work together or at the same time, (2) each did not make the same type or amount of contribution, or (3) each did not make a contribution to the subject matter of every claim of the patent.[116]

The Manual of Patent Examining Procedure states that "[s]ome quantum of collaboration or connection is required in order for persons to be 'joint' inventors under 35 U.S.C. § 116, and thus individuals who are completely ignorant of what each other has done until years after their individual independent efforts cannot be considered joint inventors."[117]

2.2.4.5. Inventive Activity Abroad

Prior to 1994, Section 104 of the Patent Act precluded an inventor from using inventive activity abroad (*i.e.*, conception and reduction to practice) to establish priority under Section 102(g). However, GATT/TRIPS (Trade Related Aspects of Intellectual Property Rights) and NAFTA amended Section 104 to allow applicants to rely on foreign inventive activity to prove date of invention.[118] For GATT/TRIPS, the amendment is effective as of January 1, 1996; the effective date for reliance on inventive activity in a NAFTA country is December 8, 1993.

---

[115] *Id.* at § 3.08[2].

[116] Prior to 1984, courts applied the "all-claims rule," which required each named inventor to contribute to every claim. The 1984 Amendments to § 116 did away with this requirement.

[117] MANUAL OF PATENT EXAMINING PROCEDURE [hereinafter MPEP] § 605.07 (rev. 1995).

[118] *See* 35 U.S.C. § 104 (as amended by P.L. 103-182, Dec. 8, 1993, § 331, 107 Stat. 2113; P.L. 103-465, Dec. 8, 1994, § 531(a), 108 Stat. 4982).

2.3. Loss of Right: Statutory Bars

2.3.1. Section 102(b) — On-Sale and Public Use Bars

According to Section 102(b), an inventor may be statutorily barred from obtaining a patent, even though he was the first to invent, if "the invention was ... in public use or on sale in [the United States], more than one year prior to the date of application for patent in the United States."[119] Such a statutory bar may be viewed as a back-handed grant of a one-year grace period "during which an inventor may perfect his invention and prepare and file his application, testing it in public, if necessary. Section [102(b)] actually encourages earlier disclosure, publication, or public use of the invention, through which the public may gain knowledge of it."[120]

These restrictions differ significantly from Section 102(a) in that Section 102(b) also includes the inventor's conduct. Consequently, an inventor may preclude himself from obtaining patent rights under Section 102(b). Furthermore, Section 102(b) focuses on the filing date, rather than the date of invention. If an inventor does not file for a patent within twelve months of the on-sale or public use activity, a patent will be statutorily barred. Thus, the critical date under Section 102(b) is one year prior to the date of application.

Four policies underlying Section 102(b) have been recognized:

First, there is a policy against removing inventions from the public which the public has justifiably come to believe are freely available to all as a consequence of prolonged sales activity. Next, there is a policy favoring prompt and widespread disclosure of new inventions to the public. The inventor is forced to file promptly or risk possible forfeiture of his invention rights due to prior sales. A third policy is to prevent the inventor from commercially exploiting the exclusivity of his invention substantially beyond the statutorily authorized [twenty]-year period. The

---

[119] 35 U.S.C. § 102(b) (1994). In other words, an applicant loses the right to obtain a patent when he or a third party: (1) patents the claimed subject matter in the United States or a foreign country more than one year before the filing date; (2) describes the claimed subject matter in a printed publication in the United States or a foreign country more than one year before the filing date; (3) publicly uses the invention in the United States more than one year before the filing date; or (4) sells or offers to sell the invention in the United States more than one year before the filing date. *Id.*

[120] Palmer v. Dudzik, 481 F.2d 1377, 1387 (CCPA 1973).

"on sale" bar forces the inventor to choose between seeking patent protection promptly following sales activity or taking his chances with his competitors without the benefit of patent protection. The fourth and final identifiable policy is to give the inventor a reasonable amount of time following sales activity (set by statute as 1 year) to determine whether a patent is a worthwhile investment. This benefits the public because it tends to minimize the filing of inventions of only marginal public interest. The 1-year grace period provided for by Congress in § 102(b) represents a balance between these competing interests.[121]

2.3.1.1. Public Use

"Public use" in the United States by the inventor or a third party occurring more than one year prior to filing precludes the grant of a patent.[122] As with the on-sale bar, the one-year grace period allows an inventor a reasonable amount of time to test an invention, gauge its sales activity, and determine its potential economic value.[123] Thus, public use is any non-secret, non-experimental use of the invention. Additionally, a public use includes any use of a claimed invention "by a person other than the inventor who is under no limitation, restriction or obligation of secrecy to the inventor."[124] A public use has been found even where the third party improperly obtained the idea from the inventor.[125] To escape qualifying as

---

[121] General Electric Co. v. United States, 654 F.2d 55, 61 (Ct. Cl. 1981).

[122] 35 U.S.C. § 102(b) (1994).

[123] *See* Elizabeth v. Pavement Co., 97 U.S. 126, 134-35 (1877):
When the subject of invention is a machine, it may be tested and tried in a building, either with or without closed doors. In either case, such use is not a public use, within the meaning of the statute, so long as the inventor is engaged, in good faith, in testing its operation. ... And though, during all that period, he may not find that any changes are necessary, yet he may be justly said to be using his machine only by way of experiment .... So long as he does not voluntarily allow others to make it and use it, and so long as it is not on sale for general use, he keeps the invention under his own control, and does not lose his title to a patent.
See also Tone Bros. v. Sysco Corp., 28 F.3d 1192, 1198 (Fed. Cir. 1994).

[124] *In re* Smith, 714 F.2d 1127, 1134 (Fed. Cir. 1983).

[125] *See* Lorenze v. Colgate-Palmolive-Peet Co., 167 F.2d 423, 429 (3d Cir. 1948).

a public use, a use must be private, under the inventor's control, and not for commercial purposes.[126]

2.3.1.2. Experimental Use

A patent applicant may defeat a showing of public use by presenting evidence that the use was for experimental purposes.[127] An inventor, or any person under the inventor's direction, may experiment with an invention in order to perfect it without defeating patentability.[128] Even a blatantly public display of an invention will qualify under the exception if, due to the nature of the invention, only a public use will adequately test the invention.[129]

Although in determining whether a use is experimental one looks to the totality of the circumstances,[130] factors that a court will consider are "the length of the test period ..., whether payment is made for the device, whether a user agreed to use secretly, whether records were kept of progress, whether persons other than the inventor conducted the asserted experiments, how many tests were conducted, how long the testing period was in relationship to tests of other similar devices."[131]

2.3.1.3. On-Sale Bar

According to Section 102(b), an inventor is barred from obtaining a patent if the patent application claims subject matter that was sold or offered for sale more than one year before filing the application or is obvious in the light of what was sold or offered for sale more than one year

---

[126] *See generally* Moleculon Research Corp. v. CBS, Inc., 793 F.2d 1261, 1266-67 (Fed. Cir. 1986).

[127] *See* Lough v. Brunswick Corp., 86 F.3d 1113, 1119 (Fed. Cir. 1996).

[128] *See Elizabeth, supra,* note 132, at 135. *See also,* Seal-Flex, Inc. v. Athletic Track and Court Construction, 98 F.3d 1318, 1324 (Fed. Cir. 1996). However, "[w]hen an evaluation period is reasonably needed to determine if the invention will serve its intended purpose, the [on-sale] bar does not start to accrue while such determination is being made." *Id.*

[129] *Elizabeth, supra* note 132.

[130] *See Lough,* 86 F.3d at 1119.

[131] TP Laboratories, Inc. v. Professional Positioners, Inc., 724 F.2d 965, 972 (Fed. Cir. 1984).

before filing the patent application.[132] This restriction is known as the "on-sale" bar. An offer to sell an invention is sufficient to invoke the bar regardless of whether the offer is accepted.[133] For several years, a question of some debate was at what developmental stage must an invention be when an offer is made before the on-sale clock begins to run.

In *UMC Electronics Co. v. United States*,[134] the Federal Circuit stated: "[W]e conclude that reduction to practice of the claimed invention has not been and should not be made an absolute requirement of the on-sale bar."[135] The court used the term "substantial embodiment" when referring to the level of development of the invention, but did not attempt "to formulate a standard for determining when something less than a complete embodiment of the invention will suffice under the on-sale bar."[136] At the same time, the court noted:

> We hasten to add ... that we do not intend to sanction attacks on patents on the ground that the inventor or another offered for sale, before the critical date [*i.e.*, more than one year before the filing date of the patent application], the mere concept of the invention. ...
>
> All of the circumstances surrounding the sale or offer to sell, including the stage of development of the invention and the nature of the invention, must be considered and weighed against the policies underlying section 102(b).[137]

There was a great deal of inconsistency at the Federal Circuit with respect to this issue, with some panels embracing the UMC standard and others adhering to a reduction to practice standard.[138] In the light of this intra-circuit conflict and uncertainty surrounding the on-sale bar

---

[132] 35 U.S.C. § 102 (b) (1994).

[133] *See* RCA Corp. v. Data General Corp., 887 F.2d 1056 (Fed. Cir. 1989).

[134] 816 F.2d 647 (Fed. Cir. 1987)

[135] *Id.* at 656.

[136] *Id.* at 657.

[137] *Id.* at 656.

[138] *Compare* Seal-Flex v. Athletic Track, 98 F.3d 1318 (Fed. Cir. 1996) *and* Micro Chemical v. Great Plains Chemical, 103 F.3d 1538, *cert. denied*, 117 S.Ct. 2516 (1997).

determination, the Supreme Court granted *certiorari* in *Pfaff v. Wells*[139] and addressed the following question:

> In view of the longstanding statutory definition that the one-year grace period to an "on sale" bar can start to run only after an invention is fully completed, should the Pfaff patent have been held invalid under 35 U.S.C. § 102(b) when Mr. Pfaff's invention was admittedly not "fully completed" more than one year before he filed his patent application?[140]

The Court rejected both the reduction to practice standard and the substantial embodiment standard. According to the Court:

> The word "invention" must refer to a concept that is complete, rather than merely one that is "substantially complete." It is true that reduction to practice ordinarily provides the best evidence that an invention is complete. But just because reduction to practice is sufficient evidence of completion, it does not follow that proof of reduction to practice is necessary in every case.
>
> . . .
>
> We conclude, therefore, that the on-sale bar applies when two conditions are satisfied before the critical date. First, the product must be the subject of a commercial offer for sale. ... Second, the invention must be ready for patenting. That condition may be satisfied in at least two ways: by proof of reduction to practice before the critical date; or by proof that prior to the critical date the inventor had prepared drawings or other descriptions of the invention that were sufficiently specific to enable a person skilled in the art to practice the invention.[141]

2.3.1.4. Third-Party Activity

Third-party public use or on-sale activity may bar a patent applicant from obtaining a patent.[142] In *Evans Cooling Systems, Inc. v. General Motors*

---

[139] 119 S.Ct. 304 (1998).

[140] *Petition for Writ of Certiorari*, Pfaff v. Wells Elec., Inc., 124 F.3d 1429 (Fed. Cir. 1997), *cert. granted*, — S.Ct. —, 66 U.S.L.W. 3474 (U.S. Mar. 9, 1998).

[141] 119 S.Ct. at 311-12.

[142] *See General Electric, supra*, note 130 at 61:
Where the sale is by one other than the inventor (one not under the inventor's control), it would seem that the policy against extended commercial exploitation and the policy favoring the filing of only worthwhile inventions could be said not to apply. Nevertheless, it is well established that a placing of the invention "on sale" by an

Corp.,[143] the patentee argued that the on-sale bar should not apply when an invention is misappropriated by the alleged infringer which led to an offer for sale by third parties not involved in the theft. The Federal Circuit disagreed and held that a patent is barred when "'a public use arises from any source whatsoever.'"[144] But the court was particularly persuaded by the fact that the offers were made by innocent third parties:

> Even if we were to create an exception to the on sale bar such that third parties accused of misappropriating an invention could not invalidate a patent based upon sales by the guilty third party, GM correctly asserts that ... activities of third parties uninvolved in the alleged misappropriation raise the statutory bar, even if those activities are instigated by the one who allegedly misappropriated the invention.[145]

2.3.2. Section 102(d) Bar on Foreign Applicants

Section 102(d) is a type of statutory bar which precludes a foreign patent applicant (which may be an American company) from obtaining a United States patent if (1) the U.S. application is filed more than one year after the foreign application is filed *and* (2) the foreign patent issues before the U.S. patent issues.[146] Thus, even if a foreign patent applicant files in the U.S. more than one year after the foreign patent filing, the applicant may still obtain a U.S. patent if the foreign patent issues after the U.S. patent.

---

unrelated third party more than 1 year prior to the filing of an application for patent by another has the effect under § 102(b) of invalidating a patent directed to that invention. *See also*, Lorenz v. Colgate-Palmolive-Peet Co., 167 F.2d 423 (3rd Cir. 1948); Baxter International, Inc. v. Cobe Labs, Inc., 88 F.3d 1054 (Fed. Cir. 1996); D.L. Auld Co. v. Chroma Graphics Corp., 714 F.2d 1144 (Fed. Cir. 1983), *cert. denied*, 474 U.S. 825 (1985). *But see* W.L. Gore & Associates, Inc. v. Garlock, Inc., 721 F.2d 1540 (Fed. Cir. 1983).

[143] 125 F.3d 1448 (Fed. Cir. 1997).

[144] *Id.* at 1453.

[145] *Id.*

[146] 35 U.S.C. § 102(d) (1994). See *In re* Kathawala, 9 F.3d 942 (Fed. Cir. 1993) (foreign applicant barred under section 102(d) from obtaining a U.S. patent).

2.4. Utility

Fulfilling the constitutional purpose "to promote the Progress of ... useful Arts,"[147] Section 101 of the Patent Act restricts patentable inventions to those which are useful. Only one who "invents or discovers [a] new and *useful* process, machine, manufacture, or composition of matter, or any new and *useful* improvement thereof, may obtain a patent ... ."[148] At first glance, the utility requirement in patent law appears to be somewhat superfluous. Indeed, it is a rare occasion that lack of utility is raised as an invalidating defense in a patent litigation context. However, there is a purpose behind the utility requirement in that it secures a *quid pro quo* for society. We require the claimed invention to function for its intended purpose. Thus, before an inventor is granted the right to exclude others from practicing or selling her invention, society must be provided with an invention that operates in accordance with its intended purpose or a purpose discernible by a person of ordinary skill in the art. As the noted Nineteenth Century patent law scholar, William C. Robinson stated:

> In order that an invention may be patentable it must not only be bestowed upon the public by its inventor, but when bestowed it must confer on them a benefit. ... No recompense can properly be made to one from whom the community receives no consideration.[149]

As one may imagine, the utility requirement is not usually an obstacle for mechanical and electrical applications. These types of inventions have a certain physicality, the utility of which is manifested through the use of drawings and diagrams. In contrast, utility poses a greater concern for chemical and biological inventions. First, it is difficult to convey the utility of a chemical composition or a pharmaceutical invention by employing drawings, diagrams, or formulae. Second, unlike mechanical and electrical inventions which usually have an end result and use in mind, chemical and pharmaceutical inventions possess an evolving utility. In short, they are more like building blocks rather than a completed building. Therefore, there is a spectrum of utility, whose breadth is especially apparent in the case of chemical and biological inventions. At one end of the spectrum, some of these inventions may be viewed as having a general usefulness in

---

[147] U.S. CONST. ART. I, § 8, cl. 8.

[148] 35 U.S.C. § 101 (1994) (emphasis added).

[149] 1 WILLIAM ROBINSON, TREATISE ON THE LAW OF PATENTS 462-63 (1890).

basic research; while at the other end, some may provide specific and immediate societal utility. Whether a patent application satisfies the utility requirement depends upon where the claimed invention lies on this spectrum.

While an invention must adequately carry out its intended purpose, an invention need not be fully operational.[150] All Section 101 requires of an invention is that it be capable of performing the proposed function.[151] A lack of practical utility can only be sustained by a showing of total incapacity.[152]

For pharmaceutical inventions, an applicant can demonstrate practical utility by presenting adequate proof of pharmacological activity.[153] Because it is difficult to predict whether a novel compound will exhibit pharmacological activity, testing is often required to establish practical utility.[154] "[T]here must be a sufficient correlation between the tests and an asserted pharmacological activity so as to convince those skilled in the art, to a reasonable degree, that the novel compound will exhibit the asserted pharmacological behavior."[155]

The Federal Circuit has articulated a two-step test for determining whether the utility requirement has been met. First, the PTO "has the initial burden of challenging a *presumptively* correct assertion of utility in the disclosure." Second, "[o]nly after the PTO provides evidence showing that one of ordinary skill in the art would reasonably doubt the asserted utility does the burden shift to the applicant" to prove utility.[156]

---

[150] *See* Stiftung v. Renishaw PLC, 945 F.2d 1173, 1180 (Fed. Cir. 1991).

[151] *See* Booktree Corp. v. Advanced Micro Devices Inc., 977 F.2d 1555, 1573 (Fed. Cir. 1992).

[152] *See* Envirotech Corp. v. Al George, Inc., 730 F.2d 753, 762 (Fed. Cir. 1984).

[153] *See* Fujikawa v. Wattansin, 93 F.3d 1559, 1564 (Fed. Cir. 1996).

[154] *Id.* at 1564.

[155] *Id.*

[156] *In re* Brana, 51 F.3d 1560, 1566 (Fed. Cir. 1995). *See also* Cross v. Iizuka, 753 F.2d 1040 (Fed. Cir. 1985), in which the Federal Circuit held that *in vitro* testing of a claimed invention coupled with *in vivo* testing of structurally similar compounds satisfied the utility requirement. According to the court, *in vitro* data is

[p]resumably ... the accepted practice in the pharmaceutical industry, ... and we note that this practice has an inherent logical persuasiveness. In vitro testing, in general, is

2.5. Nonobviousness

In addition to the patentability requirements of novelty and utility, an invention must also be nonobvious. The nonobviousness requirement, embodied in Section 103 of the Patent Code, lies at the heart of our patent system and, in many ways, is the most significant obstacle that a patent applicant faces. The nonobviousness requirement casts a broader net than the novelty requirement because it recognizes that the limitations of a claimed invention may be scattered throughout more than one prior art reference, and it would not be unduly difficult for a person of ordinary skill in the art to assemble these elements in the form of the claimed invention. In such a situation, it could reasonably be said that the claimed invention was already in the public domain, albeit not in one single prior art reference.[157] Thus, even if an invention is novel, it may nevertheless be unpatentable if it is not *significantly* different (although not necessarily better than) than the prior art.[158]

Whether an invention is obvious is a question of law with several underlying factual inquiries, which were set forth in the seminal obviousness case of *Graham v. John Deere Co.*[159] The factual inquiries are (1)

---

relatively less complex, less time consuming, and less expensive than in vivo testing. Moreover, in vitro results with respect to the particular pharmacological activity are generally predictive of in vivo test results, *i.e.*, there is reasonable correlation there between. Were this not so, the testing procedures of the pharmaceutical industry would not be as they are. [We agree with the Board that] there is a reasonable correlation between the disclosed in vitro utility and an in vivo activity, and therefore a rigorous correlation is not necessary where the disclosure of the pharmacological activity is reasonable based upon the probative evidence.

Id. at 1050. The *Cross* court held that the utility requirement was satisfied because the *in vitro* data possessed "pharmacological acivity," which in turn is "generally predictive" of *in vivo* test results. That is, utility is satisfied if there is a "reasonable correlation between the disclosed in vitro utility and an in vivo activity." *Id.*

[157] *See* ROCHELLE COOPER DREYFUSS & ROBERTA ROSENTHAL KWALL, INTELLECTUAL PROPERTY 648 (1996).

[158] *See* P.J. Federico, *Commentary on the New Patent Act*, 75 J. PAT. TRAD. OFF. SOC'Y 160, 179-80 (1993) ("An invention which has been made, and which is new in the sense that the same thing has not been made before, may still not be patentable if the difference between the new thing, and what was known before is not considered sufficiently great to warrant a patent").

[159] 383 U.S. 1, 17 (1966).

the scope and content of the prior art, (2) the differences between the prior art and the claims at issue in the patented invention, (3) the level of ordinary skill in the art, and (4) any available objective evidence of nonobviousness (*i.e.*, so-called secondary considerations).[160]

2.5.1. Scope of the Prior Art

Even though Section 102 is the only source of prior art for Section 103 determinations, not just any Section 102 reference can be used for § 103 purposes. The courts have developed what is known as the doctrine of analogous and nonanalogous art. Only prior art that is considered to be analogous to the subject matter sought to be patented can be used under Section 103.[161]

> Two criteria have evolved for determining whether prior art is analogous: (1) whether the art is from the same field of endeavor, regardless of the problem addressed, and (2) if the reference is not within the field of the inventor's endeavor, whether the reference still is reasonably pertinent to the particular problem with which the inventor is involved.[162]

The reason for the analogous art doctrine is that while it is a difficult enough burden to presume that an inventor is knowledgeable of prior art in his own inventive field and fields related thereto, it is not only unfair but also unrealistic to require an inventor to be presumptively aware of non-analogous prior art.[163]

---

[160] *Id.* at 17. Although *Graham* states that secondary considerations "may have relevancy" "as indicia of obviousness or nonobviousness," the Federal Circuit has since treated secondary considerations as a fourth element. *See* Stratoflex, Inc. v. Aeroquip Corp., 713 F.2d 1530, 1538 (Fed. Cir. 1983) ("It is jurisprudentially inappropriate to disregard any relevant evidence on any issue in any case, patent cases included. Thus evidence rising out of the so-called *'secondary considerations' must always when present be considered en route to a determination of obviousness*" (emphasis added)).

[161] *See In re* Clay, 966 F.2d 656, 659 (Fed. Cir. 1992) ("Although § 103 does not, by its terms, define the 'art to which [the] subject matter [sought to be patented] pertains,' this determination is frequently couched in terms of whether the art is analogous or not, *i.e.*, whether the art is 'too remote to be treated as prior art'").

[162] *Id.*

[163] *See In re* Wood, 599 F.2d 1032, 1036 (CCPA 1979); *see also* Union Carbide Corp. v. American Can Co., 724 F.2d 1567, 1572 (Fed. Cir. 1984)(quoting *In re Wood*).

This analogous art requirement highlights a key distinction between a § 102 novelty determination and a § 103 obviousness inquiry. With respect to the former, a reference's analogous nature or lack thereof to the claimed subject matter is entirely irrelevant. To prove anticipation under § 102, one could point to *any* single prior art reference so long as it discloses the same invention including each and every limitation of the claimed invention; not so for § 103 purposes. To prove obviousness under § 103, one can combine the teachings of several prior art references.

2.5.2. Content of the Prior Art

The Federal Circuit and its predecessor, the CCPA, have made it perfectly clear on numerous occasions that before prior art references can be combined under Section 103, the references must *suggest* to a person of ordinary skill in the art that he should make the invention and, once made, would have a *reasonable expectation of success*.[164] According to the Federal Circuit:

> Where claimed subject matter has been rejected as obvious in view of a combination of prior art references, a proper analysis under § 103 requires, *inter alia*, consideration of two factors: (1) whether the prior art would have suggested to those of ordinary skill in the art that they should make the claimed composition or device, or carry out the claimed process; and (2) whether the prior art would also have revealed that in so making or carrying out, those of ordinary skill would have a reasonable expectation of success.[165]

Thus, although Section 103, unlike Section 102, permits one to combine prior art references, one must have a reason to do so. Consequently, an invention that is "obvious to try" in the light of the prior art, may nonetheless be nonobvious if the prior art does not suggest a reasonable likelihood of success.[166]

---

[164] *See In re* Dow Chemical Co., 837 F.2d 469, 473 (Fed. Cir. 1988).

[165] *In re* Vaeck, 947 F.2d 488, 493 (Fed. Cir. 1991) (citing *Dow Chemical*).

[166] *See In re* Deuel, 51 F.3d 1552, 1559 (Fed. Cir. 1995) ("'Obvious to try' has long been held not to constitute obviousness. A general incentive does not make obvious a particular result, nor does the existence of techniques by which those efforts can be carried out").

A suggestion to invent may come from the express language in the references, the knowledge held by those skilled in the art, or the very nature of the problem the invention solved.[167] Inasmuch as it is permissible to combine the teachings of several prior art references, one must look at the entire field of relevant prior art. The ingenuity of sifting through the prior art can in itself constitute invention. The Federal Circuit has denounced the use of hindsight reconstruction and the picking and choosing of isolated prior art disclosures absent some teaching or suggestion to combine the references.[168] The proper consideration is whether one skilled in the art would have selected the particular combination of prior art references at the time the invention was made, not whether the invention is obvious after reading the patent in suit and analyzing its claims according to any technological advances made in the field of invention.[169]

Occasionally, instead of suggesting a course of action leading to a claimed invention, the prior art will teach away from it. That is, upon reading a reference, a person of ordinary skill would be discouraged from following the path set out in the claimed invention.[170] Such a reference indicates nonobviousness and is a significant factor for a court to consider in making its nonobviousness determination.[171]

---

[167] See Pro-Mold and Tool Co., Inc. v. Great Lakes Plastics, Inc., 75 F.3d 1568, 1573 (Fed. Cir. 1996).

[168] See Technologies, Inc. v. Helena Laboratories Corp., 859 F.2d 878, 887 (Fed. Cir. 1988) ("A holding that combination claims are invalid based merely upon finding similar elements in separate prior art patents would be 'contrary to statute and would defeat the congressional purpose in enacting Title 35.'" (quoting Panduit Corporation v. Dennison Manufacturing Co., 810 F.2d 1561, 1577 (Fed. Cir. 1987)).

[169] See Panduit Corp. v. Dennison Mfg. Co., 774 F.2d 1082, 1090 (Fed. Cir. 1985).

[170] See In re Gurley, 27 F.3d 551, 553 (Fed. Cir. 1994) ("[I]n general, a reference will teach away if it suggests that the line of development flowing from the reference's disclosure is unlikely to be productive of the result sought by the applicant").

[171] Id. ("Although a reference that teaches away is a significant factor to be considered in determining nonobviousness, the nature of the teaching is highly relevant, and must be weighed in substance. A known or obvious composition does not become patentable simply because it has been described as somewhat inferior to some other product for the same use").

2.5.3. Persons of Ordinary Skill in the Art

The trier of fact does not consider whether a claimed invention was obvious to just anyone. Rather, the test of obviousness is an objective one; viewed through the eyes of a hypothetical person having ordinary skill in the art.[172] Although this imaginary person's level of skill in the art is ordinary, he is presumed to have complete knowledge of all pertinent prior art.[173] When determining the appropriate level of ordinary skill, a court may consider the inventor's level of education, the types of problems encountered in the art, typical solutions to those problems, rapidity with which innovations are made, sophistication of the technology involved, and the educational background of those working in the field.[174]

2.5.4. Secondary Considerations

Secondary considerations are relevant to, and sometimes determinative of, a Section 103 obviousness determination. The "real world" considerations, thought to be objective in nature, include *commercial success*, *long-felt need/failure of others*, *copying*, and *licensing/acquiescence*. As the *Graham* Court noted, these considerations "focus our attention on economic and motivational, rather than technical issues and are, therefore,

---

[172] *See* Kimberly-Clark Corp. v. Johnson & Johnson Co., 745 F.2d 1437, 1454 (Fed. Cir. 1984)(The person having ordinary skill in the art is not the inventor, "but an imaginary being possessing 'ordinary skill in the art' created by Congress to provide a standard of patentability, a descendant of the 'ordinary mechanic acquainted with the business' of [*Hotchkiss v. Greenwood*, 52 U.S. (How.) 246, 267 (1851)]." Further, "[r]ealistically, courts never have judged patentability by what the real inventor/applicant/patentee could or would do. Real inventors, as a class, vary in their capacities from ignorant geniuses to Nobel laureates; the courts have always applied a standard based on an imaginary worker of their own devising whom they have equated with the inventor").

[173] *See* Custom Accessories, Inc. v. Jeffrey-Allan Industries, Inc., 807 F.2d 955, 962 (Fed. Cir. 1986) ("The person of ordinary skill is a hypothetical person who is presumed to be aware of all the pertinent prior art"). As Judge Learned Hand stated, "[w]e must suppose the inventor to be endowed, as in fact no inventor is endowed; we are to impute to him knowledge of all that is not only in his immediate field, but in all fields nearly akin to that field." International Cellucotton Prod. Co. v. Sterilek Co., 94 F.2d 10, 13 (2d Cir. 1938).

[174] *See* Environmental. Designs, Ltd. v. Union Oil Co., 713 F.2d 693, 696 (Fed. Cir. 1983).

more susceptible of judicial treatment than are the highly technical facts often present in patent litigation."[175] Indeed, the Federal Circuit, perhaps more adamantly than the Supreme Court, has recognized the importance of secondary considerations, sometimes elevating them to a fourth *Graham* factor.[176]

2.5.4.1. Commercial Success

Commercial success is the most important and most often asserted of the secondary considerations. When a patentee asserts commercial success, he is essentially saying, "if my invention is obvious, why didn't any of my competitors have success making the invention given its significant consumer demand?" The reason, the argument goes, is that the competitors tried and failed, thus leading to the conclusion that the invention was nonobvious.

The assumption of the importance of the market is not self-evident. Commercial success may be due to, and consumer demand may be a result of, factors unrelated to the technical quality of the claimed invention (*e.g.*, clever advertising, aggressive marketing, business acumen, or significant market share). In fact, the Federal Circuit has held that raw sales data is insufficient to prove commercial success.[177] For evidence of commercial success to be persuasive, the patentee must show comparative success with

---

[175] *Graham, supra,* note 174, at 35-36.

[176] *See, e.g.,* Stratoflex, Inc. v. Aeroquip Corporation, 713 F.2d 1530, 1538-39 (Fed. Cir. 1983). In *Stratoflex,* the court stated:

It is jurisprudentially inappropriate to disregard any relevant evidence on any issue in any case, patent cases included. Thus evidence rising out of the so-called "secondary considerations" must always when present be considered en route to a determination of obviousness. ...

En route to a conclusion on obviousness, a court must not stop until all pieces of evidence on that issue have been fully considered and each has been given its appropriate weight. Along the way, some pieces will weigh more heavily than others, but decision should be held in abeyance, and doubt maintained, until all the evidence has had its say. The relevant evidence on the obviousness-nonobviousness issue, as the Court said in *Graham,* and as other courts had earlier emphasized, includes evidence on what has now been called "secondary considerations." It is error to exclude that evidence from consideration.

[177] *See* Vandenberg v. Dairy Equip. Co., 740 F.2d 1560, 1567 (Fed. Cir. 1984).

other products on the market,[178] *and* "a nexus must be established between [commercial success] and the merits of the claimed invention."[179]

2.5.4.2. Long-Felt Need and Failure of Others

The fact that there is a long-felt need in an industry and others in the industry have tried and failed to satisfy that need may imply nonobviousness. Consider Judge Easterbrook's comments in *In re Mahurkar Patent Litigation*:

> The existence of an enduring, unmet need is strong evidence that the invention is novel, not obvious, and not anticipated. If people are clamoring for a solution, and the best minds do not find it for years, that is practical evidence—the kind that can't be bought from a hired expert, the kind that does not depend on fallible memories or doubtful inferences—of the state of knowledge.[180]

As the Federal Circuit has noted, "the failure of others to provide a feasible solution to a long standing problem is probative of nonobviousness."[181]

However, the fact that there was a failure to achieve the patented solution may simply be the result of a company's complacency toward its existing technology even though such technology is not state of the art. Furthermore, certain firms may not be willing to commit the time and resources to solving identified problems within the industry. That is, economic and business decisions must be considered when one analyzes long-felt need and failure of others.

2.5.4.3. Copying

Frequently, patentees assert that a competitor copied the claimed invention, thus manifesting nonobviousness. This argument is perhaps strongest, however, when there is evidence that the competitor initially attempted to design around the patent.[182]

---

[178] *See In re* Mageli, 470 F.2d 1380, 1384 (CCPA 1973).

[179] Pentec, Inc. v. Graphic Controls Corp., 776 F.2d 309, 315 (Fed. Cir. 1985); *see also* Windsurfing International, Inc. v. AMF, Inc., 782 F.2d 995, 1000 (Fed. Cir. 1986).

[180] 831 F.Supp. 1354, 1377-78 (N.D. Ill. 1993), *aff'd*, 71 F.3d 1573 (Fed. Cir. 1995).

[181] Uniroyal, Inc. v. Rudkin-Wiley Corp., 837 F.2d 1044, 1054 (Fed. Cir. 1988).

[182] Vandenberg v. Dairy Equipment Co., 740 F.2d 1560 (Fed. Cir. 1984).

2.5.4.4. Licensing/Acquiescence

Lastly, a patentee may assert that the acceptance of a license by the defendant or other competitors is an implicit recognition that the patent is nonobvious. The rationale is that firms would not pay royalties on a patent unless it thought the patent was valid. As the Federal Circuit stated "such real world considerations provide a colorful picture of the state of the art, what was known by those in the art, and a solid evidentiary foundation on which to rest a nonobviousness determination."[183]

However, the Federal Circuit has noted:

[Licensing] programs are not infallible guides to patentability. They sometimes succeed because they are mutually beneficial to the licensed group or because of business judgments that it is cheaper to take licenses than to defend infringement suits, or for other reasons unrelated to the unobviousness of the licensed subject matter.[184]

In other words, sometimes it just makes business sense not to contest the validity of a patent even though you may have strong evidence of obviousness. As a result, the patentee must show a "nexus between the merits of the invention and the licenses of record."[185]

2.6. Statutory Subject Matter

Statutory subject matter addresses the kinds of things that may be patented. Specifically, 35 U.S.C. § 101 authorizes the issuance of patents for "any new and useful process, machine, manufacture, or composition of matter, or any new and useful improvement thereof."[186] These four

---

[183] Minnesota Mining & Mfg. Co. v. Johnson & Johnson Orthopaedics, Inc., 976 F.2d 1559, 1575 (Fed. Cir. 1992).

[184] EWP Corp. v. Reliance Universal, Inc., 755 F.2d 898, 907-08 (Fed. Cir. 1985).

[185] In re GPAC, Inc., 57 F.3d 1573, 1580 (Fed. Cir. 1995).

[186] 35 U.S.C. § 101 (1994). In the first Patent statute, in 1790, Congress authorized patents for "any useful art, manufacture, engine, machine, or device, or any improvement therein not before known or used." Act of April 4, 1790. Then, in 1793, Congress authorized patents for "any useful art, machine, manufacture, or composition of matter, or any new and useful improvement, not known or used before the application." Act of Feb. 21, 1793. The four categories recited in the 1793 statute are still used to describe the classes of patentable subject matter, except that the term "process"

categories of patentable subject matter are said to "include anything under the sun that is made by man."[187] There are, however, exceptions such as "laws of nature, natural phenomena, ... [and] abstract ideas."[188]

Patent claims can generally be separated into products and processes. Further, a single patent may encompass product claims and process claims.

2.6.1. Products

2.6.1.1. Machines, Articles of Manufacture, Compositions of Matter

Product claims encompass machines, manufactures,[189] and compositions of matter. Each is a distinct category of invention, but generally the distinctions have little substantive impact on patentability. For instance, "[t]he term machine includes every mechanical device or combination of mechanical powers and devices to perform some function

---

replaced "art" in the 1952 Patent Act. "Art" and "process" are considered to have the same meaning. *See* Diamond v. Diehr, 450 U.S. 175, 181-82 & nn. 6-7 (1981) ("Although the term 'process' was not added to 35 U.S.C. § 101 until 1952 a process has historically enjoyed patent protection because it was considered a form of 'art' as that term was used in the 1793 Act"); Corning v. Burden, 56 U.S. (15 How.) 252, 267 (1853) ("A process ...is included under the general term 'useful art'"); H.R. Rep. No. 1923, 82d Cong., 2d Sess. (1952).

[187] Diamond v. Chakrabarty, 447 U.S. 303, 309 (1980) (citing the Committee Reports, S. Rep. No. 1979, 82d Cong., 2d Sess. 5 (1952); H.R. Rep. No. 1923, 82d Cong. 2d Sess., 6 (1952); Hearings on H.R. 3760 Before Subcomm. No. 3 of the House Comm. on the Judiciary, 82d Cong. 1st Sess. 37 (1951) (testimony of P.J. Federico)).

[188] *Diamond v. Chakrabarty,* 447 U.S. at 309 ("[A] new mineral discovered in the earth or a new plant found in the wild is not patentable subject matter. Likewise, Einstein could not patent ... $E=mc^2$; nor could Newton have patented the law of gravity."); *Diamond v. Diehr,* 450 U.S. at 185 ("'A principle, in the abstract, is a fundamental truth; an original cause; a motive; these cannot be patented, as no one can claim in either of them an exclusive right'") (quoting Le Roy v. Tatham, 55 U.S. (14 How.) 156, 175 (1853); Rubber-Tip Pencil Co. v. Howard, 87 U.S. (20 Wall.) 498, 507 (1874) ("An idea is itself not patentable").

[189] The term "manufacture" is synonymous with "article of manufacture." *In re* Hruby, 153 U.S.P.Q. (BNA) 61, 65 (C.C.P.A. 1967).

and produce a certain effect or result."[190] In other words, machines are often used to affect another object or entity by way of transferring force or energy. A "manufacture" is typically anything human-made that is not a machine or composition of matter. Further, the Supreme Court stated that a manufacture is interpreted "in accordance with its dictionary definition to mean 'the production of articles for use from raw or prepared materials by giving to these materials new forms, qualities, properties, or combinations, whether by hand-labor or by machinery.'"[191] The general distinction between machines and manufactures is that machines typically involve moving parts,[192] where manufactures are static. A machine or manufacture is often referred to as an apparatus.

Generally, a composition of matter is a new substance resulting from the combination of known or new ingredients.[193] A "'composition of matter' has been construed consistent with its common usage to include 'all compositions of two or more substances and ... all composite articles, whether they be the results of chemical union, or of mechanical mixture, or whether they be gases, fluids, powders, or solids.'"[194]

In sum, products are "things" made by man whether static, dynamic, or chemical. These classes of "products" are useful in determining exactly what the invention is, but do not have any procedural or substantive legal significance during the application process or during infringement litigation.

2.6.1.2. Living Organisms

The boundaries of patentable subject matter are tested by new technologies, including biotechnology. Biotechnology is a booming field,

---

[190] Corning v. Burden, 56 U.S. (15 How.) 252, 267 (1853) (distinguishing a machine from a process).

[191] *Diamond v. Chakrabarty*, 447 U.S. at 308 (quoting American Fruit Growers, Inc. v. Brogdex Co., 283 U.S. 1, 11 (1931)).

[192] "The term machine includes every mechanical device or combination of mechanical powers and devices to perform some function and produce a certain result." Corning v. Burden, 56 U.S. (15 How.) 252, 267 (1853).

[193] *Diamond v. Chakrabarty*, 447 U.S. at 308.

[194] *Id.*

and patent law plays an important role in its growth and development.[195] One must begin with the Supreme Court case of *Diamond v. Chakrabarty*[196] when discussing the fields of biotechnology and genetics. Although the Court pointed out that a naturally occurring product cannot be patented even if its existence was unknown, it held that genetically-engineered, living microorganism constituted patentable subject matter.[197] According to the Court, "the relevant distinction was not between living and inanimate things, but between products of nature, whether living or not, and human-made inventions."[198]

2.6.2. Processes

Process claims are directed "to an act or a series of acts, performed upon the subject matter to be transformed and reduced to a different state or thing."[199] Section 100(b) provides that "[t]he term 'process' means process, art or method, and includes a new use of a known process, machine, manufacture, composition of matter, or material."[200] Thus, a process may entail a new use for a known product.[201]

---

[195] *See, e.g.,* In re O'Farrell, 853 F.2d 894 (Fed. Cir. 1988); Amgen, Inc. v. Chugai Pharmaceutical Co., Ltd., 927 F.2d 1200 (Fed. Cir. 1991); In re Bell, 991 F.2d 781 (Fed. Cir. 1993); *In re* Deuel, 51 F.3d 1552 (Fed. Cir. 1995).

[196] 447 U.S. 303 (1980)

[197] *Id.* at 309 ("[A] new mineral discovered in the earth or a new plant found in the wild is not patentable subject matter,"). Earlier, the Court stated that "[h]e who discovers a hitherto unknown phenomenon of nature has no claim to a monopoly of it which the law recognizes." Funk Bros. Seed Co. v. Kalo Inoculant Co., 333 U.S. 127, 130 (1948) (*quoted in* Gottschalk v. Benson, 409 U.S. 63, 67-68 (1972)).

[198] *Diamond v.Chakrabarty*, 447 U.S. at 313.

[199] Cochrane v. Deener, 94 U.S. 780, 787-88 (1876). More recently, the Federal Circuit has attempted to clarify the definition of process by stating that "[a] process ... is a manipulation according to an algorithm, ... doing something to or with something according to a schema." *In re* Durden, 763 F.2d 1406, 1410 (Fed. Cir. 1985).

[200] 35 U.S.C. § 100(b) (1994).

[201] A known product with a newly discovered use, on its own, would not be patentable as a product because of a lack of novelty. However, the inventor might acquire a patent for a new method of using a known product so long as the new use can be distinguished from the known use. Titanium Metals Corp. v. Banner, 778 F.2d 775, 780-81 (Fed. Cir. 1985); *In re* Bergstrom, 427 F.2d 1394, 1402-03 (C.C.P.A. 1970).

Perhaps the principal controversy surrounding patentable subject matter today concerns the mathematical characteristics of computer software.[202] Patentable subject matter issues arise with digital computers because it is essentially a process that includes steps involving mathematical formulas or algorithms. In *Diamond v. Diehr*,[203] the Supreme Court affirmed the potential patentability of such a method. Specifically, the Court stated that "[w]hile a scientific truth, or the mathematical expression of it, is not a patentable invention, a novel and useful structure created with the aid of knowledge of scientific truth may be."[204] In determining whether the use of a particular mathematical algorithm is patentable, the Court held that a claim satisfies Section 101 "when a claim containing a mathematical formula implements or applies that formula in a structure or process which, when considered as a whole, is performing a function which the patent laws were designed to protect (e.g., transforming or reducing an article to a different state or thing)."[205]

The Federal Circuit, in *State Street Bank & Trust Co. v. Signature Financial Group Inc.*,[206] took an expansive view of patentable subject matter, specifically process patent inventions that include mathematical algorithms.

---

[202] Besides computer-related process difficulties, other areas have experienced challenges. For example, from at least 1862 a patent could not be acquired for medical procedures. *See* Morton v. New York Eye Infirmary, 17 F. Cas. 879, 882-84 (C.C.S.D.N.Y. 1862) (No. 9,865) (implying that medical procedures were not patentable despite the invention being "one of the great discoveries of modern time,"); *In re* Brinkerhoff, 27 J. PAT. OFF. SOC'Y 797 (Nov. 1945) (reviewing *Ex parte* Brinkerhoff, 24 Comm'n Manuscript Decision 349 (1883) (Case No. 182) ("The methods or modes of treatment of [sic, by] physicians of certain diseases are not patentable"). In 1954, the PTO Board of Appeals ruled that a patent may be attained for a medical procedure. *Ex parte* Scherer, 103 U.S.P.Q. (BNA) 107, 108 (Pat. & Tm. Off. Bd. App. 1954). Then from 1054 to 1996, medical procedures were, theoretically, patentable and enforceable. However, after a patentee attempted to enforce a medical procedure patent, in Pallin v. Singer, 36 U.S.P.Q.2d 1050 (D. Vt. 1995) (Opinion and Order), 1996 WL 274407 (D. Vt. 1995), Congress and medical associations rallied and legislation was passed to render medical procedure patents unenforceable. *See* 35 U.S.C. § 287(c) (West Supp. 1997).

[203] 450 U.S. 175 (1981)

[204] *Id.* at 188.

[205] *Id.* at 192.

[206] 149 F.3d 1368 (Fed. Cir. 1998).

According to the court, any process, including a business method, is statutory subject matter if it possesses practical utility in producing a "useful, concrete and tangible result:"[207]

§3. FORMALITIES

The United States Patent and Trademark Office (PTO) plays a crucial role in the U.S. patent system. Patent rights do not exist unless granted by the federal government.[208] To obtain a patent, an inventor must file a patent application with the PTO. Then, the Commissioner of Patents and Trademarks is required to "cause an examination to be made of the application and the alleged new invention; and if on such examination it appears that the applicant is entitled to a patent under the law, the Commissioner shall issue a patent therefor."[209] Examination is conducted to ensure that the claimed invention is adequately disclosed (35 U.S.C. § 112), new (35 U.S.C. § 102), nonobvious (35 U.S.C. § 103), useful (35 U.S.C. § 101), and within the statutory classes of patentable subject matter (35 U.S.C. § 101). The process of obtaining a patent is called *patent prosecution*. The writing necessary for a patent application is very technical and a degree in the relevant scientific discipline or other appropriate technical background is helpful. Indeed, the patent prosecutor has an obligation to know and comprehend not only the law, but also the pertinent

---

[207] *Id.* at 1373 ("Today, we hold that the transformation of data, representing discrete dollar amounts, by a machine through a series of mathematical calculations into a final share price, constitutes a practical application of a mathematical algorithm, formula, or calculation, because it produces "a useful, concrete and tangible result").*See also In re* Alappat, 33 F.3d 1526 (Fed. Cir.1994); Arrythmia Research Technology Inc. v. Corazonix Corp., 958 F.2d 1053 (Fed. Cir.1992).

[208] In contrast, for example, copyright subsists in a work once it is "fixed in any tangible medium of expression," 17 U.S.C. § 102 (a), and federal registration is needed only to obtain certain remedies, 17 U.S.C. § 412. Similarly, property rights in trademarks are initially created by using the mark in trade, not by governmental grant or registration, while federal registration gives the owner the benefit of additional federal rights and remedies. *See In re* DC Comics 689 F.2d, 1042, 1046-55 (Fed. Cir. 1982) (opinions by Judges Rich and Nies concurring in result and reviewing the life-cycle of a trademark—beginning with initial use and ending with abandonment or genericness).

[209] 35 U.S.C. § 131 (1994).

technology. Thus, specialized training is generally required, with a few notable exceptions, for registration to practice before the PTO.[210]

The patent application, and the resulting issued patent, contains two major components: (1) the *written description* and (2) the *claims*. These two components together make up the *specification*.[211] The process by which the patent specification and especially the patent claims are shaped is of primary importance because the claims of the issued patent establish the metes and bounds of the patent owner's right to exclude:

> The U.S. is strictly an examination country and the main purpose of the examination, to which every application is subjected, is to try and make sure that what each claim defines is patentable. To coin a phrase, *the name of the game is the claim* [and] the function of claims is to enable everyone to know, without going through a lawsuit, what infringes the patent and what does not.[212]

3.1. The Patent Application & Issued Patent

Although the patent application process may be thought of as beginning with the drafting of the application itself, this is usually preceded by other events. For example, an inventor usually documents and records his conception of the invention as well as the ensuing development of the invention towards a practical embodiment — this development process is called "*reduction to practice*." In addition, substantial dialogue may occur between the inventor and the person preparing the application.

Another probable pre-filing event is a *prior art* search. "Prior art" is a term used in patent law to refer broadly to known technical information. Although an applicant is under no obligation to conduct a search prior to

---

[210] *See* 37 C.F.R. §§ 10.5, 10.6, 10.7 (1996), wherein the regulations governing the individuals practicing before the PTO are set forth. The PTO issues a pamphlet entitled "General Requirements for Admission to the Examination for Registration to Practice in Patent Cases before the U.S. Patent and Trademark Office."

[211] *See* 35 U.S.C. § 112. Although often, and incorrectly, used interchangeably, the terms "written description" and "specification" are *not* co-extensive. The specification contains the claims as well as the written description.

[212] Giles S. Rich, *The Extent of the Protection and Interpretation of Claims—American Perspectives*, 21 INT'L REV. INDUS. PROP. & COPYRIGHT L. 497, 499, 501 (1990).

filing an application,[213] a search is usually done in view of the significant cost associated with filing a patent application. A thorough search may avoid the unnecessary costs of attempting to patent a pre-existing invention. It may also help give the applicant an opportunity to make informed arguments about the patentability of the invention, and to present the written description and claims in a way favorable to patentability. This search for relevant prior patents and other technical literature may be carried out in the Public Search Room maintained by the PTO in its Arlington, Virginia, location or various satellite search locations scattered throughout the United States, or in libraries or other repositories. Today, one may conduct a prior art search using various electronic media, including on-line services and the Internet.

Each application consists of a: (1) specification (*i.e.*, the written description and at least one claim), (2) one or more drawings (if necessary), (3) an oath or declaration,[214] and (4) the required filing fees.[215] The filing date of such an application, known as a *non-provisional* application,[216] is the date on which the specification and drawings, including at least one claim, are received at the PTO or the date they were deposited in a U.S. post office as Express Mail, provided that the mailing day was one on which the PTO was open.

While there is some flexibility as to the presentation of the patent application, the PTO prefers the application to be filed as follows:

1. title;

---

[213] *See* American Hoist & Derrick Co. v. Sowa & Sons, 725 F.2d 1350, 1362 (Fed. Cir. 1984).

[214] The oath or declaration must usually be signed by the inventor, and must state that the inventor has: (1) read the application, (2) believes he is the first inventor, and (3) acknowledges the duty to disclose any material information. *See* 37 C.F.R. § 1.63 (b) (1996). 37 C.F.R. § 1.77 (1996); Patent & Trademark Office, U.S. Department of Commerce, MPEP § 601 (6th ed. 1995, rev. July 1996).

[215] *See* 35 U.S.C. § 111(a)(2), (3) (Supp. 1997).

[216] Instead of *initially* filing a non-provisional application, an applicant, as of June 8, 1995, may opt to file a "provisional application." As a provisional application does not require claims, it is not examined and cannot mature into a patent. 35 U.S.C. § 111(b) (Supp. 1997). Nevertheless, priority can still be claimed from the date of the provisional application by filing a non-provisional application within one-year from the provisional application's filing date.

2. cross-reference to related inventions;

3. statement regarding federally sponsored research;

4. background of the invention;

5. summary;

6. brief description of the drawings;

7. detailed description of the invention;

8. claims;

9. abstract of the disclosure;

10. drawings;

11. oath or declaration.

3.1.1. The Written Description

3.1.1.1. Background of the Invention

The Background section of a patent usually accomplishes three things: (1) it sets the stage for the applicant's invention by describing the state of the prior art; (2) it directly addresses the most important aspect of the invention; and (3) it points out why that aspect was an improvement over the prior art. Skilled practitioners disagree about whether to introduce the invention's improvements over the prior art in the Background section, or whether to limit the Background section to a discussion of the prior art.

The Background section should use as simple language as the invention permits, especially with respect to commercial issues. Although the law provides that a patent application should provide technical information to a "person of ordinary skill in the art" to which the invention pertains, some argue that every patent should be written with an eye to the judge, jury, and investment banker, as well as the patent examiner.

3.1.1.2. Summary of the Invention

The Summary states the invention broadly, tracking the broadest claim, but requires sufficient detail to explain and distinguish from the prior art. The Manual of Patent Examining Procedure ("MPEP") points out, "[s]ince the purpose of the brief summary of invention is to apprise the public, and more especially those interested in the particular art to which the invention relates, of the nature of the invention, the summary should be directed to the specific invention being claimed, in contradistinction to mere generalities which would be equally applicable to numerous preceding patents."[217] The MPEP also suggests that "[t]he brief summary, if properly written to set out the exact nature, operation, and purpose of the invention, will be of material assistance in aiding ready understanding of the patent in future searches."[218]

Although no one particular way to write the Summary exists, it is recommended that Section 608.01(d) of the MPEP be followed so that the patent examiner, as well as the public, knows where to look for various kinds of information.

3.1.1.3. Detailed Description of the Invention

The Detailed Description focuses on the details of the invention. Because of its comprehensiveness, it constitutes the bulk of the specification. The Detailed Description must contain a *written description* of the invention and must be in terms sufficiently full, clear, concise, and exact as to *enable* any person skilled in the art to which the invention pertains to make and use the invention.[219] The patent applicant must also disclose the *best mode* of carrying out the invention known to the inventor at the time of filing.[220] The best mode is usually described in the detailed description, and may also be represented in the drawings.

3.1.1.4. The Drawings

Title 35, Section 113, requires the applicant to "furnish a drawing where necessary for the understanding of the subject matter sought to be patented." Drawings are often instructive in teaching the essence of the invention, and are typically necessary for mechanical devices and other forms of invention. If the invention is for a process or method, then drawings usually are not required. If drawings are required, there are formal rules governing their acceptability. Photographs are not accepted, except in very limited situations.

---

[217] MPEP § 608.01(d) (rev. ed 1995).

[218] *Id.*

[219] *See* 35 U.S.C. § 112, ¶ 1 (1994).

[220] *Id.*

3.1.2. The Claims

The 1790 and 1793 Patent Acts made no mention of claims. The invention was discerned from the written description, often with a claim-like summary at the end. It was not until the 1836 Act that "claims" were mentioned by statute.

Our present Patent Code requires that "[t]he specification shall conclude with one or more claims particularly pointing out and distinctly claiming the subject matter which the applicant regards as his invention."[221] Today, the claim is the most important part of the patent, setting forth the metes and bounds of the patentee's right to exclude. The Federal Circuit has stated time and again, "[i]t is the claims that measure the invention" and "[c]laims are infringed, not specifications."[222] Indeed, claim drafting is truly an art, the importance of which cannot be overstated.[223]

Claims are usually made up of three parts: a *preamble*, a *transition phrase*, and a *body*. The preamble identifies the invention or the technical field of the invention. The transition phrase joins the preamble to the body of the claim. The transition phrase is usually made up only of the word "comprising,"[224] which means that the invention includes the listed elements, but does not exclude others.[225] The body of the claim includes a recitation of the "elements:" the steps or parts that make up the invention. It also includes the structural, physical, or functional relationship among the elements. The elements and their relationship usually define the claim,

---

[221] 35 U.S.C. § 112, ¶ 2 (1994).

[222] SRI International v. Matsushita Electric Corporation of America, 775 F.2d 1101, 1121 (Fed. Cir. 1985).

[223] Books have been devoted to teaching the patent practitioner how best to draft claims. *See, e.g.,* ROBERT C. FABER, LANDIS ON THE MECHANICS OF PATENT CLAIM DRAFTING (4th ed. 1996)[hereinafter MECHANICS OF CLAIM DRAFTING]; THOMAS J. GREER, JR., WRITING & UNDERSTANDING U.S. PATENT CLAIMS (1979); THE ART OF DRAFTING PATENT CLAIMS (Joseph G. Jackson & G. Michael Morris eds., 1966); EMERSON STRINGHAM, PATENT CLAIM DRAFTING (2d ed. 1952).

[224] "Including" and "having" sometimes replace the word "comprising."

[225] *See* Moleculon Research Corp. v. CBS, Inc., 229 USPQ 805, 812 (Fed. Cir. 1986); *see also In re* Gray, 53 F.2d 520 (C.C.P.A. 1931); *Ex parte* Jackson, 3 USPQ 314 (Pat. Off. Bd. App. 1929).

at least for apparatus or device claims. Process claims may require additional detail.

Words in a patent are not necessarily held to their ordinary meaning. Each inventor can be his own lexicographer. However, the application must define words being used in an uncommon manner.[226] As with the rest of the patent, the author of the patent can punctuate and fashion the claim in whatever manner he desires, except that each claim must be one sentence, so there can be only one period, at the end of the sentence.

A patent application generally has more than one claim. The claims of a patent may vary in scope or method of description or expression. Broad claims include fewer limitations than do narrow claims and therefore cover a wider scope. Claims are often arranged in order of decreasing scope, that is, the broadest first and the narrowest last. Claims can be in independent, dependent, or multiple dependent form. An independent claim is completely self-contained. A dependent claim refers back to an earlier claim and thus it incorporates by reference all limitations of the claim to which if refers and also includes its own limitations. A multiple dependent claim refers back in the alternative to two or more claims and is considered to include all of its own limitations as well as those of any one of the referenced claims.[227]

There are five principal ways of claiming the statutory classes of invention set forth in 35 U.S.C. § 101: composition claims, process claims, apparatus claims, product-by-process claims, and means-plus-function claim elements.

3.1.2.1. Composition Claims

Although in practice the usage is not precise, chemical compounds are viewed as "compositions of matter"; whereas chemical combinations or mixtures of ingredients are more accurately called "compositions." They may be claimed by naming the compound or the ingredients. If necessary,

---

[226] *See* Lear Siegler, Inc. v. Aeroquip Corp., 733 F.2d 881, 888 (Fed. Cir. 1984); W.L. Gore & Assocs., Inc. v. Garlock, Inc., 721 F.2d 1540, 1558 (Fed. Cir. 1983); Autogiro Co. of America v. United States, 384 U.S. F.2d 391, 376-397 (Ct. Cl. 1967).

[227] For other examples of an independent claim, see FABER, MECHANICS OF CLAIM DRAFTING, *supra*, note 238, at 17-18. For examples of a dependent claim, see *id.* at 163. For examples of multiple dependent claims, see MPEP, at § 608.01(n).

the proportions or other parameters of the composition are stated. For example:

A plasticizer composition, comprising:

(a) about 50-60% A;

(b) about 20-30% B;

(c) about 15-25% C; and

(d) a pH-modifying substance in an amount sufficient to adjust the pH to a value of about 3 to 4.5.[228]

3.1.2.2. Process Claims

Process or method claims can be divided into (1) processes or methods of *making*; and (2) processes or methods of *using*. As to the former, the typical method of *making* claim involves acts or steps performed on an object(s) or substance(s) to achieve some result. For example:

A process for making chemical compound X, comprising the steps of:

(a) *mixing* water with compound Z to form a mixture;

(b) *heating* the mixture at a temperature of about 150-160° C;

(c) *distilling* the mixture; and

(d) *permitting* the mixture to cool to room temperature.[229]

Notice the importance of gerunds in process claims.

It is the combination or sequence of acts or steps that are patented in a process claim, not the resulting product. Where there is a sequence of steps, the sequence should be described. However, nonessential steps and sequences should not be recited in a process claim lest the claim be too easily circumvented.[230]

The only way to patent a new use of an old or new product is in the form of a method claim — this would be a method of *using* claim. Consider the following typical method of use claim:

---

[228] *See* FABER, MECHANICS OF PATENT CLAIM DRAFTING, *supra*, note 238, at § 49.

[229] *Id.* at § 37.

[230] *See id.* at § 39.

The method of treating baldness, which comprises applying to the scalp an aqueous solution of sodium chloride having a concentration of 30-40 percent by weight of sodium chloride.[231]

3.1.2.3. Apparatus Claims

Apparatus claims generally are directed to mechanical structure. The preamble usually recites the purpose of the apparatus. After the transition (*e.g.*, "comprising"), each essential element of the apparatus is set forth, in outline form. The claim must sufficiently recite the connection among the elements to define clearly the apparatus. The following example illustrates a simple apparatus claim:

Apparatus for shaking articles, which comprises:

(a) a container for the articles;

(b) a base; and

(c) a plurality of parallel legs, each leg connected pivotally at one end to the container and at the other end to the base to support the container for oscillating movement with respect to the base.[232]

3.1.2.4. Product-by-Process Claims

Product-by-process claims are hybrid claims designed to facilitate the claiming of complex products whose structure or other characteristics are insufficiently known to permit adequate description of the product itself. They indirectly claim a product by reciting the process of creating the product. They usually take the form, "a product 'prepared by a process comprising the steps of ... .'"[233] For example,

The product of a process comprising the steps of:

(a) *mixing* water with compound Z to form a mixture;

(b) *heating* the mixture at a temperature of about 150-160° C;

(c) *distilling* the mixture; and

(d) *permitting* the mixture to cool to room temperature.

---

[231] *Id.* at § 42.

[232] *Id.* at § 14.

[233] SHELDON, HOW TO WRITE A PATENT APPLICATION, at § 6.4.5. The PTO views product-by-process claims as product claims. Therefore, the MPEP and several cases require that the product itself meet the requirements of patentability.

Federal Circuit precedent is inconsistent as to whether such products are limited to the process described and claimed in the patent.[234]

3.1.2.5. Means-Plus-Function Claim Elements

Title 35, Section 112, paragraph six, specifically permits "an element in a claim for a combination [to] be expressed as a means or step for performing a specified function." These claim elements are called "*means-plus-function*" elements.[235] Such a claim element defines the function of the element, rather than its structure. The statute then provides that the claim element "shall be construed to cover the corresponding structure, material, or acts described in the specification and equivalents thereof." Consider the sample apparatus claim stated above, with the added means-plus-function element:

Apparatus for shaking articles, which comprises:

(a) a container for the articles;

(b) a base;

(c) a plurality of parallel legs, each leg is connected pivotally at one end to the container and at the other end to the base to support the container for oscillating movement with respect to the base; and

(d) *means for oscillating the container on the legs to shake the articles.*[236]

Whether a claim element may properly be considered under Section 112, paragraph six, is sometimes a difficult question.[237]

---

[234] *Compare* Scripps Clinic & Research Foundation v. Genentech, Inc., 927 F.2d 1565 (Fed. Cir. 1991) (product-by-process claims not limited by process set forth in claim) *with* Atlantic Thermoplastics Co. v. Faytex Corp., 970 F.2d 834 (Fed. Cir. 1992)(process set forth serves as limitation in determining infringement). *See also,* Exxon Chemical Patents, Inc. v. Lubrizol Corp., 64 F.3d 1553 (Fed. Cir. 1995), *suggestion for rehearing and rehearing en banc denied,* 77 F.3d 450 (Fed. Cir. 1996).

[235] Section 112, paragraph six applies only to combination claims, which necessarily have two or more distinct elements, only one of which might be defined in means-plus-function language.

[236] FABER, MECHANICS OF CLAIM DRAFTING, *supra,* note 238, at § 14.

[237] *See e.g.,* Unidynamics v. Automatic Prod., 157 F.3d 1311 (Fed. Cir. 1998); Cole v. Kimberly-Clark Corp., 102 F.3d 524 (Fed. Cir. 1996); York Products, Inc. v. Central Tractor Farm & Family Center, 99 F.3d 1568 (Fed. Cir. 1996).

3.2. Procedures Before the Patent and Trademark Office

The Patent Office, renamed the Patent and Trademark Office in 1975, is recognized as the oldest federal agency in the United States, created by statute in 1836 and now one of fourteen bureaus in the Department of Commerce.[238]

3.2.1. Initial Processing of the Application

New applications are initially processed by the Application Division, which decides if an application is complete and meets all formal requirements. Any drawings accompanying the application are forwarded to the official draftsman, who checks to see if the drawings comply with the formal requirements. Any assignment of the application is forwarded to the Assignment Division, which records the assignment in its computer and microfilm records and returns it to the applicant with a notification of the reel and frame numbers in the microfilm records.

The PTO maintains a detailed classification system by which all technologies are broken down into specific categories (e.g., chemical, electrical, etc.). Within the classification system are hundreds of classes, each class having at least dozens of subclasses. The Application Division determines the appropriate technological class and subclass of the application. It then forwards the application to the examining group in charge of that class and subclass. These documents are kept in a file jacket known as a "file wrapper."

---

[238] Although it was the 1836 Act that officially created the Patent Office, it is difficult to say exactly when it was started. It was not part of the 1790 or 1793 Patent Acts. However, in 1802, Secretary of State James Madison, who was instrumental in the development of patent and copyright law during the early years of the American republic, made the Patent Office a distinct division of the Department of State and appointed the highly regarded Dr. William Thorton, the designer of the U.S. Capitol, at a salary of $1,400 a year to the full-time position of supervising the issuance of patents. Some say that it was with the appointment of Dr. Thorton in 1802 that the Patent Office was created. For a brief history of the name of the Patent and Trademark Office see S. Rep. No. 93-1399, (1974), reprinted in 1974 U.S.C.C.A.N. 7113.

3.2.2. Examination and Prosecution

3.2.2.1. Formalities and Search by the Examiner

When an application reaches an examining group, it is assigned to the appropriate art (*i.e.*, technology) unit and then to a particular examiner. The examiner first ascertains that the application contains the elements required to obtain a filing date: (1) written description; (2) claim; and (3) any required drawing.[239]

After determining that an application satisfies these requirements, the examiner conducts a search for prior art relevant to the claimed subject matter. Much of the relevant prior art is usually set forth in the patent applicant's Information Disclosure Statement submitted to the PTO along with or shortly after the filing of the application.[240] The quality and thoroughness of the examiner's search is a function of his searching skill, the time allocated for the search, and the completeness of the libraries searched.

3.2.2.2. Office Action

After this initial activity by the examiner, he communicates in writing to the applicant or to his attorney or agent, if one has been appointed. This communication is called an *Office Action*, which includes a form cover letter, on which the examiner summarizes the action by checking the appropriate boxes and filling in the correct blanks, and an explanation of the action.

3.2.2.3. Applicant's Response

Within the period of time allotted for response, which usually can be extended up to the maximum statutory period of six months upon payment of a fee, the applicant must respond to all of the examiner's rejections and objections or the application will be held abandoned.

Applicants may respond to claim rejections and objections by amendment of the claims and arguments specifically addressing the examiner's Action. Usually, a response includes both claim amendments

---

[239] *See* 37 C.F.R. § 1.53(b)(1).

[240] *See* 37 C.F.R. § 1.56.

and arguments designed to distinguish the invention as claimed from any prior art cited by the examiner.[241]

The applicant may also respond by amending the written description to include the language of an originally-filed claim if the examiner rejects or objects to a claim as not being supported by the written description. In addition, the applicant may amend the written description in response to an objection asserting that it does not describe the invention with sufficient clarity, provided that the applicant not introduce "*new matter.*"[242] New matter is substantive information not contained in the originally filed application. For the most part, there is very little an applicant can do to the written description *after* he files the application.

3.2.2.4. Reconsideration and Allowance

After the applicant submits a response to the first Office Action, the examiner reconsiders the application. If the examiner is satisfied with the response, he issues a *Notice of Allowance*, a form letter, the primary purpose of which is to inform the applicant of allowance of the application.

If the examiner is not satisfied with the response, he may issue a second Office Action. Unless a second or subsequent Office Action is based on a new ground of rejection, such as newly discovered prior art, the examiner may make the rejection "final." At any time from the issuance of the first Office Action until the issuance of a final Office Action, the applicant or applicant's representative is entitled to a personal or telephonic interview with the examiner for the purposes of clarifying the issues and of reaching an agreement leading to the allowance of the application. After a final Office Action is issued, it is within the examiner's discretion to allow interviews and to consider responses. The examiner must make the substance of the interview of record by completing an Examiner Interview Summary Record form and, unless excused by the examiner, the applicant must also file a summary of the interview. [243]

---

[241] Although the amendment may be self-explanatory, as a rule of practice the applicant should accompany the amendment with an explanation of its relevance.

[242] *See* 35 U.S.C. § 132 (1994).

[243] *See* 37 C.F.R. § 1.133(b) (1996). For a discussion of interview practice, *see* Magnivision v. Bonneau Co., 115 F.3d 956 (Fed. Cir. 1997).

3.2.2.5. Responses to a Final Office Action

After a final rejection by the examiner, the applicant is faced with a choice. The applicant can (1) abandon the application; (2) file an appeal with the Board of Patent Appeals and Interferences;[244] (3) take allowed claims and cancel the others; or (4) file a continuing application.

3.2.2.5.1. Appeals

If the applicant files an appeal with the Board, he is given two months, extendable to six months, to file an Appeal Brief. After the Appeal Brief has been filed, the examiner must file an Examiner's Answer. There is no statutory or regulatory time limit for filing the Examiner's Answer. Within one month of the Examiner's Answer, the applicant may file a Reply Brief directed only to any new points that were raised in the Examiner's Answer.

The applicant may request an oral hearing. The appeal is then placed on the board's calendar and assigned to a panel of three Administrative Patent Judges. When an appeal is set for oral hearing, the applicant is given notice of the date of the hearing and, at that point, may waive the hearing.

After oral hearing, or if no oral hearing is requested, the appeal is considered by the board. The board may affirm the decision of the examiner in whole or in part, or may reverse it. If the board affirms the examiner's decision, the applicant may abandon the application, file a continuing application, bring a civil action to obtain a patent in the District Court for the District of Columbia, or appeal the board's decision directly to the Federal Circuit. If the board reverses the examiner's decision, the examiner must issue a Notice of Allowance. The board can also order further examination or other procedures, if the case warrants.

3.2.2.5.2. Cancellation of Claims

If an applicant faces final rejection of some claims, but allowance of others, whether or not the result of an appeal, he may decide to take the allowed claims and cancel the others. A Notice of Allowance so limited would then be issued.

---

[244] The Board of Patent Appeals and Interferences is an Article I adjudicative board within the PTO. *See generally* Michael W. Bloomer, *The Board of Patent Appeals and Interferences*, AM. INTELL. PROP. L. ASS'N BULL., Dec. 1992, at 188; Paul J. Federico, *The Board of Appeals 1861-1961*, 43 J. PAT. OFF. SOC'Y 691 (1961).

3.2.2.5.3. Continuing Applications

"Continuing application" is a generic term for three types of patent applications that are entitled to the filing date of an earlier ("parent") application. The three types of continuing applications are *continuation applications*, *continuation-in-part applications*, and *divisional applications*. The requirements for claiming continuing status are that the application be filed while the parent application is still pending ("copendency"), at least one inventor must be common to the two applications, and the text of the second application must refer back to the first.[245]

If an applicant faces a final rejection of all claims in an application, or a final rejection of claims that were canceled to allow other claims to issue, the applicant may wish to file a continuing application directed to the canceled claims. In addition, there may be other reasons for filing a continuing application, as discussed below.

A *continuation application* is an application whose written description is the same as that of the parent application, but whose claims may be the same or different from those of the parent application. A continuation application is entitled to the parent's filing date as to all subject matter contained in it. A continuation might be filed to obtain further prosecution if all claims are finally rejected in the parent, but the applicant has new amendments or arguments to present. A continuation application is often appropriate if the new amendments or arguments were presented in the parent after final rejection and were not entered because they raised new issues or required further searching, but the examiner gave some indication that the amendments or arguments had some merit. A continuation might also be filed if only some claims were finally rejected in the parent. Those claims might be canceled from the parent, allowing the other claims to issue. The canceled claims may then be pursued, with or without change, in the continuation.

A *continuation-in-part application* is an application that has some subject matter in common with the parent but also has new subject matter. A continuation-in-part is entitled to the parent's filing date as to any subject matter in common, but only to its own filing date as to the new matter. A continuation-in-part might be filed if the applicant wished to add

---

[245] *See* MPEP, §§ 201.06, 201.07, 201.08, 201.11 (rev. ed. 1995).

limitations to the parent claims to distinguish a reference or references, but the added limitations were not supported by the written description of the parent and the examiner would not allow supporting material to be added to the written description because it introduced new matter. The applicant could file a continuation-in-part to include the new matter. A continuation-in-part, including newly developed information, might also be filed if the applicant has improved the invention described in the parent. A continuation-in-part may be filed at any time, regardless of the status of prosecution of the parent case, as long as the parent is still pending.

A *divisional application* is a continuing application that is based on a parent application and has the same written description except that the claims differ, usually because of a restriction requirement. An examiner issues a restriction requirement when he believes the application claims more than one invention. When an examiner issues a restriction requirement the applicant is forced to elect which invention he wants to prosecute. This does not mean that the applicant is precluded from seeking patent protection for the non-elected invention. In fact, the non-elected invention may be prosecuted by filing a divisional application. If the claims of the divisional application, however, are not patentably distinct (nonobvious) from the claims of the parent application, the examiner may reject the divisional claims based on *obviousness type double patenting*.[246] In essence, the examiner is preventing the applicant from extending his patent rights beyond the statutory term. This type of rejection had significantly more power prior to the GATT amendments to the patent law, which now measure a patent's term from date of filing (*i.e.*, twenty years from date of filing) as opposed to date of issuance (*i.e.*, seventeen years from date of issuance). Because a divisional application by definition is entitled to the same filing date as the parent application, both will terminate 20 years from the filing date of the parent application.

3.2.2.6. Publication
Prior to the American Inventors Protection Act of 1999 (AIPA), patents were kept secret by the PTO. The AIPA as codified in the United States Code and the Federal Regulations, however, authorizes publication of applications filed on or after 29 November 2000. Pursuant to 35 U.S.C.

---

[246] *See* Symbol Technologies Inc. v. Opticon Inc., 936 F.2d 1569 (Fed. Cir. 1991).

§ 122(b)(1) (2001), subject to some exceptions, "each application for a patent shall be published...promptly after the expiration of a period of eighteen months from the earliest filing date." The exceptions to publication are set forth in 35 U.S.C. § 122(b)(2) (2001). The principal exception to publication is the applicant agrees he will not seek foreign patent protection.

3.2.2.7. Foreign Priority

An applicant can claim the benefit of the filing date of an application filed abroad. Under the terms of the Paris Convention for the Protection of Industrial Property,[247] implemented in the United States under 35 U.S.C. § 119, the benefit of the filing date (referred to as "priority") from the first application for an invention filed in any member country can be claimed in a U.S. application as long as it is *filed within one year* of the first application.[248] Priority can be claimed at any time during the pendency of an application. A claim of priority is perfected by filing a certified copy of the foreign application. Whether benefit is claimed from a domestic or foreign application, materials published between the priority date and the application filing date are not prior art to the application. However, the one-year period of 35 U.S.C. § 102(b) is counted from the earliest effective U.S. filing date, not from a foreign priority date.[249]

---

[247] Priority is also available under the GATT-World Trade Organization Treaty or under bilateral agreements with individual countries. For example, the United States now has an agreement with Taiwan, as of April 10, 1996, allowing patent applications filed in Taiwan to claim priority based on the filing date of the corresponding U.S. patent applications. *See* Daisy Wang, *Taiwan-U.S. Agreement Permits Claim to Priority Based on U.S. Filing Date*, 10 WORLD INTELLECTUAL PROPERTY REPORT 173 (1996).

[248] In addition to the application filed in a member country, an applicant (in certain circumstances) may rely on an "international application" filed pursuant to the Patent Cooperation Treaty (PCT), which is administered by the World Intellectual Property Organization (WIPO). The PCT is a multilateral treaty among more than 50 nations that is designed to simplify the patenting process when an applicant seeks a patent on the same invention in more than one nation. *See* 35 U.S.C. chs. 35-37, and World Intellectual Property Organization, *PCT Applicant's Guide* (1992, rev. 1994).

[249] What effect the GATT-based provisional application's domestic priority date will have if invoked is unknown.

3.2.2.8. Interferences

If two or more applications claim the same subject matter, the applications are said to be "interfering" and the examiner, after determining patentability of the invention to each applicant, can declare an "interference" between them.[250] A patent interference is an *inter partes* proceeding in the PTO to determine which of two or more parties was the first to make the invention.[251] An interference can also be declared between a pending application and an issued patent. If the examiner does not declare the interference, the applicant can provoke an interference. An interference can relate to some or all of the claims in the application or patent.

3.2.3. Appeals to the Courts

If an applicant is dissatisfied with a decision of the Board of Patent Appeals and Interferences in an appeal from a final rejection by the examiner, he may initiate a civil action against the Commissioner of Patents and Trademarks in the U.S. District Court for the District of Columbia. A party to an interference that is dissatisfied with the decision of the Board may have remedy by civil action against the other party.[252] In the district court, the question of the applicant's or the interfering parties' right to a patent is tried *de novo*. Appeal from the decision of the district court is taken exclusively to the Federal Circuit.[253] Alternatively, an applicant may appeal directly from the PTO to the Federal Circuit.[254] In practice, a vast majority of appeals are taken directly to the Federal Circuit, which reviews the PTO's findings of fact and questions of law for clear error and *de novo*,

---

[250] *See* 37 C.F.R. § 1.605 (1996); MPEP § 2305.

[251] Changing the United States from a first-to-invent patent system to a first-to-file patent system used by almost every other country was the subject of many trade and legislative efforts in the early 1990s. As of January 24, 1994, the United States ceased negotiations regarding this change, but held open the option to convert to a first-to-file patent system in the future. *See generally U.S. Says 'Not Now' on First-to-File & Agrees with Japan on Patent Term*, 47 Pat. Trademark & Copyright J. (BNA) 285 (January 27, 1994).

[252] *See* 35 U.S.C. §§ 145, 146 (1984 & Supp. 1997).

[253] *See* 28 U.S.C. § 1295 (1994).

[254] *See* 35 U.S.C. § 141 (1994).

respectively.[255] Decisions of the Federal Circuit are subject to the *certiorari* jurisdiction of the Supreme Court.

3.3. Post-Issuance Procedures

There are procedures whereby the terms of a patent may be reconsidered *after* the patent issues. The procedures are complex and should not be relied upon to correct major flaws in prosecution. The two main procedures that the Patent Act has established to accomplish this renegotiation and correction are *reissue* and *reexamination*.

3.3.1. Reissue

Reissue's objective is to allow the patent owner to correct an inadvertent mistake. As such, this process is made available only to the patent owner. Unlike a reexamination proceeding, neither a third party nor the PTO can institute a reissue proceeding.

The Patent Act requires that the mistake sought to be corrected by reissue must be such that its presence causes the patent to be "deemed by the owner wholly or partially inoperative or invalid."[256] The courts have interpreted this requirement to include everything from a typographical error to an error in the scope of the claims.

An inventor is required to show that the mistake was unintentional or unavoidable and without deceptive intent. While the government permits the inventor some flexibility in correcting the terms of the patent through reissue, the threshold requirement, in practice, is very high.

As one may expect, the time frame for requesting reissue depends upon the nature of the request itself. Thus, an inventor who wishes to *narrow* his claim scope may do so at any time during the life of the patent. However, an inventor who attempts to *broaden* the scope of his claims through reissue may harm the public's expectations, including competitors of the patentee, who have relied on the original claim language. Therefore, a broadening reissue may be requested only within the first two years of the original patent grant. Even this two-year limitation, however, may unfairly

---

[255] *See In re* Zurko, 142 F.3d 1447 (Fed. Cir. 1997) (*en banc*), *cert. granted*, 1998 WL 596684 (U.S.) *and In re* Brana, 51 F.3d 1560 (Fed. Cir. 1995).

[256] 35 U.S.C. § 251 (1994).

impact a third party who began to make and use (or, at least, made preparations for such) the invention as originally claimed and all of a sudden finds himself infringing the reissue patent.[257] To guard against such an occurrence, the doctrine of *intervening rights* may protect the competitor's investment.[258]

3.3.2. Reexamination

Reexamination is a procedure whereby the patentee or a third party may request that the PTO reexamine any patent claim during the life of the patent. The purpose of the reexamination statute, enacted in 1980, is to strengthen "investor confidence in the certainty of patent rights by creating a system of administrative reexamination of doubtful patents."[259] Unlike a reissue proceeding, a party other than the patentee may request a reexamination, and the claims of the patent may not be broadened.[260]

§4. OWNERSHIP AND TRANSFER

Patent law acknowledges the distinction between ownership and inventorship and deals with each differently.[261] Patent rights are a form of personal property[262] and, although proprietary rights in an invention initially vest in the inventor,[263] such rights may be transferred.[264] Ownership

---

[257] For example, a patentee's competitor may capitalize on an area left unclaimed by the patent. The competitor may begin to make a significant investment within the first two years of the patent's life, only to have the reissue lay claim to this previously unoccupied area.

[258] *See* 35 U.S.C. § 252 (1994).

[259] H.R. Rep. 96-1307.

[260] *See* 35 U.S.C. §§ 301-305 (1994).

[261] *See* Beech Aircraft Corp. v. EDO Corp., 990 F.2d 1237, 1248 (Fed. Cir. 1993) ("[I]nventorship is a question of who actually invented the subject matter in a patent. Ownership, however, is a question of who owns legal title to the subject matter claimed in a patent, patents having the attributes of personal property").

[262] 35 U.S.C. § 261 (1994).

[263] *See* Teets v. Chromalloy Gas Turbine Corp., 83 F.3d 403, 407 (Fed. Cir. 1996).

[264] 35 U.S.C. § 261 (1994); *see also,* GAIA Technologies, Inc. v. Reconversion Technologies, Inc., 93 F.3d 774, 777 (Fed. Cir. 1996)("Patents ... , like other personal property, may be conveyed from the inventor ... to others").

rests with whomever owns legal title to the subject matter, regardless of who actually invented it.[265] Likewise, inventorship belongs to the person or persons who actually invented the subject matter claimed in a patent.

A person, corporation, commercial laboratory, or other legal entity may be an owner of a patent. Joint ownership is recognized and "[i]n the absence of any agreement to the contrary, each of the joint owners of a patent may make, use, offer, or sell the patented invention within the United States, ...without the consent of and without an accounting to the other owners."[266] Thus, co-owners of a patent are tenants in common. The proportion of the co-owners' shares only enters into the equation when an award is recovered for infringement. In such a circumstance, each co-owner is given his proportionate share.[267]

The Patent Act requires the actual inventor of the claimed subject matter to make or authorize the application for a patent and sign a statement, under oath, that acknowledges the duties attendant to obtaining a patent.[268] Although inventorship is held in great esteem, inventorship in itself does not carry with it the ability to grant a license, assign a share in a patent, or sue for infringement. These are characteristics of ownership.[269] The proprietary rights in a patent rest with the owner and can be conveyed to another by mutual agreement even before the invention is conceived. Thus, an owner of a patent may parcel out the rights of the patent either by assignment or license.[270] Questions relating to ownership and licensing of patent rights are matters of state contract law.[271]

---

[265] *See* Sewall v. Walters, 21 F.3d 411, 417 (Fed. Cir. 1994).

[266] 35 U.S.C. § 262 (1994).

[267] *See* Lemelson v. Synergistics Research Corp., 669 F. Supp. 642, 645 (S.D.N.Y. 1987).

[268] 35 U.S.C. §§ 111, 115 (1994).

[269] *See* Rite-Hite Corp. v. Kelley Co., 56 F.3d 1538, 1551-52 (Fed. Cir. 1995).

[270] *See* Waterman v. MacKenzie, 138 U.S. 252, 255-56 (1891). Under 35 U.S.C. § 261, the assignment must be recorded in the PTO within three months "from its date" or it will "be void as against any subsequent purchaser or mortgagee for a valuable consideration."

[271] *See* Jim Arnold Corp. v. Hydrotech Sys., Inc., 109 F.3d 1567, 1572 (Fed. Cir. 1997) ("[T]he question of who owns the patent and on what terms typically is a question exclusively for state courts"); McCoy v. Mitsuboshi Cutlery, Inc., 67 F.3d 917, 920 (Fed.

§ 5. THE RIGHTS AND LIMITATIONS OF THE PATENT GRANT

A patent grant gives the patentee several rights, but there are also certain statutory and common law limitations that circumscribe these rights. Section 154 sets forth the basic exclusion right:

[A] patent shall contain ... a grant ... of the right to exclude others from making, using, offering for sale, or selling the invention throughout the United States or importing the invention into the United States ... .[272]

Section 271(a) provides that:

whoever, without authority makes, uses, offers to sell, or sells any patented invention within the United States or imports into the United States any patented invention during the term of the patent therefor, infringes the patent.[273]

Thus, a patentee has five basic rights of exclusion: (1) making; (2) using; (3) selling; (4) offering for sale; and (5) importing.[274] Note that the patent grant does not give the patentee the right to make, use, sell, offer for sale, or import, but rather it provides a *right to exclude*.

5.1. Scope of the Right to Exclude

5.1.1. Temporal Scope: The Patent Term

Prior to June 8, 1995, the term for a United States patent was seventeen years from the date the patent issued.[275] In April 1994, the United States and several other countries concluded the Uruguay Round trade negotiation under GATT, which included an "Agreement on Trade-Related Aspects of

---

Cir. 1995) ("Whether express or implied, a license is a contract 'governed by ordinary principles of state contract law'").

[272] 35 U.S.C. § 154 (1994).

[273] 35 U.S.C. § 271(a) (1994).

[274] The "importing" and "offering for sale" provisions became effective on January 1, 1996 and were added to sections 154 and 271(a) as part of the Uruguay Round agreement of the GATT on Trade Related Aspects of Intellectual Property.

[275] The patent term of the Patent Act of 1790 was "for any term not exceeding fourteen years." The term of fourteen years was derived from the English Statute of Monopolies, which provided a patent term of fourteen years that was equivalent to two apprenticeships of seven years. *See* DONALD S. CHISUM, 5 CHISUM ON PATENTS 16-186 (1997).

Intellectual Property" (TRIPs). The TRIPs patent section provided: "The term of protection available shall not end before the expiration of a period of twenty years counted from the filing date."[276] To effectuate this language, section 154(a)(2) of the Patent Code was amended to read:

> Term.—Subject to the payment of fees under this title, such grant shall be for a term beginning on the date on which the patent issues and ending 20 years from the date on which the application for the patent was filed in the United States, or, if the application contains a specific reference to an earlier filed application or applications ... from the date on which the earliest such application was filed.

The TRIPS legislation also affects patent applications filed before its effective date, June 8, 1995. The patent term for applications filed *before* that date is (1) seventeen years from date of issuance; *or* (2) twenty years measured from the filing date of the earliest referenced application, whichever is greater. For applications filed *on* or *after* June 8, 1995, the patent term is twenty years measured from the earliest referenced application filing date. Earlier referenced applications may include continuation applications under 35 U.S.C. § 120, divisional applications under 35 U.S.C. § 121, or Patent Cooperation Treaty (PCT) applications under 35 U.S.C. § 365(c).

A patent is effective and enforceable only upon issuance.[277] Section 154 of the Patent Code specifically states that the patent's term shall begin "on the date on which the patent issues." Therefore, activity prior to issuance that would have resulted in a finding of infringement during the life of the patent is not actionable. Also, just as a patent is unenforceable *prior* to issuance, it is unenforceable after it expires.[278]

---

[276] The patent term for design patents was not affected and remains 14 years from date of issuance. *See* 35 U.S.C. § 173.

[277] *See* Marsh v. Nichols, 128 U.S. 605, 612 (1888); *see also*, GAF Building Materials Corp. v. Elk Corp of Dallas, 90 F.3d 479, 483 (Fed. Cir. 1996) ("[A] patent does not exist until it is granted. ... Patent rights are created only upon the formal issuance of the patent; thus, disputes concerning patent validity and infringement are necessarily hypothetical before patent issuance").

[278] *See* Joy Technologies, Inc. v. Flakt, Inc., 6 F.3d 770 (Fed. Cir. 1993). However, expiration of a patent during pending litigation does not deprive the court of jurisdiction. *See* Beedle v. Bennett, 122 U.S. 71 (1887).

5.1.2. *Geographic Scope*

Section 154(a)(1) grants a patentee the right to exclude others from making, using, offering for sale, or selling the claimed invention "within" or "throughout" the United States or importing the invention "into" the United States. Thus, activity in a foreign country, *in and of itself*, does not constitute an infringing act. However, acts relating to the export from the United States to a foreign country or importation into the United States from a foreign country may give rise to an infringement action. These issues present difficult questions of statutory construction.

5.1.2.1. Exporting a Claimed Invention

Clearly, a person who makes a patented invention in the United States and exports it for use or sale infringes the patent because the act of making in this situation is itself an infringement under United States patent law (the product was actually made in the U.S.). A more difficult scenario is where a person makes an incomplete version of the patented product for export, or makes only the parts of a patented machine, and thereafter exports them for assembly abroad.

As the word "make" is not defined in the patent act, the task of giving it meaning has been left to the courts. The Supreme Court, in *Deepsouth Packing Co. v. Laitram Corp.*,[279] addressed this issue, holding essentially that one who manufactured the parts of a patented machine and shipped them to customers in a foreign country who would then assemble an entire machine, was not an infringer. Competitors of the patentee could manufacture, with impunity, the parts of a patented machine in the United States and export them to a foreign country for assembly.

In 1984, Congress responded to *Deepsouth* and this apparent loophole in the patent code by adding subsection (f) to section 271, making the export of *unassembled* components an act of infringement when it is known that the components will be reassembled in an infringing way.[280]

---

[279] 406 U.S. 518 (1972).

[280] *See* "Section-by-Section Analysis of H.R. 6286, Patent Law Amendments Act of 1984," Congressional Record, Oct. 1, 1984, H10525-26 ("The ... change ... will prevent copiers from avoiding U.S. patents by supplying components of a patented product in this country so that the assembly of the components may be completed abroad"). The Federal Circuit in Pellegrini v. Analog Devices, Inc., 375 F.3d 1113 (Fed. Cir. 2004)

5.1.2.2. Importing a Claimed Invention or Products Made By a Claimed Process Invention

Importation of a patented invention, in and of itself, is an act of infringement.[281] Moreover, since February 23, 1989, importation of an unpatented product that is made in a foreign country by a U.S. patented process constitutes infringement.[282] This provision, part of the Process Patent Amendments Act of 1988, "was enacted to close a perceived loophole in the statutory scheme for protecting owners of United States patents."[283] Prior to this Act, process patent owners could only sue for infringement if others used the patented process in the United States, but not if it was used in a foreign country and the product made from the process was imported into the United States.[284]

The linchpin to protection under Section 271(g) is that the imported product is "made by" a process patented in the United States.[285] Section 271(g) provides that an imported product is not "made by" a patented

---

suggested that § 271(f) only applies when the exported components are physical. But the case of Eolas Technologies v. Microsoft, 399 F.3d 1225 (Fed. Cir. 2005), appears to have expanded the U.S. patent's geographic reach by suggesting there is no physicality requirement.

[281] 35 U.S.C. § 154. This provision was revised to conform to the TRIPs agreement from the Uruguay Round in April of 1994.

[282] 35 U.S.C. § 271(g). Previously, a patentee had to petition the United States International Trade Commission under § 337 of the Tariff Act of 1930 for an exclusionary order that prohibited importation of the product. Also, in order to recover under § 337, petitioners had the burden of showing their patented process was used "in manufacturing the imported products, that an efficiently and economically operated industry utilizing the patent exists in the United States, and that the imported product had the effect or tendency of destroying or substantially injuring the domestic industry." SENATE COMM. ON THE JUDICIARY, PROCESS PATENTS AMENDMENTS ACT OF 1987, S. REP. No. 100-83, at 37. Further, under § 337, patentees could not collect damages. Today, the revised § 271(g) provides for the patentee to exclude others from using or selling throughout the United States and importing into the United States.

[283] See Eli Lilly and Co. v. American Cyanamid Co., 82 F.3d 1568, 1571 (Fed. Cir. 1996).

[284] Id.

[285] 35 U.S.C. § 271(g).

process if: "(1) it is materially changed by subsequent processes; or (2) it becomes a trivial and nonessential component of another product."[286] Thus, the statute "permits the importation of an item that is *derived* from a product made by a patented process as long as that product is 'materially changed' in the course of its conversion into the imported item."[287] To construe whether an imported product is "materially changed," the Federal Circuit looks to "the substantiality of the change between the product of the patented process and the product that is being imported."[288]

The legislative history reflects the evolution of tests that Congress thought would provide guidance for the courts to determine whether there had been a material change. Specifically, the Senate Reports set forth a two-part test: a product will be considered to be made by the patented process (1) "if it would not be possible or commercially viable to make that product but for the use of the patented process"; and (2) "if the additional processing steps ...do not change the physical or chemical properties of the product in a manner which changes the basic utility of the product [produced] by the patented process."[289]

5.2. Limitations of the Right to Exclude

Numerous doctrines have evolved to limit the reach of the patent grant, including: the doctrine of patent misuse; the doctrines of first sale, implied license, and repair/reconstruction; experimental use exception, especially at it pertains to the pharmaceutical industry; and governmental immunity.[290]

5.2.1. The Defense of Patent Misuse

In general, a patent may be considered misused if it is used in a way that violates the antitrust laws or when it is used to expand the scope of the

---

[286] *Id.*

[287] *See Eli Lilly*, 82 F.3d at 1572.

[288] *Id* at 1573.

[289] S. Rep. No. 83, 100th Cong., 1st Sess. 51 (1987).

[290] These limitations are distinct from the traditional patent infringement defenses such as patent invalidity, inequitable conduct, etc.

patent rights in an anti-competitive fashion.[291] Such patent-related antitrust violations comprise three general categories. First, they may involve fraudulent procurement of a patent.[292] Second, an antitrust violation can occur if there is bad faith enforcement of a patent (*e.g.*, enforcing a patent known to be invalid).[293] Finally, a violation can occur where patent related conduct violates any other antitrust law. Antitrust violations are limited by the *Noerr-Pennington* doctrine, which precludes liability when private entities solicit government action to exercise a legal right.[294]

Congress, however, narrowed the patent misuse defense when it stated that a patent owner would not be denied relief for infringement or deemed guilty of patent misuse by:

> (1) deriv[ing] revenue from acts which if performed by another without his consent would constitute contributory infringement ...; (2) licenc[ing] or authoriz[ing] another to perform acts which if performed without his consent would constitute contributory infringement ...; (3) [seeking] to enforce his patent rights against infringement or contributory infringement; (4) refus[ing] to license or use any rights to the patent; or (5) condition[ing] the license of any rights to the patent or the sale of the patented product on the acquisition of a license to rights in another patent or purchase of a separate product, unless in view of the circumstances, the patent owner has market power in the relevant market for the patent or patented product on which the license or sale is conditioned.[295]

When a patent is deemed to have been misused, it is unenforceable until the improper conduct ceases and the effects are dissipated.[296]

---

[291] *See* Windsurfing Int'l, Inc. v. AMF, Inc., 782 F.2d 995 (Fed. Cir. 1986).

[292] *See* Walker Process Equipment, Inc. v. Food Machinery & Chemical Corp. 382 U.S. 172 (1965).

[293] *See* Handgards, Inc. v. Ethicon, Inc., 601 F.2d 986 (9th Cir. 1979); Handgards, Inc. v. Ethicon, Inc., 743 F.2d 1282 (9th Cir. 1984).

[294] *See* Eastern R. Conf. v. Noerr Motors, 365 U.S. 127 (1961); United Mine Workers v. Pennington, 381 U.S. 657 (1965).

[295] 35 U.S.C. § 271(d) (1994).

[296] *See* United States Gypsum Co. v. National Gypsum Co., 352 U.S. 457 (1957).

5.2.2. First Sale, Implied License, and Repair/Reconstruction

Section 271(a) gives rise to an infringement cause of action when certain acts are conducted "without authority."[297] Authority may be express or implicit. Express authority may arise, for example, in a license[298] or settlement contract.[299] Implicit authority exists, generally, under three circumstances: after the first sale of the patented invention; where the circumstances necessitate an implied licence; and where a patented product has merely been repaired, as opposed to being reconstructed.

After the first sale of a patented product, the buyer is free to use or resell that patented product, unless there is a special agreement between the buyer and seller.[300] In general, the sale of patented products follow general contract law. The sale or license contract may contain provisions that restricts conduct after the sale of the patented product. Otherwise, the sale contract of a patented product is considered to contain implied contract terms that frees the buyer from the rights afforded to patent owners with respect to further sale or transfer of the product.

Second, the facts and circumstances may cause a court to apply the equitable doctrine of implied license.[301] The categories of conduct that give rise to an implied license include acquiescence, conduct, equitable estoppel,

---

[297] 35 U.S.C. § 271(a) 1994 ("[W]hoever without authority makes, uses, offers to sell, or sells any patented invention, within the United States or imports into the United States any patented invention during the term of the patent therefor, infringes the patent").

[298] See McCoy v. Mitsuboshi Cutlery, Inc., 67 F.3d 917 (Fed. Cir. 1995).

[299] See Gjerlov v. Schuyler Labs., 131 F.3d 1016 (Fed. Cir. 1997).

[300] See Adams v. Burke, 84 U.S. (17 Wall.) 453 (1873) ("The [patented] article passes without the limit[s] of the monopoly").

[301] See Deforest Radio Tel. & Tel. Co. v. United States, 273 U.S. 236 (1927) ("No formal granting of a license is necessary to give it effect. Any language used by the owner of the patent or any conduct on his part exhibited to another from which that other may properly infer that the owner consents to his use of the patent in making or using it, or selling it, upon which the other acts, constitutes a license and a defense to an action for a tort"); Wang Laboratories v. Mitsubishi Electronics, 103 F.3d 1571, 1580 (Fed. Cir. 1997) ("[A]n implied license merely signifies a patentee's waiver of the statutory right to exclude others from making, using, or selling the patented invention").

or legal estoppel.[302] The sale of nonpatented equipment to practice a patented invention may arise if two requirements are met: "First, the equipment involved must have no noninfringing uses"; and "[s]econd, the circumstances of the sale must 'plainly indicate that the grant of a license should be inferred.'"[303]

Finally, the legal doctrine of repair/reconstruction provides for an inferred grant of authority without an express contractual grant. Generally, the authorized purchaser may repair or replace damaged or worn parts necessary for use.[304] The authorized purchaser, however, may not reconstruct a patented product from the parts of worn-out products.[305] According to the Federal Circuit:

> The authority to use and sell a purchased device, however, does not include the right to make a new device or to reconstruct one which has been spent. Reconstruction, *i.e.*, the re-creation of a patented combination, is an infringement because such activity is beyond the implied authorization to use and sell a patented device."[306]

5.2.3. Experimental Use Doctrine

Mere use of a patented product usually constitutes infringement under Section 271(a). However, there is a line of authority suggesting that use of a patented product for non-commercial, experimental purposes is not an act of infringement. This "experimental use doctrine" is particularly germane to the pharmaceutical industry. Ideally, a generic drug should be available to the public immediately upon expiration of a patent claiming the drug. However, given the lengthy FDA approval requirements, to

---

[302] *See* Wang Laboratories v. Mitsubishi Electronics, 103 F.3d 1571, 1580 (Fed. Cir. 1997).

[303] Met-Coil Systems Corp. v. Korners Unlimited, Inc., 803 F.2d 684, 686 (Fed. Cir. 1986).

[304] *See* Wilbur-Ellis Co. v. Kuther, 377 U.S. 422 (1964); Aro Mfg. Co. v. Convertible Top Replacement Co., 365 U.S. 365 U.S. 338 (1961).

[305] *See* American Cotton-Tie Co. v. Simmons, 106 U.S. (16 Otto.) 89 (1882).

[306] Hewlett-Packard v. Repeat-O-Type Stencil, 123 F.3d 1445, 1451-52 (Fed. Cir. 1997) ("[O]ne does have authority to repair a patented device that he has purchased. ... A reconstruction occurs after the patented combination, as a whole, has been spent, when 'the material of the combination ceases to exist'").

accomplish this result would require the generic drug companies to test and use the patented drug *before* the patent expires.

In *Roche Products, Inc. v. Bolar Pharmaceutical Co.*,[307] the Federal Circuit held that the experimental use doctrine did not apply to "limited use of a patented drug for testing and investigation strictly related to FDA drug approval requirements during the last six months of the term of the patent."[308]

Shortly after *Roche* was decided, Congress responded by enacting the Drug Price Competition and Patent Term Restoration Act of 1984, also known as the Hatch-Waxman Act, which added section 271(e) to the Patent Code. That provision abrogated the holding in *Roche*. Section 271(e)(1) hastened the introduction of generic equivalents into the marketplace by exempting from infringement the making, using, or selling of "a patented invention ...solely for uses *reasonably related* to the development and submission of information under a Federal law which regulates the manufacture, use, or sale of drugs."[309] The Act also created the "abbreviated new drug application" or ANDA, a streamlined application process for entities seeking Food and Drug Administration approval and wishing to market a generic equivalent of an FDA approved patented product. Further, the Act, under section 271(e)(2), provides a patent owner with a special infringement remedy against entities filing an ANDA seeking FDA approval to market a generic equivalent *before* expiration of the patent. Finally, it provided for extensions of patent terms that result from delays and the rigors of the FDA approval process.[310]

The Act was designed to promote technological innovation while at the same time enhance the public welfare, a balancing act that is at the very heart of the patent system.

---

[307] 733 F.2d 858 (Fed. Cir. 1984).

[308] *Id.* at 861.

[309] 35 U.S.C. § 271(e)(1)(emphasis added).

[310] For a discussion of the interrelationship between the Hatch-Waxman Act provisions on patent term extension, exemption of FDA data gathering for generic equivalents, and the filing of ANDAs, *see* Eli Lilly and Co. v. Medtronic, Inc., 496 U.S. 661 (1990).

5.2.4. Governmental Use

5.2.4.1. Federal Government

When the United States government makes or uses a patented invention, the patent owner's *exclusive* remedy resides in the United States Court of Federal Claims, not federal district court. According to 28 U.S.C. § 1498(a):

> Whenever an invention described in and covered by a patent of the United States is used or manufactured by or for the United States without license of the owner thereof or lawful right to use or manufacture the same, the owner's remedy shall be by action against the United States in the United States Court of Federal Claims for the recovery of his reasonable and entire compensation for such use and manufacture.
>
> . . .
>
> For the purpose of this section, the use or manufacture of an invention described in and covered by a patent of the United States by a contractor, a subcontractor, or any person, firm, or corporation for the Government and with the authorization or consent of the Government, shall be construed as use or manufacture for the United States.[311]

The second paragraph of Section 1498(a) states that the "use or manufacture" of a patented invention by an entity "with the authorization and consent of the Government shall be construed as use or manufacture for the United States." The requirement that the use or manufacture have the "authorization and consent" of the government can involve both a "product manufactured for actual delivery to the United States or a product, machine, or process used by a contractor or subcontractor doing work for the United States."[312] In the first situation, courts have held that acceptance by the government of a patented product manufactured by a

---

[311] Some courts have suggested that section 1498 is actually based on "takings" jurisprudence, wherein the government is exercising its power of eminent domain. In W.L. Gore & Associates Inc. v. Garlock Inc., 842 F.2d 1275, 1283 (Fed. Cir. 1988), the Federal Circuit stated that "[t]he patentee takes his patent from the United States subject to the government's eminent domain rights to obtain what it needs from manufacturers and to use the same. The government has graciously consented, in the same statute, to be sued in the Claims Court for reasonable and entire compensation, for what would be infringement if by a private person."

[312] DONALD S. CHISUM, CHISUM ON PATENTS 12-289 (1997).

contractor or subcontractor invokes Sectin 1498, even absent a specified authorization.[313]

The second situation poses greater difficulties. According to Professor Chisum,

> [t]he standard clause in United States Government supply contracts is limited, extending authorization and consent only where the invention is "utilized in the machinery, tools, or methods the use of which necessarily results from compliance by the Contractor or the using subcontractor with (a) specifications or written provisions now or hereafter forming a part of this contract, or (b) specific written instructions given by the Contracting Officer directing the manner of performance." On the other hand, in contracts for research and development, the government extends "greater latitude," extending authorization and consent for "all use and manufacture of any patented invention in the performance" of a contract.[314]

5.2.4.2. State Government

Generally, state governments and their agencies are subject to the patent law. However, Eleventh Amendment immunity issues present significant impediments to an infringement suit. The Amendment states:

> The Judicial power of the United States shall not be construed to extend to any suit in law or equity, commenced or prosecuted against one of the United States by Citizens of another State, or by Citizens or Subjects of any Foreign State.

In 1992, Congress enacted the Patent and Plant Variety Protection Remedy Clarification Act.[315] This Act added Section 271(h) and abrogated state immunity as it relates to the patent law. Four years later, however, the Supreme Court decided *Seminole Tribe of Florida v. Florida*,[316] which, although not dealing with intellectual property, cast the constitutionality of

---

[313] *See* TVI Energy Corp. v. Blane, 806 F.2d 1057, 1059 (Fed. Cir. 1986)(holding that a demonstration of a product pursuant to a Government bidding procurement scheme was covered by § 1498, despite the fact that the government had not issued an "authorization and consent" letter).

[314] DONALD S. CHISUM, CHISUM ON PATENTS 16-293 (1997).

[315] Pub. L. No. 102-560, 106 Stat 4230.

[316] 116 S.Ct. 1114 (1996).

the 1992 amendment into question. In *Seminole Tribe*, the Court addressed the Indian Gaming Regulatory Act, which was "passed by Congress under the Indian Commerce Clause [which, according to the Court, is not distinguishable from the Interstate Commerce Clause], U.S. Const., Art I, § 8, cl. 3."[317] The Act "imposes upon the States a duty to negotiate in good faith with an Indian tribe toward the formation of a compact, ... and authorizes a tribe to bring suit in federal court against a State in order to compel performance of that duty."[318] The Court held that Congress' attempt to abrogate the state of Florida's immunity was not passed pursuant to a valid exercise of Congressional power, and was therefore unconstitutional. According to the Supreme Court, the only legitimate avenue available to Congress in abrogating State immunity was the Fourteenth Amendment:

> Even when the Constitution vests in Congress complete law-making authority over a particular area, the Eleventh Amendment prevents congressional authorization of suits by private parties against unconsenting States ... . The Eleventh Amendment restricts the judicial power under Article III, and Article I cannot be used to circumvent the constitutional limitations placed upon federal jurisdiction.[319]

Since the fundamental power to regulate patents derives from Article I, Section 8, Clause 8, the question is whether the 1992 abrogation of immunity for patent infringement claims is constitutional. This question was resolved in *College Savings Bank v. Florida Prepaid Postsecondary Ed. Expense Bd.*,[320] wherein the Federal Circuit held that Congress, pursuant to the Fourteenth Amendment, properly abrogated the states' Eleventh Amendment immunity.[321]

---

[317] *Id.* at 1119.

[318] *Id.*

[319] *Id.* at 1131-32.

[320] 148 F.3d 1343 (Fed. Cir. 1998).

[321] The Courts of Appeal have divided on this issue and the Supreme Court must ultimately resolve it. *Compare College Savings* (an appeal from the Third Circuit) *with* Chavez v. Arte Publico Press, 157 F.3d 282 (5th Cir. 1998) (Congress could not abrogate a state's immunity to copyright infringement claim through the Due Process Clause of the 14th Amendment).

§6. INFRINGEMENT AND REMEDIES

6.1. Infringement

Section 271 of the Patent Act declares that "whoever without authority makes, uses, offers to sell, or sells any patented invention ... infringes the patent."[322]

Analyzing a patent infringement action involves determining the meaning and scope of the patent claims asserted to be infringed, and comparing the properly construed claims to the infringing device.[323] The first step, known as claim construction or claim interpretation, is decided by the court, while the second step is determined by the finder of fact.[324]

6.1.1. Claim Interpretation

Although claim interpretation is a matter of law, since a judge may not possess the requisite knowledge pertaining to the technology used in a patent, the judge may utilize supplementary sources to ascertain the meaning of obscure words or phrases. The Federal Circuit divides potential evidence into two categories: intrinsic evidence (*i.e.*, the written description, the claims, and the prosecution history); and extrinsic evidence (*e.g.*, dictionaries, technical treatises, and expert testimony).[325] Both intrinsic and extrinsic evidence are deemed proper; however, a court must look first to intrinsic evidence in interpreting a claim.[326] Intrinsic evidence is part of the public record and thus enables others to take notice of a claim's scope.[327] Only if ambiguity persists after a court has considered all available intrinsic evidence may a court consider extrinsic evidence.[328] Any extrinsic evidence which is inconsistent with the intrinsic evidence should be afforded little or no weight.[329]

---

[322] 35 U.S.C. § 271(a) (1994).

[323] *See* Markman v. Westview Instruments, Inc., 52 F.3d 967, 976 (Fed. Cir. 1995).

[324] *See* CVI/Beta Ventures, Inc. v. Tura, 112 F.3d 1146, 1152 (Fed. Cir. 1997).

[325] *See* Vitronics Corp. v. Conceptronic, Inc., 90 F.3d 1576, 1584 (Fed. Cir. 1996).

[326] *Id.* at 1582. See also, Key Pharmaceuticals, Inc. v. Hercon Lab. Corp., 161 F.3d 709 (Fed. Cir. 1998) (discussing the role of extrinsic evidence).

[327] *Id.* at 1583.

[328] *Id.* at 1584.

[329] *See Markman*, 52 F.3d at 983.

When construing claims, the court first looks to the asserted and non-asserted claims to define the scope of the patent.[330] Second, claims are given their ordinary and customary meaning unless it appears from the intrinsic evidence that the inventor chose to be his own lexicographer and used them differently.[331] Special construction of words must be clearly stated in the patent's written description or prosecution history.[332] In other words, the written description acts as a dictionary when it expressly defines terms used in the claims or when it defines terms by implication.[333] Third, the court looks to the prosecution history, which contains a complete record of all the proceedings during patent prosecution, including express representations made by the applicant regarding the scope of the claims.[334] Finally, only if the public record ambiguously describes the scope of the claims, the court may look to extrinsic evidence.[335]

Because claim construction is a matter of law, the Federal Circuit reviews claim interpretation *de novo*[336] and thus has complete discretion to accept or reject a district court's interpretation of a claim. The Federal Circuit can make an independent analysis of any intrinsic evidence on record, and can adopt or completely disregard any extrinsic evidence.

6.1.2. Literal Infringement

Patent infringement is said to occur where there is either *literal* infringement or infringement under the *doctrine of equivalents*. Literal infringement of a patent is very basic and occurs when "every limitation recited in the claim is found in the accused device."[337] For example, patentee 1 has a patent claiming a product comprising elements A, B, and C and competitor 2 makes a product comprising A, B, and C. It would then be said

---

[330] *See Vitronics*, 90 F.3d at 1582.

[331] *See id.*

[332] *Id.*

[333] *See Markman*, 52 F.3d at 979.

[334] *See Vitronics*, 90 F.3d at 1582.

[335] *See id.*

[336] *See* Cybor v. FAS, 138 F.3d 1448 (Fed. Cir. 1998)(*en banc*).

[337] Engel Industries, Inc. v. Lockformer Company, 96 F.3d 1398, 1405 (Fed. Cir. 1996).

that patentee 1's patent claim "reads on" competitor 2's product. Literal infringement is analogous to anticipation. As discussed above, to anticipate a patent, a prior art reference must disclose each and every claim limitation. In an infringement context, however, it is the accused device, not a prior art reference, that must embody each and every claim limitation. Thus, the fundamental patent law maxim: "that which infringes, if later, would anticipate, if earlier."[338]

6.1.3. Infringement Under the Doctrine of Equivalents

Although 35 U.S.C. § 112 requires the patentee to particularly point out and distinctly claim his invention, courts do not always limit the patentee to the literal meaning of the claims. To do so "would convert the protection of a patent into a hollow and useless thing."[339] The courts have, therefore, established the Doctrine of Equivalents, which permits infringement to be found even where the accused product or process does not literally infringe the patent claim, if each element of the claimed invention has a substantial equivalent in the accused product or process or if the difference between each element in the accused product or process and the claim elements are insubstantial. Thus, in determining infringement under the doctrine of equivalents, the fact-finder must employ an element by element analysis. According to the Supreme Court in *Warner-Jenkinson Co. Inc. v. Hilton Davis Chem. Co.*:[340]

> Each element contained in a patent claim is deemed material to defining the scope of the patented invention, and thus the doctrine of equivalents must be applied to individual elements of the claim, not to the invention as a whole. ... An analysis of the role played by each element in the context of the specific patent claim will thus inform the inquiry as to whether a substitute element matches the function, way, result of the claimed element, or whether the substitute element plays a role substantially different from the claimed patent.[341]

---

[338] Peters v. Active Mfg. Co., 129 U.S. 530, 537 (1889).

[339] Graver Tank & Mfg. Co. Inc. v. Linde Air Products Co., 339 U.S. 605, 607 (1950).

[340] 117 S. Ct. 1040 (1997)

[341] *Id.* at 1049.

The Federal Circuit has stated that "[t]o be a substantial equivalent, the element substituted in the accused product for the element set forth in the claim must not be such as would substantially change the way in which the function of the claimed invention is performed."[342]

The application of the Doctrine of Equivalents is, however, subservient to the "Doctrine of Prosecution History Estoppel" (PHE) and the Public Dedication Rule. With respect to the PHE, the Supreme Court has established the following rule:

> When the patentee has chosen to narrow a claim, courts may presume the amended text was composed with awareness of this rule and that the territory surrendered is not an equivalent of the territory claimed. In those instances, however, the patentee still might rebut the presumption that estoppel bars a claim of equivalence. The patentee must show that at the time of the amendment one skilled in the art could not reasonably be expected to have drafted a claim that would have literally encompassed the alleged equivalent.[343]

The patentee can meet this burden by showing the (1) equivalent was unforeseeable at the time of amendment, and therefore, could not have been claimed; (2) the rationale underlying the amendment was only tangentially related to the equivalent; or (3) some other reason suggesting the patentee could not reasonably be expected to have claimed the equivalent.[344] The public Dedication Rule further limits the Doctrine of Equivalents. This rule states that subject matter disclosed in a patent specification, but not claimed, is dedicated to the public domain.[345] For public dedication to occur the specification must be specific enough for a person having ordinary skill in art to identify and understand the disclosed

---

[342] Pennwalt Corp. v. Durand-Wayland, Inc., 833 F.2d 931, 935 (Fed. Cir. 1987)(*en banc*).

[343] Festo Corporation v. Shoketsu Kinzoku Kogyo Kabushiki Co., Ltd., 535 U.S. 722, 741 (2002).

[344] *Id.* at 740-41.

[345] Johnson & Johnson Associates, Inc. v. R.E. Service Co., Inc., 285 F.3d 1046 (Fed. Cir. 2002) (*en banc*).

unclaimed subject matter. A generic reference to in the specification does not necessarily give rise to dedication.[346]

6.1.4. Indirect Infringement

In addition to direct infringement, the Patent Act, under Sections 271(b) and (c), imposes liability for indirect infringement. Section 271(b) pertains to "active inducement," that is, where a party encourages or aids another directly to infringe a patent by, for example, providing instructions on how to practice a patented invention.[347] Two elements must be established to show inducement of infringement: (1) direct infringement by another;[348] and (2) intent to cause the acts which constituted the infringement.[349]

Section 271(c), on the other hand, concerns itself with contributory infringement. For example, the sale of a component of a patented device or composition or the sale of a component for use in practicing a patented process. That section requires that the alleged contributory infringer sell his component "knowing the same to be especially made or especially adapted for use in an infringement of such patent." In *Aro Mfg. v. Convertible Top Replacement Co.*,[350] the Supreme Court stated that "§ 271(c) does require a showing that the alleged contributory infringer knew that the combination for which his component was especially designed was both patented and infringing."[351] Furthermore, section 271(c) codifies prior case law which refused to find contributory infringement where the component sold had a noninfringing use.[352] The statute uses the phrase "substantial noninfringing use," which "relates ...to whether the portion of the invention

---

[346] Toro Co. v. White Consolidated Industries, Inc., 383 F.3d 1326 (Fed. Cir. 2004).

[347] *See* Hewlett-Packard Co. v. Bausch & Lomb, Inc., 909 F.2d 1464 (Fed. Cir. 1990).

[348] *See* Serrano v. Telular Corp., 111 F.3d 1578, 1583 (Fed. Cir. 1997).

[349] *See* Water Tech. Corp. v. Calco, Ltd., 850 F.2d 660, 668 (Fed. Cir. 1988).

[350] 377 U.S. 476 (1964).

[351] *Id.* at 488-90.

[352] As the Supreme Court stated, "Undoubtedly a bare supposition that by a sale of an article which, though adopted to an infringing use, is also adopted to other and lawful uses, is not enough to make the seller a contributory infringer. Such a rule would block the wheels of commerce." Sidney Henrey v. A.B. Dick Co., 224 U.S. 1, 48 (1912).

supplied by the contributory infringer ... has a use other than to be combined with other items that together fall within the metes and bounds of the claims of the patent."[353]

6.2. Remedies

Once liability in an infringement action has been found, the focus turns to an assessment of damages or equitable relief. An infringement remedy may take the form of compensatory relief (lost profits or reasonable royalties), equitable relief (preliminary and permanent injunctions), and an award of attorney fees. Section 284 of the Patent Act allows a successful patent owner to recover "damages adequate to compensate for the infringement."[354] Although computing the exact damage caused by an infringing product can be complex, the patentee is entitled to no less than a "reasonable royalty."[355]

6.2.1. Compensatory Damages

A patent owner may seek any reasonably foreseeable damages that were proximately caused by an infringing product.[356] A reasonably foreseeable damage may entail lost profits due to captured sales, eroded prices, or increased expenses in producing the patented invention.[357] In addition, recovery is sometimes available for component parts normally sold with a patented invention if the parts act to complete a functional machine under the "entire market rule."[358] Calculation of monetary damages is generally measured as lost profits or reasonable royalty.

To recover the lost profits, a patent owner must show a causal link between the lost profits and the infringement.[359] *Panduit Corp. v. Stahlin Bros. Fibre Works*[360] set forth four elements that must be proven in a lost

---

[353] Lucas Aerospace, Ltd. v. Unison Indus., 899 F. Supp. 1268, 1287 (D.Del. 1995).

[354] 35 U.S.C. § 284 (1994).

[355] *Id.*

[356] *See* Rite-Hite Corp. v. Kelley Co., 56 F.3d 1538, 1549 (Fed. Cir. 1995).

[357] *See* Lam, Inc. v. Johns-Manville Corp., 718 F.2d 1056, 1065 (Fed. Cir. 1983).

[358] *See Rite-Hite*, 56 F.3d at 1549-50.

[359] *Lam, Inc.*, 718 F.2s at 1065.

[360] 575 F.2d 1152 (6th Cir. 1978).

profit analysis: (1) a demand for the patented product, (2) the absence of acceptable non-infringing substitutes for the patented product, (3) the patent owner's manufacturing and marketing capability to exploit the demand for the patented product, and (4) the amount of profit the patent owner would have expected in the absence of infringement.[361] A patent holder must establish each criterion to recover lost profits.[362]

In the event that a patent owner cannot show lost profits, a court may impose a reasonable royalty to provide adequate compensation.[363] A district court has discretion in choosing a method to calculate a reasonable royalty.[364] The court may calculate a reasonable royalty based on an established royalty, or rely on the standards of the pertinent industry.[365] This method is commonly referred to as the analytical approach.[366]

An alternative is for a court to determine the reasonable royalty that a willing licensor and a willing licensee would agree upon during a hypothetical negotiation.[367] A court must be flexible in applying this approach, for to focus solely on a standard fictitious negotiation "would be to pretend that the infringement never happened."[368] When establishing a reasonable royalty, a court should consider the specific factors that "normally prudent businessmen would, under similar circumstances take into consideration ... ."[369]

---

[361] *Id.* at 1156.

[362] *See* Smithkline Diagnostics, Inc. v. Helena Laboratories Corp., 926 F.2d 1161, 1165 (Fed. Cir. 1991).

[363] *See* Dowagiac Mfg. Corp. v. Minnesota Moline Plow Co., 235 U.S. 641, 648-49 (1915).

[364] *See* TWM Mfg. Co. v. Dura Corp., 789 F.2d 895, 900 (Fed. Cir. 1986).

[365] *See* Armco, Inc. v. Republic Steel Corp., 707 F.2d 886, 891 (6th Cir. 1983).

[366] *See* TWM Mfg., 789 F.2d at 898.

[367] *See* Minco, Inc. v. Combustion Engineering, Inc., 95 F.3d 1109, 1119 (Fed. Cir. 1996).

[368] *TWM Mfg.,* 789 F.2d at 900.

[369] Georgia-Pacific Corp. v. United States Plywood Corp., 318 F. Supp. 1116, 1121 (S.D.N.Y. 1970).

6.2.2. Exemplary Damages

A district court may award up to three times the assessed damages in the event of willful infringement.[370] Deliberately copying the invention of another, bypassing a reasonable investigation to determine the validity of a patent, and behaving improperly during litigation suggest bad faith on the part of an infringer.[371] "The law of willful infringement does not search for minimally tolerable behavior, but requires prudent, and ethical, legal and commercial actions."[372] Once a district court finds clear and convincing evidence of willful infringement, it looks to the totality of the circumstances to assess the appropriate increase in damages.[373]

Although not specifically mentioned under Section 284 of the Patent Act, a district court has the discretion to award prejudgment interest. Notwithstanding this grant of discretion, it has been held that a court should award prejudgment interest unless there is a sound reason to withhold the interest.[374] Also, adequate compensation for infringement customarily entails post-judgment interest, which is controlled by 28 U.S.C. § 1961.

6.2.3. Injunctive Relief

A district court can prevent possible ongoing infringement of a patent prior to a finding of infringement by granting a preliminary injunction.[375] *Smith International, Inc. v. Hughes Tool Co.*[376] set forth four factors a district court must weigh before granting a preliminary injunction. First, whether the party seeking the injunction (the movant) has sufficiently established a reasonable likelihood of success on the merits. This requirement includes a showing that the patent is not invalid and is infringed. Second, whether

---

[370] *See* 35 U.S.C. § 284 (1994). *See also* Sensonics, Inc. v. Aerosonic Corp., 81 F.3d 1566, 1574 (Fed. Cir. 1996).

[371] *See Lam, Inc., supra,* note 374, at 474.

[372] SRI Int'l, Inc. v. Advanced Tech. Labs., Inc.,127 F.3d 1462, 1464 (Fed. Cir. 1997).

[373] *See* State Indus., Inc. v. Mor-Flo Indus., 883 F.2d 1573, 1575 (Fed. Cir. 1989).

[374] *See* General Motors Corp. v. Devex Corp., 461 U.S. 648, 656 (1983).

[375] *See* 35 U.S.C. § 283 (1994).

[376] 718 F.2d 1573 (Fed. Cir. 1983).

the movant would suffer irreparable harm if an injunction was not granted. A presumption of irreparable harm can be made by a strong showing of both validity and infringement, regardless of the solvency of the infringer. Third, whether a balance of hardships tips in the movant's favor. This analysis entails comparing the potential harm to the patent owner if the injunction is withheld, with the potential harm to the alleged infringer if the injunction is granted. The final consideration is whether an injunction will impair the public interest. Although the public interest is generally concerned with protecting patent rights, the true focus of this element is whether the public would be injured by granting preliminary relief.[377] None of the four factors is dispositive. Rather a "district court must weigh and measure each factor against the other factors and against the form and magnitude of the relief requested."[378]

After finding infringement, a court generally grants a permanent injunction unless there is a sufficient countervailing reason.[379] Similar to preliminary injunctions, a public interest concern may delay or prevent a permanent injunction; e.g., a transition period may be required to allow the industry to adjust,[380] or the defendant to respond to an injunction.[381]

§ 7. DESIGN PATENTS

One may obtain a design patent on a "new, original, and ornamental design for an article of manufacture."[382] The Patent & Trademark Office has defined a design patent as follows:

The design of an object consists of the visual characteristics or aspects displayed by the object. It is the appearance presented by the object which creates an impression, through the eye upon the mind of the observer.[383]

---

[377] See Hybritech Inc. v. Abbott Lab., 849 F.2d 1446, 1458 (Fed. Cir. 1988).

[378] Id. at 1451.

[379] See Richardson v. Suzuki Motor Co., 868 F.2d 1226, 1246-47 (Fed. Cir. 1989).

[380] See, e.g., Schneider AG v. SciMed Life Sys, Inc., 852 F. Supp. 813, 850-51, 860-61 (D. Minn. 1994).

[381] See, e.g., Polaroid Corp. v. Eastman Kodak Co., 228 U.S.P.Q. (BNA) 305, 342 (D. Mass. 1985).

[382] 35 U.S.C. § 171 (1994).

[383] MPEP § 1502 (3d Rev. 1977).

The term of a design patent is fourteen years from the date of issuance.[384] Like a utility patent, a design patent must meet the requirements of patentability (*e.g.*, novelty, etc.).

Section 171 requires that a design patent be ornamental, "the product of aesthetic skill and artistic conception ...,"[385] but not necessarily "pleasing to the eye." Although one may obtain a design patent on a useful invention,[386] a design is unpatentable if it is "primarily functional rather than ornamental" or "is 'dictated by' the use or purpose of the article."[387]

A court will first construe the claim of the design patent, and then compare it to the accused device.[388] Infringement occurs

> if, in the eye of an ordinary observer, giving such attention as a purchaser usually gives, two designs are substantially the same, if the resemblance is such as to deceive such an observer, inducing him to purchase one supposing it to be the other, the first one patented is infringed by the other.[389]

The Federal Circuit has held that "[b]eyond the substantial similarity requirement, ... design patent infringement requires that the accused product 'appropriate the novelty in the patented device which distinguishes it from the prior art.'"[390] The substantial similarity must pertain to the novel features of the design.

Only the ornamental features of the patented design can be infringed.[391] If the patented design comprises both ornamental and functional elements, "to prove infringement a patent owner must establish

---

[384] *See* 35 U.S.C. § 173 (1994).

[385] Blisscraft of Hollywood v. United Plastics Co., 294 F.2d 694, 696 (2nd Cir. 1961).

[386] *See* Avia Group Int'l, Inc. v. L.A. Gear California, Inc., 853 F.2d 1557, 1563 (Fed. Cir.1988).

[387] Power Controls Corp. v. Hybrinetics, Inc., 806 F.2d 234, 237 (Fed. Cir. 1986); *see also*, Bonito Boats, Inc. v. Thunder Craft Boats, Inc., 489 U.S. 141, 148 (1989).

[388] *See* Elmer v. ICC Fabricating, Inc., 67 F.3d 1571, 1577 (Fed. Cir.1995).

[389] Gorham Co. v. White, 81 U.S. (14 Wall.) 511, 528 (1871).

[390] Sun Hill Indus., Inc. v. Easter Unlimited, Ltd., 48 F.3d 1193, 1197 (Fed. Cir. 1995)(quoting Litton Sys. v. Whirlpool Corp, 728 F.2d 1423, 1444 (Fed. Cir. 1984)).

[391] *See* Lee v. Dayton-Hudson Corp., 838 F.2d 1186, 1188 (Fed. Cir. 1988); KeyStone Retaining Wall Sys., Inc. v. Westrock, Inc., 997 F.2d 1444, 1450 (Fed.Cir.1993).

that an ordinary person would be deceived by reason of the common features in the claimed and accused designs which are ornamental."[392]

---

[392] Read Corp. v. Portec, Inc., 970 F.2d 816, 825 (Fed. Cir. 1992).

Part III: Trademark

§ 1. SOURCES OF POWER

1.1. Common Law Approach

As a Common Law jurisdiction, trademark protection in the United States is premised upon prior adoptio n and use rather than prior registration as is generally the case in civil law jurisdictions. The concept of trademark protection in the United States is also completely distinct from both patents or copyrights in the United States. Whereas the United States Constitution provides the grounding for both patents and copyrights,[1] trademarks do not enjoy such recognition. In fact, when confronted with the issue, the United States Supreme Court expressly held that the Patent and Copyright Clause of the Constitution did not envision protection of trademarks.[2]

Rather than being based on the Patent and Copyright Clause, federal trademark protection in the United States is premised upon Congress' authority to regulate commerce via the Commerce Clause of the United States Constitution.[3] This is why interstate commerce or "use" of a trademark is necessary for federal protection.[4] In the United States, trademark protection is a common law concept that exists independent of any statute. In fact, the legislative history of the Lanham Act,[5] the current trademark law, shows that it purports to be only a registration statute codifying common law and not a statute which creates new rights.[6]

---

[1] U.S. CONST. art. I, § 8, cl. 8.

[2] The Trademark Cases, 100 U.S. 82, 94 (1879).

[3] U.S. CONST. art. I, § 8, cl. 3.

[4] In 1988, the Lanham Act was amended to provide registration and significant rights to be established based on a bona fide "intent" to use a mark in commerce. 15 U.S.C. § 1051(b)(1988). *See also infra,* §4.2.2. Intent-to-Use Registration.

[5] 15 U.S.C. § 1051 *et seq.*

[6] In fact, the first draft of the Lanham Act included section 34 which stated:
Nothing in the Act shall entitle the registrant to interfere with or restrain the use by any person of the same trade-mark or of a similar trade-mark for the same or like goods or services when such person by himself or his predecessors in business has continuously used such trade-mark from a date prior to the use or registration, whichever is earlier, by the registrant or his predecessors.
Trade-mark: Hearings on H.R. 9041 Before Subcomm. on Trade-marks of the House Comm. on Patents, 75th Cong. 3d Sess. 6 (1938) (reading of the bill H.R. 9041 into the record).

The United States Supreme Court has reasoned that trademarks do not "depend upon novelty, invention, discovery, or any work of the brain. It requires no fancy or imagination, no genius, no laborious thought. Trademarks are simply founded on priority of appropriation." [7]

Trademark jurisprudence has developed over centuries of time. The use of a mark to identify the source of a product actually began at least 3500 years ago when potters made scratchings on the bottom of their creations to identify the sources. The first judicial recognition of trademarks in a common law system did not come, however, until 1584 in what is known as "Sandforth's Case." [8] From this rather inauspicious beginning where a mark owner was protected from economic loss due to the deceit of another, it soon became a well accepted judicial notion in England that a mark deserved protection at common law to indicate source or origin of goods. Moreover, judicial interpretation has significantly expanded federal protection of unregistered marks under Section 43(a) of the Lanham Act.

The United States Trademark Association interpreted this to mean that "nothing in this Act shall affect any common-law rights acquired by a third party prior to the use or registration of the registrant." *Id.* at 64.

[7] *Trademark Cases*, 100 U.S. at 94.

[8] Sandforth's Case, Cory's Entries, BL MS. Hargrave 123, fo. 168 (1584) (providing a fairly complete portion of the complaint), reprinted in J.H. Baker & S.F.C. Milsom, Sources of English Legal History - Private Law to 1750 615-18 (1986); HLS MS. 2071, fo. 86 (providing a brief abstract of the case), reprinted in Baker & Milsom, supra, at 615-18; HLS MS. 5048 fo. 118v. (formerly catalogued as HLS MS. Acc. 704755, fo 118v.) (providing another brief abstract of the case), reprinted in Baker & Milsom, supra, at 615. Other unpublished references to the case are found in CUL MS. Ii 5. 38, fo. 132; HLS MS. 2074, fo. 84v.; and BL MS. Lansdowne 1086, fo. 74v. For an extremely helpful analysis of the history and significance of this case, see Keith M. Stolte, *How Early Did Anglo-American Trademark Law Begin? An Answer to Schechter's Conundrum* , 8 FORDHAM I. P., MEDIA & ENT. L.J. 505 (1998)(relying on the above cited research to correct the erroneous, but well accepted, view that Southern V. Howe, 79 Eng. Rep 1244 (1618), had been the first Common Law trademark case.) *See generally* FRANK I. SCHECTER, THE HISTORICAL FOUNDATIONS OF THE LAW RELATING TO TRADEMARKS (1925).

1.2. The Lanham Act

The American concept of trademark law followed this English common law notion.[9] Today, the common law has been codified in the Lanham Act. The Lanham Act defines trademarks as any "word, name, symbol, or device or any combination thereof ... used ... to indicate the source of the goods ... ."[10] Although the Lanham Act was intended primarily as a registration statute codifying common law rights, in reality, the Act does create a right of incontestability[11] and now, protection against "dilution,"[12] two concepts that were not widely accepted at common law.

As a common law jurisdiction, the United States provides essentially two parallel avenues of concern for trademark owners. The first is whether the common law would recognize a mark as a valid trademark; the second is whether such a mark is registerable. Although today validity for registration on the Principle Registry and validity for enforcement purposes in a federal court receive essentially the same analysis, there are times when the common law will still prevail. For example, a decision to register a mark by the Patent and Trademark Office Examining Attorneys is not binding on a court that is faced with the question of the mark's validity and a federal court has the power to correct the registry by canceling marks as it deems appropriate.[13]

Even though the source of trademark protection in the United States is state common law, the Lanham Act does provide many meaningful additional protections that make registration necessary for anyone seeking the fullest protection of their trademarks in the United States.

---

[9] *Trademark Cases*, 100 U.S. at 92.

[10] 15 U.S.C. § 1127 (1997) (Lanham Act § 45).

[11] 5 U.S.C. §§ 1064, 1065, 1115. *See* Kenneth L. Port, *The Illegitimacy of Trademark Incontestability*, 26 IND. L. REV. 519 (1993) (arguing that incontestability was not recognized at common law and a codification of such a concept was an expansion of the common law).

[12] 15 U.S.C. § 1125(c) (Lanham Act § 42). *See* Kenneth L. Port, *The "Unnatural" Expansion Of Trademark Rights: Is A Federal Dilution Statute Necessary?*, 18 SETON HALL LEGIS. J. 433 (1994)(arguing that the federal dilution statute is not justified in a common law system and converts the trademark right to a property right when the common law never treated it as such).

[13] 15 U.S.C. § 1119 (Lanham Act § 37).

1.2.1. Nationwide Protection.

Once a trademark is registered, nationwide protection is conferred on the owner of the registration as of the date of the registration, even if the use has not been nationwide. Intent-to-Use[14] registrations similarly enjoy a constructive nationwide first-use date. This date is the date of the filing of the application with the PTO.

1.2.2. Evidentiary Presumptions

A registered trademark is also prima facie evidence of the validity of the registered mark, of the registration, of the registrant's ownership of the mark, and of the registrant's exclusive right to use the registered mark in commerce on or in connection with the goods or services specified in the registration.[15] Once a mark is used for five years and a section 15 affidavit is filed appropriately with the PTO—or becomes incontestable[16]— the registration becomes conclusive evidence of the validity of the registered mark, of the registration, of the registrant's ownership of the mark, and of the registrant's exclusive right to use the registered mark in commerce on or in connection with the goods or services specified in the registration.[17]

1.2.3. Warning Function

Once a trademark is registered, the owner may use the symbol (R) or "Registered Trademark" to designate that the mark is registered with the United States Patent and Trademark Office. This clearly notifies all other would-be users of the mark of the firstcomer's rights. It should therefore act as a general deterrent to prevent innocent and unintentional infringing.

1.2.4. Damages

In very egregious cases, the statute allows for a trebling of damages if the mark infringed is a registered trademark.

Therefore, although the United States is a use-based, priority system based on common law, and not a registration-based system, there are still extremely important reasons why any trademark user in the United States should seriously consider filing for a federal registration.

---

[14] *See infra,* at § 4.2.2. Intent-to-Use Applications.

[15] 15 U.S.C. § 1115(a) (Lanham Act § 33(a)).

[16] 15 U.S.C. § 1065 (Lanham Act § 15).

[17] 15 U.S.C. § 1115(b) (Lanham Act § 33(b)).

1.3. Significant Amendments to the Lanham Act
1.3.1. Trademark Clarification Act of 1984

The Trademark Clarification Act of 1984[18] added the following language to the Lanham Act:

The primary significance of the registered mark to the relevant public rather than purchaser motivation shall be the test for determining whether the registered mark has become the generic name of goods or services on or in connection with which it has been used.[19]

This amendment was added to the Lanham Act because the Ninth Circuit insisted on using the purchaser motivation test to arrive at the a result that made the famous trademark MONOPOLY[20] for a board game to be generic and therefore unenforceable. It is one of the rare instances where the United States Congress has specifically overruled a court on a trademark matter using an amendment to the Lanham Act.

1.3.2. Trademark Counterfeiting Act of 1984

The Trademark Counterfeiting Act of 1984[21] was the most extensive set of amendments to the Lanham Act in its first forty years.[22] Congress amended the Lanham Act to provide both federal prosecutors and trademark holder with the "essential tools" for combating counterfeiters.[23] In what it called the "insidious and rapidly growing form of commercial fraud,"[24] the Act changed Sections 34, 35, and 36 of the Lanham Act and granted the courts the power to grant *ex parte* seizure orders and monetary remedies in cases of counterfeiting of registered marks, including lessening the burden to establish treble damages.[25] It did this in a new paragraph of

---

[18] Trademark Clarification Act of 1984, Pub. L. No. 98-620, § 102, 98 Stat. 3335 (1984) (codified at 15 U.S.C. § 1064(3) (1984)).

[19] 15 U.S.C. § 1064(3) (1984).

[20] Anti-Monopoly, Inc. v. General Mills Fun Group, 684 F.2d 1316 (9th Cir. 1982), *cert. denied*, 459 U.S. 1227 (1983).

[21] Trademark Counterfeiting Act of 1984, Pub. L. No. 100-667, 102 Stat. 3935 (1988) (codified at 15 U.S.C. §§ 1117, 1118, 1119 (Lanham Act §§ 35, 36, 37).

[22] *See* S. Rep. No. 100-515, at 2 (1988), *reprinted in* 1988 U.S.C.C.A.N. 5577, 5578.

[23] S. Rep. No. 98-526, at 1 (1984), *reprinted in* 1984 U.S.C.C.A.N. 3627, 3627.

[24] S. Rep. No. 98-526, at 1 (1984), *reprinted in* 1984 U.S.C.C.A.N. 3627, 3627.

[25] S. Rep. No. 98-526, at 2-3 (1984), *reprinted in* 1984 U.S.C.C.A.N. 3627, 3628-9.

Section 35: that provision states that a court shall award "three times...profits or damages, whichever is greater" in the case of any violation that consists of "intentionally using a mark or designation, knowing such mark or designation is a counterfeit mark...in connection with the sale, offering for sale, or distribution of goods or services."[26] It created a presumption of damages in cases of counterfeiting toward an award of treble damages and placed the burden upon the potential defendant to demonstrate the defense of "extenuating circumstances."[27] It also added criminal trademark anti-counterfeiting penalties for the first time.[28]

1.3.3. Trademark Revision Act of 1988

The Trademark Revision Act of 1988[29] made two rather profound changes to the Lanham Act and the way trademarks are protected in the United States, by redefining "use" and allowing for an "intent-to-use" registration.

1.3.3.1. New Definition of Use

Until the Trademark Revision Act of 1988, mere "token" use was sufficient to establish that the applicant had used a mark in interstate commerce and had therefore met one of the primary prerequisites to federal registration. The Revision Act did away with token use and now requires "use in the ordinary course of trade."[30] This is a flexible standard. It requires use that is commensurate with the goods or services identified on the application. Therefore, if one sold candy bars, significantly more sales would be necessary compared to an applicant who claimed use of a mark on or in connection with the sale of highly sophisticated machine tools.

---

[26] 15 U.S.C. § 1117(b) (Lanham Act § 35(b)). *See also* Thomas P. Olson, An Analysis of the Trademark Counterfeiting Act of 1984, *in New and Extraordinary Relief in Intellectual Property Cases*, at 21 (*PLI Pat., Copyrights, Trademarks, and Literary Prop. Course, Handbook Series* No. G4 3765, 1985).

[27] 15 U.S.C. § 1117(d) (Lanham Act § 35(d)).

[28] 18 U.S.C. § 2320 (2001).

[29] Trademark Revision Act of 1988, Pub. L. No. 100-667 § 132, 102 Stat. 3935, 3946 (codified at 15 U.S.C. § 1125 (1989)).

[30] 15 U.S.C. § 1127 (Lanham Act § 45).

1.3.3.2. Intent-to-Use Registration

The more significant change, concomitant with abolition of token use, was to adopt an intent-to-use registration system.[31] Because use (even though it was token use) was required prior to the amendment, some companies were prejudiced by having to wait until they actually got some sort of product to market before they could obtain a United States Patent and Trademark Office ruling on whether the mark was valid. This delay was considered excessive and made American industries less competitive.

Also, under the language of Section 44 of the Lanham Act in effect at that time, a mark registered in a foreign country could be used as the basis for priority and for registration in the United States if that application is filed in the United States within one year of the issuance of the registration in the foreign country.[32] Therefore, owners of trademark registrations in many civil law countries could obtain a federal registration in the United States based on that foreign registration without ever using the mark in commerce in the United States. Foreign trademark owners, therefore, received an undue advantage over United States applicants.

For these reasons and many more, it was perceived that a United States trademark owner should be able to reserve rights in a mark it intends to use as well as a mark it actually uses. Therefore, Section 1051(b) was added to the Lanham Act which allows for the federal registration of marks which the owner had a "bona fide intention" to use.[33]

1.3.4. North American Free Trade Agreement Implementation Act

Prior to the North American Free Trade Agreement ("NAFTA") Implementation Act,[34] if a mark was determined to have secondary meaning, it could be placed on the principal register even if it was "primarily geographically deceptively misdescriptive." Additionally, it could be placed on the secondary register without a showing of secondary meaning. The NAFTA Implementation Act amended Section 2 of the

---

[31] *See infra*, §4.2.2. Intent-to-Use Applications. Naturally, both foreign and domestic corporations may fine intent-to-use applications.

[32] 15 U.S.C. § 1126 (1988).

[33] 15 U.S.C. § 1051(b) (Lanham Act § 1).

[34] North American Free Trade Agreement Implementation Act, Pub. L. No. 103-182, 107 Stat. 2057 (codified at U.S.C. § 1052(f) (1993)).

Lanham Act[35] to no longer allow such registrations.[36]

1.3.5. Uruguay Round Agreements Act

Congress enacted the Uruguay Round Agreements Act[37] to bring the Lanham Act in accordance with the Agreement on Trade-Related Aspects of Intellectual Property Rights ("TRIPS Agreement").[38] The Act amended the Lanham Act Section 2[39] to prohibit registration of a geographical mark for wine or liquor that identifies a place other than the actual origin of the product.[40] The Act also amended Section 45[41] to bring abandonment definitions in-line with international norms as set by the TRIPS Agreement.[42]

1.3.6. Federal Trademark Dilution Act of 1995

Perhaps the most controversial[43] amendment to the Lanham Act came most recently. In 1996, President Clinton signed into law the Federal Trademark Dilution Act of 1995.[44] This law essentially provided for a new section to be added to the Lanham Act and requires courts to recognize a new cause of action never recognized by the Lanham Act before. In the new Section 43(c) of the Lanham Act, injunctive relief may be granted if a trademark (registered or not) is "diluted" by the use of another mark. Section 43(c) is available only to owners of "famous" marks. Whereas trademark infringement is available only when there is competition between the parties' products or services, 43(c) allows for injunctive relief even when there is no competition and therefore no confusion is possible. The

---

[35] 15 U.S.C. § 1052(f) (Lanham Act § 2(f)).

[36] See infra, Ch. 3, § 2, I. Use Applications.

[37] Uruguay Round Agreements Act, Pub. L. No. 103-465, 108 Stat. 489 (codified as amended at U.S.C. §§ 1052(f), 1127 (1994).

[38] Uruguay Round Agreements Act, S. Rep. No. 103-412, at 226 (1994).

[39] 15 U.S.C. § 1052(f) (Lanham Act § 2(f)).

[40] Uruguay Round Agreements Act, S. Rep. No. 103-412, at 226 (1994).

[41] 15 U.S.C. § 1127.

[42] Uruguay Round Agreements Act, S. Rep. No. 103-412, at 226 (1994).

[43] See e.g., Kenneth L. Port, The "Unnatural" Expansion Of Trademark Rights: Is A Federal Dilution Statute Necessary?, 18 SETON HALL LEGIS. J. 433 (1994).

[44] Federal Dilution Act of 1995, Pub. L. No. 104-98, 109 Stat. 985 (1996), codified at 15 U.S.C. §§ 1051, 1125-1127 (1996).

examples in the legislative history include Buick Brand Aspirin and the like. Where the owners of Buick may not be able to establish confusion because of the lack of competition between the manufacturer of an automobile and a pain reliever, they may be able to show a likelihood that there would be a lessening of the distinctive qualities of the famous mark.[45]

Although prior documentation of the concept exists,[46] Frank Schechter is generally given credit for raising the idea of dilution within the United States. Schechter's revolutionary claim was that trademarks themselves sell products and therefore trademarks themselves deserve protection. That is, Schechter's implicit claim is that there is an unacceptable gap in trademark protection. Section 43(c) was intended to plug this gap. Certainly, 43(c) grants new trademark rights not previously contemplated by the Lanham Act. It remains to be seen how significant 43(c) will actually be on the practice of trademark law in the United States. The Trademark Trial and Appeal Board has indicated that dilution shall *not* be ground for cancellation of an existing registration nor grounds for denying registration.[47] Before the Anticybersquatting Consumer Protection Act,[48] when a "cybersquatter" purposefully registered a famous trademark as a domain name, injured parties would look to Section 43(c) to provide the remedy.[49] Yet, it took years before an instance where HAHA was held to dilute WAWA as used on convenience stores was no longer the most important case on dilution.[50]

---

[45] 15 U. S. C. § 1125(c) (Lanham Act § 43(c)).

[46] *See* Judgement of September 11, 1924, Landgericht Elberfeld, 25 Juristiche Wochemschrift 502, XXV Markenschutz and Wettbewerb (M.U.R.) 264.

[47] Babson Bros. Co. v. Surge Power Corp., 39 U.S.P.Q.2d (BNA) 1953 (T.T.A.B. 1996) (Lanham Act 43(c) does not provide authority for the T.T.A.B. to hear cancellation or opposition claims).

[48] *See infra*, Ch. 1, § 3, VII, Anticybersquatting Consumer Protection Act of 1999.

[49] *See, e.g.,* Intermatic, Inc. v. Toeppen, 947 F.Supp. 1227 (N.D. Ill. 1996) (Defendant's reservation of domain names for "famous marks" in order to sell or lease them to trademark owners created confusion providing a basis for relief).

[50] Wawa, Inc. v. Haaf, 40 U.S.P.Q.2d 1629 (E.D. Pa. 1996) (WAWA held to be "famous" and therefore protectable under § 43(a) of the Lanham Act).

1.3.7. Anticounterfeiting Consumer Protection Act of 1996

The Anticounterfeiting Consumer Protection Act[51] strengthened the remedies created under the Trademark Counterfeiting Act of 1984.[52] Congress created the Act to supplement the Trademark Counterfeiting Act of 1984 because it had proven to be an inadequate remedy for the explosive growth of criminal commercial counterfeiting.[53]

The Act amended Section 34(d) of the Lanham Act[54] to ensure that any federal law enforcement or local law enforcement agent can execute a seizure order in a civil action. The Act's Legislative history indicates that it had also granted courts the extreme authority, under certain conditions, to seize an aircraft, vehicle, or vessel used in connection with a violation of the Lanham Act.[55] In addition, the Act created a new Section 34(a) of the Lanham Act that requires the seizure and destruction of counterfeit goods imported into the United States.[56] It also provides for civil fines against persons who aid in the importation of counterfeit goods that are seized.[57]

The Act also amends Section 35 of the Lanham Act to allow trademark owners to opt for judicially determined statutory damages in civil cases, rather than actual damages and profits.[58]

---

[51] Anticounterfeiting Consumer Protection Act, Pub. L. No. 104-153, 110 Stat. 1386 (codified as amended at U.S.C. §§ 1116(d), 1117(c) (1996)).

[52] *See supra*, § 1.3.3, Trademark Revision Act of 1988; *infra*, Damages for Counterfeiting § 8.3.2.2.

[53] Anticounterfeiting Consumer Protection Act of 1996, H.R. Rep. No. 556, at 2 (1006), *reprinted in* 1996 U.S.C.C.A.N. 1074, 1075.

[54] 15 U.S.C. § 1116(d)(9) (Lanham Act § 34).

[55] *See* Anticounterfeiting Consumer Protection Act of 1996, H.R. Rep. No. 104-556, at 11 (1996), *reprinted in* 1996 U.S.C.C.A.N. 1074, 1084.

[56] A part of the Act that was not codified into the Lanham Act allowed for an altruistic alternative to destroying the counterfeit goods: "Where the counterfeit goods do not present a health risk and the trademark owner consents, the goods (or proceeds from the sales of the goods) may be distributed to an appropriate charity or governmental agency." H.R. Rep. No. 104-556, at 8 (1996), *reprinted in* 1996 U.S.C.C.A.N. 1074, 1081.

[57] Anticounterfeiting Consumer Protection Act, Pub. L. No. 104-153, 110 Stat. 1386 (1996).

[58] Anticounterfeiting Consumer Protection Act, Pub. L. No. 104-153, 110 Stat. 1386 (1996).

1.3.8. Trademark Law Treaty Implementation Act of 1998

In 1994, the international community bound together to create a treaty that would standardize and simplify trademark registration in all signatory countries. The result of these efforts was the Trademark Law Treaty of 1994 (TLT). The TLT was ratified by the United States Senate in June of 1998.[59] The legislation implementing the TLT and amending the Lanham Act in compliance with the requirements of the TLT was signed into law by President Clinton on October 30, 1998.[60]

Most of the Lanham Act was already in compliance with the TLT provisions; however, some technical amendments were required to Sections 1, 8, 9, 10, 12(b) and 44 of the Lanham Act.[61]

For example, Section 10 of the Lanham Act[62] was amended to clarify that documents filed with the Patent and Trademark Office pursuant to the requirements of TLT Article 11 would be "recorded" for the purposes of Section 10. Currently, the PTO requires that a complete copy of the assignment document be filed for recording. Under the TLT (Article 11(b)(2)), only an extract from the assignment document need be recorded as evidence of the change in ownership. This amendment to Section 10 of the Lanham Act was necessary to allow an assignee to file a mere extract of the assignment document rather than the entire document for recording purposes with the United States Patent and Trademark Office.

Section 9[63] of the Lanham Act was amended to delete the requirement of continued use as the basis for a renewal of the registration. Article 13 of the TLT specifically prohibits any member from requiring proof of use as an element necessary for the renewal of a registration. In order to accommodate this provision and still eliminate "deadwood" from the Principal Register, Sections 8 and 9 of the Lanham Act were both amended. Pursuant to the amendments, Section 9 renewals will now issue without proof of continued use; however, Section 8 now requires that Continuing Use Affidavits be filed not only between the fifth and sixth years of registration, but also between the ninth and tenth year, nineteenth and

---

[59] 56 Patent, Trademark and Copyright Journal 278 (1998).

[60] 57 Patent, Trademark and Copyright Journal 12 (1998).

[61] 15 U.S.C. §§ 1051, 1058, 1059, 1060, 1062(b), and 1126.

[62] 15 U.S.C. 1060.

[63] 15 U.S.C. Sec. 1059.

twentieth year, etc. By separating these two requirements, the intent is to allow the United States to remain faithful to its use-based system while adhering to the technical language of Article 13 of the TLT.

Section 44(e) of the Lanham Act[64] was also amended. That section previously required that a certified copy of the foreign certificate of registration accompany the application for registration in the U.S. Article 3 of the TLT sets out a comprehensive list of filing requirements. All applications filed with Contracting States must be granted a filing date if the application satisfies the requirements of Article 3. Article 3 does not include a certified copy of a foreign certificate of registration. Therefore, to be in compliance with Article 3, Section 44(e) was amended to no longer require that a certified copy of the foreign certificate of registration accompany the application in the United States.[65]

1.3.9. Trademark Amendments Act of 1999

The Trademark Amendments Act of 1999[66] intended to clarify and broaden existing trademark law.[67] The Trademark Amendments Act was signed into law by President Clinton on 5 August 1999.[68] First, the Act amends Section 43(c) of the Lanham Act to include dilution as a ground for opposition under Section 13(a) and a ground for cancellation under Section 14.[69] While dilution is not a basis for an *ex parte* refusal to register a mark

---

[64] 15 U.S.C. 1126(e).

[65] Section 44(e) now reads as follows: "Such applicant shall submit, within such time period as may be prescribed by the Commissioner, a certification or a certified copy of the registration in the country of origin of the applicant."

[66] Trademark Amendments Act of 1999, Pub. L. No. 106-43, 113 Stat. 218 (1999) (codified at 15 U.S.C. §§ 1051, 1052, 1060, 1063, 1064, 1092, 1114, 1116, 1117, 1118, 1122, 1125, 1127, 1501). This Act also eliminated the old use of the word "trade-mark" in the Lanham Act and replaced all uses with "trademark."

[67] *See generally* John L. Welch, *Modernizing for the Millennium: the 1999 Amendments to the Trademark Law*, 13 INT'L. LAW PRACTICUM 34 (New York State Bar Assoc. 2000).

[68] *Id.* at 34.

[69] *See infra*, § 6.4.3.

under Section 2 of the Lanham Act,[70] the Act provides that injunctive relief[71] is available in dilution action, but that monetary recovery[72] and/or destruction of infringing articles[73] will be available only in the case of "willful violations."[74]

Second, the Act eliminates the federal government's immunity from suit for violation of the Lanham Act. It expands the definition of "any person" in Sections 32 and 45 to include the United States, its agencies, instrumentalities, and any entities or persons acting for it.[75] The Act specifically changes Section 40 to expressly state that the United States waives sovereign immunity.[76]

Third, the Act amends Section 43(a) to provide that, in a civil action for infringement of trade dress not registered on the principal register, the party that asserts trade dress protection has the burden to prove non-functionality.[77]

1.3.10. Anticybersquatting Consumer Protection Act of 1999

In 1999, Congress passed a bill that, in effect, extended trademark law into cyberspace. On 29 November 1999, President Clinton signed into law an appropriations bill that included the Intellectual Property and Communications Omnibus Reform Act of 1999.[78] The Anticybersquatting

---

[70] 15 U.S.C. § 1052; *see* John L. Welch, *Modernizing for the Millennium: the 1999 Amendments to the Trademark Law*, 13 INT'L. LAW PRACTICUM 34 (New York State Bar Assoc. 2000).

[71] 15 U.S.C. § 1116(a) (Lanham Act § 34(a)).

[72] 15 U.S.C. § 1117 (Lanham Act § 35).

[73] 15 U.S.C. § 1118 (Lanham Act § 36).

[74] The Lanham Act refers to counterfeiting as a "willful violation" under § 43(c). *See* 15 U.S.C. § 1118.

[75] *See* Trademark Amendments Act of 1999, Pub. L. No. 106-43, 113 Stat. 218 (1999).

[76] *See* Trademark Amendments Act of 1999, Pub. L. No. 106-43, 113 Stat. 218 (1999).

[77] *See* Trademark Amendments Act of 1999, Pub. L. No. 106-43, 113 Stat. 218 (1999); *see also* John L. Welch, *Modernizing for the Millennium: the 1999 Amendments to the Trademark Law*, 13 INT'L. LAW PRACTICUM 34, 34 (New York State Bar Assoc. 2000).

[78] Steven R. Borgman, *The New Federal Cybersquatting Laws*, 8 INTELL. PROP. L.J. 265, 265 (2000).

Consumer Protection Act ("ACPA")[79] was Title III of this omnibus appropriations bill. Congress created the ACPA to

> protect consumers and American businesses, to promote the growth of online commerce, and to provide clarity in the law for Trademark owners by prohibiting the bad-faith and abusive registration of distinctive marks as Internet domain names with the intent to profit from the goodwill associated with such marks.[80]

The ACPA protects trademark owners against a new harm in cyberspace—"cybersquatting"[81]—when a party registers a domain name that is identical or confusingly similar to a trademark for the purpose of creating confusion as to the source of the domain name. The ACPA added a new section 43(d)[82] to the Lanham Act, which again pushed the Lanham Act beyond its common law origins.[83] The most obvious change that Section 43(d) brings to the Lanham Act is that it designates domain names for Lanham Act protections. Section 43(d) of the Lanham Act does not give trademark-like protections to domain names; however, for holders of registered trademarks, Section 43(d) gives them protections against those who register identical or confusingly similar domain names in bad faith:[84] Section 43(d)(1) creates this new "bad faith" cause of action against cybersquatters;[85] Section 43(d)(2) creates an *in rem* cause of action for cybersquatting;[86] and Section 43(d)(3) expressly provides that the new causes of action under Sections 43(d)(1) and 43(d)(2) may be brought in addition to any other civil action or remedy otherwise applicable.[87]

[79]Anticybersquatting Consumer Protection Act of 1999, Pub. L. No. 106-113, § 3002(a), 113 Stat. 1501, 1537 (1999) (codified at 15 U.S.C. §§ 1114, 1116, 1117, 1125(d), 1127 & 1129).

[80]Anticybersquatting Consumer Protection Act, S. Rep. No. 106-140, at 4 (1999).

[81]*See infra*, § 2.2.6.

[82]15 U.S.C. § 1125(d).

[83]*See supra*, § 1.3.3.1, 1.3.5.

[84]15 U.S.C. § 1125(d). Anticybersquatting Consumer Protection Act of 1999, Pub. L. No. 106-113, § 3002(a), 113 Stat. 1501, 1537 (1999). *See infra*, § 6.5.

[85]15 U.S.C. § 1125(d)(1). Anticybersquatting Consumer Protection Act of 1999, Pub. L. No. 106-113, § 3002(a), 113 Stat. 1501, 1537 (1999). *See infra*, § 6.5.1.

[86]15 U.S.C. § 1125(d)(2). Anticybersquatting Consumer Protection Act of 1999, Pub. L. No. 106-113, § 3002(a), 113 Stat. 1501, 1537 (1999). *See infra*, § 6.5.2.

[87]15 U.S.C. § 1125(d)(3). Anticybersquatting Consumer Protection Act of 1999, Pub. L. No. 106-113, § 3002(a), 113 Stat. 1501, 1537 (1999). *See infra*, §8.3.2.3.

1.3.11. Madrid Protocol Implementation Act of 2002

Introduced in 2001, the Madrid Protocol Implementation Act of 2002[88] serves as the implementing legislation for the Madrid Protocol. In general terms, the Madrid Protocol reformed the earlier international effort to allow international trademark registration— called the Madrid Agreement. The Madrid Protocol Implementation Act of 2002 gives a succinct explanation of how (1) the Madrid Protocol would make up for the shortcomings of the Madrid Agreement, and (2) how the Lanham Act would need to change to accommodate the Madrid Protocol:

> Practically speaking, the Protocol "updated" the Madrid Agreement, in many respects by conforming its contents to existing provisions in U.S. law. For example, under the Protocol, applications for international trademark extension can be completed in English; ... applications under the Agreement are required to be completed in French. Moreover, under the Protocol, an international application may be based on a country of origin application - as opposed to an actual registration - thus allowing U.S. applicants to seek international protection at the same time they file a U.S. application, including an application based on a *bona fide* intention to use a mark in commerce. The Protocol also permits an extended eighteen month period in which a country may refuse to give effect to an international registration and allows for higher filing and renewal fees, both of which conform with the effective pendency and fee structure of the U.S. Patent and Trademark Office.
>
> Finally, the Protocol modifies the so-called "central attack" provision of the Madrid Agreement. Under the Madrid Agreement, if during the first five years of an international registration, the national application or registration upon which the international registration is dependent is limited or cancelled, all rights obtained in the member countries of the Madrid Agreement based on extensions of that registration are similarly limited or cancelled. This is known as "central attack." With the Protocol, in the event of a "central attack" on the home mark and the subsequent cancellation of the international registration, the international registration may be "transformed" into a series of national applications in the designated countries, all of which will retain the original filing date (i.e., the international registration date) and any priority claimed. So, a U.S. trademark owner whose mark is cancelled in the United States will still be able to retain a priority in other countries in which it is seeking

---

[88]Pub. L. No. 107-273, § 13401, 116 Stat. 1758, 1913-1920 (2002) (codified at 15 U.S.C. § 1141).

protection.[89]

In essence, the Act adds title XII, Sections 60-74 of the Lanham Act, to allow for trademark filers to make international trademark registrations through the USPTO.[90]

1.4. State Trademark Protection

In addition to the federal scheme of protection, each state in the United States also has its own common law as well as statutory schemes of registration and protection of trademarks. Most state registration statutes still do not give the registrant priority of use state-wide,[91] require no substantive review of the marks they register,[92] and are not often times taken as seriously as federal registrations. The three types of state statutes most relevant are the state trademark protection acts, deceptive trade practices acts, and state dilution statutes.

1.4.1. State Trademark Statutes

Most state trademark statutes follow the Model State Trademark Bill.[93] This Bill is not significantly different from the protections recognized at common law and under the Lanham Act. The purpose of state trademark statutes is to protect marks which are not used sufficiently to be deemed used in interstate commerce for the purposes of the Lanham Act. That is, the state statutes operate as a fallback position for most trademark owners in the event they fail to obtain protections granted in federal court under the Lanham Act.

---

[89]Madrid Protocol Implementation Act, S. Rep. No. 107-46, at 3 (2001), 1991 WL 84058, at *3.

[90]15 U.S.C. § 1441.

[91] *See* Burger King of Florida, Inc. v. Hoots, 403 F.2d 904 (7th Cir. 1968) (common law trademark rights limited to a small geographical area surrounding defendants existing business establishment).

[92] *See e.g.,* Leon's Frozen Custard, Inc. v. Leon Corp., 513 N.W.2d 636 (Wis. Ct. App. 1994)(Wisconsin does not review trademark registration applications for similarity to existing registrations).

[93] RESTATEMENT (THIRD) UNFAIR COMPETITION Ch. 3 (1995).

1.4.2. Deceptive Trade Practices Statutes

State statutes based on the Model State Deceptive Trade Practices Act have slightly more teeth than the state trademark statutes. These statutes contemplate not only protection against conduct not necessarily prohibited by common law trademark law or the Lanham Act, but they also usually provide a possibility (if not a requirement) that the appropriate State Attorney General enforce the Act.[94] The Illinois Uniform Deceptive Trade Practice Act is perhaps representative of these types of statutes. Not all states have adopted these statutes but most have. The Illinois statute provides as follows:

A person engages in a deceptive trade practice when, in the course of his business, vocation or occupation, he:

(1) passes off goods or services as those of another;

(2) causes likelihood of confusion or of misunderstanding as to the source, sponsorship, approval or certification of goods or services;

(3) causes likelihood of confusion or of misunderstanding as to affiliation, connection or association with or certification by another;

(4) uses deceptive representations or designations of geographic origin in connection with goods or services;

(5) represents that goods or services have sponsorship, approval, characteristics, ingredients, uses, benefits or quantities that they do not have or that a person has a sponsorship, approval, status, affiliation or connection that he does not have;

(6) represents that goods are original or new if they are deteriorated, altered, reconditioned, reclaimed, used or secondhand;

(7) represents that goods or services are a particular standard, quality or grade or that goods are a particular style or model, if they are of another;

(8) disparages the goods, services or business of another by false or misleading representation of fact;

(9) advertises goods or services with intent not to sell them as advertised;

(10) advertises goods or services with intent not to supply reasonably expectable public demand, unless the advertisement discloses a limitation of quantity;

(11) make false or misleading statements of fact concerning the reasons for, existence of or amounts of price reductions;

(12) engages in any other conduct which similarly creates a likelihood of confusion or of misunderstanding.

In order to prevail in an action under this Act, a plaintiff need not prove

---

[94] *See e.g.,* 815 Ill. Comp. Stat. 510/2 (2004).

competition between the parties or actual confusion or misunderstanding.[95]

1.4.3. State Dilution Statutes

Thirty-five states have adopted dilution statutes[96] and three states

---

[95] 815 Ill. Comp. Stat. 510/2 (2004).

[96] Alabama: ALA. CODE § 8-12-17 (1998)
Alaska: ALASKA STAT. § 45.50.180 (West, Westlaw through 2003 sess.)
Arizona: ARIZ. REV. STAT. § 44-1448.01 (2002)
Arkansas: ARK. CODE ANN. § 4-71-213 (1999)
California: CAL. BUS. & PROFESSIONS CODE § 14330 (West, Westlaw through 2004 sess.) (elec. update)
Connecticut: CONN. GEN. STAT. § 35-11i(c) (2003)
Delaware: DEL. CODE ANN. tit. 6, § 3313 (2003)
Florida: FLA. STAT. ANN. § 495.151 (West 2002)
Georgia: GA. CODE ANN. § 10-1-451(b) (1993)
Hawaii: HAW. REV. STAT. § 482-32 (2001)
Idaho: IDAHO CODE § 48-501 (Michie 2004)
Illinois: 765 ILL. COMP. STAT. 1036/65 (1998)
Iowa: IOWA CODE § 548.113 (West, Westlaw through 2004 sess.)
Kansas: KAN. STAT. ANN. § 81-214 (West, Westlaw through 2003 sess.)
Louisiana: LA. REV. STAT. ANN. § 51:223.1 (West 2004)
Maine: ME. REV. STAT. ANN. tit. 10, § 1530 (West, Westlaw through 2004 sess.)
Massachusetts: MASS. GEN. L. ANN. ch. 110B, § 12 (West 2003)
Missouri: MO. ANN. STAT. § 417.061 (West 2001)
Montana: MONT. CODE ANN. § 30-13-334 (2003)
Nebraska: NEB. REV. STAT. ANN. § 87-140 (Michie 2000)
New Hampshire: N.H. REV. STAT. ANN. § 350-A:12 (1992)
New Mexico: N.M. STAT. ANN. § 57-3B-15 (Michie 1997)
New York: N.Y. GEN. BUS. LAW § 360(1) (West, Westlaw through 2004 sess.) (elec. update)
Oregon: OR. REV. STAT. § 647.107 (2003)
Pennsylvania: 54 PA. CONS. STAT. ANN. § 1124 (West 1996)
Rhode Island: R.I. GEN. LAWS § 6-2-12 (West, Westlaw through 2003 sess.)
South Carolina: S.C. CODE ANN. § 39-15-1165 (Law. Co-op. 2004)
Tennessee: TENN. CODE ANN. § 47-25-513 (2000)
Texas: TEX. BUS. & COM. CODE ANN. § 16.29 (Vernon 2002)
Washington: WASH. REV. CODE ANN. § 19.77.160 (West 2003)
West Virginia: W. VA. CODE § 47-2-13 (1996)
Wyoming: WYO. STAT. ANN. § 40-1-115 (Michie 1997).

include dilution as part of their common law.[97] The typical state dilution statute states that the court "may consider" whether the mark is registered or whether a likelihood of confusion exists[98] in granting injunctive relief to the holder of a trademark.[99]

Unfortunately, statutory dilution language is not applied consistently

---

[97] Michigan is considered a common law dilution state based on the following cases which issued injunctions based on a dilution theory but all of these cases were coupled with confusion and trademark infringement. It is far from clear whether a plaintiff would succeed on a pure dilution common law cause of action in Michigan. *See* O M Scott & Sons Co. v. Surowitz, 209 F. Supp. 59 (E.D.Mich 1962); Koffler Stores, Ltd. v. Shoppers Drug Mart, Inc. 434 F. Supp. 698 (E.D.Mich. 1976); Consolidated Freightways, Inc. v. Central Transport, Inc., 201 U.S.P.Q. (BNA) 524 (E.D.Mich. 1978).

New Jersey common law has recognized common law dilution. *See* Chanel, Inc. v. Casa Flora Co., 241 A.2d 24, (N.J. 1967), *cert. denied,* 242 A.2d 381 (1968); *but c.f.* Great Atlantic & Pacific Tea Co. v. A&P Trucking Corp., 149 A.2d 595 (N.J. 1959) (injunction issued even though there was no competition but court required and found a reasonable likelihood of confusion). Therefore, it is also quite unlikely that a plaintiff would prevail in under New Jersey common law in a pure dilution cause of action. *See also* Caesars World, Inc. v. Caesar's Palace, 490 F. Supp. 818 (D.N.J. 1980).

Ohio also appears to recognize a common law cause of action for dilution. Ameritech, Inc. v. American Info. Tech. Corp., 811 F.2d 960, 965 (6th Cir. 1987).

[98] The typical state dilution statute lists a number of factors in considering dilution: these factors mirror the likelihood of confusion factors used in considering infringement. *Compare* the Illinois dilution statute *infra* note 4, with *infra,* § 8.1.1.

[99] *See, e.g.,* the Illinois dilution statute, which reads as follows:
(a) The owner of a mark which is famous in this State shall be entitled, subject to the principles of equity and upon such terms as the court deems reasonable, to an injunction against another person's commercial use of a mark or trade name, if the use begins after the mark has become famous and causes dilution of the distinctive quality of the mark, and to obtain such other relief as is provided in this Section. In determining whether a mark is distinctive and famous, a court may consider factors such as, but not limited to: (1) the degree of inherent or acquired distinctiveness of the mark in this State; (2) the duration and extent of use of the mark in connection with the goods and services with which the mark is used; (3) the duration and extent of advertising and publicity of the mark in this State; (4) the geographical extent of the trading area in which the mark is used; (5) the channels of trade for the goods or services with which the mark is used; (6) the degree of recognition of the mark in the trading areas and channels of trade in this State used by the mark's owner and the person against whom the injunction is sought; (7) the nature and extent of use of the same or similar mark by third parties; and (8) whether the mark is the subject of a State registration in this State, or a federal registration under the Act of 3 March 1881, or under the Act of 20 February 1905, or on the principal register. 765 Ill. Comp. Stat. 1036/65 (1998).

from state to state. For example, some New York courts today require evidence of confusion even though the New York statute clearly dictates that dilution may be found regardless of confusion,[100] while Illinois courts will refuse to find dilution if there is confusion because "[a] trademark likely to confuse is necessarily a trademark likely to dilute."[101] Therefore, New York courts require confusion while Illinois courts preclude dilution remedies when there is confusion. To make matters worse, the New York dilution statute and the Illinois dilution statute were identical until 1997.[102] In addition, many other states have identical dilution statutes.[103]

The state statutes are consistent in requiring that the marks be famous prior to protecting them from dilution.

§ 2. SUBJECT MATTER OF PROTECTION

2.1. Introduction

The Lanham Act defines trademarks as "word, name, symbol, or device or any combination thereof ... used ... to indicate the source of the goods ... ."[104] United States courts have been taking this statement more and more literally. Therefore, if "any" aspect of a product indicates the source or origin of that product, courts today in the United States are very likely to recognize it as a trademark. Hence, the scope of trademark protection is theoretically unlimited, confined only by the requirement that the trademark act to identify source (and otherwise not be violative of the Lanham Act). Thus, the inside of a restaurant might be distinctive enough

---

[100] Beverly Pattishall, *The Dilution Rationale for Trademark-Trade Identity Protection, Its Progress and Prospects*, 71 Nw. U. L. Rev. 618, 624, n.47 and references cited therein (1976).

[101] James Burrough Ltd. v. Sign of the Beefeater, Inc., 540 F.2d 266, 274-75 n. 16 (7th Cir. 1976) (claims for confusion and dilution examined on an economic basis and both claims considered to be within the same economic context).

[102] *Compare* 765 Ill. Comp. Stat. 1035/15 (repealed 1998) *with* N.Y. Gen. Bus. Law § 368-d (repealed in 1997).

[103] *See, e.g.*, Ariz. Rev. Stat. § 44-1448.01 (2002); Ark. Code Ann. § 4-71-213 (1999); 765 Ill. Comp. Stat. 1036/65 (1998); Kan. Stat. Ann. § 81-214 (West, Westlaw through 2003 sess.); Minn. Stat. § 333.285 (2004); Mont. Code Ann. § 30-13-334 (2003); Neb. Rev. Stat. Ann. § 87-140 (Michie 2000); 54 Pa. Cons. Stat. Ann. § 1124 (West 1996); Tenn. Code Ann. § 47-25-513 (2000).

[104] 15 U.S.C. § 1127 (1997).

to warrant trademark protection,[105] the color alone of a product or a feature of a product,[106] or even the sound a motorcycle makes when idling[107] might warrant protection if it has come to identify a consistent source of that product.

United States trademark law generally protects trademarks, collective marks, certification marks, service marks, trade and business names if they indicate source and are used on products, and trade dress.[108]

A trademark identifies the source of goods or services. The source itself need not be known; rather, it is important that a source is consistently recognized and associated with a particular good or service.[109] In addition to source identification, a trademark represents the goodwill of a business, the reputation of the producer of goods or services. The consumer comes to rely upon an established level of quality in purchasing a particular good or service.[110] Trademarks become the embodiment of this goodwill.

---

[105] Two Pesos, Inc., v. Taco Cabana International, Inc., 505 U.S. 763 (1992)("Mexican theme" of bright colors, paintings and artifacts has acquired secondary meaning and is distinctive).

[106] Qualitex Co. v. Jacobson Prod. Co., 514 U.S. 159 (1995).

[107] See U.S. Trademark Application Serial No. 74/485,223, in the name of Harley-Davidson (filed 1 February 1994) (claiming the sound of a Harley-Davidson motorcycle to be distinctive and indicating Harley-Davidson, Inc. as the source of motorcycles in the minds of consumers) (on file with the United States Patent and Trademark Office); see also Kawasaki Motors Corp., U.S.A. v. H-D Mich., Inc., 43 U.S.P.Q.2d 1521 (T.T.A.B. 1997) (attacks against Harley-Davidson's bid to register sound of motorcycle exhaust).

[108] 15 U.S.C. §§ 1127, 1053 (service marks); § 1054 (collective and certification marks).

[109] 15 U.S.C. § 1127 (1997); see also International Kennel Club of Chicago, Inc. v. Mighty Star, Inc., 846 F.2d 1079 (7th Cir. 1988) (International Kennel Club is distinctive and recognized as a source of information on pure bred dogs and registrations).

[110] A particular level of quality is not specified by the Lanham Act. The quality expectation of the consumer is one of continuity. The association between the consumer and the business is developed by the businesses efforts in establishing and maintaining a particular level of quality. Quality itself may be high or low, but the consumer knows that it will always be the same when identified by the trademark associated with a particular product. It is this expectation and fulfilment which establishes the good will that is protected by trademark law. See Coca-Cola Co. v. Koke Co., 254 U.S. 143, 146 (1920) (holding that the expectation behind the COCA-COLA name is "a single thing coming from a single source"); Mishawaka Rubber & Woolen Mfg. Co. v. S.S. Kresge Co., 316 U.S. 203, 205 (1942) ("The protection of trade-marks is the protection of

2.2. Categories of Marks
2.2.1. Trademarks

The Lanham Act defines trademarks as "any word, name, symbol, or device, or any combination thereof (1) used by a person, or (2) which a person has a bona fide intention to use in commerce and applies to register on the principle register established by this chapter to identify or distinguish his or her goods ... ."[111]

A mark may be registered on the Principle Register provided it satisfies 15 U.S.C. § 1052. Section 1052 actually serves as a list identifying marks which are prohibited from being registered. Thus, any mark which is not statutorily prohibited by Section 1052 should be registrable.[112]

Section 1052 prohibits the following types of marks from being registered:

(a) Marks which comprise immoral, deceptive, or scandalous matter.

This prohibition has proven to be difficult to apply. The test is whether the applicant's mark is "shocking to the sense of ... decency or propriety."[113] But what is "shocking" today may not be even amusing in a few years. What one court might find shocking now, ten or twenty years later may not be shocking at all and may even have become a mainstream colloquialism. The standard seems quite subjective. The key to application of 1052(a) seems to be whether an appreciable segment of the population at the time the matter is raised finds the mark to be shocking to their sense of decency.[114]

---

symbols...A trade-mark is a merchandising short-cut which induces a purchaser to select what he wants, or what he has been led to believe he wants...Once this is attained, the trade-mark owner has something of value. If another poaches upon the commercial magnetism of the symbol he has created, the owner can obtain legal redress.").

[111] 15 U.S.C. § 1127 (Lanham Act § 45).

[112] *See In re* McGinley, 660 F.2d 481 (C.C.P.A.1981) (mark of nude woman and man kissing and embracing in manner that exposed the man's genitalia held scandalous); *In re* Mavely Media Group Ltd., 33 F.3d 1367 (Fed. Cir.1994) (for marks considered scandalous under 15 U.S.C. § 1052(a)).

[113] *In re* McGinley, 660 F.2d 481 (C.C.P.A. 1981)(picture of a man and woman embracing in a manner that exposed the man's genitalia was scandalous).

[114] Harjo v. Pro Football, Inc., 30 U.S.P.Q.2d 1828 (T.T.A.B. 1994) trademark which exposes an appreciable segment of the population to public ridicule is not registrable), *rev'd*, 284 F.Supp.2d 96 (D.D.C. 2003) (trademark cancellation is warranted if "substantial composite" of those referred to is depreciated or degraded).

(b) A mark that consists of or comprises a flag or coat of arms of the United States, any State in the United States or any other foreign nation.

(c) A mark that consists of or comprises a name, portrait or signature identifying a particular living individual except with that individual's consent or the name, signature or portrait of a deceased President of the United States during the life of the Widow without the Widow's consent.

(d) Marks that are likely to cause confusion with a mark previously registered on the Principle Register. Marks that are likely to cause confusion as to the source of the goods or services or appear to create some false sense of sponsorship are also not registrable.[115]

(e) Marks that are merely descriptive,[116] merely geographic terms, are primarily merely of surname significance and primarily geographically deceptively misdescriptive terms are not registrable. Merely geographic marks are not registrable.[117] However, words that also have geographic significance are registrable if there is no "goods/place" association in the minds of the consumers. Therefore, the mark NANTUCKET for use on T-shirts is registrable because the place called Nantucket is not generally associated as the place from where T-shirts emanate.[118]

Marks which are merely of surname significance are not registrable unless they also act to identify the source or origin of some good or service. Therefore, although Taylor is the name of a person once connected with the manufacture and sale of wine, the mark TAYLOR WINE is also acts to identify source and therefore constitutes a valid trademark.[119]

(f) Secondary meaning

The term used to describe when a mark which is otherwise violative of Section 1052(e) is registrable is "secondary meaning." A mark is said to have secondary meaning when the mark has two functions. One may be to be descriptive of the goods or services, to merely be of geographic

---

[115] *See infra*, Section 8.1.

[116] Merely descriptive marks are marks which simply describe the product or attribute of the product and do not connote source to the relevant consuming public. *See* Park 'N Fly, Inc. v. Dollar Park & Fly, Inc., 469 U.S. 189 (1985).

[117] *See* DONALD S. CHISUM & MICHAEL A. JACOBS, UNDERSTANDING INTELLECTUAL PROPERTY LAW, § 5C[1][c][ii](2).

[118] *In re* Nantucket, Inc., 677 F.2d 95 (C.C.P.A. 1982).

[119] The Taylor Wine Co., Inc. v. Bully Hill Vineyards, Inc., 590 F.2d 701 (2^d Cir. 1978).

significance, or to merely name a surname. The other function may be to identify source. It is this second function that is necessary for any mark to overcome a Section 1052(e) rejection and still be registrable.[120]

Generally speaking, a trademark must exhibit three qualities: it must embody the definition provided in section 1127 and be determined allowable by the Patent and Trademark Board; it must be in use or be intended for use in commerce; and it must be able to distinguish the goods or services of the manufacturer.[121]

2.2.2. Collective Marks

Collective marks may be registered on the principle register under 15 U.S.C. §1054. A collective mark is defined as a trademark or servicemark,

(1) used by a person other than its owner, or

(2) which its owner has a bona fide intention to permit a person other than the owner to use in commerce and files an application to register on the principle register established by this Act, to certify regional or other origin, material, mode of manufacture, quality, accuracy, or other characteristics of such person's goods or services or that the work or labor on the goods or services was performed by members of a union or other organization.[122]

Collective marks are unique in certain respects. A collective mark must be registered by the group who exercises or intends to exercise control over use of the mark.[123] An individual member of the collective is not allowed to register the mark.[124] A collective mark may be either a collective membership mark or a collective organization mark. A collective membership mark is used by a group to signify membership in an organization. A collective organization mark is used by a group which serves as an umbrella over other groups. The umbrella group may promote

---

[120] International Kennel Club of Chicago, Inc. v. Mighty Star, Inc., 846 F.2d 1079 (7th Cir. 1988) (International Kennel Club has acquired secondary meaning).

[121] 1 JEROME GILSON, TRADEMARK PROTECTION AND PRACTICE § 1.02[1].

[122] 15 U.S.C. § 1127 (Lanham Act § 45).

[123] Control and registration is indicative of ownership.

[124] F.R. Lepage Bakery v. Roesch Bakery Products Co., 851 F.2d 351 (Fed. Cir. 1988) (collective trademark canceled upon assignment to an individual), *vacated on other grounds*, 863 F.2d 43 (Fed. Cir. 1988).

goods on behalf of its members.[125] As opposed to a trademark, a collective mark may be geographically descriptive.

2.2.3. Certification Marks

Certification marks should not be confused with collective marks. A certification mark serves a very specific and unique purpose. A certification mark is owned and registered by an entity which exists to provide certification of other products or services. Certification marks cannot be used as trademarks by the entity that owns the mark.[126] A certification mark may be used (under the authority of the owner) *by others* on products or services which meet the standards and specifications established by the owner of the mark. A good example of a certification mark is Underwriters Laboratory (UL). UL specifies standards that must be met by manufactures in order to affix the UL mark to their product. This certification is relied upon by consumers to indicate a consistent level of quality. The use of the UL mark on goods and services is a great advantage in the marketplace.

Certification may only be used for certifying the goods or services of others. In addition, a certification mark owner must exercise control over the use of the mark. Failure to exercise control may result in cancellation of the mark.[127]

2.2.4. Service Marks

Service marks have the same rights to registration as trademarks.[128] The definition applied to service marks is nearly identical to that of a trademark.[129] The primary distinction is that a service mark is specifically designated to cover services. Service marks, like trademarks, must be used in commerce in order to qualify for registration. Unlike trademarks, use in advertising is generally sufficient to constitute use of a service mark. Some courts, however, have held that advertisement is sufficient use to avoid a

---

[125] 1 McCarthy, Trademarks and Unfair Competition at § 19.99 (4th ed. 2004).

[126] Consolidated Dairy Prods. Co. v. Gildner & Schimmel Inc., 101 U.S.P.Q. 465, (1954). *See also* 1 McCarthy Trademarks and Unfair Competition § 19.94 (4th ed. 2004).

[127] 15 U.S.C. § 1064(e)(1) (Lanham Act § 14(e)(1)).

[128] 15 U.S.C. § 1053 (Lanham Act § 3); *In Re* Dr. Pepper, 836 F.2d 508 (U.S. App. 1987) (lottery does not constitute a "service").

[129] 15 U.S.C. § 1127 (Lanham Act § 45).

finding of abandonment, but use of the service mark through actual sales is still necessary to *secure* registration of service marks.[130]

Trademarks and service marks are essentially interchangeable. A business may choose to use an identical mark for both its products and its services.[131] It is important to note, however, that a service mark must be used on services and a trademark on products.[132] It is simple to define what a product is. A product constitutes any tangible article sold by the owner in commerce. A service, however, is more difficult to define. A service mark is being used when title to the goods in question are not transferred but only molded, fit, or otherwise worked upon.

2.2.5. Trade Names

Trade names are the actual names of corporations which themselves might own a host of trademarks or service marks. Trademark protection is technically not available to trade names unless they are also used on or in the connection with the sale of some goods or services in interstate commerce.[133] Trade names must adhere to the same requirements as trademarks in order to gain protection.[134] Simply registering a corporate name with the Secretary of State where business is conducted (also known as "qualifying to do business") does not result in the creation of any trademark rights. Only use as a trademark can result in trademark rights.[135]

The owner of a trade name may prevail in a suit for infringement when the trade name is used by another as a trademark if confusion is likely

---

[130] Kinark Corp. v. Camelot Inc., 548 F. Supp. 429 (D.N.J. 1982) (advertising sent out prior to use for new hotel not yet in operation is not sufficient to confer rights).

[131] 1 GILSON, TRADEMARK PROTECTION AND PRACTICE § 1.02[1][b] (pub. 726, rel. 52, 2004).

[132] *In re* Forbes, 31 U.S.P.Q. 1315 (T.T.A.B. 1983).

[133] American Steel Foundries v. Robertson, 269 U.S. 372 (1926) (use of trademark "Simplex" when applied to actual goods is sufficient to secure rights); 1GILSON, TRADEMARK PROTECTION AND PRACTICE § 2.15 (pub. 726, rel. 52, 2004).

[134] Goodyear's India Rubber Glove Mfg. Co. v. Goodyear Rubber Co., 128 U.S. 598 (1888) (generic names not protected); Safeway Stores, Inc. v. Safeway Properties, Inc., 307 F.2d 495 (2d Cir. 1962) (descriptive marks have limited protection); North American Aircoach Sys., Inc. v. North American Arats, Inc., 231 F.2d 205 (9th Cir. 1955) (geographically descriptive marks not protected).

[135] George Washington Mint, Inc. v. Washington Mint, Inc., 349 F. Supp 255 (S.D.N.Y. 1972) (prior establishment as corporation name does not confer rights).

in the minds of the relevant consumer even if it has not actually used its trade name as a trademark. Conversely, the owner of a trademark may prevail in a suit for infringement if its trademark is used as a trade name by a third party and would confuse purchasers as to source. Protection extends to related businesses which may not be direct competitors, provided there is a likelihood the plaintiff will bridge the gap between the products.[136] In all cases, likelihood of confusion is the standard upon which a determination of infringement will be made.

Names used in non-commercial manners are also protectable. Religious groups, professional associations, fraternal, and benevolent groups are included in this category. The basis for protection in this instance is to maintain an established reputation and to prevent confusion among persons wishing to associate with or make contributions to such groups.[137]

2.2.6. Domain Names

A domain name is not a trademark. The Lanham Act defines a domain name as

> any alphanumeric designation which is registered with or assigned by any domain name registrar, domain name registry, or other domain name registration authority as part of an electronic address on the Internet.[138]

Trademark law encounters problems in cyberspace. One must understand how the symbols of the Internet work: the Internet has its own lexicon that

---

[136] Standard Oil Co. v. Standard Oil Co., 56 F.2d 973 (10th Cir. 1932) (second comer activity in Mexico not sufficiently distant from senior user's reasonable geographical expansion when both users engage in manufacturing, production and marketing of petroleum products).

[137] American Gold Star Mothers, Inc. v. National Gold Star Mothers, Inc., 191 F.2d 488 (D.C. Cir. 1951) (uses which tend to divert membership and gifts are injurious); American Legal Aid, Inc. v. Legal Aid Services, Inc., 176 U.S.P.Q. 131 (Wyo. 1972) (use of "legal aid" went beyond defendants description of business in incorporation papers and was injurious to established association); National Board of YWCA v. YWCA of Charleston, S.C., 335 F. Supp 615 (D.S.C. 1971) (ability to raise money and maintain established reputation is undermined when there is a confusing mark in use).

[138] 15 U.S.C. § 1127 (Lanham Act § 45).

complicates analysis of relevant legal issues.[139]

Now that the Internet has become a household tool, most everyone has a basic understanding of what it is. Most people in the U.S. understand that the "Internet is not a physical or tangible entity, but rather a giant network which interconnects unnumerable smaller groups of linked computer networks."[140] Unlike other communications utilities, no single person or commercial or government entity controls the operation of the Internet.[141] The Internet "exists and functions as a result of the fact that hundreds of separate operators...independently decided to use common data transfer protocols to exchange communications and information."[142] "The resulting whole is a decentralized, global medium of communications ... that links people, institutions, corporations, and governments around the world."[143]

This computer network relies on consistent standards to communicate and share data. Each computer accessing the Internet has a corresponding Internet protocol ("IP") address, which is comprised of four groups of numbers, with each group separated by a decimal point.[144] Instead of requiring Internet users to use IP addresses, the developers of the Internet devised a system of domain names.

A domain name "identifies a more specific area on the Internet, and as with IP numbers, is separated by a 'dot'."[145] For example, in the U.S. Supreme Court's domain name, <supremecourtus.gov>, "gov" is the generic top-level domain (gTLD), and is a country code or identifier that may signify the country or, in the case of some gTLDs, the type of information at the resultant web site. The "supremecourtus" portion of the domain name is the second-level domain. "All second level domains are

---

[139]Colby B. Springer, *Master of the Domain (Name): A History of Domain Name Litigation and the Emergence of the Anticybersquatting Consumer Protection Act and Uniform Dispute Resolution Policy*, 17 Santa Clara Computer & High Tech L.J. 315, 317 (2001).

[140]Am. Civil Liberties Union v. Reno, 929 F.Supp. 824, 830 (E.D. Pa.), *aff'd*, 521 U.S. 844 (1997).

[141]*Id.* at 832.

[142]*Id.*

[143]*Id.* at 831.

[144]*See* NSI v. Umbro Int'l, Inc., 529 S.E.2d 80, 83 (Va. 2000).

[145]*Id.*

unique, and frequently contain the corporate or trade name of the domain name holder."[146] This is because domain names do not yet teach the Internet-user the precise context of use, which is what makes trademarks unique. Second-level domains are selected and requested by the domain name registrant.[147]

Under trademark law, more then one party may hold the rights to the same mark,[148] but in cyberspace only one party may hold the registration for a particular domain name.[149] To cite a frequently noted example, although United Airlines and United Van Lines both have valid trademark rights in "United" for their respective goods and services, only one party can register <united.com>.[150]

The conceptual underpinning of the nature of harm on the Internet holds certain assumptions about how commerce operates in the Internet. The Anticybersquatting Consumer Prevention Act (ACPA) presupposes two things. First, it presupposes that consumers seeking a good or service will use second-level domains[151] as an indicator of source: "If an internet user knows the domain name for a particular Web site ... the user can type the name in to a Web browser and access that site directly without having to conduct what may be a time consuming search."[152] Second, the ACPA presupposes that holders of trademarks, specifically word marks, will want to create domain names using the word mark as the second-level domain

---

[146]MTV Networks v. Curry, 867 F.Supp. 202, 204 n. 2 (S.D.N.Y. 1994) (finding that domain names are unique).

[147]See NSI v. Umbro Int'l, Inc., 529 S.E.2d 80, n. 6 (Va. 2000).

[148]See infra, §6.2.4.

[149]MTV Networks v. Curry, 867 F.Supp. 202, 204 n. 2 (S.D.N.Y. 1994) (finding that domain names are unique).

[150]Example from Lisa M. Sharrock, *The Future of Domain Name Dispute Resolution: Crafting Practical Legal Solutions from within the UDRP Framework*, 51 DUKE L.J. 817, 820 (2001).

[151]"Second-level domains are selected and requested by the domain name registrant." NSI v. Umbro Int'l, Inc., 529 S.E.2d 80, n. 6 (Va. 2000).

[152]Panavision Int'l, L.P. v. Toeppen, 945 F.Supp. 1296 (C.D. Cal., 1996), *aff'd*, 141 F.3d 1316 (9th Cir. 1998).

in a domain name.[153] In other words, domain names are valuable because they can not only function as an address, but also a symbol of the information to which they point.[154]

2.3. Signs Which May Serve as Trademarks
2.3.1. Words, Letters, and Slogans

Words, letters and slogans may act as trademarks when they designate the source of a good or service.[155] All three categories are sufficiently similar and allow discussion as a common group. Words or letters which merely *designate differences* in colors, grades, styles, or types of products are not eligible for protection as trademarks.[156] Such designations are not capable of distinguishing source as they are used to describe a particular attribute of a specified product.

In the instance that a letter alone or in combination with others, serving to identify grade or style is recognized as an identification of source, it will receive trademark protection to the extent it identifies the source of the good or service. In addition, an arbitrary number which does not indicate grade, style or type is eligible for protection.[157] This is true of single letter and combination letter marks as well. If it is merely descriptive of the product, as to ingredients or merely an abbreviation, it will not be protected.[158]

---

[153]For example, Microsoft holds the registration to <microsoft.com>, Coca-cola holds the registration to <coca-cola.com>, and Burger King holds the registration to <burgerking.com>. *See* Dan L. Burk, *Trademarks along the Infobahn: A First Look at the Emerging Law of Cybermarks*, 1 RICH. J.L. & TECH. 1 (1995).

[154]*See* NSI v. Umbro Int'l, Inc., 529 S.E.2d 80, 82 (Va. 2000).

[155] 15 U.S.C. § 1127, (Lanham Act § 45).

[156] 1 GILSON, TRADEMARK PROTECTION AND PRACTICE § 2.05 (pub. 726, rel. 52, 2004).

[157] Worthington Products, Inc. v. Lister Industries, Inc., 215 N.Y.S.2d 783 (1961) (random number system created by plaintiff for particular colors confusing when used by defendant); Shaw Stocking Co. v. Mack, 21 Blatchf. 1, 12 F. 707 (C.C.D.N.Y. 1882) (use of arbitrary numbering system is protected).

[158] Singer Mfg. Co. v. Singer Upholstering & Sewing Co., 130 F. Supp. 205 (D. Pa. 1955) (Singer's use of "S" is an indication of source); Hypertherm Inc. v. Precision Products Inc., 832 F.2d 697 (1st Cir. 1987) (use of imaginative designations protected); Shaw Stocking Co. v. Mack, 12 F. 707 (N.D.N.Y. 1882) (numbering system not indicative of any particular ingredient or quality and therefore protected as trademarks).

2.3.1.1. Personal Names

Because a personal name is inherently descriptive (i.e., it describes the person not the source or origin of a good or service) it cannot function as a trademark unless it has acquired secondary meaning. In some instances, a celebrity may register her name with the USPTO, usually to brand a line of goods that the celebrity sponsors (for example, *George Foreman* for use on propane and natural gas barbeque grills and stands for grills (Reg. No. 2,566,646).

In the context of abusive registration of domain names, both the federal ACPA[159] and the international Uniform Dispute Resolution Policy specifically mention protecting personal names. To receive protection they both require the personal name to function as an indicator of source. [160]

With personal names, a fair use defense arises to allow one to use her own name. In the face of a strong mark, this defense is very limited.

2.3.2. Nonverbal Marks

2.3.2.1. Alphanumeric Symbols

Letters and numbers are sometimes combined to create marks and, when not descriptive of the product, can be protected. Arbitrary combinations of numbers and letters are given the highest protection.[161] Alphanumeric marks are infringed when another user adopts nearly the

---

[159] *See* Intellectual Property and Communications Omnibus Reform Act of 1999, *H.R. Conf. Rep.* No. 106-464 (1999), 1999 WL 1095089, at *109,

Protection under Section 43 of the Lanham Act has been applied by the courts to personal names which function as marks, such as service marks, when such marks are infringed. Infringement may occur when the endorsement of products or services in interstate commerce is falsely implied through the use of a personal name, or otherwise, without regard to the goods or services of the parties. This protection also applies to domain names on the Internet, where falsely implied endorsements and other types of infringement can cause greater harm to the owner and confusion to a consumer in a shorter amount of time than is the case with traditional media.

[160] WIPO, Report of the Second WIPO Internet Domain Name Process, *The Management of Internet Names and Addresses: Intellectual Property Issues*, ¶ 199 (3 September 2001), http://arbiter.wipo.int/processes/process2/report/html/report.html: ("Persons who have gained eminence and respect, but who have not profited from their reputation in commerce, may not avail themselves of the UDRP to protect their personal names against parasitic registrations.")

[161] Standard Brands, Inc. v. Smidler, 151 F.2d 34 (2d Cir. 1945) ("V-8" arbitrary for vegetable juice).

identical mark on a similar good or service.[162]

Telephone mnemonics, a telephone number which has replaced some numerals with letters, are becoming more and more popular in advertising. For example, the phone number 800-DENTIST would most likely be descriptive of dental services and therefore not registrable. There is currently a split within the circuits on whether this type of mark can be protected.[163] The PTO has determined that it will deny registration for any mnemonic that is generic.[164] However, a mnemonic which as a composite contains a generic word and a numeral may acquire protection if it has secondary meaning.[165]

2.3.2.2. Color

Historically, a color alone was not protected as a trademark. A general belief that the number of colors would become depleted and that it is impossible for the human eye to distinguish between fine shades of colors provided for denying protecttiont.[166] The courts reasoned that allowing the use of a color as a trademark would prevent another manufacturer from utilizing a necessary tool in marketing a product. In the mid 1980's a split in the circuits developed over this issue.[167] The split was resolved in 1995

---

[162] Nabisco Brands, Inc., v. Kaye, 760 F. Supp. 25 (D. Conn. 1991) (substituting the number "2" for the number one in "A-1" for meat sauce is confusing with "A-1").

[163] Dial-A-Mattress Franchise Corp. V. Page, 880 F.2d 675 (2d Cir. 1989) (telephone number spelling a generic term is protected); Murrin v. Midco Communications, Inc. 726 F. Supp. 1195 (D. Minn. 1989)(telephone number spelling LAWYER protected in a particular geographic area); Dranoff-Perlstein Associates v. Sklar, 967 F.2d 852 (3d Cir. 1992) (telephone numbers spelling generic terms are not protectable; secondary meaning must be demonstrated with descriptive terms).

[164] TMEP § 1209.03(i) (3rd ed. 2002).

[165] Dranoff-Perlstein Associates v. Sklar, 967 F.2d 852 (3d Cir. 1992) (sufficient evidence of secondary meaning in telephone number spelling INJURY-1 justifies ites protection as a trademark).

[166] Nutra-Sweet Co. v. Stadt Corp., 917 F.2d 1024 (7th Cir. 1990), *cert. denied*, 499 U.S. 983 (1991) (blue color of packaging for "Nutra-Sweet" not distinguishable from blue color of packaging for "Equal").

[167] *In re* Owens-Corning Fiberglass Corp., 774 F.2d 1116 (Fed. Cir. 1985) (use of the color pink for insulation is distinctive); Nutra-Sweet Co. v. Stadt Corp., 917 F.2d 1024 (7th Cir. 1990) (inability to distinguish between similar colors of blue packaging for artificial sweeteners precludes protection).

when the Supreme Court ruled that a color alone was capable of protection.[168]

However, a color which is functional[169] is not protected.[170] More specifically, a color which is used on a product to enhance a particular feature will not be protected.[171] The Second Circuit has qualified the *Qualitex* ruling by stating that a color is protected only after acquiring secondary meaning.[172]

Color has been and continues to be protected when used in combination with other colors or as part of a design.[173] It is important to note that when assessing a combination of colors or color(s) and designs, the general rule of trademark distinctiveness applies.[174] The greater the distinctiveness, the greater the likelihood of protection. In addition, the more arbitrary the symbol used in association with the color, the greater the

---

[168] Qualitex Co. v. Jacobson Prods. Co., 514 U.S. 159 (1995) (green gold color of press pads distinctive).

[169] Functionality may be aesthetic or utilitarian. Aesthetic functionality is concerned with color that is used merely to "decorate" products and not as a source indicator. Functionality can also be described as utilitarian; application of a color only to serve a useful purpose. Brunswick Corp. v. British Seagull, 35 F.3d 1527 (Fed. Cir. 1994), *cert. denied*, 514 U.S. 1049 (1995) (black color of motor used to de-emphasize size not protectable).

[170] *Id.* at 1162-1163.

[171] Deere & Co. v. Farmland, Inc., 560 F. Supp. 85 (S.D. Iowa 1982)(customer preference for matching implements not sufficient to confer rights in use of a particular color); Sazerac Co. v. Skyy Spirits, 37 U.S.P.Q.2d (BNA) 1731 (E.D. La. 1995) (no distinctiveness in blue color used to attract customers attention).

[172] Fabrication Enters. v. Hygenic Corp., 64 F.3d 53 (2d Cir. 1995)(color scheme on rubber bands to denote resistance has acquired secondary meaning and is protectable); Mana Prods. v. Columbia Cosmetics Mfg., 65 F.3d 1063 (2d Cir. 1995)(no secondary meaning for black compacts in ordinary shapes used within the industry as a whole); Knitwaves Inc. v. Lolytogs Ltd., 71 F.3d 996 (2d Cir. 1995) (ecological design on sweaters is distinctive).

[173] Barbasol Co. v. Jacobs, 160 F.2d 336 (7th Cir. 1947) (combination of blue-white-red-white is protectable); Brunswick-Balke-Collender Co. v. American Bowling & Billiard Corp., 150 F.2d 69 (2d Cir. 1945) (use of red crown design on neck of pin is protectable).

[174] *See infra*, §3.1. Distinctiveness.

likelihood of protection.[175]

A unique extension of color protection can be found in the application of protection to non-specified colors. A color or one of several colors used consistently with a non-specified color as part of a product design may be protected.[176]

As with numbers and letters, colors cannot be used to differentiate grade or size if other manufactures require the same colors to make the same differentiation.[177] If different colors are used by different manufacturers of the same type of products, the use of color to distinguish grade and style is acceptable.[178]

The inquiry into color protection is highly factual and hinges upon consideration of several factors, including the type of use, the association of the color with source, and the availability of color to other producers.

2.3.2.3. Fragrance

In 1990, fragrance was added to the list of types of marks which can be registered.[179] Fragrance is limited in application to use as an additive to a product.[180] It may not in and of itself be protected. This limitation prevents product scents from obtaining registration. A product which is manufactured and sold as a scent or primarily associated with a scent is not allowed registration.[181]

---

[175] Radio Corp. Of America v. Decca Records, Inc., 51 F. Supp. 493 (S.D.N.Y. 1943) (red color of phonograph label is not sufficiently distinctive for "RED SEAL" records).

[176] A.T. Cross Co. v. TPM Distributing, Inc., 226 U.S.P.Q. (BNA) 521 (D. Minn. 1985). *But see* Keystone Camera Products Corp. v. Ansco Photo-Optical Corp., 667 F. Supp. 1221 (N.D.Ill. 1987)(unspecified combination of colors is not protectable when there is not a consistent design utilizing the color combination).

[177] Coats v. Merrick Thread Co., 149 U.S. 562 (1893)(designation on embroidery floss denoting length and ply thickness not infringed).

[178] Barnes Group, Inc., v. Connell Ltd. Partnership, 15 U.S.P.Q.2d (BNA) 1100 (D. Del. 1990) (color of die springs which denote particular load strength not protected).

[179] *In re* Clarke, 17 U.S.P.Q.2d 1238 (T.T.A.B. 1990) (scented yarn held to be distinctive).

[180] *Id.*

[181] *Id.*

2.3.2.4. Designs

A design that is not inherently distinctive must have acquired secondary meaning[182] to be registered on the principle register. A design which is not sufficiently distinctive to obtain registration on the principle register may be registered on the supplemental register.[183]

A design may be either pictorial or three dimensional.[184] Either embodiment must meet the distinctiveness test. Pictorial designs may be used as backgrounds for word marks provided the background design creates a "separate commercial image" apart from the word mark itself.[185] A background design which utilizes a commonly used shape is unlikely to obtain protection due to the extensive use of such shapes in the promotion of products. Such shapes are generally not considered to have inherent distinctiveness.[186]

Designs which are merely descriptive of a product are not eligible for registration.[187] If a design meets the definition of fanciful,[188] it need not acquire secondary meaning to be registered. A fanciful background design which is not normally associated with a particular type of product may be registered without secondary meaning provided it also meets the separate commercial impression test.[189]

A repeated design used to cover a package or label may also be

---

[182] See infra, §3.1.2. Non-Inherently Distinctive Marks.

[183] In re David Crystal, Inc. 296 F.2d 771 (C.C.P.A. 1961); In re Dassler, 134 U.S.P.Q. 265 (T.T.A.B. 1962) (design of shoe had acquired sufficient secondary meaning for registration).

[184] In re Yahama International Corp. v. Hoshino Gakki Co., 231 U.S.P.Q. (BNA) 926 (T.T.A.B. 1986)(registration allowed for guitar peg head configuration), aff'd, 840 F.2d 1572 (Fed. Cir. 1988).

[185] In re Hillerich & Bradsby Co., 204 F.2d 287 (C.C.P.A. 1953) (oval line on baseball and softball bats not protected).

[186] Seabrook Foods, Inc., Bar-Well Foods, Ltd., 568 F.2d 1342 (C.C.P.A. 1977) (stylized leaf background not protected).

[187] Ginger Group, Ltd, v. Beatrice Cos., 678 F. Supp. 555 (E.D.Pa. 1988) (background with half or whole apple for juice not protected); In re Underwater Connections, Inc. 221 U.S.P.Q. (BNA) 95 (T.T.A.B. 1983) (illustration of underwater air tank descriptive for diving equipment).

[188] See §3.1.1. Inherently Distinctive Marks.

[189] Hygenic Products Co. v. Coe, 85 F.2d 264 (D.C.Cir. 1936) (yellow rectangle with blue border used as background is not descriptive of toilet cleaning powder).

registered, provided it meets the separate commercial impression test and is inherently distinctive.[190]

2.3.3. Trade Dress
2.3.3.1. Generally

Trade dress protection is granted under Section 43(a) of the Lanham Act and state law on unfair competition in addition to protections granted if it satisfies the definition of trademark under Section 45 of the Lanham Act.[191] Trade dress protection extends to the total compilation and image presented by a product configuration or packaging.[192] "'[T]rade dress' includes the total look of a product and its packaging and even includes the design and shape of the product itself."[193]

Trade dress protection does not extend to promotion and advertising.[194] Further, the unique "style" depicted in a particular expression of a product is not protected.[195] In addition, trade dress protection must satisfy the parameters established by trademark law. Trade dress must be distinctive, either inherently or through secondary meaning, and it must identify the source of the product.

In *Wal-Mart Stores v. Samara Bros., Inc.*, the Supreme Court limited what constitutes protectable trade dress and distinguished three trade dress categories: product design, product packaging, and a third category, called the "tertium quid." The Court further stated that a showing of secondary

---

[190] Vuitton et Fils S.A. v. J. Young Enterprises, Inc., 644 F.2d 769 (9th Cir. 1981) (design comprised of letters "LV" and surrounded by flower like symbols repeated over fabric is distinctive).

[191] Compco Corp. v. Day-Brite Lighting, Inc., 376 U.S. 234 (1964); Sears, Roebuck & Co. v. Stiffel Co., 376 U.S. 225 (1964).

[192] Two Pesos, Inc. v. Taco Cabana, Inc. 505 U.S. 763 (1992) ("Mexican theme" of a restaurant protected); Blue Bell Bio-Medical v. Cin-Bad, Inc., 864 F.2d 1253 (5th Cir. 1989)(blue and off-white medical carts not protected due to absence of confusion); John H. Harland Co. v. Clarke Checks, Inc., 711 F.2d 966 (11th Cir. 1983) (overall style of memory check stub products protected).

[193] 1 MCCARTHY, TRADEMARKS AND UNFAIR COMPETITION § 8:4.

[194] Haagen-Dazs, Inc. v. Frusen Gladje, Ltd., 493 F.Supp 73 (S.D.N.Y. 1980) (Scandinavian theme used in advertising and marketing not protected).

[195] Contra Romm Art Creations, Ltd. v. Simcha Int'l, Inc., 786 F. Supp. 1126 (E.D.N.Y. 1992)(posters and limited editions protected when they are not merely an established "style" of expression).

meaning was required in all cases of product design trade dress, and such a showing was only sometimes required for product packaging trade dress. To reconcile this decision with the Court's earlier holding in *Two Pesos*, the Court determined that *Two Pesos* was a case of product packaging and some other undefined third category, or tertium quid.[196] If the trade dress sought to be protected is the configuration or design of a product itself, secondary meaning will have to be shown as a prerequisite for registration.

If one claims the design or portion of the trade dress as a trademark, it must be nonfunctional. If the trade dress is not registered as a trademark with the USPTO, the party claiming trade dress rights has the burden to show that the trade dress is nonfunctional.[197]

If one seeks to protect the design or the configuration of the product, and that feature is the subject of a utility patent, then there will be a strong presumption that the feature is functional and, therefore, not protectable as trade dress.[198]

2.3.3.2. Functionality

Trade dress which is functional is not protected. Functionality is determined in light of the "utility" that the trade dress may play on any given product. The utility of any given trade dress is determined by considering the superiority of design and this determination is based on whether the trade dress is essential to competition. The factors courts will consider to determine if a trade dress is functional include: (1) the existence of an expired utility patent which discloses the utilitarian advantage of the design sought to be registered as trade dress; (2) the trade dress owner itself claim there are no alternatives available;[199] (3) the trade dress contributes to more efficient use, adds durability, or aids in manufacturing or distribution.[200] Common use of an item on packaging will also limit trade

---

[196]*See* Wal-Mart Stores, Inc. v. Samara Bros., Inc., 529 U.S. 205 (2000) (holding that a line of children's clothing with decorative features was not distinctive).

[197]15 U.S.C. § 1125(a) (3). *See supra*, § 3.3.9.

[198]*See* TrafFix Devices, Inc. v. Marketing Displays, Inc., 532 U.S. 53 (2001).

[199] *In re* Morton-Norwich, 671 F.2d 1332 (C.C.P.A. 1982)(shape of spray bottle not functional).

[200] Bayline Partners L.P. v. Weyerhaeuser Co., 31 U.S.P.Q.2d (BNA) 1051 (N.D. Cal. 1994) (box features related to efficiency of use and are functional).

dress protection.[201] This is commonly referred to as "utilitarian functionality."

The real question in determining whether a particular trade dress is functional is to determine whether or not competitors need that specific trade dress to compete effectively in the market or if granting the trade dress to one entity would result in essentially a monopoly on the goods in question and thereby grant a "backdoor" patent to the claimant. Courts are to view trade dress as a whole in determining whether it is functional.[202] There are two types of functionality: utilitarian (or mechanical) functionality and aesthetic functionality.

Unlike utilitarian functionality, aesthetic functionality is not protectable if the design feature contributes to or enhances a product's consumer appeal.[203] In the rather famous *Pagliero*[204] case, the Ninth Circuit held that if the particular feature was an important ingredient in the commercial success of the product, the interest in free competition would permit its imitation in the absence of a patent or copyright. However, if the feature or design was a mere arbitrary embellishment, a form of dress for the goods primarily adopted for purposes of identification and individuality and therefore was unrelated to any need of a competitor to market or sell the same or similar product, imitation may be actionable if the owner can show secondary meaning.

Recently, however, some courts have rejected the important ingredient test and have preferred a more general analysis of competitive need. If the plaintiff is seeking protection "for a precise expression of a decorative style"[205] it is more likely to prevail than if it is attempting to protect "basic elements of style that are part of the public domain."[206] After all, the

---

[201] Mana Prods. v. Columbia Cosmetics Mfg., 65 F.3d 1063 (2d Cir. 1995)(black cosmetic compacts used throughout the industry not protected).

[202] Fuddruckers Inc. v. Doc's B.R. Others Inc., 826 F2d 837, 843 n.7 (9th Cir. 1987) (overall decor including menus, layout and style of service protected).

[203] *See* Pagliero v. Wallace China Co. Ltd., 198 F2d 339, 343 (9th Cir. 1952) (designs which are a response to consumer demand are not protected).

[204] *Id.*

[205] Wallace International Silversmiths, Inc. v. Godinger Silver Art Co. Inc., 916 F.2d 76 (2d Cir. 1990) (no protection for basic elements of style that are necessary to create common type of silverware), *cert. denied,* 499 U.S. 976 (1991).

[206] *Id.*

Restatement (Third) of Unfair Competition states that a "design is functional because of its aesthetic value only if it confers a significant benefit that cannot be practically duplicated by the use of alternative designs."[207] Therefore, although still alive and strong, analysis under the aesthetic functionality doctrine is more likely to be focused on overall competitive need of the trade dress and less on whether or not the claimed trade dress is an important ingredient of a product or service.

§ 3. CONDITIONS OF PROTECTION
3.1. Distinctiveness

The first consideration in determining whether a trademark is protectable in the United States is to determine whether or not the mark is distinctive of the products or services on which the mark is used. Distinctiveness is either "inherent" in the trademark itself, or acquired through secondary meaning.[208] A trademark which merely describes the product or service it is used on is not distinctive, but merely descriptive.[209] Marks which are inherently distinctive may be immediately registered on the Principle Register provided they do not violate any of the prohibitions as stated in Section 2 of the Lanham Act.

Most U.S. courts look to the "continuum" of trademarks: all trademarks fit somewhere on a continuum from generic (not protectable at all) to inherently distinctive marks. Inherently distinctive marks include those that are arbitrary, fanciful, or suggestive.[210] Marks which are not inherently distinctive require secondary meaning to be registered.[211] The categories include generic marks, descriptive marks, suggestive marks, and fanciful or arbitrary/inherently distinctive marks.

Where a trademark falls within this continuum will determine how much protection is will be afforded by the courts. This determination is a question of fact.[212]

---

[207] RESTATEMENT (THIRD) UNFAIR COMPETITION, Ch. 3 § 17 (1995).

[208] *See infra*, § 3.1.2.1. Descriptive Marks.

[209] *Id.*

[210] 15 U.S.C. § 1052 (Lanham Act § 2).

[211] 15 U.S.C. § 1052(f) (Lanham Act § 2(f)).

[212] G. Heileman Brewing Co. v. Anheuser-Busch, Inc., 873 F.2d 985, 992 (7th Cir. 1989) (characterizing a mark is an issue of fact).

3.1.1. Inherently Distinctive Marks
3.1.1.1. Arbitrary Marks

Arbitrary marks are words or symbols which already exist in the language, but are used as trademarks on goods or services with which they are not normally associated. For example "APPLE" for computers, or "IVORY" for soap. Arbitrary marks do not describe the good or service in any manner and do not convey any characteristic, ingredient or function of the good. Arbitrary marks are considered inherently distinctive and do not require secondary meaning to be registered.[213]

An arbitrary mark is created by using a common word, symbol or name in association with a good in an arbitrary manner. Use of a common word in an arbitrary manner does not diminish the strength of the trademark.[214] In fact, arbitrary marks are considered strong.[215]

A mark is arbitrary if the consumer makes no association between the mark and the product/service. Although the word or words that comprise an arbitrary mark may appear in a dictionary and therefore actually be a common part of the English (or other) language, the mere fact that the word(s) appears in the dictionary is not dispositive in determining whether a mark is arbitrary.[216] Rather, the key is whether the consumer makes no mental association between the mark and the goods or services upon viewing the mark for the first time. If there is such a mental association, the mark is not arbitrary..

3.1.1.2. Fanciful Marks

Fanciful marks are "coined" or "invented" words which do not exist in any language. Fanciful marks, like arbitrary marks, do not require secondary meaning to be registered or protected because they are considered inherently distinctive. A fanciful mark is created solely for the purpose of using the term as a trademark. Fanciful marks are considered to be the strongest type of mark because they have no relation whatsoever to

---

[213] Mobil Oil Corp. v. Pegasus Petroleum Corp., 818 F.2d 254(2d Cir. 1961).

[214] Fleischman Distilling Corp. v. Maier Brewing Co., 314 F.2d 149 (9th Cir. 1963) ("Black and White" for Scotch whiskey held to be arbitrary).

[215] Abercrombie & Fitch Co. v. Hunting World, Inc., 537 F.2d 4 (2d Cir. 1976) (stating arbitrary marks are strong marks).

[216] Wynn Oil Co. v. Thomas, 839 F.2d 1183 (6th Cir. 1988) (words that are found in the dictionary are not per se weak).

330

the good or service on or in connection with which they are used.[217] Fanciful marks are purely made-up words.[218]

Examples of fanciful marks include, KODAK[219] for photographic equipment, EXXON[220] for oil and gas products and CLOROX[221] for bleach. Coined terms are considered to be the strongest mark possible because they are not only distinctive of the product or service on which they are used, but they are also distinctive of any other words in any language. For this reason, fanciful marks are accorded the strongest protection available to trademarks.[222]

3.1.1.3. Suggestive Marks

A mark is "suggestive" when it suggests the goods or services but does not go so far as to actually describe them. A suggestive mark is one that requires the consumer to "conjure up" an image of the product and does not think of the product or service immediately upon confronting the mark.[223] This distinction separates a merely descriptive mark[224] from a suggestive mark, which can be registered on the Principle Register without establishing secondary meaning providing it is not violative of Section 1052.

As with all marks, in determining which category is appropriate, one must also consider the goods and services on which the mark is used because a mark may be suggestive if used on one type of good but

---

[217] Abercrombie & Fitch Co. v. Hunting World, Inc., 537 F.2d 4 (2d Cir. 1976) (fanciful marks do not relate to the goods or services with which they are associated).

[218] Fanciful marks are not limited to words. They may be symbols, numbers or letters as well.

[219] Spraying Sys. Co. v. Delavan, Inc., 975 F.2d 387 (7ᵗʰ Cir. 1992) (coined words such as "Kodak" are fanciful).

[220] Exxon Corp. v. Xoil Energy Resources, Inc., 552 F. Supp. 1008 (S.D.N.Y. 1981) (stating "Exxon" is a coined term).

[221] Sara Lee Corp. v. Kayser-Roth Corp., 81 F.3d 455 (4ᵗʰ Cir.), *cert. denied*, 117 S. Ct. 412 (1996) (stating but not holding that "Clorox" is a fanciful mark).

[222] *Id.* at 464.

[223] Stix Products, Inc. v. United Merchants & Manufacturers, Inc., 295 F. Supp. 479, 488 (S.D.N.Y. 1968) (suggestive terms require imagination; descriptive terms give an immediate idea of produce composition).

[224] Descriptive marks must have acquired secondary meaning to be registered on the principle register. *See infra*, § 3.1.2. Non-Inherently Distinctive Marks.

descriptive or even arbitrary if used on another type of good. For example, ORANGE CRUSH has been held to be suggestive (not merely descriptive) when used on a flavored soda beverage[225] and BROWN-IN-BAG has been held to be suggestive when used on a plastic bag used to cook meat.[226]

The line between suggestive marks and descriptive marks is, of course, not clearly drawn.[227] An underlying consideration in making this determination is whether or not the mark is necessary for competition. This fundamental policy decision will often be rather influential for courts when they make a determination about whether a specific mark is suggestive or descriptive. If the mark is a word necessary for effective competition in the industry, it is much more likely to be found descriptive by the courts.[228]

3.1.2. Non-Inherently Distinctive Marks
3.1.2.1. Descriptive Marks

Descriptive marks are not registrable and will not be afforded protection without establishing secondary meaning. The Lanham Act states:

No trademark by which the goods of the applicant may be distinguished from the goods of others shall be refused registration on the principle register on account of its nature *unless* it—

(e) consists of a mark which, (1) when used on or in connection with the goods of the applicant is merely descriptive ...

(f) ... nothing herein shall prevent the registration of a mark used by the applicant which has become distinctive of the applicant's goods in commerce.[229]

A descriptive mark immediately conveys information regarding qualities, characteristics, or ingredients of the product without requiring

---

[225] Orange Crush Co. v. California Crushed Fruit Co., 297 F. 892 (D.C. Cir. 1924).

[226] Reynolds Metals Co., 480 F.2d 902 (C.C.P.A. 1973) ("Brown-In-Bag" bags were used for other purposes and as such could not be construed to conjure up the sole descriptive use of the good).

[227] Franklin Knitting Mills, Inc. v. Fashonit Sweater Mills, Inc., 297 F. 247 (S.D.N.Y. 1923) (no clear demarcation exists between suggestive and descriptive marks, but "the validity of the mark ends where suggestion ends and description begins").

[228] Miller Brewing Co., v. Heileman Brewing Co., 561 F.2d 75 (7th Cir. 1977), *cert. denied*, 434 U.S. 1025 (1978) ("light" held to be descriptive for low calorie beer and necessary for other beer brewers to use in describing the nature of low calorie beer).

[229] 15 U.S.C. § 1052 (Lanham Act § 2).

any imagination on the part of the consumer.[230]

Descriptive marks are not protectable because they consist of information that competitors need in order to sell the relevant goods or services. In this sense, descriptive marks are said to be incapable of identifying a consistent source for the goods or services because the mark may appear on the goods or services of others in order to describe the goods or an attribute of the goods or services. The trademark DOUBLE CERTIFIED ORGANIC was refused registration by the PTO because it describes what the service accomplishes. If the mark was registrable, other producers wishing to use a repetitive certification process may be prevented from labeling the product as such.[231] Giving one producer the right to use a descriptive term as a trademark stifles competition, which is contrary to the fundamental purpose of the Lanham Act.

Composite marks may escape designation as descriptive if the combination of their parts is not in totality descriptive. In other words, when terms normally considered descriptive on their own, are combined to create a mark, the total image of the mark will be examined.[232] In addition, if there are parts of a mark which are not descriptive, the mark as a whole will not be held to be descriptive.[233]

Abbreviations or acronyms are not exempt from the analysis used to determine whether marks are descriptive. If an abbreviation or acronym merely describes a good or produces an immediate association with a characteristic or quality of the good, it will be held descriptive.[234]

---

[230] Franklin Knitting Mills, Inc. v. Fashonit Sweater Mills, Inc., 297 F. 247 (S.D.N.Y. 1923) ("FASHIONIT" merely descriptive of fashionable knit clothing).

[231] *In re* Eden Foods, 24 U.S.P.Q.2d (BNA) 1757 (T.T.A.B.1992) (refusal to register "DOUBLE CERTIFIED ORGANIC" as suggestive because it prevents other producers form claiming the same process for their pasta products).

[232] *In re* Disc Jockey, 23 U.S.P.Q. 2d (BNA) 1715 (T.T.A.B.1992) ("DJDJ" determined to be non-descriptive based upon the combination of the two separate DJ terms. Other users would still be able to utilize the well know acronym "DJ" in reference to Disc Jockey).

[233] Minnesota Mining & Mfg. Co. v. Johnson & Johnson, 454 F.2d 1179 (C.C.P.A. 1972) ("SKINVISIBLE" tape, a combination of two descriptive terms, skin and invisible, held not to be descriptive as a combination term).

[234] Bristol-Meyers Squibb Co. v. McNeil-P.P.C., Inc., 973 F.2d 1033 (2d Cir. 1992) ("PM" determined to be descriptive of the use of the cold remedy at night).

3.1.2.2. Secondary Meaning

Descriptive marks may qualify for registration under the Lanham Act if they have acquired secondary meaning. Secondary meaning may be statutorily acquired through continuous and exclusive use of the mark for a period of five years.[235] Use of the mark over a period of years creates the opportunity for an association as to source to be established between the good and the mark. If consumers come to know the mark as an indication of a source, and immediately associate the mark in this manner, secondary meaning has been successfully created and the registrant/owner need not wait five years to prove it.

A mark has secondary meaning when, in addition to the descriptive usage of the term, it has also come to indicate source.

The burden of proving secondary meaning is always the responsibility of the party asserting it. Proof must be clear and convincing in order to succeed in registration.[236] Courts will consider the following evidence in determining whether a mark has secondary meaning:

-Consumer surveys
-Success in the market
-Duration of continuous use
-Duration of exclusive use
-Attempts to imitate
-Amount spent on advertising[237]

None of these factors are dispositive in the determination of secondary

---

[235] 15 U.S.C. § 1052(f) (Lanham Act § 2). A mark may acquire secondary meaning prior to the 5 years required under 2(f) if sufficient evidenced is presented. Marks which are merely descriptive, and thus not able to be registered on the Principle Register may be registered on the Supplemental Register if they are capable of distinguishing the owners goods. *See infra*, §4.2.3. Supplemental Register.

[236] Application of Meyer & Wenthe, Inc., 267 F.2d 945 (C.C.P.A. 1959) (level of proof required to show secondary meaning is clear and convincing).

[237] International Kennel Club of Chicago v. Mighty Star, Inc., 846 F.2d 1079 (7th Cir. 1988); Eagle Snacks v. Nabisco Brands, Inc., 625 F. Supp. 571 (D.N.J. 1985) (expenses in promoting a good will lend credibility to the claim of secondary meaning, but will not necessarily prove it exists); Mattel, Inc. v. Azrak-Hamway Int'l, Inc. 724 F.2d 357 (2d Cir. 1983) (surveys important way to determine secondary meaning); Maternally Yours, Inc. v. Your Maternity Shop, Inc., 234 F.2d 538 (2d Cir. 1956) (secondary meaning found even though there was rapid development in a short period of time).

meaning. Courts will look at this range of elements and make their determination based the impact on competition and whether or not the attempts to create secondary meaning have actually been effective.

3.1.2.3. Generic Marks

Another non-inherently distinctive mark is a generic mark. Generic marks are words that are found in the English (or other) language and amount to the very noun required for a specific product. Trademarks can be generic from inception or they can become generic through use. To make matters even more interesting, a mark can move over time on the continuum from generic to distinctive and then back again. The resolution of the precise position depends on the consumer's perception.

Regardless of whether the mark was generic from inception or became generic through use, the test today is what is the primary significance to the relevant consumer. If the primary significance to the consumer is to identify source, the mark is valid; if the primary significance of the mark is to identify the product, the mark is generic and invalid.[238]

Generic terms are never granted protection; acquisition of secondary meaning will not serve to make a generic mark distinctive. Granting protection to a generic term will prevent competitors from using a term necessary to identify their own goods. In the famous SHREDDED WHEAT case, the court determined that the term "shredded wheat" was generic for the product itself and that other producers needed this term to sell their own version of the same good.[239] To deny other competitors the right to use the word for the product itself would essentially grant a new patent to the owner. The trademark LITE for use on a beer with allegedly fewer calories is also an example of a mark that was deemed generic from its inception.[240]

Marks can also become generic through use. This happens when the relevant mark comes to identify the goods themselves and not the producer. Examples of this are many. The most famous include the mark ASPIRIN[241] for use on a pain reliever and CELLOPHANE[242] for use on a plastic wrap.

---

[238] 15 U.S.C. § 1064 (Lanham Act § 14).

[239] Kellogg Co. v. National Biscuit Co., 305 U.S. 111 (1938).

[240] *See supra*, note 153.

[241] Bayer Co. v. United Drug. Co., 272 F. 505 (S.D.N.Y. 1921).

[242] DuPont Cellophane Co. v. Waxed Prods. Co., 85 F.2d 75 (2d Cir. 1936), *cert. denied*, 299 U.S. 601 (1936).

Trademark owners in the United States must be vigilant to avoid genericism of their marks because courts are not concerned with the intent of the trademark owner; they are concerned with the effect on the market place and the minds of the consumers.

§ 4. FORMALITIES
4.1. Adoption and Use

Federal trademark rights in the United States are premised upon the adoption and use of the mark in interstate commerce.[243] Priority of rights is determined by first use, not registration (although the intent to use registration is a singular exception to this rule). Therefore, the first party to use a mark in the ordinary course of trade will have priority over others who may want to use that same or similar mark on the same or similar goods. However, concurrent use is possible in remote geographic locations where no consumers will be confused. Federal registration codifies those rights obtained via common law through priority of adoption and use.

4.1.1. Priority—First to Use

Because the U.S. trademark system is based upon use it is important to establish priority in the use of a mark in order to obtain and enforce trademark rights. The first to use requirement is strict. Prior common law rights, based on prior use, will not be defeated by subsequent federal registrations. Use sufficient to establish priority for purposes of the Lanham Act requires that the use be in the ordinary course of trade[244] and not merely to secure or maintain trademark rights.[245] Merely picking out, or creating a mark, without actually using it in commerce, is not sufficient to acquire use-based rights in the mark.[246]

Constructive nationwide first use priority will be conferred upon the successful applicant of an intent-to-use application. Use priority is

---

[243] 15 U.S.C. § 1051(a) (Lanham Act § 1(a)).

[244] 15 U.S.C. § 1127 (Lanham Act § 45).

[245] Proctor & Gamble Co. v. Johnson & Johnson, Inc., 485 F. Supp. 1185 (S.D.N.Y. 1979) (trademarks may not be reserved for future use), aff'd, 636 F.2d 1203 (2d Cir. 1980).

[246] Hanover Star Milling Co. v. Metcalf, 240 US 403 (1916) (Tea Rose on flour limited to the geographic area where actual use is established).

conferred by the Lanham Act.[247] This is addressed in more detail in Section 4.2.2 below.

4.1.2. Sufficient Use

In order to gain priority in a mark, use of the mark must be "sufficient" to confer rights. For sales to constitute the requisite use, they must be at "arms length," meaning that the sale is actually one representing a commercial transaction and not merely an internal business deal.[248]

Sale of a product to which the mark is attached may or may not be sufficient, depending upon the purpose and circumstances of the sale. A minimal number of sales spread over a long period of time is not necessarily sufficient to confer priority.[249] Initial sales of a product in an effort to establish a market for the good may be sufficient to acquire rights if that use is in the ordinary course of trade.[250] A transaction undertaken only to get the mark before the public but not an actual sale, will not be enough to confer rights.[251]

Under the 1988 Trademark Revision Act, the definition threshold for "use" under the Lanham Act was raised. Prior to 1988, "token use" was sufficient to establish rights under the Act. After November 16, 1989, the effective date of the 1988 amendments, use must be in the ordinary course of trade before rights will be established under the Lanham Act. Because the Act reads "ordinary course of trade" there is no objective amount of sales that any trademark user must attain before registration is allowed. Instead, each product in each industry is analyzed to determine if the use amounted to the subjective amount of use of the applicant's product in that relevant market. For example, many thousands of candy bars would have to be sold

---

[247] 15 U.S.C. § 1057(c) (Lanham Act § 7).

[248] Florida v. Real Juices, Inc., 330 F. Supp. 428 (M.D. Fla. 1971) (shipment of six cans of grapefruit juice not "at arms length" transaction sufficient to establish use).

[249] Sweetarts v. Sunline, Inc., 380 F.2d 923 (8th Cir. 1967) (minimal mail order sales of candy made in several states not enough to confer rights in those states).

[250] International Telephone and Telegraph Corp. v. International Mobile Machines Corp., 800 F.2d 1118, 231 USPQ (BNA) 142 (Fed. Cir. 1986) (single sale sufficient to confer rights).

[251] Blue Bell v. Farah Mfg. Co., 765 F.2d 1097(Fed. Cir. 1985) (use of trademark on goods not intended to be sold under that trademark does not confer rights in the trademark).

in order to constitute use in the amount ordinary for the candy bar industry; however, in the machine tool industry, only one sale of a one million dollar machine tool may establish requisite use for that industry.

4.1.3. Affixation

To satisfy the affixation requirement, a mark need only be used on or in connection with the sale of a good or service. At common law it was necessary to "mark" or physically affix the trademark to the good itself.[252] With adoption of the Lanham Act, this requirement became much more liberal in application. A mark need not be actually affixed to the product, but may be part of the packaging, attached tags or prominently displayed close to the product.[253] A further relaxation in the requirement came with the 1988 Trademark Revision Act. If the mark is used on "documents associated with the goods or their sale" when "the nature of the goods makes such placement impracticable,"[254] this would still be sufficient affixation for purposes of the Lanham Act.

4.1.4. Interstate and Foreign Commerce

The Lanham Act is grounded in the Commerce Clause of the United States Constitution.[255] The Commerce Clause states that the United States Congress has the authority to regulate interstate commerce.[256] Therefore, to establish or protect trademark rights under the Lanham Act, there must not only be use of a mark but that use must be in interstate or foreign commerce; mere intra-state use is insufficient.[257]

Interstate commerce is often defined as merely sales of goods over state lines. This is the easiest and most obvious case. The definition of interstate

---

[252] Western Stove Co. v. George D. Roper Corp., 82 F. Supp. 206 (S.D. Cal. 1949) (affixation on goods held to have priority over use of mark in promotion).

[253] 15 U.S.C. § 1127 (Lanham Act § 45); *In re* Castelton China, Inc., 156 U.S.P.Q. (BNA) 691 (T.T.A.B. 1968) (display close to goods and instantly associated with the goods sufficient to meet the affixation requirement; mere advertising not sufficient).

[254] S. Rep. No. 100-515, 100th Cong., 2d Sess. 45 (1988).

[255] U.S. CONST. art. I, § 8, cl. 3.

[256] Heart of Atlanta Motel, Inc. v. United States, 379 U.S. 241 (1964) (intrastate commerce which has an effect on interstate commerce is subject to regulation by Congress).

[257] 15 U.S.C. § 1051 (Lanham Act § 1).

commerce, however, is broader than that for the purposes of the Lanham Act. Under the Act, one point of sale of restaurant goods and services could constitute interstate commerce if the goods sold were transported across state lines and thereby "effected" interstate commerce.[258] Goods imported for sale in the U.S. are judged by the movement through commerce upon entering the U.S. market.[259]

4.1.5. Eleventh Amendment

Trademark Law encounters special problems when a state is a party to a Lanham Act claim.[260] In 1992 Congress passed the Trademark Remedy Clarification Act, which attempted to remove the Eleventh Amendment immunity of a state or state agency from being sued in federal court for trademark infringement under the Lanham Act.

In 1999, the Court struck down the portion of the Trademark Remedy Clarification Act that authorized Lanham Act false advertising claims against a state,[261] finding that a state could not be sued in federal court for false advertising in violation of Lanham Act § 43(a). The court also rejected the argument that the state waived its Eleventh Amendment immunity by participating in commercial activities.

4.2. Lanham Act Registration

Registration of trademarks is accomplished through the Lanham Act either as an application based on actual use or as an application based on the owner's intent-to-us e the mark. Prior to the 1988 amendments, only use-based applications were allowed in the United States. Subsequent to the implementation date of the 1988 amendments, a trademark owner can either claim actual use as grounds for the federal registration or a bona fide intention to use the mark as grounds for the application. Both types of registrations confer nationwide protection and constructive notice of trademark rights to others. The applicant must choose and clearly state

---

[258] Larry Harmon Pictures Corp. v. Williams Restaurant Corp., 929 F.2d 662 (Fed. Cir. 1991), *cert. denied,* 502 U.S. 823 (1991).

[259] *In re* Silenus Wines, 557 F.2d 806 (C.C.P.A. 1977).

[260] *See generally,* 4 McCarthy, McCarthy on Trademarks and Unfair Competition §§ 25.64-25.66 (4th ed. 2000).

[261] Coll. Sav. Bank v. Florida Prepaid Postsecondary Educ. Expense Bd., 527 U.S. 666 (1999).

whether its application is a use-based application or an intent-to-use application. Applications made under both provisions will be rejected.[262]

4.2.1. Use Applications

Use-based applications may be applied for when a mark has already been adopted and used in commerce in the United States. The user (or licensor of such use) is the only eligible party who can register a mark.[263] All applications are filed with the United States Patent and Trademark Office (PTO) in Washington, D.C. Applications must be in writing and include the following:

1. The date of first use;
2. The date of first use in commerce;
3. A description of the goods on which the mark is used;
4. A statement by the owner or a qualified representative that the mark is owned by the applicant and is not confusing with another mark;[264]
5. A drawing of the mark;
6. A specimen or reproduction of the mark; and
7. The required fee.[265]

The description of the goods on which the mark is used is critical. The scope of the registration once issued is determined by the "identification" of the goods or services. Although at common law, when enforcing a trademark against an alleged infringer, this identification of the goods or services, and the International Classification to which the mark is assigned, is not binding on any court and plays no role in the determination of infringement, claiming the appropriate goods or services is significant for many reasons. Perhaps the most important reason involves incontestability. Once a trademark has been registered and used for five years, the registration may become incontestable. Once the registration becomes incontestable, the registration itself serves as "conclusive proof" of, among other things, the owner's right to use the mark on or in connection with the sale of the goods or services identified in the registration. Clearly, if inappropriate goods are claimed in the identification of goods, the scope of the conclusive proof may be significantly narrowed.

---

[262] *In re* Gillier, 18 U.S.P.Q.2d (BNA) 1973 (Comm'r of Pat. & TM 1991).

[263] 15 U.S.C. § 1051(a) (Lanham Act § 1(a)).

[264] *See infra*, §6.2.4. Concurrent Registration.

[265] 15 U.S.C. § 1051(a)(1-2) (Lanham Act § 1(a)(1-2)).

All applications are reviewed by the PTO to determine whether the mark meets the requirements for registration. Only trademarks which are barred by Section 2 of the Lanham Act will be denied registration. The statutory bars to registration include the following:

a. Immoral, deceptive, scandalous marks;[266]

b. Marks which represent any national insignia;[267]

c. Marks which represent a living individual without that person's permission[268] or represent a deceased President of the United States during the lifetime of his widow without the widow's consent;[269]

d. Marks which are confusingly similar to another registered mark;[270]

e. Marks which are merely descriptive, deceptively misdescriptive,[271] geographically misdescriptive[272] or geographically deceptively misdescriptive[273] of the applicants goods or are of merely surnames significance.[274]

f. Marks that are functional.[275]

Marks which are merely descriptive, deceptively misdescriptive, geographically misdescriptive or geographically deceptively misdescriptive may be registered on the principle register upon acquiring secondary meaning.[276] Geographically descriptive terms may not be used as an appellation of origin for wines pursuant to the GATT Uruguay Round Treaty.[277] Under the NAFTA Implementation Act, geographically deceptively misdescriptive marks cannot be registered even if secondary

---

[266] 15 U.S.C. § 1052(a) (Lanham Act § 2(a)).

[267] 15 U.S.C. § 1052(b) (Lanham Act § 2(b)).

[268] 15 U.S.C. § 1052(c) (Lanham Act § 2(c)).

[269] 15 U.S.C. § 1052(c) (Lanham Act § 2(c)).

[270] 15 U.S.C. § 1052(d) (Lanham Act § 2(d)).

[271] 15 U.S.C. § 1052(e)(1) (Lanham Act § 2(e)(1).

[272] 15 U.S.C. § 1052(e)(2) (Lanham Act § 2(e)(2).

[273] 15 U.S.C. § 1052(e)(3) (Lanham Act § 2(e)(3).

[274] 15 U.S.C. § 1052(e)(4) (Lanham Act § 2(e)(4).

[275] 15 U.S.C. § 1052(e)(4) (Lanham Act § 2(e)(5)).

[276] *See infra*, § 3.1.2.2. Secondary Meaning.

[277] Agreement on Trade-Related Aspects of Intellectual Property Rights, 15 April 1994, 33 I.L.M. 81 (1994).

meaning can be shown.[278] None of the other statutory bars can be overcome with secondary meaning.

A foreign applicant or U.S. citizens not possessing United States postal addresses are required to appoint a representative from the U.S. Any such designation is required to be identified in the application.

Upon review and acceptance by the PTO, a mark will be published in the Official Gazette.[279] Any party who believes they will be damaged by a registration may file an opposition.[280] Absent opposition, or a successful attempt to oppose a mark, the mark will be registered.[281] The entire registration process, from application to registration usually takes about eighteen months. Occasionally, marks are registered more quickly, and if any problems or oppositions are raised the process may take even longer.

4.2.2. Intent-to-Use Applications

The Trademark Revision Act of 1988 created an opportunity to obtain trademark rights based upon intent-to-use ("ITU") applications.[282] This represents a significant change from previous statutory codification of common law. Prior to the 1988 amendments, there were no courts which expressly recognized a common law intent-to-use claim. Although all other rights in the United States system are based on actual use, this provision alone is based on the applicant's intent to use the mark in commerce. In intent-to-use situations, all rights are created upon the registration of that intent, not on the actual use. Subsequent to the 1988 amendments, only one court had adopted a common law intent-to-use cause of action where the intent to use the mark was implicitly protected without a registration.[283]

The intent to use application is similar to the actual use application.

---

[278] *See supra*, § 3.3.4.

[279] 15 U.S.C. § 1062 (Lanham Act § 12).

[280] 15 U.S.C. § 1063(a) (Lanham Act § 13(a)). Oppositions must be filed within 30 days of publication in the Official Gazette. Additional 30 day extensions may be granted by the PTO for good cause. *Id.*

[281] 15 U.S.C. § 1063(b) (Lanham Act § 13(b)).

[282] 15 U.S.C. § 1051(b) (Lanham Act § 1(b)).

[283] Maryland Stadium Authority v. Becker, 806 F. Supp. 1236 (D.Md. 1992), *aff'd*, 36 F.3d 1093 (4th Cir. 1994) (use of "Camden Yards" in advertising and promotion prior to baseball stadium being built held to be sufficient to confer rights), *aff'd*, 36 F.3d 1093 (4th Cir. 1994) (unpublished table decision).

All of the information required in the use application is also required in the ITU application, except that the dates for first use and first use in commerce are omitted. Instead, the applicant must state a bona fide intention to use the mark.[284] Naturally, because no actual use has occurred, the applicant may also not be able to provide a specimen of use.

If actual use occurs before any action on the application by an examiner (usually within three months of the actual filing date), the applicant may file an amendment to the ITU application claiming that actual use has taken place[285] and convert the application to a standard use-base application.

All ITU applications are examined and published by the PTO in the same manner as actual use applications and, if there is no successful opposition, a Notice of Allowance is issued rather than a Certificate of Registration.[286]

Within six months of the date of the Notice of Allowance, the applicant must file either an affidavit claiming actual use (known as a "Statement of Use") or file a Request for an Extension of Time in which to file a Statement of Use. This time period can be extended for an additional six months without showing cause and an additional aggregate of twenty-four additional months by showing cause (for a total of thirty-six months) if the Requests for Extension of Time are timely filed.[287] Upon completion of the review process, all ITU applications are also published in the Official Gazette[288] and are at that point open for opposition by parties who believe they will be harmed by the registration.

4.2.3. Supplemental Register

Trademarks which are "capable of distinguishing applicants goods or services and not registrable on the Principle Register" may be registered on the Supplemental Register.[289] Generally speaking, marks which are not inherently distinctive and do not yet possess secondary meaning are

---

[284] *Id.*

[285] 15 U.S.C. § 1051(c) (Lanham Act § 1(c)).

[286] 15 U.S.C. § 1063(b)(2) (Lanham Act § 13(b)(2)).

[287] 15 U.S.C. § 1051(d)(2) (Lanham Act § 1(d)(2)).

[288] 15 U.S.C. § 1062(a) (Lanham Act § 12(a)).

[289] 15 U.S.C. § 1091(a) (Lanham Act § 23(a)).

considered appropriate for the Supplemental Register. Of course, in the United States system, use of the trademark determines how courts will categorize the mark. Therefore, even if a mark is only registered on the Supplemental Register, this has no binding effect on a court's determination of whether the mark has come, through use subsequent to the registration, obtained secondary meaning or even become inherently distinctive.[290]

The Supplemental Register is available only to use-based applications and not intent to use applications. Once use is claimed in a Statement of Use, the applicant can amend its application and choose the Supplemental Register instead of the Principal Register. A mark which is placed on the Supplemental Register is not published for opposition but is published in the Official Gazette. As any other trademark, a mark registered on the Principal Register is subject to cancellation upon a finding of confusion with another registered mark. A mark on the Supplemental Register which is found to have been abandoned will be canceled and removed from the register.[291]

4.3. Maintenance

Marks registered on the Principal Register must be maintained or they will be canceled by the PTO.

4.3.1. Registration Duration and Initial Renewal

The term of protection provided under the Lanham Act is ten years. Marks registered prior to the effective date of the 1988 amendments (November 16, 1989) were valid for twenty years. Provided the registered mark is used on or in connection with the goods or services identified in the registration, the registration may be renewed for an unlimited number of ten year periods. If a renewal application is not filed with the PTO during the period that commences six months prior to the expiration date of the registration and ends three months after the expiration date of the registration, the PTO will cancel the registration.[292]

---

[290] California Cooler, Inc. v. Loretto Winery, Ltd., 774 F.2d 1451 (9th Cir. 1985) (registration of "California Cooler" on Supplemental Register does not preclude owner from asserting proof of secondary meaning later).

[291] 15 U.S.C. § 1092 (Lanham Act § 24).

[292] 15 U.S.C. § 1059 (Lanham Act § 9).

4.3.2. Continuing Use Affidavits

In the initial term of registration, each registrant must file a Continuing Use Affidavit (also known as a "Section 8 Affidavit") during the fifth year of registration. Effective October 30, 1999, Section 8 Affidavits are also required in the final year of registration prior to an application to renew the mark on the Principal Register. If a Section 8 Affidavit is not timely filed, the PTO will cancel the registration.[293] A Section 8 Affidavit must claim that the mark is still being used in commerce on or in connection with the goods or services identified in the registration. Any gaps in continued use must be explained by the owner. Only non-use due to special circumstances will be excusable.[294] A Section 8 Affidavit must be filed only in the initial term of registration. During subsequent terms of registration, Section 8 Affidavits are not required.

4.3.3. Loss of Trademark Rights

4.3.3.1. Abandonment

Abandonment of a mark is grounds for any party to move the PTO to cancel a registered trademark. Abandoned trademarks are also not protectable under the common law. Abandonment is defined under the Lanham Act as discontinuing use of a mark with an intent not to resume such use.[295] An intent to abandon will be inferred if the mark is not used for a period of three years. Use of a mark means the bona fide use of a mark in the ordinary course of trade and not mere token use to reserve rights in or to a mark.

Abandonment differs from acquiescence. Acquiescence is a claim made by one party in a particular suit, while abandonment represents a complete loss of trademark rights and commits the trademark at issue to the public domain.[296]

4.3.3.2. Voluntary Termination

Any trademark registration may be voluntarily surrendered by

---

[293] 15 U.S.C. § 1058(a) (Lanham Act § 8(a)).

[294] 15 U.S.C. § 1058(b)(2) (Lanham Act § 8(b)(2)).

[295] 15 U.S.C. § 1127 (Lanham Act § 45).

[296] Defiance Button Machine Co. v. C&C Metal Products Corp., 759 F.2d 1053 (2d Cir. 1985) (explaining abandonment as a complete loss of rights), *cert. denied*, 474 U.S. 844 (1985).

voluntary cancellation[297] or an intentional discontinuation of use.[298] If the registrant specifically intends to terminate the registration, the registrant need only surrender the registration to the PTO for cancellation and the PTO will correct the Principle Register accordingly.

4.3.3.3. Involuntary Termination

Involuntary termination of a registration occurs primarily when a registered mark becomes a generic term and ceases to indicate source. As stated above, a mark is generic when it primarily identifies the product on which it is used and not the source.[299]

A petition to cancel a registered trademark must be filed within five years of the date of registration. It may be filed by any person who feels they will be damaged by the registration. Such cancellation petition my be filed more than five years after the date of registration if it is based on the following grounds:

1. The registered mark has become the generic term for the goods or services identified in the registration;

2. The mark has been abandoned;

3. The registration was obtained fraudulently;

4. If a collective mark, the mark has been used by the collective on its own goods or services; if a certification mark, the registrant does not control the mark, the registrant engages in the production or marketing of goods on which the certification mark is used, permits use of the certification mark for reasons other than to certify and/or discriminately refuses to certify;

5. The mark violates sections (a) (scandalous or deceptive marks), (b) (marks consisting of or comprising a flag, coat of arms or other national insignia), and (c) (marks which comprise or consist of the name or portrait of a particular living individual or the name, signature or portrait of a deceased president without the widow's consent) of Section 1052 of the Lanham Act.

---

[297] 15 U.S.C. § 1057(e) (Lanham Act § 7).

[298] La Maur v. Block, 176 U.S.P.Q. (BNA) 218 (T.T.A.B. 1972) (mark abandoned for tax reasons).

[299] 15 U.S.C. § 1127 (Lanham Act § 45).

§ 5. OWNERSHIP AND TRANSFER

5.1. Initial Ownership

As indicated above, trademarks in the United States are "owned" by the entity that first adopts, fixes and uses a trademark in commerce. However, in a common law system such as the United States, the mark itself is not subject to property ownership. Rather, the first user of a mark in the United States owns the right to exclude others from using the mark to the extent they have used the mark themselves.

The federal trademark registration issues to the owner of this trademark right (the right to exclude others). If a registration issues to a second user, the first user can oppose the application or move the PTO within five years of the date of registration to cancel the registration. Once the mark is canceled, the first user can then file its own trademark registration application.

Although the proper owner of the trademark right is usually determined simply by ascertaining who used the mark in interstate commerce first, occasionally two or more entities may have concurrently used a trademark. For example, if a musical band adopts a trademark, writes and records songs, and then splits up, often the issue of who owns the rights to the mark is an open question. In most instances, the party that controlled the mark would be considered the owner. However, in *Bell v. Streetwise Records, Ltd.*,[300] the court determined that in such a situation, if neither party had registered the mark, ownership should be determined by the consuming public. Therefore, if the consuming public came to associate the band members themselves, for example, as the source of the goods or services, rather than the producer, the band members would be considered the owners of the mark regardless of how much time and money the producer invested in promoting the band.

5.2. Assignment of Trademarks

Contrary to many civil law systems such as Japan,[301] France, and Germany, trademarks in the United States are not assignable in gross. That is, in most Civil Law systems, the trademark can be assigned without assigning the goodwill associated with the specific trademark. In the United States, an assignment of a trademark without the appurtenant goodwill is

---

[300] 640 F. Supp. 575 (D. Mass. 1986).

[301] *See* KENNETH L. PORT, JAPANESE TRADEMARK JURISPRUDENCE (1998).

invalid and, if coupled with a cessation of use by the assignor, will usually result in an abandonment of the trademark.

An ITU application may not be assigned until a statement of use is filed with the PTO and it is converted to a use-based application. The trademark in the United States is a right to use a mark and the right to exclude others from using the mark. Therefore, unless actual use occurs and at least some goodwill is established, there is nothing to assign because all rights in the United States are said to be premised on use, not registration.

5.3. Licensing of Trademarks

Trademarks may be licensed to third parties, but the licensor must retain the right to control the quality of the resulting products. This provision is known as "quality control" and must be expressly included in the language of any license agreement. If the licensor does not expressly retain quality control rights, a "naked" license results. A naked license may be inferred if a trademark owner does not police the use of its mark and allows others to use it without providing oversight.[302] In either case, an abandonment will result and the trademark owner will loose all trademark rights.

The quality control requirement envisioned in the Lanham Act does not require that the licensor actually control the business of the licensee.[303] Rather, it is merely necessary either to have the latent ability to control the use of the mark or to actually control the use of the mark to the extent reasonably necessary to ensure that the consumer will be able to rely on an established level of quality.[304]

---

[302] Yokum v. Covington, 216 U.S.P.Q. (BNA) 210 (T.T.A.B. 1982) (original owner of mark "Pied Pipers" abandoned the trademark by failing to monitor the mark's use by others).

[303] Oberlin v Marlin American Corp., 596 F.2d 1322 (7th Cir. 1979) (Lanham Act did not intend to create an agency requirement for licensors; day to day oversight is not required).

[304] Kentucky Fried Chicken Corp. v. Diversified Packaging Corp., 549 F.2d 368 (5th Cir. 1977) (KFC's monitoring of packaging producers is sufficient to show control).

§ 6. SCOPE OF EXCLUSIVE RIGHTS
6.1. Incontestability

"Incontestability" under the Lanham Act is premised on the notion that at some point, trademark owners ought be able essentially to quiet title and rely on the registration as proof that no other party has superior rights in or to the relevant trademark. Therefore, section 33(a) of the Lanham Act states that once a trademark has been registered for at least five years and certain formalities addressed below are completed by the registrant, the registration becomes conclusive evidence of the validity of the mark, the validity of the registration, the registrant's ownership of the mark and the registrant's exclusive right to use the mark on or in connection with the identified goods or services.[305] As will be made clear below, there are many strategic reasons why all trademark registrants should take the necessary steps to take advantage of incontestablity.

6.1.1. Mechanics

A trademark registration may become incontestable if the mark is used for five continuous years in commerce in the United States and the registrant files what is known as a Section 15 Affidavit after Section 15 of the Lanham Act.[306] Section 15 Affidavits are not reviewed in the same manner as an application. The PTO acknowledges the affidavit and records the filing but does not substantively review the claims in the Section 15 Affidavit for accuracy and requires no supporting documentation or other evidence corroborating the claim made.[307] Although actual abuse of this fact appears rare, many significant rights are granted the registrant via an incontestable registration in response to the Section 15 Affidavit.

6.1.2. Defensive Use of Incontestable Registrations

There are two ways a registrant might use an incontestable registration: offensively to claim its mark is strong and defensively to claim that its mark is immune from certain attacks.[308] The rationale behind the defensive use of incontestability centers on the fact that incontestability was

---

[305] 15 U.S.C. § 1115(b) (Lanham Act § 33(b)).

[306] 15 U.S.C. § 1065 (Lanham Act § 15).

[307] TMEP § 1604 (1986).

[308] Park 'N Fly, Inc. v. Dollar Park & Fly, Inc., 469 U.S. 189 (1985) (a mark which is incontestable is not subject to cancellation on "merely descriptive" challenges).

349

originally envisioned as a way to insulate registered trademarks from frivolous claims of invalidity. Although the word "incontestable" is used, it is not intended to be absolutely incontestable. The following conditions apply even to incontestable registrations:

1. The registration may be canceled if it or the incontestable right was obtained fraudulently;
2. The registration may be canceled if the mark has been abandoned by the registrant;
3. The registration may be canceled if the mark is being used to misrepresent the source or origin of the identified goods or services;
4. An incontestable mark may still be used by any third party if such use is in a fair use, descriptive manner;
5. The owner of an incontestable registration may not interfere with rights created in third parties via use by the third party prior to the registration of the mark;
6. The owner of an incontestable registration does not have absolute rights over a previously registered and used trademark in regional areas;
7. The owner of an incontestable registration may not use the mark to violate the antitrust laws of the United States;
8. Equitable principles such as laches, estoppel and acquiescence apply to incontestable registrations as well.
9. The trademark has become functional.[309]

6.1.3. Offensive Use of Incontestabilty

The mere use of an incontestable mark by a defendant is not *per se* infringement. Even incontestable marks require proof of infringing conduct. In determining whether a mark is infringed, the courts consider whether there is a likelihood of confusion; this in turn requires consideration, among other things, of whether the plaintiff's mark is strong or weak. A strong mark will receive more protection than a weak mark.

There is uncertainty in the federal circuits regarding the offensive use of an incontestable trademark.[310] Some circuits find that if the plaintiff's registered trademark is incontestable, the mark is presumptively a strong

---

[309] 15 U.S.C. § 1115(b) (Lanham Act § 33(b)).

[310] Kenneth L. Port, *The Illegitimacy of Trademark Incontestabilty*, 26 IND. L. REV. 519, 570 (1993).

mark[311]; some other circuits find that incontestability has no bearing on whether a mark is strong or weak during an infringement analysis.[312]

Therefore, based on the evidentiary advantage that incontestabilty provides a registrant with regard to challenges to the registration's validity, the registrant is strongly advised to seek incontestability as soon as possible. Moreover, there is enough uncertainty in the application of incontestabilty in an offensive manner in infringement litigation that all plaintiffs should be encouraged to obtain incontestabilty before filing suit to claim whatever advantages may be available in the jurisdiction.

6.2. Territorial Scope of Trademark Rights
6.2.1. The Common Law Market Penetration Rule

Under the common law, the first user of a trademark has the right to use the mark and exclude others from using a trademark to the extent the firstcomer has both horizontally and vertically used the mark.[313] Vertical use refers to market analysis. Different vertical use implies that one party uses the mark in, for example, the retail market and the other party uses the mark in the wholesale market.[314] Horizontal use implies geographic or regional use. Therefore, a subsequent user under the common law could enter the market using the same or similar mark on the same or similar goods and not infringe the firstcomer's rights if the use was either horizontally or vertically remote. Unless there is a showing of intentional adoption of another's mark to injure the prior user, there is no infringement at common law.[315]

Therefore, even if a first user adopted a mark in the eastern part of the

---

[311] Dieter v. B. & H. Indus. of Southwest Florida, 880 F.2d 322 (11th Cir. 1989), *cert. denied*, 498 U.S. 950 (1990) ("Shutterworld" as an incontestable mark is held to be at least "descriptive with secondary meaning and therefore a relatively strong mark"), *cert. denied*, 498 U.S. 950 (1990).

[312] Munters Corp. v. Matsui America, Inc., 909 F. 2d 250 (7th Cir.), *cert. denied*, 498 U.S. 1016 (1990) (incontestability of trademark registration is not conclusive evidence of mark's strength), *cert. denied*, 498 U.S. 1016 (1990).

[313] Hanover Star Milling Co. v. Metcalf, 240 U.S. 403 (1916) (territory where use has been established carves out rights in all segments of trade).

[314] Dawn Donut Co. v. Hart's Food Stores, Inc., 267 F.2d 358 (2d Cir. 1959) (sales in retail and wholesale markets).

[315] Hanover Star Milling Co. v. Metcalf, 240 U.S. 403 (1916).

United States on certain drugs, the common law would not prevent the use of the same or similar mark on the same or similar goods by a third party in, for example, the southern part of the United States if such adoption and use was not done intentionally for purposes of unfair competition.[316] Similarly, if a mark is used only in wholesale, such prior use may not be a bar to a subsequent user from adopting the same or similar mark for use on the same or similar goods or services in the retail market for those goods or services.[317]

6.2.2. Scope of Concurrent Use Common Law Rights
6.2.2.1. Good Faith

If a junior user adopts the same or similar mark with the intention of unfair competition, its rights to the mark may be limited despite the market penetration rule. Analysis of good faith is made at the point of adoption and first use of the mark.[318] Good faith has not been uniformly defined within the circuits. The Tenth Circuit states that knowledge alone is not indicative of bad faith in adopting a mark, and that some evidence of intent to confuse must be present in order to find bad faith.[319]

6.2.2.2. Remoteness

Remoteness has taken on a different meaning as time has passed. At the time of the *Hanover Star Milling* decision[320] the ability to transport goods and the ability to communicate with the consumers were limited. In 1916, Tennessee may have appeared to be "remote" from the Northeast. Today, remoteness is much more difficult to establish because most consumers are extremely mobile in their pursuit of goods or services.

---

[316] United Drug Co. v. Theodore Rectanus Co., 248 U.S. 90 (1918) (adoption of "Rexall" by junior user was in an area distant to senior user and done without intention to trade on the good will of the senior user).

[317] Dawn Donut Co. v. Hart's Food Stores, Inc., 267 F.2d 358 (2d Cir. 1959) (senior user may expand into a different segment of the market at a later time once rights are established).

[318] Allied Telephone Co., Inc. v. Allied Telephone Systems Co., 565 F.Supp 211 (S.D. Ohio. 1982) (at the time the junior user adopted the mark, the senior user was using another name).

[319] GTE Corp. v. Williams, 904 F.2d 536 (10th Cir. 1990), *cert. denied*, 498 U.S. 999 (1990) (intent to benefit from a senior user is required).

[320] Hanover Star Milling Co. v. Metcalf, 240 U.S. 403 (1916).

Furthermore, the Internet also allows virtually immediate presence for any competitor in any market. The north woods of Minnesota is no longer "remote" if one has a cellular telephone and a computer. Therefore, many businesses today will be conferred a rather large geographic area of expansion and the common law market penetration rule may very well be soon obsolete.[321]

6.2.2.3. Market Penetration

The common law scope of protection is defined by the degree to which the trademark owner has penetrated the market. Each circuit court tends to use different factors in analyzing the extent to which the market has been penetrated. For example, the Eighth Circuit implements the following four factor test: volume of sales; customer ratio to population; growth potential; and duration of any lapse in significant sales.[322] On the other hand, the Fourth Circuit will analyze sales volume; identification of any growth trends; population in relation to potential customers; and product advertising.[323]

In the end, the analysis is essentially the same: the common law allows trademark owners the right to exclude others, but only to the extent the owner itself has used the mark. Therefore, there needs to be some objective criteria to determine to what extent the owner of the mark has penetrated the market and, therefore, the extent to which it deserves common law protection.

6.2.2.4. Natural Zone of Expansion

In addition to the actual extent of market penetration, most courts in the United States will also allow for a natural zone of expansion to protect not only the actual extent of the trademark owner's use, but also to protect the next logical step in the marketing and selling of its goods or services. However, all circuit courts are not in accord with what factors to analyze when considering the natural zone of expansion and what weight to give

---

[321] Travelodge Corp. v. Siragusa, 228 F. Supp. 238 (N.D. Ala. 1964) (expansion "concept" held to be sufficient to prove expansion is likely).

[322] Sweetarts v. Sunline, Inc., 436 F.2d 705 (8th Cir. 1971) (Sweetarts market penetration into several states was not sufficient to usurp Sunline's concurrent expansion).

[323] Natural Footwear Ltd., v. Hart, Schaffner & Mark, 760 F.2d 1383 (3d Cir. 1985) (no market penetration established by junior user), cert. denied, 474 U.S. 920 (1985).

each element. For example, the Eleventh Circuit draws the boundary for trademark rights rather liberally and draws the line of natural expansion rather broadly. This court has stated that if a senior user can demonstrate that the junior user resides in an area which they can reasonably expand, the senior user even reserves rights in that area.[324] A more narrow view is stated by the First Circuit, which has held that if a senior user fails to register its trademark and it is subsequently innocently adopted by a junior user, the senior user's rights will be very narrowly construed.[325]

6.2.2.5. Relevance of State Boundaries

Although the court in *Hanover Star Milling* claimed that state boundaries had some significance in determining the scope of rights in common law marks, today, state boundaries would appear to be inconsequential.[326] Today, the real consideration is the extent to which consumers have been exposed to the relevant trademark. Because the nature of commerce in the United States has changed so radically in the last fifty years with technological advances in transportation, communication and marketing, state boundaries are becoming less and less relevant in determining the geographic scope of unregistered trademarks.[327]

6.2.2.6. Secondary Meaning Marks

Trademarks without secondary meaning are merely descriptive marks, not afforded the protections of either the common law or the Lanham Act. If a mark lacks secondary meaning, it will not get the expansion of protection considered above. Just as secondary meaning must be established to gain protection of the mark, it must also be established in

---

[324] Tally-Ho, Inc. v. Coast Community College District, 889 F.2d 1018 (11th Cir. 1989) (proof of a natural bridge to "related use" markets solidifies the rights of the senior user).

[325] Raxton Corp. v. Anania Associates, Inc., 635 F.2d 924 (1st Cir. 1980), *on remand*, 668 F.2d 662 (1st Cir. 1982) (senior user was unable to establish any prior use or reputation in the area of the junior user's business).

[326] Burger King of Florida Inc. v. Hoots, 403 F.2d 904 (1968) (senior user in Illinois limited to a small geographic area of priority).

[327] Spartan Food Systems, Inc. v. HFS Corp., 813 F.2d 1279(4th Cir. 1987).

order to form a basis for expansion of the rights in or to that mark.[328]

If a mark is inherently distinctive (a suggestive, fanciful or arbitrary mark), courts are likely to give the mark broad protection even if the mark lacks secondary meaning;[329] however, the courts have been inconsistent in articulating a definition of inherently distinctive trade dress. In *Wal-Mart Stores, Inc. v. Samara Bros., Inc.*,[330] the Supreme Court created at least two categories of trade dress: product design and product packaging. A showing of secondary meaning was required in all cases of product design trade dress, and such a showing was only sometimes required for product packaging trade dress. In *Wal-Mart*, the court distinguished *Taco Cabana, Inc. v. Two Pesos, Inc.*,[331] an earlier case that determined that trade dress could be inherently distinctive. The Court determined that *Taco Cabana, Inc. v. Two Pesos, Inc.*[332] was a case of product packaging or some other undefined third category – a "tertium quid."

6.2.3. Effects of Federal Registration

Federal registration affords important benefits to the registrant, affecting the power and scope of the mark.

6.2.3.1. Constructive Notice: Post Registration Use

Registration of a trademark on the Principle or Supplemental Registers provides nationwide constructive notice of the owner's claim to rights in the mark.[333] Once registered, all subsequent applications for registration that would cause confusion, mistake or deception (as well as all other bars enumerated in Section 2 of Lanham Act) should be denied registration by the PTO. For intent-to-use applications, the effective date of the notice reverts back to the date the application was filed once a Notice of Allowance

---

[328] Shoppers Fair of Arkansas, Inc. v. Sanders Co., Inc, 328 F.2d 496 (8th Cir. 1964) (lack of secondary meaning in the new market will preclude a finding of rights in the mark).

[329] Two Pesos, Inc. v. Taco Cabana International, Inc., 505 U.S. 763 (1992), *reh'g denied*, 505 U.S. 1244 (1992).

[330] 529 U.S. 205, 120 (2000).

[331] 505 U.S. 763 (1992) (holding that the festive decor of a Tex-Mex restaurant was inherently distinctive and did not require a showing of secondary meaning).

[332] 505 U.S. 763 (1992) (holding that the festive decor of a Tex-Mex restaurant was inherently distinctive and did not require a showing of secondary meaning).

[333] 15 U.S.C. § 1072 (Lanham Act § 22).

issues. Once a plaintiff's mark is registered, the defense of innocent infringement is usually no longer available to the defendant in an infringement cause of action. Some courts strictly interpret the effect of registration. The Second Circuit has held that if the plaintiff's mark is registered, it is impossible for a subsequent user to adopt the same or similar mark for use on the same or similar goods in good faith.[334] That is, in some settings, courts will infer bad faith or wrongful intent for adopting a mark that was previously registered by another party. It is thought that this evidentiary advantage reduces the number of conflicting marks by encouraging applicants to search the PTO's records *prior* to filing their trademark applications.

6.2.3.2. Freezing the Junior User's Market

One of the most important results of registration under the Lanham Act is that five years after registration is effected, a trademark registration may become incontestable as discussed above.[335] Once a registration is incontestable, the provisions of Section 33(b)(5) apply. Therefore, if party A uses a mark first in commerce in the United States, party B subsequently uses the same or similar mark on the same or similar goods, and party A registers the mark after party B first uses the mark but before party B registers the mark, the full effect of nationwide rights granted under the Lanham Act take effect on the date A's trademark application is published for opposition. Accordingly, on the date of publication, B's common law rights to use the mark are terminated except to the extent B has continuously used the mark up to the date of A's mark is published. Subsequent to that date, B will be required to relinquish all market share and use that it may have obtained.[336]

---

[334] Dawn Doughnut Company, Inc. v. Hart's Foods Stores, Inc., 267 F.2d 358 (2d Cir. 1959) (§ 1072 eliminates the good faith defense by providing constructive notice of use).

[335] *See supra,* § 6.1. Incontestability.

[336] Burger King of Florida, Inc. v. Hoots, 403 F.2d 904 (7th Cir. 1968) (junior user limited to the small geographic area where they have established business); Thrifty Rent-A-Car System v. Thrift Cars, Inc., 831 F.2d 1177 (1st Cir. 1987) (limited exception of use in remote area established by junior user after senior user but prior to senior user's federal registration).

6.2.4. Concurrent Lanham Act Registration

If two different entities establish rights in the same or similar mark on the same or similar goods through concurrent use of a mark but no confusion is likely because the relevant uses have be geographically remote, the Lanham Act allows two or more parties to own such "concurrent" registrations.[337] The test in this regard remains whether the consumer is likely to be confused. Given the nature of markets and consumers today, concurrent registrations should probably be granted only in the most extreme cases.

6.2.4.1. First User's Rights

If a subsequent user attempts or even succeeds in registering its trademark prior to the first user, the first user can oppose the application or petition the PTO to cancel the mark within five years from the date of the registration. In the United States, all rights are supposed to be derived from use. Therefore, the first party to use a mark in commerce should have the right to register the mark first. However, in some rare instances, if both parties have established mark awareness in geographically remote areas, the PTO may grant concurrent use registration. A concurrent use registration effectively carves up the nation and assigns each party a particular area in which they can use the mark.[338]

6.2.4.2. Correction of the Register by Federal Courts

Contrary to most civil law jurisdictions where the courts do not have the authority to cancel registered trademarks or issue orders affecting the relevant trademark registry,[339] the Lanham Act allows any federal court to order that the Principle Register be corrected to conform with its holdings regarding concurrent use.[340] The Sixth Circuit has held that federal courts may hear and decide concurrent use controversies.[341] Once a court has ordered the issuance of a concurrent use registration, the PTO enforces the decision by issuing the necessary concurrent use registrations.[342]

---

[337] 15 U.S.C. § 1052(d) (Lanham Act § 2(d)).

[338] In re Beatrice Foods Co., 429 F.2d 466 (C.C.P.A. 1970).

[339] KENNETH L. PORT, JAPANESE TRADEMARK JURISPRUDENCE (1997).

[340] 15 U.S.C. § 1052(d), (Lanham Act § 2(d)).

[341] Old Dutch Foods, Inc. v. Dan Dee Pretzel & Potato Chip Co., 477 F.2d 150 (6th Cir. 1973).

[342] Holiday Inn v. Holiday Inns, Inc., 534 F.2d 312 (C.C.P.A. 1976).

6.3. Product and Service Scope

The trademark rights in the United States are premised on the basic common law understanding that mark users may exclude others from using the mark to the extent that they, the first user, have used the mark. Therefore, as discussed above, the scope of trademark protection is not absolute. Rather, if a second comer's use is geographically remote, the prior user may not be able to interfere with that use. Likewise, if the products on which a third party uses the mark are sufficiently distinct so that no competition is likely between the sellers of the two relevant products, the first comer should not be able to prevent such use either.

That is, in the United States, confusion is supposed to be impossible unless the two parties are in competition.[343] This is because trademark law is a subset of the larger unfair competition law. Trademark protection is justified in the United States only in connection with the basic mandate that producers must compete fairly so that consumers are not harmed by the resulting confusion as to the source or origin of the relevant goods or services.

6.4. Dilution

The only exception to this common law rule is found in the new provisions of Section 43(c)[344] of the Lanham Act, which provides for a federal cause of action for trademark dilution. As stated above, dilution is defined as the lessening of the capacity of a famous mark to identify or distinguish the goods or services regardless of competition between the

---

[343] Determining when two parties are in competition has been a particularly vexing issue for courts. Initially, head-to-head competition was required before trademark infringement was allowed. This changed with Aunt Jemima Mills Co. v. Rigney & Co., 247 F. 407 (2d Cir. 1917). Now known as the "Aunt Jemima Doctrine," this case stands for the proposition that two companies need not be in head-to-head competition for precisely the same products. Rather, if the consumer believes the two products at issue come from the same source, the definition of competition for confusion analysis has been satisfied. This has now been expanded into the "bridging the gap" doctrine where even if a company is not selling in the defendant's market at all, if it had real plans to do so, this would be sufficient to satisfy the definition of competition for the confusion analysis. Therefore, the use of the word "competition" in this sentence is meant in this context.

[344] 15 U.S.C. §1125(c) (Lanham Act § 43(c)).

parties or the likelihood of confusion, mistake or deception.[345] If a second comer's mark is likely to cause dilution, the owner of a famous mark may sue to obtain an injunction of such use.

There have been three kinds of dilution identified by the courts: dilution by tarnishment, dilution by blurring, and dilution by alteration. Tarnishment occurs when a plaintiff's trademark is associated with products of lesser quality or is presented to the consumer in some derogatory manner.[346] In such a case, the plaintiff's reputation may suffer in the minds of its consumers. Blurring involves the "whittleing away of an established trademark's selling power through unauthorized use by others upon dissimilar products."[347] Alteration dilution occurs when one entity in the process of comparative advertising alters the trademark of another and presents it to consumers in that altered form whether or not it is coupled with the intent to tarnish.[348]

The drafters of Section 43(c) considered the use of "Buick" on aspirin or "Kodak" on pianos as examples of dilution. Once a mark has become very well known, if others merely use the mark on unrelated products, such use will drastically lessen the distinctiveness of the well known mark. Kodak is a very distinctive mark for the very reason that one sees no other use of the mark on products not emanating from Kodak. If there were many examples of Kodak brand pianos, Kodak brand bicycles, Kodak brand tires, etc., the distinctiveness of Kodak as a trademark to identify one source would be lessened and its value as a trademark would correspondingly decrease.

---

[345] 15 U.S.C. § 1127 (Lanham Act § 45).

[346] Academy of Motion Picture Arts and Sciences v. Creative House Promotions, Inc., 944 F. 2d 1446, 1457 (9th Cir. 1991)(if the appearance of the defendant's STAR awards is poor or cheap, the Oscar's value as a "symbol of excellence ... is threatened").

[347] Mead Data Central, Inc. v. Toyota Motor Sales, U.S.A., Inc. 875 F.2d 1026, 1031 (2d Cir. 1989).

[348] Deere & Co. v. MTD Products, Inc., 41 F.3d 39 (2d Cir. 1994). Incidentally, if the dilution rationale is intended to apply to companies not in competition, it is, of course, totally paradoxical why we need a dilution cause of action to address the ills of comparative advertising. Presumably, if the defendant engaged in comparative advertising, it ought to be estopped from claiming that it is not in competition with the plaintiff. Clearly, dilution will continue to expand as creative American lawyers in the common law system zealously represent the interests of their clients.

6.4.1. Fame

Like all trademark rights, the right to claim one's mark has been diluted is not absolute. The most important fact requirement is that only "famous" marks can take advantage of Section 43(c). Underthat section courts are to consider the following factors in determining if a mark is famous for purposes of applying the dilution prohibitions:

1. The degree of distinctiveness of the mark;

2. The duration and extent o f use of the mark;

3. The duration and extent of advertising an d publicity of the mark;

4. The geographical extent of the trading area in which the mark is used;

5. The channels of trade for the goods or services with which to mark is used;

6. The degree of recognition of the mark in the trading areas and channels of trade used by the marks' owner and the person against whom the injunction is sought;

7. Whether the trademark is registered.[349]

Unfortunately, the application of the rule that marks need to be famous before the dilution principles apply has been, to say the least, rather inconsistent. For example, the Ninth Circuit has found that "Fruit" as in "Fruit of the Loom" is not famous for purposes of dilution,[350] whereas the district court in Pennsylvania has held that the mark "WAWA" for use on convenient stores is famous enough to apply the dilution rationale.[351]

6.4.2. Dilution Likelihood

The test for whether or not the injunction contemplated under Section 43(c) should issue was first articulated in a concurring opinion (discussing New York law) in *Mead Data Central v. Toyota Motor Sales, U.S.A., Inc.*[352]

Today, proving dilution is still difficult, and the dilution doctrine

---

[349] 15 U.S.C. § 1125(c) (Lanham Act § 43(c)).

[350] Fruit of the Loom, Inc. v. Girouard, 994 F.2d 1359 (9th Cir. 1993) (fruit generic for "result of effort" and loom generic for "a machine producing clothes" renders the mark non famous).

[351] WAWA, Inc. v. Haaf, 1996 U.S. Dist. (Lexis 11494 (extensive use in convenience stores for over ninety years supports finding of famous mark), *aff'd*, 116 F.3d 471 (3d Cir. 1997) (unpublished table opinion).

[352] 875 F.2d 1026 (2d Cir. 1989).

remains puzzling. Before *Moseley v. V Secret Catalogue*[353] the federal circuits were split on two points concerning dilution: (1) whether the Dilution Act requires proof of "actual dilution;" and (2) whether dilution (actual dilution or a likelihood of dilution) must be proven directly or by circumstantial evidence.[354]

To determine a likelihood of dilution, courts had looked to the following factors:
1. Renown of senior mark;
2. Similarity of marks;
3. Similarity of products;
4. Predatory intent;
5. Renown of junior mark;
6. Sophistication of buyers.

In *Moseley* the Supreme Court held that the Dilution Act "unambiguously requires a showing of *actual* dilution, rather than a *likelihood* of dilution."[355] However, the Court also stated "that direct evidence of dilution such as consumer surveys will not be necessary if actual dilution can reliably be proven through circumstantial evidence."[356]

6.4.3. Note on Dilution

Perhaps because of the newness of the doctrine and perhaps because the concept of dilution does not fit within the conceptual justifications of trademark protection in the United States, its application by courts has been confused and unpredictable at best. Therefore, all practitioners in the United States should be aware of the problems inherent in this system. The Dilution Act did not by its terms add dilution as one of the grounds for opposition to trademark registration under Section 13 of the Lanham Act. The Trademark Amendments Act amended Section 43(c) of the Lanham Act to include dilution as a ground for opposition under Section 13(a).[357]

---

[353] 537 U.S. 418 (2003).

[354] *See* Thomas R. Lee, *Demystifying Dilution*, 84 B.U. L. REV. 859, 863 (2004).

[355] Moseley v. V Secret Catalogue, 537 U.S. 418, 434 (2003).

[356] Moseley v. V Secret Catalogue, 537 U.S. 418, 433 (2003).

[357] The new statute amended the Lanham Act's provision on "Opposition to registration" to provide that "[a]ny person who believes that he would be damaged by the registration of a mark upon the principal register, including as a result of dilution under Section 1125(c) of this title, may...file an opposition." 15 U.S.C. § 1063(a).

The House Judiciary Committee specifically referred to *Babson Bros. Co. v. Surge Power Corp.*,[358] a case where the T.T.A.B. held that dilution is not a grounds for cancellation or opposition to registrations, as "illuminat[ing] the need for further legislation."[359] The question before Congress was whether second comers should bear the risk of uncertainty created by possible dilution claims. Congress felt that unfair competition policy required that the PTO resist creating uncertain rights, and, therefore, the PTO should have the ability to refuse to register marks based on dilution:

> [The Amendments to the Dilution Act are] necessary for several reasons. Resolution of the dilution issue before the Board, as opposed to Federal District Court, would result in more timely, economical, and expeditious decisions. Resolving the issue at the Board would provide certainty to competing trademark interests, before the applicant has invested significant resources in its proposed mark, and before dilution-type damage has been suffered in the marketplace by the owner of the famous mark. Also, the Board would give guidance to litigants and the Trademark Bar, through precedent, with respect to such issues as what qualifies as a "famous" mark, and what constitutes dilution, whether by blurring or tarnishment.[360]

The issue of the "fame" of the mark becomes central if the holder opposes registration of a subsequent mark.[361] The senior mark's "fame" cuts off the junior user's rights to a concurrent use registration,[362] depriving the junior user of a right to register with the U.S.P.T.O. to protect the area of the market that the junior user has penetrated.[363]

---

[358] Babson Bros. v. Surge Power Corp., 39 U.S.P.Q. (BNA) 1953 (T.T.A.B. 1996).

[359] Trademark Amendments Act of 1999, H.R. Rep. No. 106-250, at 5 (1999), 1999 WL 528534, at *5.

[360] Trademark Amendments Act of 1999, H.R. Rep. No. 106-250, at 5-6 (1999), 1999 WL 528534, at *5-6.

[361] *See* Enterprise Rent-A-Car Co. v. Advantage Rent-A-Car, Inc., 330 F.3d 1333, 1343 (Fed. Cir. 2003) ("Because there can be no dilution under the [Dilution Act] where the allegedly famous mark did not achieve fame prior to any use by the accused infringer, there can be no opposition."), *cert. denied*, 124 S. Ct. 958 (2003) (mem.).

[362] 15 U.S.C. § 1052.

[363] *See* Enterprise Rent-A-Car, Co. v. Advantage Rent-A-Car, Inc., 330 F.3d 1333, 1343 (Fed. Cir. 2003) ("There is not a provision in the Lanham Act to allow for concurrent use registrations in the dilution context. In fact, when Congress

The Dilution Act creates great uncertainty for the junior user, so much that one may advise a junior user fearful of diluting another's mark to take a defensive posture in state court first, allowing it to carve out local territory without the threat of cancellation. Likewise, the plaintiff in a dilution claim will likely rush to the federal courts to oppose registrations, to take advantage of the Dilution Act's opposition provisions. However, a plaintiff may prefer to file in state courts to establish a dilution cause of action under a likelihood of dilution burden rather than face the much more difficult (and puzzling) *Moseley* actual confusion burden.

6.5. Cybersquatting

Because domain names are registered on a "first-come, first-served" basis, a party may register a domain name containing its competitor's or another's mark.[364] Such conduct clearly causes consumer confusion and would amount to trademark infringement.[365] This predatory registration is the kind of harm the Lanham Act protects against. If this were the only harm, Article 43(d) of the Lanham Act would not be necessary.[366]

Parties may abuse the domain name registration process in other ways that do not fit so neatly into typical Lanham Act analysis. While this practice first arose in humorous anecdote,[367] the harm has become more common, more organized, and more severe.[368]

The legislative history of the Act gives various examples: for instance, a party may register a domain name that is identical or confusingly similar

---

amended...the Lanham Act in 1999 to add dilution under [the Dilution Act] as a ground for opposition, it also amended Section 1052, the section that grants the Board the power to issue concurrent use registrations, to make clear that dilution could not be considered in proceedings brought under that section.").

[364] *See supra*, § 3.2.6.

[365] 4 McCarthy, McCarthy on Trademarks and Unfair Competition § 25.76 (4th ed. 2000) (explaining how the use of a domain name may be a form of infringement).

[366] *Id.*

[367] *See* Dan L. Burk, *Trademarks along the Infobahn: A First Look at the Emerging Law of Cybermarks*, 1 Rich. J.L. & Tech. 1 (1995) (Princeton Review offers to transfer the <kaplan.com> domain name to the Kaplan Review in exchange for a case of beer).

[368] *See* Press Release, World Intellectual Property Organization, Record Number of Alleged Cybersquatting Cases Filed in May (2000) *at* http://www/wipo.int/edocs/prdocs/en/2000/wipo_und_2000_ 100_html.

to another's mark with the intent to extort money from the holder of the mark and prevent the holder of the mark from reflecting its mark on the Internet, to create confusion, to divert the mark holder's customers to the cybersquatter's own (often pornographic) site for commercial gain, or to defraud the public.[369] All of these domain name registrations are actionable under Section 43(d) of the Lanham Act if the mark holder can demonstrate that its trademark predates the registration of the domain name, and the domain name registree had a bad faith intent to profit from the registration of a domain name that is identical or confusingly similar to the trademark holder's mark.

Section 43(d)(1) provides as follows:

(A) A person shall be liable in a civil action by the owner of a mark, including a personal name which is protected as a mark under this section, if, without regard to the goods or services of the parties, that person

(i) has a bad faith intent to profit from that mark, including a personal name which is protected as a mark under this section; and

(ii) registers, traffics in, or uses a domain name that -

(I) in the case of a mark that is distinctive at the time of registration of the domain name, is identical or confusingly similar to that mark;

(II) in the case of a famous mark that is famous at the time of registration of the domain name, is identical or confusingly similar to or dilutive of that mark; or

(III) is a trademark, work, or name protected by reason of Section 706 of title 18, United States Code, or Section 220506 of title 36, United States Code.[370]

6.5.1. Bad Faith Requirement

New Section 43(d)(1)(B)(i) provides a nonexclusive list of nine factors that courts may consider when determining whether a person has the requisite bad faith intent under Section 43(d)(1)(A):

(B)(i) In determining whether a person has a bad faith intent described under subparagraph (A), a court must consider factors such as, but not limited to

(I) the trademark or other intellectual property rights of the person,

---

[369]The Anticybersquatting Consumer Protection Act, S. Rep. No. 106-140, at 6-7 (1999), 1999 WL 594571.

[370]15 U.S.C. § 1125(d)(1)(A).

if any, in the domain name;

(II) the extent to which the domain name consists of the legal name of the person or a name that is otherwise commonly used to identify that person;

(III) the person's prior use, if any, of the domain name in connection with the bona fide offering of any goods or services;

(IV) the person's *bona fide* noncommercial or fair use of the mark in a site accessible under the domain name;

(V) the persons' intent to divert consumers from the mark owner's online location to a site accessible under the domain name that could harm the goodwill represented by the mark, either for commercial gain or with the intent to tarnish or disparage the mark, by creating a likelihood of confusion as to the source, sponsorship, affiliation, or endorsement of the site;

(VI) the person's offer to transfer, sell, or otherwise assign the domain name to the mark owner or any third party for financial gain without having used, or having an intent to use the domain name in the *bona fide* offering of any goods or services, or the person's prior conduct indicating a patter of such conduct;

(VII) the person's provision of material and misleading false contact information when applying for the registration of the domain name, the person's intentional failure to maintain accurate contact information, or the person's prior conduct indicating a pattern of such conduct;

(VIII) the person's registration or acquisition or multiple domain names which the person knows are identical or confusingly similar to marks of others that are distinctive at the time of registration of such domain names, or dilutive of famous marks of others that are famous at the time of registration of such domain names, without regard to the goods or services of the parties; and

(IX) the extent to which the mark incorporated in the person's domain name registration is or is not distinctive and famous within the meaning of subsection (c)(1) of Section 43.[371]

In practice, the first four factors indicate a lack of bad faith and the last five factors indicate the presence of bad faith.[372] The legislative history recognizes that presence or absence of any of these factors may not be

---

[371] 15 U.S.C. § 1125(d)(1)(B)(i)

[372] Anticybersquatting Consumer Protection Act, S. Rep. No. 106-140, at 9 (1999), 1999 WL 594571.

determinative.[373] For example, a parodic use does not preclude bad-faith, and the provision of erroneous registration information does not necessarily show bad faith.[374] Instead, the legislative history regards these as "balancing factors," recognizing not only that caveats could exist for (B)(i)(IV) and (B)(i)(VIII) but for all of the balancing factors.[375]

The list of bad-faith balancing factors is "nonexclusive and nonexhaustive."[376] In addition to factor (IV) in Section 43(d)(1)(B)(i), Section 43(d)(2)(B)(ii) provides that bad faith shall not be found "in any case in which the court determines that the person believed and had reasonable grounds to believe that the use of the domain name was a fair use or otherwise lawful."[377]

6.5.1.1. Reverse Domain Name Hijacking under the UDRP

The legislative history indicates that Congress was concerned that trademark holders may employ the ACPA in bad faith.[378] Where a *bona fide* domain name registration existed first, an interloper could register a trademark that was identical or confusingly similar to the domain name and then assert the provisions of Section 43(d). An unsuspecting domain name holder could find itself under attack from a second-comer holding a trademark registration. To address this concern, Section 43(d)(1)(A)(ii)(I) states that the mark needs to be distinctive at the time of the domain name registration.

---

[373] Anticybersquatting Consumer Protection Act, S. Rep. No. 106-140, at 9 (1999), 1999 WL 594571.

[374] Anticybersquatting Consumer Protection Act, S. Rep. No. 106-140, at 9 (1999), 1999 WL 594571.

[375] Anticybersquatting Consumer Protection Act, S. Rep. No. 106-140, at 9-10 (1999), 1999 WL 594571.

[376] Anticybersquatting Consumer Protection Act, S. Rep. No. 106-140, at 10 (1999), 1999 WL 594571.

[377] 15 U.S.C. § 1125(d)(1)(B)(jj) (Lanham Act § 43(d)(1)(B)(ii)).

[378] This section ... protects against the rights of domain name registrants against overreaching trademark owners. Under a new section subparagraph (D)(iv) in Section 32(2), a trademark[ ]owner who knowingly and materially misrepresents to the domain name registrar or registry that a domain name is infringing shall be liable to the domain name registrant for damages resulting from the suspension, cancellation, or transfer of the domain name.

6.5.2. In rem Jurisdiction Over Domain Names

Due to the ease of registering domain names beyond territorial boundaries, Congress was concerned that domain name registrees may not be subject to personal jurisdiction in this country.[379] Another concern was that registrees would intentionally provide false information to avoid service of process and evade personal jurisdiction. The ACPA creates an *in rem* cause of action by adding Section 43(d)(2) to the Lanham Act:

> The owner of a mark may file an *in rem* civil action against a domain name in the judicial district in which the domain name registrar, domain name registry, or other domain name authority that registered or assigned the domain name is located if -
>
> (i) the domain name violates any right of the owner of a mark registered in the Patent and Trademark Office, or protected under subsection (a) or (c); and
>
> (ii) the court finds that the owner -
>
> (I) is not able to obtain *in personam* jurisdiction over a person who would have been a defendant in a civil action under paragraph (1); or would have been a defendant in a civil action under paragraph (1); or
>
> (II) through due diligence was not able to find a person who would have been a defendant in a civil action under paragraph (1) by -
>
> (aa) sending a notice of the alleged violation and intent to proceed under this paragraph to the registrant of the domain name at the postal and e-mail address provided by the registrant to the registrar; and
>
> (bb) publishing notice of the action as the court may direct promptly after filing the action.[380]

In an *in rem* action, a domain name is deemed to have its *situs* in the judicial district where the domain name registrar that registered or assigned

---

[379] Additionally, some have suggested that dissidents and others who are online incognito for legitimate reasons might give false information to protect themselves and have suggested the need to preserve a degree of anonymity on the Internet particularly for this reason. Allowing a trademark owner to proceed against the domain names themselves, provided they are, in fact, infringing or diluting under the Trademark Act, decreases the need for trademark owners to join the hunt to chase down and root out these dissidents or others seeking anonymity on the Net.

Anticybersquating Consumer Protection Act, S. Rep. No. 106-140, at 11 (1999), 1999 WL 594571.

[380] 15 U.S.C. § 1125(d)(2).

the domain name is located, or where documents sufficient to establish control and authority regarding the disposition and use of the domain name are deposited with the court.[381] A court that does not have jurisdiction over the *situs* will also lack jurisdiction in the ACPA proceeding.[382]

6.5.3. Domain Name Registrars

In *Lockheed-Martin v. Network Solutions, Inc.*,[383] Lockheed sued NSI for contributory infringement because of its registration of the <skunkworks.com> domain name. Lockheed held the trademark registration for *Skunkworks* for an aircraft design and construction laboratory, which gave it nationwide priority for the mark. Lockheed also argued that its PTO registration of the Skunkworks mark gave NSI constructive notice of Lockheed's rights in the *Skunkworks* mark. Therefore, by registering the <skunkworks.com> domain name, NSI contributed to the domain name registree's infringement. The court specifically held that domain name registrars could *not* be held liable for domain name registrations.[384]

Because registrars are not liable for contributory trademark infringement,[385] a registrar need not inquire into whether a party is registering a domain name that contains another's mark, or even if that party has any rights in the domain name.

6.5.4. Domain Name Dispute Resolution

While the U.S. created federal law to resolve disputes involving the Internet, the Internet Corporation for Assigned Names and Numbers ("ICANN") created a dispute resolution protocol as part of its mandate to facilitate the coordination and management of specific technical,

---

[381] 15 U.S.C. §§ 1125(d)(2)(C)(i), 1125(d)(2)(C)(ii) (Lanham Act §§ 43(d)(2)(C)(i), 43(d)(2)(C)(ii).

[382] "Court in New York does not have jurisdiction when the registrar is located in Maryland. Trademark owner cannot file suit in a venue of its choosing and unilaterally relocate the domain name's legal situs to that venue 'to buttress that choice'." McCarthy, Trademarks and Unfair Competition § 25:79 (4th ed. 2004) *construing* Mattel, Inc. v. Barbie-Club.com, 310 F.3d 293 (2d Cir. 2002).

[383] 194 F.3d 980 (9th Cir. 1999).

[384] *Id.* at 985.

[385] *See* 15 U.S.C. § 1114(2)(D) (Lanham Act § 32(2)(D)); *See infra*

managerial and policy development tasks that require central coordination.[386]

Because the United States government had been involved in the early development of the Internet, many parts of the domain name system were either performed by U.S. government agencies or pursuant to contracts by U.S. government agencies.[387]

On July 1, 1997, as part of the Administration's Framework for Global Electronic Commerce, ... President [Clinton] directed the Secretary of Commerce to privative the management of the domain name system in a manner that increased competition and facilitated international participation in its management.[388]

In a "White Paper"[389] addressing the management of Internet names and addresses, the United States Chamber of Commerce encouraged the U.S. government to end involvement. One of the suggestions on how to remove the administration of the Internet from the U.S. was to form a private corporation with oversight capabilities. In 1998, ICANN was formed.[390]

ICANN is a nonprofit, private California corporation created expressly to assume responsibility for the IP address space allocation, protocol parameter assignment, domain name system management, and root server system management functions previously performed under U.S. government contracts.[391]

As part of its domain name system management responsibilities,

---

[386] *See* ICANN Fact Sheet, *at* http://www.icann.org/general/fact-sheet.htm (Last modified 12 January 2004).

[387] Image Online Design, Inc. v. Core Assoc., 120 F.Supp.2d 870 (C.D. Cal. 2000).

[388] Memorandum of Understanding Between the U.S. Department of Commerce and Internet Corporation for Assigned Names and Numbers, *available at* http://www.ican.org/general/incann-mou-25nov98.htm (last modified 31 December 1999).

[389] *See* Management of Internet Names and Addresses, 63 Fed. Reg. 31741 (1998), *available at* http://www.ican.org/general/white-paper-05jun98.htm (last updated 22 July 2000).

[390] Image Online Design, Inc. v. Core Assoc., 120 F.Supp. 2d 870 (C.D. Cal. 2000).

[391] *Id.*

ICANN created a dispute resolution policy in October 1999,[392] called the Uniform Dispute Resolution Policy ("UDRP" or "Policy").[393] The UDRP applies to the following generic top-level domains ("gTLDs"): .aero, .biz, .com, .coop, .info, .museum, .name, .net, and .org.[394] In other words, to receive accreditation from ICANN, registrars (that register these gTLDs) must agree to administer and abide by the UDRP.[395] "Under the UDRP, accredited registrars are bound to refrain from taking any action regarding complaints received from trademark holders on the impact of registered domains until instructed to do so by the domain registrant or by an appropriate court or independent arbitrator."[396] Where holders of trademarks allege that a registrant has committed an abusive registration of a domain name, and the mark holder chooses to arbitrate the dispute, the registration agreement obliges the registrant to submit to arbitration. This mandatory administrative agreement requires the proceeding be conducted before one of the approved administrative-dispute-resolution service providers.[397] There are currently four such providers: the World Intellectual Property Organization ("WIPO"), the National Arbitration Forum ("NAF"), CPR Institute for Dispute Resolution, and the Asian Domain

---

[392] See Timeline for the Formulation and Implementation of the Uniform Domain-Name Dispute-Resolution Policy, at http://www.ican.org/udrp/udrp-schedule.htm (last updated 5 February 2002).

[393] See generally Domain Name Dispute Resolution Policies, at http://www.icann.org/udrp/#udrp (last updated 30 January 2004).

[394] Id.

[395] Other gTLDs are governed by other policies. These policies are similar to the UDRP. In the case of country code top-level domains (ccTLDs), the local administrator decides what policy to adopt. For a list of list of country codes and links to ccTLD administrators see IANA, Root-Zone Whois Information, at http://www.iana.org/cctld/cctld-whois.htm (Last modified 28 April 2004). If an administrator of a ccTLD adopts the UDRP; in other words, the UDRP has no requirement that the ccTLD registrant have any affiliation with the country assigned that ccTLD. Potential registrants with media-related websites have created a large demand for the country of Tuvalu's ".tv" ccTLD.

[396] See John Magee, Domain Name Disputes: An Assessment of the UDRP as Against Traditional Litigation, 2003 U, ILL. J.L. TECH. & POL'Y 203, 205 (2003).

[397] Uniform Domain Name Dispute Resolution Policy (UDRP), available at http://www.icann.org/dndr/udrp/policy.htm (last modified 17 May 2002).

Name Dispute Resolution Centre ("ADNDRC").[398] The complainant in UDRP proceedings has the opportunity to select the service provider.[399]

6.5.4.1. Resolving Disputes Under the UDRP

The UDRP prohibits the abusive registration of domain names.[400] Paralleling the ACPA, the UDRP protects trademark holders from those who, in bad faith, register domain names that are identical or confusingly similar to the holder's mark.[401] In the case where a party alleges that a domain name registrant has abused the domain name registration process, the registration agreement obliges the registrant to submit to the jurisdiction of the UDRP as well.

To file a claim under the UDRP, the holder of the mark files a complaint with one of the approved administrative-dispute-resolution service providers.[402] The provider commences the action by notifying the holder of the disputed domain name[403] that an administrative action is pending concerning the disputed domain name. In addition, the provider notifies the registrar of the domain name, and the registrar puts an administrative lock on the domain name--preventing transfer of the domain name.

---

[398] Approved Providers for Uniform Domain-Name Dispute-Resolution Policy, *at* http://www.icann.org/dndr/udrp/approved-providers.htm (last modified 1 March 2002).

[399] John Magee, *Domain Name Disputes: An Assessment of the UDRP as Against Traditional Litigation*, 2003 U. Ill. J.L. Tech. & Pol'y 203, 205 (2003).

[400] WIPO, Final Report of the WIPO Internet Domain Name Process, The Management of Internet Names and Addresses: Intellectual Property Issues, ¶¶ 170-171 (30 April 1999), *at* http://arbiter.wipo.int/processes/process1/report/finalreport.html ("Because of the elastic meaning of cybersquatting in popular terminology, we have therefore chosen to use a different term – abusive registration of a domain name – in order to attribute to it a more precise meaning.").

[401] *Compare* 15 U.S.C. § 1125(d) (Lanham Act § 43(d)) *with* Uniform Domain Name Dispute Resolution Policy, *at* http://www.icann.org/dndr/udrp/policy.htm (last modified 17 May 2002).

[402] *See supra*, § 6.5.4. In referring to the parties in a UDRP proceeding, the author will refer to the holder of the mark as "complainant" and the holder of the domain name registration as "respondent."

[403] As determined by the domain name's *Whois* registration information. *See*, e.g., http://www.networksolutions.com/en_US/whois/index.jhtml (Network Solutions Enhanced WHOIS Directory).

The scope of the UDRP is narrow; it is only to resolve abusive registrations of domain names. To succeed on a UDRP claim, a complainant must demonstrate: (1) that it has rights in a trademark or service mark and the disputed domain name is identical or confusingly similar to complainant's mark, (2) that the respondent has no rights or legitimate interests in the domain name, and (3) the respondent has registered and used the disputed domain name in bad faith.[404]

6.5.4.2. Complainant's Rights in a Mark and Similarity Under the UDRP

Paragraph 4(a)(i) requires a complainant to establish that it has rights in a mark that is identical or confusingly similar to the disputed domain name to bring an action under the UDRP.[405] A complainant may establish rights in a domain name by providing evidence of a USPTO registration.[406] Most panels read that paragraph as a UDRP "standing requirement."[407] The other important element under 4(a)(i) is that complainant's rights must predate respondent's domain name registration.[408]

Absent a PTO registration, panels have permitted complainants to establish common law rights in a mark.[409] To establish common law rights, a complainant must demonstrate that the mark has acquired secondary meaning.[410]

To establish that the disputed domain name is identical or confusingly similar, a complainant need only make a facial comparison of the two. In fact, the burden for similarity under the UDRP is less than the burden for

---

[404] See UDRP ¶ 4(a).

[405] UDRP ¶ 4(a)(i).

[406] See Nike v. Azumano Travel, WIPO Case No. D2000-1598 (17 February 2001) (finding that Nike's registration with the USPTO gave it rights under ¶ 4(a)(i) of the UDRP).

[407] See Spacy v. Alberta Hot Rods, NAF Case No. FA 114437 (1 August 2002).

[408] See Intermark Media, Inc. v. Wang Logic Corp., NAF Case No. FA 139660 (19 February 2003).

[409] See British Broadcasting Corp. v. Renteria, WIPO Case No. D2000-0050 (23 March 2000) (holding that its history indicates that the UDRP "does not distinguish between registered and unregistered trademarks and service marks").

[410] See Galatasaray Spor Kulubu Dernegi v. Maksimum Iletisim A.S., WIPO Case No. D2002-0726 (15 October 2002).

similarity under federal trademark law: all the complainant need demonstrate is that the domain name includes the trademark.[411]

It is under 4(a)(i) that panels consider whether appending "sucks" to a trademark constitutes a resultant domain name that is confusingly similar to the mark.[412] Some do this to gripe about the trademark holder; this is appropriately called "cybergriping." In "sucks" cases, various panels have warned against excessive rigidity when regarding similarity in reference to

---

[411]*See* Kirkbi AG v. Dinoia, WIPO Case No. D2003-0038 (9 March 2003) The test of confusing similarity under the Policy is confined to a comparison of the disputed domain name and the trademark alone, independent of the other marketing and use factors usually considered in trademark infringement or unfair competition cases.

[412]In Full Sail, Inc. v. Spevack, WIPO Case No. D2003-0502 (3 October 2003), the panel summarized five different rationales for finding that "sucks" appended to a mark creates a confusingly similar domain name. First, a domain name is confusingly similar to a trademark "when the domain name includes the trademark, or a confusingly similar approximation, regardless of the other terms of the domain name." *See* Wal-Mart Stores, Inc. v. MacLeod, WIPO Case No. 2000-0662 (21 September 2000); Kendall/Hunt Publ. Co. v. Headhunterbob, NAF Case No. FA 102247 (14 January 2002). Second, appending "sucks" to a domain name will lead to a diversion of customers because it will be pulled up by search engine queries for the trademark. *See* Wal-Mart Stores, Inc. v. Walsucks, WIPO Case No. D2000-0477 (25 July 2000). Third, the consumer may mistake the resultant websites at the "-sucks.com" domain name for the trademark holder's official complaint site. "Given the apparent mushrooming of compliant sites identified by reference to the target's name, can it be said that the regulation would be recognized as an address plainly dissociated from the complainant's?", Direct Line Group Ltd. v. Purge I.T. Ltd, WIPO Case No. D2000-0583 (16 August 2000). Fourth, non-English speakers may not be familiar with the pejorative nature of the word "sucks," and, therefore, will be confused about the source of origin of the "-sucks.com" domain name. *See* ADT Servs. v. ADTSucks.com, WIPO Case No. D2001-0213 (26 April 2001). Fifth, some panels have noted that in certain situations the disputed domain name may not be employing the word "sucks" in the pejorative sense, i.e., "Nothing sucks like Electrolux." Vivendi Universal v. Scallen, WIPO Case No. D2001-1121 (7 November 2001). But, as *Full Sail* also notes, some panels have held that both "common sense and a reading of the plain language of the [UDRP] supports the view that a domain name combining the trademark with the word "sucks" or other language clearly indicating that the domain name is not affiliated with the trademark owner cannot be confusingly similar to the trademark." Lockheed Martin Corp. v. Parisi, WIPO Case No. D2000-1015 (31 January 2001).

"sucks" sites: emerging technologies require a different approach.[413] However, panels often find that cybergriping sites are confusingly similar to the trademarks that they criticize.[414]

6.5.4.3. Rights and Legitimate Interests under the UDRP

To establish that a respondent has abused the domain name registration process, a complainant must make a *prima facie* showing that the holder of the domain name does not have legitimate rights or interests in the domain name.[415] The burden then shifts to the respondent to demonstrate that it has rights and legitimate interests.[416] Paragraph 4(c) of the UDRP establishes three ways in which a respondent can establish rights or legitimate interests in the domain name pursuant to paragraph 4(a)(ii):

> (i) before any notice to you of the dispute, your use of, or demonstrable preparations to use, the domain name or a name corresponding to the domain name in connection with a *bona fide* offering of goods or services; or
>
> (ii) you (as an individual, business, or other organization) have been commonly known by the domain name, even if you have acquired no trademark or service mark rights; or
>
> (iii) you are making a legitimate noncommercial or fair use of the domain name, without intent for commercial gain to misleadingly divert consumers or to tarnish the trademark or service mark at issue.[417]

The history of the UDRP indicates that paragraph 4(c) holds "safe harbor"

---

[413] *See* Nat'l Alliance for the Mentally Ill Contra Costa v. Fouts, NAF Case No. FA 204074 (6 December 2003) (citing Brookfield Communications, Inc. v. W. Coast Enter. Corp., 174 F.3d 1036, 1054 (9th Cir. 1999)).

[414] *See*, e.g., InfoSpace, Inc. v. Sunwave Communications, NAF Case No. FA 198015 (10 November 2003).

[415] *See* Intocast AG v. Lee Daeyoon, WIPO Case No. D2000-1467 (17 January 2001).

[416] *See* Do The Hustle, LLC v. Tropic Web, WIPO Case No, D2000-0624 (21 August 2000) (finding that once complainant asserts that respondent has no rights or legitimate interests with respect to the domain, the burden shifts to respondent to provide "concrete evidence that it has rights to or legitimate interests in the domain name at issue").

[417] *See* IDRP ¶ 4(c).

provisions.[418] Basically, the respondent may demonstrate that its use of the domain name does not bump into the complainant's goodwill.

Panels consider paragraph 4(c)(i) and 4(c)(iii) together: the operative question is whether respondent is attempting to usurp complainant's goodwill. Claims may fail under paragraph 4(c)(i) if the respondent can demonstrate that its use is *bona fide* (i.e., absent bad faith),[419] it has concurrent rights in the mark,[420] or it was doing business as the domain name[421] (a sub-set of this is that it is a generic domain name reseller).[422] Under 4(c)(iii), parody,[423] complaint,[424] and hobby sites may prevail,[425] as

---

[418]ICANN, Second Staff Report on Implementation Documents for the Uniform Dispute Resolution Policy, Submitted for Board meeting of 24 October 1999, ¶ 4.6 (25 October 1999), available at http://www.icann.org/udrp/udrp-second-staff-report-24oct99.htm.

[419]*See* Scholastic Inc. v. Master Games Int'l, Inc., WIPO Case No. D2001-1208 (3 January 2002) (finding that respondent's use of the disputed domain name for a website regarding chess tournaments, particularly because the domain name appropriately described both the target users of respondent's services and the nature of respondent's services, was a *bona fide* use of the domain name).

[420]*See* Kelly v. Qsoft Consulting Ltd., WIPO Case No. D2003-0221 (30 April 2003) (finding that respondent had concurrent rights and legitimate interests in the <mygaydar.com> domain name where, at the time that the administrative proceeding was commenced, both parties had "homonymous trademark rights to the *Gaydar* mark" through their respective use of the mark in the U.S. and the U.K.).

[421]*See* K2r Produkte AG v. Trigano, WIPO Case No. D2000-0622 (23 August 2000) (finding that respondent had rights and legitimate interests in the domain name <k2rr.com> where he registered the domain name for a website in connection with his mother's store, "Kirk et Rosie Rich").

[422]*See* Fifty Plus Media Corp. v. Digital Income, Inc., NAF Case No. FA 94924 (17 July 2000) (finding that complainant failed to prove that respondent had no rights in the domain name and had registered and used the domain name in bad faith where respondent is an Internet business which deals in selling or leasing descriptive/generic domain names).

[423]*See* Robo Enters., Inc. v. Tobiason, NAF Case No. FA 95857 (24 December 2000) (holding that in order to qualify as a protected "parody," which would confer rights or a legitimate interest, the domain name itself must signify critical purposes, as opposed to imitation of the service mark).

[424]*See* New York Press v. New York Press, NAF Case No. FA 94428 (18 May 2000) (finding that respondent's use of its website for review and criticism of the New York press and its pending USPTO registration for the *New York Press* mark for use with his online publication is evidence that he began to use the domain name for a legitimate

long as there is no evidence of commerce.[426]

Paragraph 4(c)(ii) allows for a respondent who has built up a reputation around a domain name to keep it if it can demonstrate that it is commonly known by that domain name.[427]

6.5.4.4. Bad Faith Under the UDRP

Paragraph 4(b) of the UDRP lists four nonexclusive factors to determine if a respondent's registration or use of a domain name is in bad faith pursuant to Policy 4(a)(iii):

(i) circumstances indicating that you have registered or you have acquired the domain name primarily for the purpose of selling, renting, or otherwise transferring the domain name registration to the complainant who is the owner of the trademark or service mark or to a competitor of that complainant, for valuable consideration in excess of your documented out-of-pocket costs directly related to the domain name; or

(ii) you have registered the domain name in order to prevent the owner of the trademark or service mark from reflecting the mark in a corresponding domain name, provided that you have engaged in a pattern of such conduct; or

(iii) you have registered the domain name primarily for the purpose of disrupting the business or a competitor; or

(iv) by using the domain name, you have intentionally attempted to attract, for commercial gain, Internet users to your web site or other on-line location, by creating a likelihood of confusion with the complainant's mark as to the source, sponsorship, affiliation, or endorsement of your web site or location or of a product or service on your web site or

---

noncommercial use).

[425]*See* Mattel v. Knox, NAF Case No. 245916 (21 April 2004) (finding that respondent's use of the <ukbarbie.com> domain name was to share its *Barbie* doll collection with the UK doll-collecting community was noncommercial and, therefore, fair use).

[426]*See* Lockheed Martin Corp. v. Etheridge, WIPO Case No. D2000-0906 (24 September 2000) (finding that respondent has rights in the <missionsuccess.net> domain name where it was using the domain name in connection with a noncommercial purpose).

[427]*See* Puky GmbH v. Agnello, WIPO Case No. D2001-1345 (3 January 2002) (holding that respondent's invoice, which demonstrated that it had been planning to trade under the name *Purkhon Ki Yaden,* was evidence that respondent had rights or legitimate interests in the disputed domain name).

location.[428]

Panels have generally regarded paragraph 4(b) to require evidence of bad faith registration *and* use.[429]

Paragraph 4(b)(i) protects against what the history of the ACPA referred to as "piracy," and the history of the UDRP refers to as the predatory and parasitical practices of exploitation.[430] In its inception, ICANN intended for 4(b)(i) to protect against domain name registrants who intended to profit off of the holder of the identical or confusingly similar mark.[431] Panels have expanded 4(b)(i) to construe any attempted sale of a disputed domain name as evidence of bad faith.[432] In addition, panels have even held a respondent's attempts to sell a disputed domain name in bad faith when complainant initiated the offer.[433] However, some panels have found that those who are in the business of selling domain names, and conduct bulk domain name registrations, do not evidence bad

---

[428]UDRP ¶ 4(b).

[429]*See* ICANN, Second Staff Report on Implementation Documents for the Uniform Dispute Resolution Policy, Submitted for Board meeting of 24 October 1999, ¶ 4.6 (25 October 1999), *available at* http://www.icann.org/udrp/udrp-second-staff-report-24oct99.htm; *see also* Dow Jones & Co. v. Hephzibah Intro-Net Project Ltd., WIPO Case No. D2000-0704 (4 September 2000):
("It may be that the Policy needs to be reviewed, particularly in relation to the requirement for showing use and registration in bad faith. It may seem inappropriate that a person with no legitimate right or interest in a name should be able to register it as a domain name adversely to one who has demonstrated such rights and interests[;] but the panel is bound to apply the Policy as it is.").

[430]*Compare* The Anticybersquatting Consumer Protection Act, S. Rep. No. 106-140, at 6-7 (1999), 1999 WL 594571, *with* WIPO, Final Report of the WIPO Internet Domain Name Process, The Management of Internet Names and Addresses: Intellectual Property Issues, Paragraph 23 (30 April 1999), *available at* http://arbiter.wipo.int/processes/process1/report/finalreport.html.

[431]WIPO, Final Report of the WIPO Internet Domain Name Process, The Management of Internet Names and Addresses: Intellectual Property Issues, ¶ 170 (30 April 1999), *at* http://arbiter.wipo.int/processes/process1/report/finalreport.html.

[432]*See* Am. Anti-Vivisection Soc'y v. "Infa dot Net" Web Serv., NAF Case No. FA 95685 (6 November 2000) ("[G]eneral offers to sell the domain name, even if no certain price is demanded, are evidence of bad faith.").

[433]*See* Marrow v. IceT.com, WIPO Case No. D2000-1234 (22 November 2000) (stating that a panel should not "put much weight on the fact that it was the complainant who contacted respondent to *see* if it was interested in selling the domain name").

faith under 4(b)(i) by selling those domain names.[434]

Complainant's find paragraph 4(b)(ii) difficult to assert. Panels are split whether "prevention ... from reflecting the mark in a corresponding domain name" limits claims under 4(b)(ii) to instances of whether respondent's activity prevents the mark holder from registering a domain name that is identical to its mark.[435] Other construe "corresponding" not to require that the "preventing" domain name be identical to the mark. Additionally, complainants rarely establish the requisite pattern required by the "prevention ... and pattern" requirement of 4(b)(ii). Evidence that respondent holds multiple domain name registrations is not persuasive under 4(b)(ii);[436] however, evidence that previous panels have ruled against respondent is very persuasive evidence that respondent has engaged in a pattern.[437] In an instance where the requisite bad faith exists under 4(b)(ii), a complainant will almost always be able to establish either 4(b)(iii) or 4(b)(iv).[438]

---

[434]See Lumena s-ka zo.o. v. Express Ventures LTD, NAF Case No. FA 94375 (11 May 2000) (finding no bad faith where the domain name involves a generic term, and there is no direct evidence that Respondent registered the domain name with the intent of capitalizing on Complainant's trademark interest).

[435]See Sanrio Co. v. Lau, WIPO Case No. D2000-0172 (20 April 2000) (finding that respondent's registration of <sanriosurprises.com> precluded complainant from registering its registered *Sanrio Surprises* mark as a domain name).

[436]See Ingersoll-Rand Co. v. Gully, WIPO Case No. D2000-0021 (9 March 2000):
The panel is not persuaded that the registration of three very similar or identical domain names arises to the "pattern of conduct" required by [Policy ¶] 4(b)(ii), and although respondent appears to have realized commercial gain by intentionally attracting Internet users searching for the web site of Ingersoll-Rand Co. and by offering links to pornographic web sites where services were available for fees, it is highly unlikely that such Internet users, who were seeking the web site of a long-standing United States corporation, were likely to be confused that complainant would deign to sponsor such links as <tasteless.net> or <rascals.net>, or endorse the [pornography] offered there.

[437]Sony Corp. v. Zuccarini, NAF Case No. 109041 (23 May 2002) ("Complainant has provided evidence that respondent has a history of registering infringing domain names that incorporate the trademarks and service marks of others.").

[438]See Ingersoll-Rand Co. v. Gully, WIPO Case No. D2000-0021 (9 March 2000) (finding that although respondent's act of registering multiple domain names did not constitutes bad faith registration and use pursuant to policy ¶ 4(b)(ii), its practice of appropriating a complainant's mark to redirect Internet traffic to pornography constituted bad faith registration and use pursuant to policy ¶ 4(b)(iv)).

Panels have interpreted paragraph 4(b)(iii) to protect the complainant's mark. A bad faith claim under paragraph 4(b)(iii) pivots on evidence of competition.[439] The panels' definition of competition is a lot broader than under U.S. trademark law, and panelists rarely consider the domain name holder's proximity to the mark holder as indicative of whether the parties are in competition.[440] Panels have even found the existence of competition where the disputed domain results in a directory service that offers links to complainant's competitors.[441] In addition, panelists rarely consider proximity or any other of the infringement factors; quite simply, 4(b)(iii) does not require that a complainant establish a likelihood of confusion, only competition.

Panels have interpreted paragraph 4(b)(iv) to protect the consumers. Unlike a 4(a)(iii) claim, a 4(a)(iv) claim pivots on the existence of confusion, as well as commercial gain. However, unlike under U.S. trademark law, proving confusion under 4(b)(iv) requires only a showing of similarity (proven under 4(a)(i)). In other words, the mark's scope of use is of little importance.[442] Paragraph 4(b)(iv) looks partially like a dilution claim, finding, for instance, because of the fame of complainant's *Britannica* mark, respondent's use of the <britannica.com> domain name

---

[439] *See* Mission KwaSizabantu v. Rost, WIPO Case No. D2000-0279 (7 June 2000) (interpreting "competitor" in the Policy to mean "one who acts in opposition to another and the context does not imply or demand any restrict meaning such as commercial or business competitor"). *But see* Tribeca Film Ctr., Inc. v. Brusasco-Mackenzie, WIPO Case No. D2000-1772 (10 April 2001) (rejecting the *Mission KwaSizabantu* approach and holding that "a respondent can 'disrupt the business of a competitor' only if it offers goods or services that can compete with or rival the goods or services offered by the trademark owner").

[440] *See*, e.g., S. Exposure v. S. Exposure, Inc.. NAF Case No. FA 94864 (18 July 2000) (finding respondent acted in bad faith by attracting Internet users to a website that competes with complainant's business).

[441] *See* Six Continents Hotels, Inc. v. Asia Ventures, WIPO Case No. D2003-0659 (14 October 2003) (finding that redirecting Internet users seeking complainant's mark to a website that lists competing services is evidence of bad faith registration and use pursuant to policy ¶ 4(a)(iii)).

[442] *See supra*, 6.5.4.2; *See also* Goto.com, Inc. v. Walt Disney Co., 200 F.3d 1199, 1206 (9th Cir. 2000) ("With respect to Internet services, even services that are not identical are capable of confusing the public.").

to promote gambling is evidence of bad faith registration and use.[443] Panelists commonly justify findings under Policy ¶ 4(b)(iv) by asserting that respondents could easily sell their products without appropriating complainant's mark, rather than the respondent's actions erode the distinctiveness of complainant's mark.[444]

In determining "commercial gain" under 4(b)(iv) panelists often infer pecuniary benefit even if there is no evidence of sales at the resultant website.[445] Panels find this benefit in inferred revenues from advertising, links, and directory services at the resultant website as well as redirection from the disputed domain note to other domain names.[446]

The factors under 4(b) are non-exclusive.[447] A panel may consider the general intent of ¶ 4(a)(iii) to determine bad faith. Typosquatting– preying on consumers typographical erros– falls under the general application of Policy ¶ 4(a)(iii).[448] "Passive holding"–domain name inactivity that

---

[443] See Encyclopaedia Britannica Inc. v. Shedon.com, WIPO Case No. D2000-0753 (6 September 2000) (finding that respondent violated policy ¶ 4(b)(iv) by using the domain name <britannica.com> to hyperlink to a gambling site).

[444] See State Farm Mut. Auto. Ins. Co. v. Northway, NAF Case No. FA 95464 (11 October 2000) (finding that respondent can accomplish his stated purpose of providing news and information about State Farm without the use of State Farm's trademark in a name).

[445] See Bank of Am. Corp. v. Out Island Props., Inc., NAF Case No. FA 154531 (3 June 2003) (because that the disputed domain names resolved to search engines, and the panel inferred that respondent received payment for pop-up advertisements, the domain names were registered and used in bad faith pursuant to Policy ¶ 4(b)(iv).

[446] Types of legitimate benefits that typosquatters abuse include "click-through fees," which pay the referring website for customer's visits and "affiliate programs," which allow websites to act as promoters, usually through banner advertising, of another merchant's goods and services.

[447] See Do the Hustle, LLC v. Tropic Web, WIPO Case No. D2000-0624 (21 August 2000) ("[T]he examples [of bad faith] in Paragraph 4(b) are intended to be illustrative, rather than exclusive.").

[448] See Nat'l Ass'n of Prof'l Baseball League, Inc. v. Zuccarini, WIPO Case No. D2000-1011 (21 January 2003) ("Typosquatting...is the intentional misspelling of words with [the] intent to intercept and siphon off traffic from its intended destination, by preying on Internauts who make common typing errors. Typosquatting is inherently parasitic and of itself evidence of bad faith.").

amounts to bad faith– also arises under this application of 4(a)(iii).[449]

§ 7. RIGHTS IN UNREGISTERED MARKS
7.1. Lanham Act Section 43(a)
7.1.1. Generally

Apart from available state law claims, the owner of an unregistered mark may seek federal enforcement of rights under Section 43(a) of the Lanham Act against one who uses that mark in a manner which may cause confusion as to the origin or sponsorship of goods or services. Section 43(a) also provides remedies where conduct by another misrepresents the nature, characteristics, qualities or geographic origin of that person's or another's goods or services.

7.1.2. Endorsement and Sponsorship Confusion—Section 43(a)

Section 43(a) states that any person who, on or in connection with any goods or services, or any container for goods, uses any word, term, name, symbol, or device which is likely to cause confusion, mistake or deception as to the affiliation, connection or association of such a person with another or the origin of the goods or services will be subject to the remedies outlined in the Lanham Act.[450]

Section 43(a) is most widely used to to enforce rights in trade dress. It has been applied to a wide variety of identifiers of source, including the inside of a Mexican restaurant,[451] color alone,[452] product configuration,[453] and a host of other unregistered trade dress to prevent consumers from being mislead about the origin or sponsorship of goods or services. In reality, competitors are clearly using the broad provisions of Section 43(a)

---

[449] *See* Telstra Corp. v. Nuclear Marshmallows, WIPO Case No. D2000-0003 (18 February 2000) ("[I]t is possible, in certain circumstances, for inactivity by the respondent to amount to the domain name being used in bad faith").

[450] 15 U.S.C. § 1125(a)(1) (Lanham Act § 43(a)(1)).

[451] Two Pesos, Inc. v. Taco Cabana, Inc., 505 U.S. 763, *reh'g denied*, 505 U.S. 1244 (1992) (trade dress applicable to "Mexican theme" of restaurant).

[452] Qualitex Co. v. Jacobson Products Co., 514 U.S. 159 (1995) (green-gold press pads held sufficiently identifying source to warrant trademark protection).

[453] Pagliero v. Wallace China Co., 198 F.2d 339 (9th Cir. 1962) (designs which are not functional or an aesthetic change in response to commercial desires are protected).

to raise the cost of market entry and/or competition for market share. The two limitations on Section 43(a) claims are that the plaintiff's trade dress actually operates as a trademark to identify source and that the trade dress is not functional. The Supreme Court in 1992 stated that trade dress cases brought under Section 43(a) should be analyzed exactly like any other trademark case.[454] In addition, Section 43(a) may be applied to protect any registered or unregistered, distinctive mark (not only trade dress) from the likelihood of confusion as to origin, source or sponsorship.[455]

7.2. False Advertising

Section 43(a) also makes actionable the use of any commercial representation which in commercial advertising or promotion, misrepresents the nature, characteristics, qualities, or geographic origin of his or her or another person's goods, services, or commercial activities.[456] This section makes actionable false advertising about your own or another's goods or services.

Comparative advertising alone is not actionable under the Lanham Act. Truthful comparative advertising is perfectly acceptable as it assists consumers in making rational choices in the market place. However, misleading consumers by stating untrue claims regarding a competitor's product should be actionable because the competitor may not know of the advertisement or would incur the costs of other advertising to overcome the false association planted in the minds of the consumers by the untrue advertising. Section 43(a) recognizes how important producer reputation is and also how fragile that reputation is in the minds of the consumers.

§ 8. INFRINGEMENT AND REMEDIES

The owner of a trademark has the exclusive right to use the mark in commerce.[457] This right includes the right to use the mark itself on or in connection with identified goods or services as well as the right to license this right to third parties. Any attempt to use the mark by others not

---

[454] Two Pesos, Inc. v. Taco Cabana, Inc., 505 U.S. 763 , *reh'g denied*, 505 U.S. 1244 (1992) (trade dress and trademark are protected under the same statute and there is no textual basis for analyzing them differently).

[455] Allen v. National Video, Inc., 610 F. Supp. 612 (S.D.N.Y. 1985)

[456] 15 U.S.C. § 1125(a)(1)(B) (Lanham Act § 43(a)(1)(B)).

[457] *See supra,* § 6.2.4. Concurrent Lanham Act Registration.

licensed by the owner of the mark, or adoption of a similar mark on similar goods or services, may give rise to an infringement claim by the registrant or first user. Section 32 of Lanham Act provides as follows:

(1) Any person who shall, without the consent of the registrant—

a) use in commerce any reproduction, counterfeit, copy, or colorable imitation of a registered mark in connection with the sale, offering for sale, distribution, or advertising of any goods or services on or in connection with such use is likely to cause confusion, or to cause mistake, or to deceive; or

(b) reproduce, counterfeit, copy or colorably imitate a registered mark and apply such reproduction, counterfeit, copy or colorable imitation to labels, signs, prints, packages, wrappers, receptacles or advertisements intended to be used in advertising of goods or services on or in connection with such use is likely to cause confusion, or to cause mistake, or to deceive.

shall be liable in a civil action by the registrant for the remedies hereinafter provided.[458]

8.1. Likelihood of Confusion
8.1.1. The Analytical Factors

In order to prevail under Section 32 of the Lanham Act, and, for unregistered marks under Section 43(a), the plaintiff must show there is a likelihood that the consumer will be confused, mislead, or deceived regarding the source or origin of the goods or services. That is, the plaintiff must show only a *likelihood* of confusion and need not establish *actual* confusion. Likelihood of confusion is the central requirement in actions both at common law and under the federal trademark statute.[459] While each circuit has adopted its own list of elements and tests for determining likelihood of confusion, they are remarkably similar. The Second Circuit's version, set out in 1961 in *Polaroid Corp. v. Polarad Electronics Corp.*,[460] is perhaps the most comprehensive and the most popular. It established eight factors to be considered in determining if a there is a likelihood of confusion and therefore a finding of infringement:

1. Strength of plaintiff's mark;
2. The degree of similarity of the marks;

---

[458] 15 U.S.C. § 1114(1) (Lanham Act § 32(1)).

[459] Polaroid Corp. v. Polarad Electronics Corp., 287 F.2d 492 (2d Cir. 1961).

[460] *Id.*

3. The proximity of the products or services in the marketplace;

4. The likelihood that the plaintiff will bridge the gap (narrowing significant market differences);

5. Evidence of actual confusion;

6. Defendant's good faith in adopting the mark;

7. The quality of the defendant's product or service; and

8. The sophistication of the buyers.[461]

These criteria are not intended to be exhaustive nor is any one of the criterion intended to be dispositive.[462] Furthermore, no specific combination of these criteria will guarantee a specific outcome. Rather, each case will be determined by the peculiar facts presented the court. The relevant test for likelihood of confusion is intended only as a guide for courts to follow to consider all of the circumstances of a particular case and not make their decision based on one fact.

For example, in *Polaroid v. Polarad*,[463] the plaintiff claimed that Polarad infringed its trademark. Polaroid, of course, makes and sells photographic cameras and films. Polarad's primary line of business included microwave apparatus and television studio equipment. The *Polaroid* court held that with the elements of strength of Polaroid's mark and the similarity of the two marks, Polaroid prevailed. Howerver, analysis of the other factors was either inconclusive or dictated a finding of no confusion. That is, a particular finding on one or two elements will not be sufficient to support a finding of confusion.[464]

8.1.1.1. Circuit Variations

Each federal circuit has adopted its own list of factors to be taken into consideration when determining the likelihood of confusion.
The First Circuit considers the following:

1. Similarity of the marks;

2. Similarity of the goods;

3. The relationship between the parties' channels of trade;

---

[461] *Id.* at 495.

[462] *Id.* at 494. It should be said that all of the circuits note this same caveat. It is rare to see a court incorporate factors beyond those stated in *Polaroid* although the courts have provided the latitude to do so.

[463] 287 F.2d 492 (2d Cir. 1961).

[464] *Id.* at 494.

4. The relationship between the parties' advertising;

5. The classes of prospective purchasers;

6. Evidence of actual confusion;

7. The defendants intent in adopting the mark;

8. The strength of the plaintiff's mark[465]

The Third Circuit will consider the following:

1. The degree of similarity between the marks;

2. The strength of the plaintiff's mark;

3. The price of the relevant goods;

4. The duration during which defendant used the mark without any actual confusion arising;

5. The intent of the defendant;

6. Evidence of actual confusion;

7. Channels of trade;

8. Extent of overlap in targeted markets;

9. Similarity of functions of the marks;

10. Other factors that might make the consumer believe or expect the defendant's goods emanate from the plaintiff.[466]

The Fourth Circuit will consider the following:

1. Strength or distinctiveness of the mark;

2. Similarity of the two marks;

3. Similarity of the goods or services on which the mark is used;\

4. Similarity of the two businesses;

5. Similarity in advertising;

6. Intent of the defendant;

7. Actual confusion.[467]

The Fifth Circuit will consider the following elements:

1. Similarity of the products;

2. Identity of retail outlets and purchasers;

3. Identity of advertising media;

4. Strength of the mark;

5. Defendant's intent;

6. Similarity of design of the marks;

---

[465] Keds Corp. v. Renee International Trading Corp., 888 F.2d 215 (1st Cir. 1989).

[466] Interpale Corp. v. Lapp, Inc., 721 F.2d 460 (3d Cir. 1983).

[467] Pizzeria Uno Corp. v. Triple, 747 F.2d 1522 (4th Cir. 1984).

7. Actual confusion.[468]

The Sixth Circuit will consider the following factors:

1. Strength of the plaintiff's mark
2. Relatedness of the goods;
3. Similarity of the marks;
4. Actual confusion;
5. Marketing channels;
6. Likely degree of purchaser care;
7. Defendant's intent in selecting the mark;
8. Likelihood of expansion of the product lines.[469]

The Seventh Circuit will consider the following elements:

1. Similarity of mark;
2. Similarity of products;
3. Area and manner of concurrent use;
4. The degree of care likely to be exercised by consumers;
5. The strength of the plaintiff's mark;
6. Actual confusion;
7. Intent of the alleged infringer.[470]

The Eighth Circuit applies the following test:

1. The strength of the plaintiff's mark;
2. Similarity of the marks;
3. The degree to which the products compete;
4. Defendant's intent;
5. Actual confusion;
6. Degree of purchaser care.[471]

The Ninth Circuit panels have been inconsistent in their application of the test they will apply. The broadest test lists the following considerations:

1. Strength of the mark;
2. Proximity of the goods;
3. Similarity of the marks;
4. Actual confusion;

---

[468] Roto-Rooter Corp. v. O'Neal, 513 F.2d 44 (5th Cir. 1975).

[469] Frisch's Restaurant, Inc., v. Shoney's Inc., 759 F.2d 1261 (6th Cir. 1985).

[470] Helene Curtis Industries, Inc. v. Church & Dwight Co., In., 560 F.2d 1325 (7th Cir. 1977), *cert. denied*, 434 U.S. 1070 (1978).

[471] Squirtco. v. Seven Up Co., 628 F.2d 1086 (8th Cir. 1980).

    5. Marketing channels;

    6. Degree of care exercised by purchasers;

    7. Defendant's intent;

    8. Likelihood of expansion of the product lines.[472]

The Tenth Circuit largely follows the factors listed in the Restatement of Torts.[473] The Restatement provides the following elements to be considered in making determining likelihood of confusion:

    1. Appearance of the marks;

    2. Pronunciation of the words used;

    3. Verbal translation of the pictures or designs involved;

    4. What the marks suggest.[474]

Finally, the Eleventh Circuit applies the following factors:

    1. The nature of the plaintiff's mark;

    2. Similarity of the marks;

    3. Similarity of the products;

    4. Similarity of the parties' retail outlets and customers;

    5. Nature of the parties' advertising;

    6. Defendant's intent;

    7. Extent of actual confusion.[475]

Virtually all of the courts above list at least the following common denominators in their analysis of a likelihood of confusion.

8.1.1.2. Mark Similarity

When considering whether two marks are similar, courts look at the similarity in sound, meaning and appearance of the marks.[476] Any one, or any combination of these can be influential in determining the similarity of a mark. It is not necessary for a mark to be *exactly* like another in order to be infringing. The Supreme Court has stated that if there is enough similarity to create confusion as to the source of the goods or services, the

---

[472] AMF Inc., Sleekcraft Boats, 599 F.2d 341 (9th Cir. 1979).

[473] Beer Nuts, Inc. v. Clover Club Foods Co., 711 F.2d 934 (10th Cir. 1983).

[474] RESTATEMENT OF TORTS § 729 (1938).

[475] Wesco Mfg. Inc. v. Tropical Attractions of Palm Beach Inc., 833 F.2d 1484 (11th Cir. 1987).

[476] RESTATEMENT (THIRD) UNFAIR COMPETITION § 21(a) (1995).

mark is infringing.[477] The similarity test should focus on the total effect of the mark, rather than on a comparison of individual features of the mark.[478] Similarity in sound is examined by verbalizing the mark. If the two marks are close in sound as spoken, even in the absence of any spelling similarity, the marks may be considered similar.[479]

Similarity in appearance involves a visual analysis of the marks. Analyzing a mark by sight is especially appropriate for picture and graphic marks[480] but also naturally deals with whether two word marks are spelled the same, have the same dominant features, or use the same type of script.

Similarity in meaning is examined through definition, context and association. If two marks create the same association, they can be found similar in meaning.[481] A mark may not be similar in sound or appearance, but if it means the same as the plaintiff's mark it may be adjudicated as similar.[482]

Foreign word marks are translated into English and assigned their meaning in English. In addition, word marks may infringe picture marks if the meaning is the same or closely related.[483]

---

[477] Saxlehner v. Eisner & Mendelson Co., 179 U.S. 19 (1900) (general resemblance of the marks likely to mislead).

[478] Mutual of Omaha Insurance Co. v. Novak, 836 F.2d 397, 399 (8th Cir. 1987) (Mutant of Omaha found to be similar in overall appearance to Mutual of Omaha), cert. denied, 488 U.S. 933 (1988).

[479] Esso, Inc. v. Standard Oil Refining Co., 363 F.2d 945 (5th Cir. 1966, cert. denied, 385 U.S.1007 (1967) ("Esso" and "S.O." verbally similar); G.D. Searle & Co. v. Chas. Pfizer & Co., 265 F.2d 385 (7th Cir. 1959) ("Bonamine" and "Draminine" verbally similar).

[480] In examining picture and graphic marks, the T.T.A.B. looks at the overall visual impression of the mark. Lacoste Alligator S.A. v. Everlast World's Boxing Headquarters, 204 U.S.P.Q. (BNA) 945 (T.T.A.B. 1979) (noting that a flying dragon was not similar to an alligator).

[481] Hancock v. American Steel & Wire Co. 203 F.2d 737 (C.C.P.A. 1953), (CYCLONE and TORNADO for wire fencing confusing as to similarity).

[482] Standard Oil Co. v. Standard Oil Co., 252 F.2d 65 (10th Cir. 1958).

[483] Mobil Oil Corp. v. Pegasus Petroleum Corp., 818 F.2d 254 (2d Cir. 1987) (PEGASUS found to infringe Mobil's logo which constitutes a flying horse).

8.1.1.3. Mark Strength

It is axiomatic in American trademark law that strong marks deserve more protection than weak marks. In determining whether a trademark is strong, most courts consider whether the mark is arbitrary, fanciful, suggestive or descriptive. The more arbitrary or fanciful the mark is, the stronger it will be. In determining if a mark is strong, some courts will also consider whether the mark is registered and whether that registration has become incontestable. The objective with analyzing a mark's strength is to determine the extent to which a mark has come to identify the source or origin of goods or services in the minds of the relevant consuming public. If a mark has a high degree of consumer recognition, it will be considered a strong mark. If there is a low degree of consumer recognition, it will be considered a weak mark.

8.1.1.4. Similarity of the Goods or Services

When considering the similarity of the goods or services, United States courts will be most concerned with the amount of direct competition between goods. If the goods are in direct competition, the amount of similarity of the actual products necessary to support an injunction and/or damages will be lower.[484] That is, courts will conduct a detailed, side-by-side analysis of the goods or services at stake. However, the most important concern will usually be whether the relevant goods or services are in competition. If they are in competition, the showing necessary to support a finding of a likelihood of confusion will be lessened.

8.1.1.5. Channels of Trade and Advertising (Proximity)

Courts will also consider whether or not the relevant goods or services are confronted by the same or similar consumer in the same or similar time, place or manner. This is also known as proximity of the products or services. This is largely a structural economic analysis of the relevant goods and services and how they get to the consumer. Proximity of the goods or

---

[484] HRL Associates, Inc. v. Weiss Associates, Inc., 12 U.S.P.Q. (BNA) 1819 (T.T.A.B. 1989), aff'd, 902 F.2d 1546 (Fed. Cir. 1990); Borden Ice Cream v. Borden's Condensed Milk Co., 201 Fed. 510 (7th Cir. 1912) (stating that the likelihood of confusion between ice cream and milk is low due to the fact that the products do not directly compete).

services could address the physical location of a product in a store,[485] whether the plaintiff's goods are sold only at wholesale and the defendant's goods or services are sold at retail,[486] or whether the goods or advertising flows through commerce in a similar chain of control. Similarity of the products themselves is also part of this analysis.

8.1.1.6. Consumer Sophistication and Care

When courts consider the consumer level of sophistication, they are primarily concerned with the comparative nature of the consumers who purchase the relevant goods or services. If both parties' consumers are impulse buyers making purchasing decisions with little or no care or concern, it will be significantly easier to establish confusion than if the purchasers make buying decisions only after in-depth study or analysis implementing training or experience in the process.[487]

8.1.1.7. Actual Confusion—Survey Evidence

Evidence of actual confusion is only one element in the analysis of whether there is a likelihood of confusion. That is, it is possible (and in actual practice happens rather frequently) for there to be actual evidence of actual confusion and yet no likelihood of confusion. Although evidence of actual confusion is not a requirement in proving infringement, it weighs heavily in favor of the plaintiff.[488] Proof of actual confusion is required,

---

[485] For example, snack foods such as potato and corn chips are placed in the same general area, often in the same aisle in grocery stores, whereas a soda product is not likely to be placed next to a powered soft drink. *See*, e.g., Vitarroz Corp. v. Borden, Inc., 644 F.2d 960 (2d Cir. 1981). The greater the "space" between the two products the less likely the confusion.

[486] Dawn Doughnut Company, Inc. v. Hart's Foods Stores, Inc., 267 F.2d 358 (2d Cir. 1959) (retail and wholesale markets distinguished in determining likelihood of confusion).

[487] E. & J. Gallo Winery v. Consorzio Del Gallo Nero, 782 F. Supp 457 (N.D. Cal. 1991),*citing* Taylor Wine Co. v. Bully Hill Vineyards, Inc., 569 F.2d 731, 196 U.S.P.Q (BNA) 593 (2d Cir. 1978) (stating that purchasers of inexpensive wine are not connoisseurs who have any knowledge of wine selection).

[488] Maternally Yours, Inc. v. Your Maternity Shop, Inc., 234 F.2d 538 (2d Cir. 1956) (confusion of directory assistance operators and misdirected mail evidence of actual confusion).

however, when damages are claimed.[489] The premise behind this difference is that if a party seeks to collect damages, he must show that damage occurred via a loss of sales due to consumers being confused.[490]

Courts have recognized that it is difficult to find incidences of actual confusion[491] and it is reversible error for a judge to ignore evidence of actual confusion in decision making.[492] Evidence of actual confusion must show that the confusion was somehow caused by the defendant and not merely the product of consumer error. For example, if a customer misreads a phone book in calling a junior user, it is considered consumer error and not actual confusion.[493]

Evidence of actual confusion will not guarantee a finding of infringement. Instances of actual confusion must constitute a sufficient basis upon which to determine infringement has occurred. Actual confusion which is minimal is weighted accordingly by the court.[494]

Surveys are most commonly used to determine the existence of actual confusion in the marketplace. To be admissible evidence, surveys must be performed objectively without leading or misleading questions, they must be independently drafted and conducted, and they must not cause prejudice. Even when surveys are conducted with the utmost of care, there will still be objections by the party not submitting the survey. However, surveys are exceptionally important in infringement litigation. Some courts will presume that the result of a survey would have been against a party who refused to commission a survey to support that party's position.[495]

---

[489] *See infra*, § 8.3.2. Damages.

[490] Brunswick Corp. v. Spinit Reel Co., 832 F.2d 513 (10th Cir. 1987), (in order to recover damages a plaintiff must show loss of sales due to actual confusion). *But see,* Taco Cabana Int'l, Inc. v. Two Pesos, Inc., 932 F.2d 1113 (5th Cir. 1991) , *aff'd*, 505 U.S. 763 (1992) (volatility of the restaurant business and application of the "headstart" theory negate need to provide evidence of actual lost sales).

[491] AMF, Inc. v. Sleekcraft Boats, 599 F.2d 341 (9th Cir. 1979).

[492] Frostig v. Saga Enterprises, Inc., 272 Or. 565, 539 P.2d 154 (1975) (actual confusion cannot be ignored by a judge in cases where similarity is slight).

[493] Lang v. Retirement Living Publications Co., 949 F.2d 576 (2d Cir. 1991).

[494] *Id.* (actual confusion which does not create an injury is insufficient to show likelihood of confusion).

[495] Pebble Beach Co. v. Tour 18, Ltd., 942 F. Supp. 1513, 1560 (S.D. Tex. 1996), *aff'd*, 155 F.3d 526 (5th Cir. 1998); Gillette Co. v. Norelco Consumer Prods. Co., 946 F. Supp. 115, 130 (D. Mass. 1996).

8.1.1.8. Intent

Courts have given inconsistent weight to the element of intent. Historically, intent was required in order to find confusion under common law.[496] According to Judge Learned Hand, the intent to misdirect consumers from the plaintiff to the defendant was "the Law and Prophet" of the subject.[497] However, this strict reading of unfair competition law is clearly far too rigid.[498] Today, courts define the trademark right far more broadly than requiring actual predatory intent, and focus on the effect on the marketplace. The intent of the defendant, therefore, is only one element of this analysis just as "actual confusion" is only one element of the analysis.

Although a showing of actual predatory intent is not necessary to prevail in an infringement case in the United States, a lack of predatory intent is not an absolute defense.[499] Again, the point of infringement analysis is to determine the "likely" effect on the marketplace. If actual predatory intent was an absolute requirement or if the lack of predatory intent was an absolute defense, the focus would be shifted to the conduct of the defendant and away from the effect the defendant's conduct had on the marketplace. The effect on the marketplace is the primary consideration of United States trademark law.

Historically, none of the prior federal trademark statutes required actual predatory intent to prove infringement.[500] A distinction has been made between the occurrence of confusion and the intent of one producer

---

[496] McLean v. Fleming, 96 U.S. 245 (1878) (intent not required where infringement is clear).

[497] Yale Electric Corp. v. Robertson, 26 F.2d 972 (2d Cir. 1928).

[498] *See* Kenneth L. Port, *Learned Hand's Trademark Jurisprudence: Legal Positivism and Myth of the Prophet*, 27 PAC. L. J. 221 (1996) (criticizing Learned Hand's rigid adherence to the old common law notion that predatory intent was necessary for a finding of infringement).

[499] President & Trustees of Colby College v. Colby College - New Hampshire, 508 F.2d 804 (1st Cir. 1975) (when likelihood of confusion is found, expression of "good faith" is not a defense).

[500] Elgin Nat'l Watch Co. v. Illinois Watch Case Co., 179 U.S. 665 (1901) (1881 Act in effect). Thaddeus Davids Co v. Davids Mfg. Co., 233 U.S. 461 (1914) (1905 Act in effect). Fleischmann Distilling Corp. v. Maier Brewing Co., 314 F.2d (9th Cir.), *cert. denied*, 374 U.S. 830 (1963) (1946 Trademark Act in effect).

to trade off of the good will of another.[501] Finally, the Lanham Act itself does not require that actual predatory intent be established before a finding of infringement would be appropriate.[502]

8.1.1.9. Likelihood of Bridging the Gap

When the goods or services of the parties to an infringement case are not in competition, most courts will also consider the likelihood that the plaintiff will bridge the gap between its goods or services and the defendant's goods or services. Such likelihood of bridging the gap can be established two ways. The easiest way is to argue that although the plaintiff is not currently selling the defendant's products, the defendant's goods amount to a natural expansion of the plaintiff's line of business. The second method of establishing the likelihood that the plaintiff will or would bridge the gap is to show actual evidence of an actual intent by the plaintiff. That is, although they actually intended to bridge the gap, the presence of the defendant in that market makes such expansion difficult or would thereby cause confusion in the minds of the consumer.[503]

8.1.2. Second Comer Doctrine

Trademark protection is based upon first use. Any producer who enters the market with a mark which is similar to that of a producer who is already established in the marketplace runs the risk of being charged with infringement. Therefore, a new entrant must take time to investigate the availability of its intended mark or whether its intended mark will be too similar to an existing mark. Failure to investigate does not remove liability from the new user.[504]

---

[501] Lois Sportswear, U.S.A., Inc. v. Levi Strauss & Co., 799 F.2d 867 (2d Cir. 1986).

[502] 15 U.S.C. §§ 1114(1)(a) (Lanham Act § 32(1)(a)) and 1117 (Lanham Act § 35). Under the Lanham Act intent is required to obtain certain damages resulting from a finding of infringement. Lanham Act § 32(1)(b) and 32(2) (innocence in infringement activity directed by another party limits action to injunction on future printing of infringed mark).

[503] AMF Inc. v. Sleekcraft Boats, 599 F.2d 341 (9th Cir. 1979) (both parties being engaged in diversification of product lines leads to the strong possibility that each will enter the other's market).

[504] San Fernando Electric Mfg. Co. v. JFD Electronics Components Corp., 565 F.2d 683 (C.C.P.A. 1977) (it is well established in trademark law that junior users are subject to the rights of senior users and failure to search prior to adopting a mark does not

In fact, evidence that shows a junior user had knowledge of a senior user prior to his own adoption weighs more heavily against the junior user in an infringement action. This is particularly true when the senior user has established a strong presence in the market.[505]

8.1.3. Question of Law or Fact—Standard of Review

In the United States, the standard by which an appellate court will review what the lower courts have done is sometimes as important as the merits of the case itself. Courts fundamentally consider all questions raised on appeal as either questions of law or questions of fact. Questions of law are reviewed *de novo* (meaning the court need not give deference to the lower court opinion because, presumably, the appellate court knows at least as well, if not better, what the law of any given subject is). Questions of fact are reviewed under the clearly erroneous standard (meaning unless the lower court made some clear error in its finding of facts the appellate court will not disturb that finding because the lower court judge is present during the presentation of all evidence and can assess its credibility on a first hand basis).

Likelihood of confusion is usually considered a question of fact and therefore reviewed under the clearly erroneous standard.[506] In fact, the Restatement (Third) of Unfair Competition (1993) also classifies infringement as a question of fact. However, a number of courts now consider infringement to be a question of law and therefore reviewable under the *de novo* standard.[507] Even others consider it a mixed question of law and fact where the analysis and evidence of each of the elements leading to the conclusion of infringement are questions of fact but the actual

---

relieve a junior user of liability). *See also* Big O Tire Dealers, Inc. v. Goodyear Tire & Rubber Co., 561 F.2d 1365 (10th Cir 1977), *cert. dismissed*, 434 U.S. 1052 (1978).

[505] J & J Snack Foods Corp. v. McDonald's Corp., 932 F.2d 1460 (Fed. Cir. 1991) (it is reasonable to expect that a newcomer will take sufficient care in adopting a mark when a well-known senior user exists).

[506] *See, e.g.*, Dieter v. B&H Industries, Inc., 880 F.2d 322 (11th Cir. 1989), *cert. denied*, 498 U.S. 950 (1990); Smith Fiberglass Products, Inc. v. Ameron, Inc., 7 F.3d 1327 (7th Cir. 1993).

[507] *See, e.g..* Giant Food, Inc. v. Nation's Foodservice, Inc., 710 F.2d 1565 (Fed. Cir. 1983).

finding of confusion itself is a question of law.[508]

Because the standard of review is such an important issue, one would prefer to have one, consistent rule in the United States. However, no such rule appears forthcoming. Each circuit's rule on this issue must be analyzed each time a case is appealed. The benefit of not having a nationwide, rigid rule on the appropriate standard of review is that in each case a good faith argument can be made by counsel that one or the other standard should prevail.

8.1.4. Reverse Confusion

By definition, trademark confusion results when consumers come to believe that products emanating from a second comer are actually those of the entity with prior rights. When trade is diverted in this manner, consumers are confused, the market is upset and therein lies the justification for an injunction and/or damages.

However, if the second comer devotes substantial resources in advertising and marketing the line of goods associated with the mark, consumers can be lead to the belief that the first comer is the entity causing this confusion and believe that the first comer's products emanate from the second comer.[509]

This type of confusion is called reverse confusion. A specific example works best to describe this issue. In *Sands, Taylor & Wood Co. v. Quaker Oats Co.*,[510] Quaker Oats was originally ordered to pay over $43 million in a reverse confusion case. In that case, Quaker Oats adopted the trademark "Gatorade is Thirst Aid" for use on its isotonic beverages. However, the plaintiff had already used and registered THIRST-AID for a variety of products including beverages. When Gatorade flooded the market with its "thirst-aid" commercials, purchasers of the plaintiff's goods came to the incorrect conclusion that the plaintiff's goods came from or were sponsored by Gatorade.

This is a classic case of reverse confusion. Quaker Oats was enjoined and initially (although reduced on appeal) ordered to pay $43 million

---

[508] *See* Bristol-Meyers Squibb Co. v. McNeil-P.P.C., Inc., 973 F.2d 1033 (2d Cir. 1993).

[509] 320.Sands, Taylor & Wood Co. v. Quaker Oats Co., 978 F.2d 947 (7th Cir. 1992), *cert. denied*, 507 U.S. 1042 (1993).

[510] *Id.*

dollars in damages, prejudgment interest and attorneys fees.[511]

However, the doctrine of reverse confusion will not allow mark holders to assert trademark law to protect expired copyrights.[512] In *Dastar Corp. v. Twentieth Century Fox Film Corp.*,[513] Dastar repackaged and sold a war movie, originally produced by Twentieth Century Fox, with an expired copyright. Part of Dastar's repackaging was to remove Twentieth Century Fox's mark and affix the Dastar mark to the movie. The court held that the false origin of goods language in Lanham Act Section 43(a)(1)(A) does not cover fast designations of the producer or creator of a creative or communicative work, such as a movie. Specifically, the Court refused to allow Section 43(a)(1)(A) to limit the right of the public to copy and use works on which the copyright had expired.[514]

8.2. Defenses

There are multiple defenses available in an infringement case. Any affirmative defense not raised in the answer is considered waived,[515] therefore, it is important to consider all available defenses at the outset of any infringement claim.

8.2.1. Invalidity of Plaintiff's Mark

The first and usually the best defense is to claim that the plaintiff's mark is invalid. If the plaintiff's trademark is not valid, a defendant cannot be liable for infringement. The plaintiff may use federal registration as prima facie evidence of validity;[516] if the mark has become incontestable, as conclusive evidence of validity;[517] or claim that an unregistered mark is inherently distinctive. The defendant then has the burden of proof (a

---

[511] Sands, Taylor & Wood v. The Quaker Oats Co., 18 U.S.P.Q.2d 1457 (N.D. Ill. 1990) (award includes 10% profits on sales of defendant's product along with pre-judgment interest, attorney fees and costs).

[512] Thereby melding trademark law into copyright law to extend a concept of moral rights, a concept not protected in U.S. Copyright law.

[513] 539 U.S. 23, 123 (2003).

[514] *Id.*

[515] U.S. Olympic Comm. v. Bata Shoe Co., 225 U.S.P.Q. (BNA) 340 (T.T.A.B. 1984).

[516] 15 U.S.C. § 1115(a) (Lanham Act § 33(a)).

[517] 15 U.S.C. § 1115(b) (Lanham Act § 33(b)).

preponderance of the evidence) to show that the mark is not valid.[518]

The most common ground for invalidity is that the plaintiff's mark is or has become generic. A mark is generic if the primary significance of the mark is to identify the product and not the producer.

In addition to these two popular defenses, Section 33(b) of the Lanham Act lists several other defenses. These include fraudulently obtained marks, abandonment, deceptive use, marks used in violation of antitrust laws, and defenses such as latches and estoppel.[519] Abandonment,[520] descriptiveness,[521] and functionality[522] are also legitimate defenses.

8.2.2. Fraud

Fraud in obtaining a federal registration is grounds for cancellation of a trademark registration at any time, including after incontestability has been established. However, some courts have found that common law rights asserted under § 43(a) of the Lanham Act are not affected even by a finding that a mark was fraudulently registered.[523]

The elements of fraud are as follows:

1. A false representation regarding a material fact.[524]

2. Knowledge or belief that the representation is false.

3. Intent to induce action or prevent action in reliance of the misrepresentation.

4. Reasonable reliance of the misrepresentation.

5. Damage resulting from the reliance on the misrepresentation.[525]

---

[518] GTE Corp. v. Williams, 904 F.2d 536 (10th Cir.), *cert. denied*, 498 U.S. 998 (1990) (registration by the PTO without requiring any showing of secondary meaning raises the presumption that a mark is arbitrary, fanciful, or suggestive).

[519] *Id.*

[520] *See supra*, § 4.3.2.

[521] *See supra*, § 6.2.2.

[522] *See supra*, § 2.2.3.

[523] Orient Express Trading Co. v. Federated Dept. Stores, Inc., 842 F.2d 650 (2d Cir. 1988) (assertion of common law rights are not precluded by fraudulent federal registration).

[524] Material misrepresentations are those that would have prevented registration had they been disclosed at the time of registration. Pennwalt Corp. v. Sentry Chemical Co., 219 U.S.P.Q. (BNA) 542 (T.T.A.B. 1983).

[525] *See* 5 MCCARTHY, TRADEMARKS § 31:61 (4th ed. 2004), *construed in* San Juan Prods., Inc. v. San Juan Pools of Kan., Inc., 849 F.2d 468 (10th Cir. 1988).

Misrepresentation must be made with knowledge of falsity. Mere inaccuracies will not support a fraud claim.[526] Similarly, an innocent mistake made during prosecution can rescue a registration if corrected.[527]

8.2.3. Antitrust Violations

In order to claim antitrust violations as a defense to infringement, the trademark use must be more than incidental; it must be directly involved in the antitrust violation.[528] The only party who is able to assert an antitrust claim is the party who is directly affected by such behavior.[529]

8.2.4. Fair Use

If the mark is not generic, another popular defense is fair use. The fair use defense arises when the plaintiff's mark is descriptive in nature (not a fanciful or coined term)[530] and the defendant uses it in a way to describe its goods or services and not to identify source.[531]

8.2.5. Laches, Acquiescence, and Estoppel

Failure or unreasonable delay in acting against a junior user or an infringer can be viewed as acquiescence in allowing another to use the same or a confusingly similar mark. The court is not obliged to enforce

---

[526] King-Size, Inc. v. Frank's King Size Clothes, Inc., 547 F. Supp. 1138 (S.D. Tex. 1982)(good faith belief of use sufficient for registration statement; use of honest but inaccurate statements do not prove fraud) .

[527] Universal Overall Co. v. Stonecutter Mills Corp., 379 F.2d 983 (C.C.P.A. 1967) (original application based upon fraudulent information will not defeat registration when amendment was made prior to publication).

[528] Carl Zeiss Stifting v. VEB Carl Zeiss, Jena, 298 F. Supp. 1309 (S.D.N.Y. 1969), *modified*, 433 F.2d 686 (2d Cir. 1970), *cert. denied*, 403 US 905 (1971).

[529] Central Ben. Mut. Ins. Co. v. Blue Cross & Blue Shield Assoc., 711 F. Supp. 1423 (S.D. Ohio 1989).

[530] Zatarains, Inc. v. Oak Grove Smokehouse, Inc. 698 F.2d 786 (5th Circuit 1983) ("Fish-fri" is descriptive and necessary for others to use in describing their products). *But cf.* Car-Freshener Corp. V. S.C. Johnson & Son, Inc. 70 F. 3d 267 (2d Cir. 1995) (whether plaintiff's mark is descriptive is less important; focus should be on whether defendant used the mark in a descriptive and non-trademark manner).

[531] Munters Corp. v. Matsui, American Inc., 909 F.2d 280 (7th Cir.1990) (use determined to be fair and in good faith to describe their own product), *cert. denied*, 498 U.S. 1016 (1990).

trademark rights under these circumstances.[532] Use of an acquiescence defense is premised upon the senior party's knowledge and acceptance of a junior user's use of a mark.

Equitable estoppel is available to a defendant when a plaintiff has led the defendant to believe the plaintiff will not assert its rights, and the defendant has relied upon this assertion. The defendant must show that reliance creates a material prejudice against it.[533]

The principle of laches is based upon the plaintiff's unreasonable delay in bringing an action of infringement against a defendant. Laches is closely related to acquiescence in that both assert the plaintiff has failed to enforce rights in a timely manner. Factors which may be considered in determining whether laches should apply include: harm to plaintiff; good faith of the defendant's assertion of ignorance of the plaintiff's rights; competition between the parties; and harm to the defendant.[534] Without a statute of limitations, laches can create a limitation on claims.[535] Laches will not necessarily cure deliberate infringement.[536]

8.3. Remedies

Available remedies for trademark infringement include injunctive relief, damages, and, exceptional cases, the award of costs and counsel fees.

8.3.1. Injunctive Relief

Injunctions are a form of equitable relief which has been codified in the Lanham Act.[537] Injunctions are issued in order to prevent continued

---

[532] Conan Prop., Inc. v. Conano Pizza, Inc., 225 U.S.P.Q. (BNA) 379 (5th Cir. 1985)(delay in asserting a right does not automatically defeat rights if the delay does not operate to evaporate the right).

[533] Menendex v. Holt, 128 U.S. 514 (1888); Flowers Indus., Inc. v. Interstate Brands Corp., 5 U.S.P.Q.2d (BNA) 1580 (T.T.A.B. 1987) (consideration of the factors does not indicate sufficient evidence to find laches, there is no reasonable finding that the delay caused harm).

[534] 5 MCCARTHY, § 31:1 (4th ed. 2004). Clamp Mfg. Co. Enco Mfg. Co. 870 F.2d 512 (9th Cir. 1989), cert denied, 493 U.S. 872 (1989).

[535] Clamp Mfg. Co. Enco Mfg. Co. 870 F2d 512 (9th Cir.), cert denied, 493 U.S. 872 (1989) (laches used to determine damage limitations on infringement claim).

[536] My-T Fine Corp. v. Samuels, 69 F.2d 76 (2d Cir. 1934) (intentional copying overrides the two year delay in filing suit).

[537] 15 U.S.C. 1116(a) (Lanham Act § 34(a)).

wrongful actions. One of the requirements for injunctive relief is the unavailability or inadequacy of exiting remedies. Inadequacy usually refers to the idea that money damages will not be an adequate remedy for the infringement activity. As such, injunctions serve a critical purpose in trademark infringement actions.

Trademark damages are somewhat unique in that they normally involve loss of business or business reputation due to the infringing use. This type of loss is not adequately addressed by the payment of damages.[538]

Injunctive relief must be applied with careful consideration to the circumstances and facts at issue in a particular case.[539] Upon a finding of infringement, a court may order a defendant to make disclaimers,[540] discontinue use,[541] or take steps to distinguish its goods or services from plaintiff's goods or services.[542] Destruction of packaging and any related tagging materials may also be ordered.[543]

Injunctive relief may be ordered prior to actual infringement. Preliminary injunctions seek to prevent imminent damage which would result without the injunction.[544] Conversely, injunctions may be ordered after a formal finding of infringement. Permanent injunctions can be modified when the facts and circumstances warrant such changes.[545]

---

[538] International Kennel Club, Inc. v. Mighty Star, Inc., 846 F.2d 1079 (7th Cir. 1988).

[539] ALPO Petfoods v. Ralston Purina Co., 913 F2d 958 (D.C. Cir. 1990) (injunction narrowed to provide definition of advertising to that which complies with Lanham Act § 43(a) definitions).

[540] Kentucky Fried Chicken Corp. v. Famous Recipe Fried Chicken, Inc., 157 U.S.P.Q. (BNA) 697 (N.D. Ohio 1968) (defendant required to disclaim any association with "Kentucky Fried Chicken").

[541] S.S. Kresge Co. v. Tabacco, 173 U.S.P.Q. (BNA) 222 (E.D. Mich. 1972).

[542] Kellogg Co. v. National Biscuit Co., 305 U.S. 111, reh'g denied, 305 U.S. 674 (1938) (Kellogg may use "Shredded Wheat" and the pillow shaped biscuit if they distinguish themselves from other producers).

[543] 15 U.S.C. § 1118 (Lanham Act § 36).

[544] Standard Oil Co. v. Standard Oil Co., 56 F.2d 973 (10th Cir. 1932) (longstanding recognition of Standard Oil would be disrupted without an injunction preventing use of a similar name).

[545] United States v. Swift & Co., 286 U.S. 106 (1932) (removal of threat of monopoly sufficient to modify injunction) .

8.3.1.1. Injunctive Relief Against Domain Name Registrars

The Lanham Act encourages domain name registrars to cooperate with the courts and establish the court's authority regarding abusive registrations of domain names. Subsection 32(D)(i)(II) makes registrars subject to injunctive relief if they have: (1) not expeditiously deposited documents with the court "to establish the courts control and authority regarding the disposition of the registration and use of the domain name," (2) transferred, suspended, or modified the domain name in the pendency of the action, except upon order of the court, or (3) willfully failed to comply with any such court order in regard to the domain name.[546] The ACPA provides protections for registrars that create policies and procedures to allow cooperation with the courts.[547] If a registrar takes the action of refusing to register, removing from registration, transferring, temporarily disabling, or permanently canceling a domain name, the Act provides immunity. Registrars receive immunity from both monetary relief and limited immunity from injunctive relief for registrars that are (1) in compliance with at court order under Section 43(d), (2) in the implementation of a reasonable policy to prohibit the registration of domain name that is identical to, confusingly similar to or dilutive of another's mark.[548] "Thus, the Act protects a registrar when it complies with a court order under Section 43(d) and disables, transfers, cancels, or removes from registration, a domain name as part of a "reasonable policy" prohibiting the registration of domain names that are identical to, confusingly similar to, or cause dilution of another's mark."[549] This immunity extends to the registrar (except where the registrar does not cooperate with the court as determined in 32(2)(D)(i)(II))[550] regardless of whether the domain name is ultimately determined to infringe or dilute the mark.[551]

In addition, Section 32(2)(D) exempts domain name registrars from liability from the registration process. Registrars of domain names are not

---

[546]15 U.S.C. § 1114(2)(D)(i)(II).

[547]*See supra*, § 8.3.1.1.

[548]15 U.S.C. § 1114(2)(D)(ii).

[549]Steven R. Borgman, *The New Federal Cybersquatting Laws*, 8 TEX. INTELL. PROP. L.J. 265, 272 (2000).

[550]*See supra*, § 8.3.1.1.

[551]15 U.S.C. § 1114(2)(D)(i)(I) (Lanham Act § 32(2)(D)(i)(I).

liable for the registration or maintenance of a domain name of another absent a showing of bad faith intent to profit from such registration or maintenance of the domain name.[552] If a party makes a "knowing and material misrepresentation" to a registrar, and the registrar refuses to register or removes, transfers, disables, or cancels a domain name, then the party shall be liable,[553] and the court may also grant injunctive relief to the domain name registrant.[554] In the context of these actions by the registrar, the registrant of the domain name may file a civil action to establish that its registration or use of the domain name is not unlawful, and the court may grant injunctive relief to the domain name registrant.[555]

8.3.2. Damages

Damages refer to the various forms of monetary recovery available upon a finding of infringement. Damages can include lost profits, business losses, punitive damages, costs and attorney's fees. Damages have been held to include the cost of corrective advertising; in other words, the amount that would be necessary to correct the consumer misperception that had been created by the infringement.[556] In actions based on Section 43(c) of the Lanham Act, damages are not available unless the plaintiff can show, essentially, that the defendant willfully intended to trade on the plaintiff's reputation. In such cases, monetary damages may be increased to three times the actual damages as the court deems just.[557]

8.3.2.1. Profits

Profits are awarded based upon the premise that infringing profits rightfully belong to the senior user. Award of profits is an equitable form of relief. Damages to the plaintiff may include all profits realized by the

---

[552]15 U.S.C. § 1114(2)(D)(iii) (Lanham Act § 32(2)(D)(iii).

[553]15 U.S.C. § 1114(2)(D)(iv) (Lanham Act § 32(2)(D)(iv).

[554]15 U.S.C. § 1114(2)(D)(iv) (Lanham Act § 32(2)(D)(iv); *see supra*, § 8.3.1.1.

[555]15 U.S.C. § 1114(2)(D)(iv).

[556] Big O Tire Dealers, Inc. v. Goodyear Tire & Rubber Co., 408 F. Supp. 1219 (D.Colo. 1976), *cert. denied*, 434 U.S. 1052 (1978) ($2.8 million awarded to plaintiff in damages).

[557] 15 U.S.C. § 1117 (Lanham Act § 35).

defendants stemming from sales of the infringing goods,[558] but profits are not awarded automatically. It is up to the court to determine if and how much should be awarded based upon lost profits.

Supreme Court decisions have indicated that an "intent" is required in order for profits to be awarded.[559] Absent intent to palm off or commit fraud, an injunctive remedy is sufficient.

8.3.2.2. Damages for Counterfeiting

Damages can be awarded for counterfeiting of trademarks as well as for infringement. Lanham Act § 34(d) provides:

(c) In case involving the use of a counterfeit mark (as defined in section 34(d) in connection with the sale, offering for sale, or distribution of goods or services, the plaintiff may elect, at any time before final judgment is rendered by the trial court, to recover, instead of actual damages and profits under subsection (a), an award of statutory damages for any such use in connection with the sale , offering for sale, or distribution of goods or services in the amount of—

(1) not less than $500 or more than $100,000 per counterfeit mark per type of goods or services sold, offered for sale, or distributed, as the court considers just; or

(2) if the court finds that the use of the counterfeit mark was willful, not more than $1,000,000 per counterfeit mark per type of goods or services sold, offered for sale, or distributed, as the court considers just.[560]

8.3.2.3. Damages for Cybersquatting

Sections 34(a) and 35(a) of the Lanham Act expressly allow courts to grant the same injunctive and monetary relief for cybersquatting that is currently allowed for trademark infringement, trademark dilution, and false advertising under the Lanham Act.[561] In addition, the Act adds Section 35(d),[562] which allows the plaintiff to collect statutory damages:

In a case involving a violation of Section 43(d)(1) of this title, the

---

[558] Polo Fashions, Inc. v. Craftex, Inc., 816 F.2d 145 (4th Cir. 1987) (award of profits from sales of infringing use properly trebled).

[559] Lindy Pen Co. v. Bic Pen Corp., 982 F.2d 1400 (9th Cir. 1993) (no willfulness in exploiting the trademark precludes award of profits).

[560] 15 U.S.C. § 1117(c) (Lanham Act § 35(c)).

[561] See supra, § 8.3.2.

[562] 15 U.S.C. § 1117(d).

plaintiff may elect, at any time before final judgement is rendered by the trial court, to recover, instead of actual damages and profits, an award of statutory damages in the amount of not less than $1,000 and not more than $100,000 per domain name, as the court considers just.[563]

In addition to these remedies, Section 43(d)(1)(C) of the Lanham Act, provides that "a court may order the forfeiture or cancellation of the domain name or the transfer of the domain name to the owner of the mark."[564]

The remedies available in an *in rem* action are limited to an order for forfeiture or cancellation of the domain name, or its transfer to the owner of the mark.[565]

8.3.3. Other Forms of Relief

Additionally, the Lanham Act allows for a recovery of costs and attorney fees in exceptional cases.[566]

---

[563] 15 U.S.C. § 1117(d) (Lanham Act § 35(d)).

[564] 15 U.S.C. § 1125(d)(1)(C) (Lanham Act § 43(d)(1)(C)).

[565] 15 U.S.C. § 1114(2)(D)(i) (Lanham Act § 32(2)(D)(i)).

[566] 15 U.S.C. § 1117 (Lanham Act § 35).

INDEX: PATENT
(References are to Section Numbers)

INDEX: TRADEMARK

(References are to Section Numbers)